25.00

GERMANS OF
LOUISIANA

German settlements and place names in Louisiana. *Map by Raymond Calvert.*

GERMANS OF LOUISIANA

BY ELLEN C. MERRILL

FOREWORD BY DON HEINRICH TOLZMANN

PELICAN PUBLISHING COMPANY
Gretna 2005

The word "Pelican" and the depiction of a pelican are trademarks
of Pelican Publishing Company, Inc., and are registered in the
U.S. Patent and Trademark Office.

Library of Congress Cataloging-in-Publication Data

Merrill, Ellen C.
Germans of Louisiana / by Ellen C. Merrill ; foreword by Don
Heinrich Tolzmann.
    p. cm.
Includes bibliographical references and index.
ISBN 1-58980-244-6 (hardcover : alk. paper)
1. German Americans—Louisiana—History. 2. Immigrants—
Louisiana—History. 3. German Americans—Louisiana—Social life
and customs. 4. Louisiana—Ethnic relations. 5. Louisiana—
Civilization. 6. Louisiana—Emigration and immigration. 7.
Germany—Emigration and immigration. I. Title.

    F380.G3M47 2004
    976.3'00431—dc22

                          2004012615

Printed in Canada
Published by Pelican Publishing Company, Inc.
1000 Burmaster Street, Gretna, Louisiana 70053

This work is dedicated to all of the German immigrants who have passed through the port of New Orleans in hopes of finding a better life in the United States. We are, indeed, the richer for their coming.

Contents

Foreword

As John Fredrick Nau observed, the Germans' part in building an important presence in the lower Mississippi valley has been overshadowed to a great extent by the work of the French and the Spanish. Indeed, in the 1950s, Nau observed that considerable surprise is often registered "when one ventures to suggest that other Europeans besides the French and Spanish have had a part in the forging of New Orleans life, among these, the immigrants from Germany." A second reason given by Nau for the lack of general awareness of Louisiana's German heritage can be found in the two world wars, which obscured the German dimension in American history. Nau noted that this was a problem not unique to the history of Louisiana but pertained to American history in general (*The German People of New Orleans, 1850-1900*, Leiden: E. J. Brill, 1958). Reinhardt Kondert observed that "despite the recognized significance of the German element among Louisiana's colonial officials, historians of Louisiana have displayed an amazing ignorance of that fact." He also noted that only in the recent past "have scholars come to admit that the Germans played a crucial role in the development" of the state ("Germans in Louisiana, 1720-1803," *Yearbook of German-American Studies,* vol. 16, Lawrence: University of Kansas Press, 1981).

This recent awareness of the role of the German heritage in American history is due to the ethnic heritage/roots revival of the 1960s and 1970s. In addition to the twenty states where German-Americans are the largest ethnic group, there are a number of other areas where the German heritage is especially strong, e.g., in Texas, California, and Florida. However, the one state that has usually been overlooked is Louisiana. Recent work dealing with Louisiana's German heritage has contributed greatly to rectifying this oversight and has also reestablished continuity with the valuable German-American historical publications completed before World War I.

Louisiana has a long history with regard to its German heritage, which reaches back to the early 1700s. Indeed, the first Germans arrived in 1722. The German immigration became concentrated in an area near New Orleans that, at that time, became known as the German Coast. In 1803 the colonial prefect of Louisiana wrote that the German Coast was "the most industrious, the most populous, the most at ease, the most upright, the most respected part" of the French colony.

New Orleans is especially important for the history of German immigration to the United States, as it was one of the four major ports of entry, along with New York, Philadelphia, and Baltimore. Although most immigrants moved north into the Mississippi River valley, or east along the Ohio River, many remained in Louisiana, particularly in and around New Orleans.

The first book in German dealing with Louisiana was a translation of Louis Hennepin's work, entitled *Die Landschafft Louisiana* (Nürnberg: Andrea Otto, 1689). In the next century the early German settlements in Louisiana were not only well known in Germany but were providing the basis for literary works. Heinrich Zschokke published his novel, *Die Prinzessin von Wolfenbüttel,* based on the legend of a German princess who immigrated to Louisiana and supposedly established a German colony (see Paul C. Weber, *America in Imaginative German Literature in the First Half of the Nineteenth Century,* New York: Columbia University, 1926). Paul Wilhelm, Duke of Württemberg, visited New Orleans during his travels in the new world and described the city as "a gathering place of many nations," which had "a cosmopolitan population similar to that of the large transatlantic seaports." He also described his visits there with prominent German-Americans, such as Vincent Nolte, and mentioned the presence of German-American churches and institutions (*Reisen in Nordamerika, 1822-24 [Travels in North America, 1822-24]*, trans. W. R. Nitske, Norman: University of Oklahoma, 1973). After Charles Sealsfield (Karl Postl), the famous German-American author, paid an extended visit to Louisiana, he noted that there were a great number of Germans in New Orleans, "either planters, farmers, merchants, or mechanics" (*Sämtliche Werke,* Hildesheim: Olms, 1972).

In the middle of the century Ludwig von Reizenstein published his notorious novel, *Die Geheimnisse von New Orleans* (trans. Steve Rowan, St. Louis: University of Missouri, 1998), which created interest in New Orleans and its German element. During this century another version of the fictional princess of Wolfenbüttel appeared (Gustav Brühl, *Charlotte: Eine Episode aus der Kolonialgeschichte Louisianas,* Cincinnati: Mecklenbourg and Rosenthal, 1883).

New Orleans had indeed developed a flourishing German-American community by the mid-nineteenth century. After 1840 German immigration increased substantially. Documentation sets the number of Germans arriving at the port of New Orleans at 250,000, while informed estimates place the total for the century at a third of a million. In 1847 the German Society of New Orleans was founded to assist the recently arrived immigrants. In 1860 there were 25,000 German-born residents in Louisiana, most of whom resided in and around New Orleans. During the Civil War the Louisiana Germans placed eleven military companies into the field. More than fifty German-language newspapers and journals were published in the state. By 1870 one-fifth of the population was German speaking. There were a large number of German-American religious congregations as well as numerous German-American societies and associations. All through the nineteenth century Germans who had arrived at Northern ports moved to Louisiana to take advantage of the favorable agricultural conditions. Because New Orleans was one of the major port cities for German immigration, many German-Americans living in the West and Midwest had immigrated through New Orleans and continued to maintain ties to the city. Clearly, New Orleans was the major German-American center in the South.

The presence of many fine German singing societies led to the sponsorship in New Orleans in 1890 of the national *Sängerfest* of the North American *Sängerbund*. This drew both national and international attention to New Orleans as a German-American cultural center. At the turn of the century, German immigrants were actively recruited by the state through German-language brochures advertising the advantages of Louisiana as a place to settle. By the early 1900s there were over 250 German-American societies in the state, mainly in New Orleans, with Germans making up about 12 percent of the state's population. In 1909 a state branch of the German-American National Alliance was formed, which united the German-American societies of Louisiana under one central organization. German-language schools were numerous, with German instruction being available in the public schools as well as in the private and parochial schools maintained by German-American secular and religious institutions.

These cultural associations were strengthened historically by the Mississippi River, which connected New Orleans with cities, towns, and settlements throughout its river valley and that of the Ohio River. All of these factors, together with the 1890 *Sängerfest* and the German-

American Alliance of Louisiana, contributed to making New Orleans a well-recognized German-American cultural center before World War I. Another important factor was the presence in New Orleans of one of the major German-American historians of the pre-world-war era, who was also one of the foremost spokesmen for the German element in America, Prof. J. Hanno Deiler (1849-1909).

In 1879 Deiler accepted a position as professor of German at Tulane University, a position he held for twenty-eight years. It was Deiler who not only organized the 1890 *Sängerfest* in New Orleans but also played an active role in the German-American communities of the state. In 1895 he became president of the German Society of New Orleans and, at the 1899 annual convention of the North American *Sängerbund* in Cincinnati, was elected national president. This honor was an indication of his reputation in the German-American communities of the nation. He was without question one of the most distinguished figures in the cultural life of his time and was well known for "his unbounded energy, his genial attitude toward students and his untiring enthusiasm" (Nau, op. cit., p. 133).

Following on the heels of this period was the tragedy of World War I. As such a large ethnic group, the Louisiana Germans could not escape becoming a target for the anti-German hysteria of the war. The severity of this hysteria in Louisiana was reflected in the laws passed in 1918 by the Louisiana state legislature. Teaching the German language in the public, parochial, and private schools, colleges, and other institutions in the state was prohibited, as was printing any material in German. Speaking the language, flying the German flag, and even selling or exhibiting German-made products also became illegal acts, punishable by fines and prison sentences up to sixty years. These draconian laws obviously struck a blow to the German heritage of Louisiana, as they eliminated German instruction in the educational institutions and forced German organizations, businesses, and religious congregations to disband, go underground, or assume an "American" identity. Fortunately these acts were repealed by the state legislature in 1921.

Nationally the decade of the 1920s was a time of recovery and rebuilding after the devastating years of the anti-German hysteria of World War I. An important occasion took place in 1927 for the Germans of New Orleans with the celebration of the eightieth anniversary of the German Society. To celebrate this occasion, Louis Voss, pastor of the First German Presbyterian Church of New Orleans, published his

History of the German Society of New Orleans, with an Introduction Giving a Synopsis of the History of the Germans in the United States, with Special Reference to Those in Louisiana (New Orleans: Sendker, 1927). The next year the Deutsches Haus was founded to bring the German-Americans of the city and their societies under one umbrella organization. A large building was purchased and renovated, which still today serves as a central point for the many German-related activities of the area.

In 1935 Karl J. R. Arndt accepted a position as professor of German at Louisiana State University. During his twelve-year tenure at L.S.U. Arndt began his research on the German-American press. This resulted in the publication in 1961 of a major work in the field of German-American studies, which listed state by state and city by city the German-American newspapers and journals that had been published from 1732 to 1955 (Karl Arndt and May Olson, *German-American Newspapers, 1732-1955: History and Bibliography,* Heidelberg: Quelle and Meyer, 1961). Not surprisingly Arndt became interested in Louisiana's fascinating German heritage and investigated several German communities in the state. He was especially interested in Germantown in northwestern Louisiana, a communitarian settlement similar to other German communities in Pennsylvania and Ohio.

When John Fredrick Nau wrote in the 1950s his *German People of New Orleans, 1850-1900,* he observed that the Germans of the city were still inspired by the same determination and loyalty that had motivated them to build their communities in the former century. He found this to be apparent in the continuation of their churches, schools, and singing and benevolent societies as well as in their businesses and industries, many of which are still in operation. He noted that "the influence of the Germans upon the city of New Orleans still lives, while German-American contributions to the building of New Orleans are visible on every hand." Nau commented that, in the research for his history of the New Orleans Germans, he repeatedly found that German-Americans "helped to make New Orleans a city of commerce, industry and business. They built New Orleans." He concluded, "To read the history of New Orleans and Louisiana aright, it is important to consider carefully the part played by the German element of the city in molding the culture and life of this city."

As elsewhere in the nation, interest in German heritage was again on the upswing by the late 1950s. In 1958 the national *Sängerfest* of the North American *Sängerbund* was held in New Orleans for the second time. In the 1960s and 1970s the German heritage of the area was further recognized as part of the national revival of interest in America's ethnic roots. A recently published directory of German-American societies listed a variety of organizations in Louisiana, an indication of continued and growing interest in the German heritage (J. Richley, *Adressbuch deutsch-amerikanischer Vereine und Gesellschaften in den USA,* Chicago: Richley, 1989).

The annual *Volksfest* parade, abandoned after the Civil War, has been revived in New Orleans. On German-American Day, October 6, speeches and ceremonies are held by the major German heritage organizations of the area. *Oktoberfest* is celebrated by the Deutsches Haus during five public weekends of German food, music, dancing, and general revelry. The German Seamen's Mission holds a monthly German-language church service; the German Heritage Festival Association hosts an annual Oktoberfest parade and a gourmet Christmas dinner. Additionally the German American Cultural Center was opened in Gretna by the National Park Service. Recently the former German Society was revived, attracting 300 members in its first year. These and other German-oriented activities, too numerous to mention, attest to the continuing interest within this region in all things German.

DON HEINRICH TOLZMANN, PH.D.
President, Society for German-American Studies
University of Cincinnati

Preface

Through funding supplied by the Louisiana Endowment for the Humanities and the National Park Service I have had the opportunity to bring together a wealth of material on the German heritage of Louisiana. Because of the scope of the task I had not considered attempting it until these opportunities arose. In creating this work I concentrated on researching the resources covering the major periods of German immigration to the New Orleans region. The scholars in the field recognize three major eras, the *Colonial Period; the Period through the Civil War,* within which immigration peaked (1853); and the *Post-Civil War Period* of the gradual decline of this "Golden Age" of German culture. The end of the last wave of immigration to Louisiana coincided with improving conditions in Germany, which resulted from the 1871 unification of the various states into one nation. Even the two world wars within the twentieth century and the resulting displacement of large population groups did not produce a significant effect upon the cultural landscape of Louisiana. Although references to this period are included, the scope of this work primarily covers the eighteenth and nineteenth centuries, when there was a direct German impact on the cultural milieu of the lower Mississippi delta region of Louisiana. During these centuries the German influence could be objectively determined by examining the historical documents of the colonial period and records of the many German institutions, churches, schools, businesses, societies, etc., that flourished in the following century. The present-day interest in the German heritage of the state, which has arisen as a result of the national ethnic revival of the 1960s and 1970s, is evidence of the impact that German immigration and settlement had upon this region (see chapter 2).

I have consulted primary and secondary sources in public libraries, archives, and private collections, other public and private records such as city directories, newspapers, pamphlets, oral histories, etc.—in short, everything I could find that shed some light on the Germans of Louisiana. There are, no doubt, omissions, since an effort such as this is never complete. First of all I want to thank my husband and research associate, Raymond Calvert, who not only worked with me throughout this project but also illustrated a number of the figures. I also wish to express my thanks to the following librarians and archivists, who provided me with assistance and access to fragile materials in special collections: Colin Hamer of the New Orleans Public Library; at Tulane University: Wilbur Meneray, university librarian for special collections, and his co-worker Courtney Page; Joan Caldwell of the Louisiana Collection, assisted by Carole Hampshire; Lee Miller, manuscripts librarian, and co-worker Mary LeBlanc; Robert Sherer, university archivist; and, finally, Gary Van Zante and his colleague Kevin Williams at Tulane's Southeastern Architectural Archive. At the Hill Memorial Library, Louisiana State University in Baton Rouge, I would like to thank Faye Phillips, assistant dean of libraries for special collections; Charles Thomas, curator of the Louisiana and Lower Mississippi Valley Collection; and Judy Bolten, in charge of public services in the reading room. Special thanks are due to Christina Riquelmy of the McIlhenny Collection at the Hill Library, who provided suggestions as well as a great amount of assistance. Thanks also go to John Magill of the Williams Research Center at the Historic New Orleans Collection and his assistants Sally Stassi, Siva Blake, and Mary Lou Eichhorn. Finally, thanks are due to Florence Jumonville, director of the Louisiana/Special Collections, and John Kelly, digital librarian, both at the Earl K. Long Library of the University of New Orleans.

GERMANS OF LOUISIANA

Robert de La Salle, John Law, and Karl Darensbourg. *Drawings by Raymond Calvert.*

CHAPTER ONE

The German Coast of Louisiana

THE FRENCH COLONIAL PERIOD

The *Côte des Allemands* under the *Compagnie des Indes*

For decades France neglected Louisiana, that huge area between the
Great Lakes and the Gulf Coast, which Robert Cavelier, Sieur de La
Salle claimed for France in 1682. France had been almost continually
at war since La Salle's claim and had no means at its disposal to retain
the vast territory of its newly acquired colony. In addition Louis XIV
was opposed to sending his citizens to French possessions overseas. He
valued his population, if for no other reason than as a source for taxation. In hopes of discouraging England and Spain from encroaching on
his possession, in 1712 the king granted a fifteen-year trade monopoly
for the development of Louisiana to Antoine Crozat. Crozat at that time
was perhaps the wealthiest man in France, easily in a position to
finance this great enterprise. However, after losing more than two million *livres* in prospecting for precious metals and gems in Louisiana, in
1717 he returned his charter to France. From 1682 until the king's
death in 1715 fewer than four hundred emigrants were permitted to settle
in Louisiana, partly explaining the failure of Crozat to develop the
colony.

Louis XIV's successor, the regent duc d'Orleans, faced empty royal
coffers, drained by constant warfare and the extravagances of the Sun
King and his court. In desperation the duke seized upon a scheme
developed by the professional gambler John Law, a Scotsman who had
fled murder charges in his homeland. Law first created a private bank
that issued paper money, a novelty at that time. The next year Law saw
a great opportunity in the charter just returned by Crozat to the crown.
He persuaded the regent that the development of Louisiana was far too
large an undertaking for any individual and should be entrusted to a
company owned by stockholders.

So the Company of the West was born, headed by none other than
John Law. The company received a trade monopoly for twenty-five

19

years with the right to lease and sell the land, to control the forts, ships, and weapons already existing in Louisiana, to conscript soldiers, and to appoint officers and officials. The contract obligated the company to bring 6,000 whites and 3,000 blacks into Louisiana within ten years. Law could issue virtually unlimited amounts of stock in the Company of the West. Through this leverage he promised the French government the liquidation of state debt. Because of the clever salesmanship of the company, large population segments wanted to buy stock in Louisiana. A true craze of speculation ensued, stemming from shameless descriptions of the many riches to be found in Louisiana. In a short time the stock rose to astronomic values. Two years later Law issued 100,000 more shares of stock when he merged the Company of the West with the East Indies and China companies to become the *Compagnie des Indes.* Frantic buying of the stock by French investors continued, all expecting to share in the mineral riches of Louisiana. The regent was so pleased with Law's financial successes that he made Law's private bank the official Bank of France, with Law as director general.

Meanwhile colonization was pushed by the company. If Louisiana was going to develop, it needed people, white settlers and black slaves. It became the policy of the *Compagnie des Indes* to give large land grants to wealthy Frenchmen. The concessionaires were themselves responsible for acquiring settlers to farm the land as *engagés,* indentured workers who legally stood between being free men and slaves. In 1718, 300 concessionaires agreed to leave France to develop the riches on the Louisiana plantation sites granted to them. Another hundred were to come the next year. It was obvious, however, that voluntary immigration would never produce the 6,000 white *engagés* required of the *Compagnie des Indes.* So the company turned to the unwanted elements of French society as a population source. Well over a thousand of the dregs of society were rounded up the next year. Criminals, drunks, prostitutes, the penniless, even the mentally ill and infirm were enlisted by force, put under special guard, and shipped to Louisiana.

As could be expected, these immigrants comprised just as undesirable a workforce in Louisiana as they had in France. Gov. Jean Baptiste Le Moyne, Sieur de Bienville complained so bitterly to the company that the practice was stopped within a year. Consequently a new policy for populating Louisiana was developed, borrowed by Law from another director of the *Compagnie des Indes.* This person was Jean-Pierre Purry, a Swiss businessman who proposed recruiting Germans and German-speaking Swiss for Louisiana. These people would have just the qualities needed for settlers in a new colony, being of sturdy stock, honest, and hardworking. Although the regent had reservations about importing foreigners who might challenge French control of Louisiana, he reluctantly agreed to Law's plan.

Purry was put in charge of recruitment, which was to reach to the far corners of the German states and German-speaking Switzerland. Much of Europe at this time was still in economic ruin caused by the Thirty Years War and Louis XIV's wars for the Rhineland. Peasant farmers had little hope of more than scraping together a meager living in their homeland. Agents of the *Compagnie des Indes* circulated recruitment brochures in these areas, promising a tropical paradise filled with gold, silver, copper, and lead deposits. The German recruits, all of whom expected to become workers indentured to John Law, signed up in droves. Law had obtained three land grants, one in New Biloxi, another on the east bank of the Mississippi at English Turn, and a third, elevated to a principality, on the Arkansas River near its juncture with the Mississippi. The recruitment efforts of the *Compagnie des Indes* were far more successful than had been expected. Caravans made up of entire villages led by the mayor left their homeland. Estimates vary from 4,000 to 10,000, including those headed for the Louisiana Swiss regiment and workers assigned to the army. The number of emigrants recruited for Louisiana was probably somewhere in between these two figures. Many were discouraged by the long journey to the French ports, while others were stopped at the border by the threat of having their property confiscated and losing their citizenship. Some settled in France rather than await uncertain embarkation, while others returned to their homeland.

Embarkation at Lorient

When these emigrants began to arrive at the port of embarkation in July of 1720, the transport ships to take them to Louisiana were not yet ready. No provision had been made by the *Compagnie des Indes* for the unexpected thousands who continued to arrive in Lorient, the French port where they were to embark. On the outskirts a makeshift camp was set up around a fountain to supply water. Of the 3,991 emigrants known to have arrived in Lorient, up to 2,000 died in an epidemic, thought to be cholera, which broke out in this crowded and unsanitary holding pen.

The first ship to depart for Louisiana, the *Deux Frères,* sailed in mid-November of 1720 after a five-month delay. But the contagion of the camp was carried aboard by the passengers, and half died in transit, with only 130 Germans and about 30 Swiss reaching Louisiana. Also that month 141 Swiss soldiers of the Merveilleux Company departed on the *Mutiné* and arrived in Old Biloxi, luckily without mishap. The next ship to sail, the *Garonne,* departed two months later, again with ill passengers. First it stopped in Brest so that the Germans on board could be treated. After three months at sea, the ship was captured by pirates in Santo Domingo and the passengers held captive for six weeks. When finally released and transported to Louisiana by the *Durance,* only 50 Germans had survived. The fourth ship, the *Charente,* sailed in early February of 1721 but, proving un-seaworthy, had to return to port, where it was later auctioned. Its passengers were probably loaded onto the *Portefaix,* which sailed in early March and brought the 300 on board safely to Old Biloxi.

Of note was the passenger Karl Friedrich Darensbourg, who later was to serve for forty-eight years as the commander of the German Coast of Louisiana. Darensbourg had been born in the German section of Stockholm, Sweden. His parents were of noble lineage, originating from Arensbourg on the Swedish island of Oesel. As a young man he entered a military academy and was commissioned as an officer in the Swedish military. In 1721 he enlisted with John Law's *Compagnie des Indes* as a captain-at-half-pay and sailed to Louisiana. There he was made commandant of the German Coast, a position that had both military and civil duties. In this capacity he served as commander of the militia as well as civil judge and mediator for the grievances of the colonists.

In April the *Venus* departed with 65 Swiss, the rest of the Merveilleux Company, and reached Old Biloxi safely. Two more ships sailed in early May, the *Saint-André* and the *Durance.* On the *Saint-André* 53 of the 158 Germans died of contagion before reaching Louisiana. The *Durance* fared better, losing only 8 passengers and bringing 100 Germans to Old Biloxi. The last ship to sail, the *Saône,* was delayed for seven months and probably did not transport any Germans. In May of 1721 about 400 Germans, still waiting in the ill-fated tent city at Lorient, were finally given a small travel stipend and sent back to their homeland. These Germans were probably those who were to have sailed on the *Saône.* Six hundred Germans in Lorient remain unaccounted for. No doubt they were among those who settled elsewhere in France or returned to their homeland before May of 1721. This date marks the end of the *Compagnie des Indes'* attempts to bring

German settlers to Louisiana, an effort that can only be characterized as a disaster. Of the 4,000 Germans known to have arrived in Lorient with the purpose of emigrating to Louisiana as workers or soldiers, only about 1,000 reached their destination.

In Old Biloxi, east of the Mississippi, no provisions had been made for the care of the arriving immigrants. Bienville ordered the Swiss worker/soldiers to go inland and find food and shelter on their own. But of those would-be *engagés* left on the beaches, half died from sunstroke, thirst, or starvation or from eating poisonous weeds or spoiled oysters, which had washed up on the sand. The local Indians, hearing of their plight from the Swiss, could save only some of them by supplying corn and deer meat. One group of Germans was transferred by Bienville to Law's concession in New Biloxi on the north shore of the gulf, where conditions were better. Those Germans still alive, who had arrived on board the *Deux Frères,* were transported to Law's large Arkansas concession. This group was comprised of about fifty German and a larger number of French *engagés.* The perilous voyage up the Mississippi against the strong current of the river took several months. Upon arrival in early August of 1721 they began clearing and planting the land and building shelter for the winter. Within two months, however, they were informed by a group of Swiss soldiers that John Law had gone bankrupt and fled from France.

Already in May of 1720 the price of the stock issued by the *Compagnie des Indes* had begun to tumble. By December it had become virtually worthless, destroying the Bank of France and bankrupting thousands of French investors. France immediately confiscated Law's French property but let matters drift concerning Louisiana. Those German *engagés* on Law's Arkansas property, originally recruited by the *Compagnie des Indes,* were now uncertain of their status. Most of them abandoned the settlement and floated downstream to New Orleans, where they hoped to be repatriated or at least resettled in a less remote area. However, the governor and the administrators in Louisiana as well as the directors of the *Compagnie des Indes* in France were indecisive about the future of Louisiana. No one seemed to know what to do with the settlers.

In the meantime more Germans had arrived in Old Biloxi on the *Durance, Saint-André,* and *Portefaix.* Passengers on the *Portefaix* confirmed the news of John Law's bankruptcy. However, the paralysis of the administration again left this large group of Germans stranded on the inhospitable beaches of Old Biloxi. By the end of 1721 the majority of

these approximately five hundred Germans had died of disease, expo-
sure, or starvation. With the return of the Arkansas Germans to New
Orleans, Bienville realized that he must act. First he consulted with
Darensbourg, a former captain in the Swedish army who had been put
in charge of the German immigrants. Then he resolved to take inland
all the surviving Germans plus the few Swiss from the *Deux Frères*.
Longboats were requisitioned to transport these survivors to the west
bank of the Mississippi, about thirty miles above New Orleans. The
transfer was completed by February of 1722.

Settlement on the German Coast

This area, already consigned but neglected by its French owner, was
granted by Bienville to the new arrivals. The land extended between
present-day Lucy and Hahnville and covered a large area, which was
not known ever to have flooded. It was choice land, described as beautiful and fertile, and had already been partially cleared and cultivated
by two Indian tribes. The settlers were located on the inner (west) bank
of the Bonnet Carré bend, which was connected by a bayou to *Lac des
Ouachas.* This large lake, located approximately five miles southwest
of the German colony, was later named *Lac des Allemands* and the
colony itself *Aux Ouacha* or *le Village des Allemands*.

The settlers were no longer *engagés* for Law's large concessions but
now had the status of *habitants,* that is, concessionaires of the company
in their own right. Penniless as they were, the Germans received only
small land grants, which they did not yet fully own. The Superior Council,
which had been created by the *Compagnie des Indes* as the ruling body in
Louisiana, now controlled the developing economy. The new arrivals
were forced to sell their products to the company and, in turn, would
receive the necessities of life, such as food and tools, all at fixed prices.

Preparations for settlement of these German colonists were begun in
late 1721. By the next year the Germans had established three villages,
Hoffen, Marienthal, and Augsburg. Together there were 69 men, 79
women, and 99 children for a total of 247 persons. An earlier census
had estimated 330 settlers but had incorrectly included about 80 temporary workers sent by the *Compagnie des Indes* to assist the newcomers. Within a year they had already planted rice, corn, and other
vegetables. Tobacco was also to be grown at the insistence of the
Compagnie des Indes, to which the crop was pledged.

The five-acre concession where Karl Darensbourg, the *Kommandant
des Allemands,* lived was named Karlstein in his honor (now Killona

on the river's west bank). Both Karlstein and Hoffen were located directly on the Mississippi. The two other settlements, Marienthal and Augsburg, were located on the former Indian fields, which were easy to cultivate. One was established by fourteen families about seven-tenths of a mile away from the river, the second by twenty-one families about a mile and a half distant from the Mississippi. A graveyard lay on the common ground between the two neighboring villages. It bordered the rear portion of Darensbourg's grant, which stretched about half a mile along the river but was shallow in depth. This homestead was the largest land grant on the coast, befitting the newly appointed commandant of the Germans.

Since the plots on the Mississippi were assigned according to the contour of the river, the size of each plot was determined by the river frontage. The depth of the plots was always the same, namely forty linear *arpents,* an old French land measurement equaling about a mile and a half. Therefore a plot of five *arpents,* approximately the size of most of the land grants allotted to the German settlers, contained somewhat less than five acres in the form of a narrow rectangle. The term *côte* or *anse,* hence *Côte des Allemands,* designated the concave bank of the river bend. Those land grants on the concave bank had the advantage of their shore-lines being built up by the river, while the grants on the convex banks, which were given the term *île* or *pointe,* lost land through erosion. The extension of the German colony to the East Bank, directly across the river from the *Côte des Allemands,* was delayed by this phenomenon.

The Germans immediately set about building homes and clearing and planting the land, assisted by workers supplied by the *Compagnie des Indes.* The necessary lumber, tools, and seeds were also supplied by the company, showing how much faith Bienville had in the future of the German settlement. Perhaps he had foreseen its productivity when he located these Germans just upriver from the future capital of the Louisiana colony.

In September of 1722 a devastating hurricane inundated the area, destroyed the crops, and drowned a number of the colonists. The hurricane drove masses of water from *Lac des Allemands* over the Germans' fields and into their villages. After the flood most of the citizens of Augsburg and Marienthal moved to high ground in Hoffen. It was a bitter experience to learn that only those areas that lay directly on the river could be safely farmed.

The census taken in 1724 counted 56 German families in the German settlement, altogether 169 people. Almost a third of the original settlers had been dispersed or drowned. Because of this catastrophe some of the German colonists acquired new concessions farther downriver. Thirteen families became *engagés* on Governor Bienville's land, and a few may have returned to Europe. Most of the Germans now lived on the river in the village of Hoffen. One of the other two villages was now only half-populated with fourteen families, while the second village retained only three hardy settlers.

The 1724 census noted that all of the German families had planted vegetables and grain and were able to feed their cattle. In addition they were building levees on the river frontage of their properties. Although the German farmers were supposed to sell their products at fixed prices only to the *Compagnie des Indes,* by 1724 they were bringing their excess to market in the capital. From the beginning of the settlement the Germans began providing a dependable source of food for the population center in New Orleans.

However, the commentary to this same census recognized the endangered position of these colonists (*Archives Nationales, Ministère des Colonies,* Series C 13 C):

> If these German families, the survivors of a far greater number, are not helped by Negroes in their work, gradually they will perish. For what can a man and his wife achieve with a piece of land if they must go to the grist [grinding] mill instead of being able to eat their dinner and rest after their day of strenuous labor. This work [grinding rice into flour] is hard and dangerous for both men and women. Many get hurt; especially the women suffer serious injury. If one of the two gets sick, the other has to do all the work alone, and so both finally die. The soil is unrelenting in the lower portion of the colony. The weeds grow so fast and so thick that, after a short time, it looks as if no work has been accomplished. The land is covered with tree trunks and stumps, but these people have no draft animals so they cannot work with a plow, only with hoes or pick-axes. This, plus the hard labor of grinding rice, destroys these poor people who are good and willing workers. They want nothing more than to be able to remain in a country where they are free from the high taxes imposed on the farmers in Germany. They would consider themselves very lucky if they could obtain one or two Negroes. . . . The German colonists could feed their Negroes well from the grain they plant. They also could sell a great amount of foodstuffs to the large concessions, which, when regularly supplied, could devote themselves to growing indigo, lumbering and other activities useful for export to France and Santo Domingo.

Because the German colony had been so badly stricken by the cata-
strophic flood of 1722, it developed slowly. By 1724 most of the
inhabitants in Hoffen had prepared only about an acre for planting.
Nevertheless, together they had managed to clear well over a hundred
acres. On their small plots of land the Germans planted primarily corn
and rice, which had to be protected from pests. To frighten away these
predators the colonists beat on pots and pans during the day and kept
fires burning at night. The size of the crops, however, was quite small
because of the spring floods and the damage done by birds and rodents.
Hulling and grinding rice was a very laborious task requiring a whole
day to produce enough flour for bread for two days at the most.
Additionally there was the strenuous work of building levees to prevent
the repeated flooding.

Nevertheless the German settlers assumed the function of supplying
the market of New Orleans during the early years of hardship. The distance to the capital, about thirty miles, was not too far for them to bring
their produce in their *pirogues* (a type of canoe) on weekends. Early on,
a decree by the Superior Council was needed to protect their products
from seizure on the river by hungry soldiers. With their limited number of dray animals and lack of slaves the German colonists could produce only grain and vegetables rather than commercial crops.
However, it took only several years until they could contribute to the
supplies for New Orleans.

As early as 1725 there was conflict with the Catholic Church over
the presence of Protestants in the colony. Father Raphael, the Capuchin
Superior of Missions in Louisiana, strongly objected to the commander of the German Coast being a Lutheran. He accused Darensbourg of
having a concubine and several illegitimate children and demanded his
removal. These allegations were, no doubt, a distortion of the facts by
Father Raphael in order to expel a Protestant from a position of command. The census of 1724 had listed an orphan boy as the only inhab-
itant of Karlstein other than Darensbourg himself. The concubine was
probably Marguerite Metzer, a girl of twenty-one who had arrived with
her family in 1721 on the *Saint André*. The "illegitimate children" may
have been several of the two sons and six daughters born of her union
with Darensbourg, solemnized by marriage in 1725. Continued complaints by Raphael finally resulted in an official inquiry, but whatever
happened had no consequences for Darensbourg. Bienville had
appointed him as commandant of the German Coast and had nothing
but respect for his governance. This appointment was perpetuated by

all of the French governors. Darensbourg held the position for forty-eight years, until his removal at the beginning of Spanish rule.

Father Raphael also claimed that Darensbourg had been an obstacle to conversion among the Germans, although there were only ten Protestant families on the entire *Côte des Allemands*. Nevertheless this priest was relentless in his propagation of the Catholic faith. Because of his continued agitation the *Compagnie des Indes* finally agreed to assign a Capuchin priest to the German Coast so that the residents no longer had to journey to the capital to participate in Catholic rites.

The census of 1726 showed that whatever property remained in the two villages set back from the river had been given up and that those colonists had moved to the riverbanks. Only three settlers had a few field workers or cattle; none had slaves or horses. Apparently nothing had been done by the *Compagnie des Indes* to help the German colonists, who still were able to clear sizeable amounts of land on their own. It was most remarkable that Darensbourg had already planted over eight acres and the other German colonists two to five acres. This census showed that the *Village des Allemands* had 152 settlers, a loss of only 17 settlers, who may have moved elsewhere.

The censuses taken in the first ten years of German colonization on the lower Mississippi showed that most of the Germans from Bienville's concession had again resettled upriver with their country-men. By this time all the land from below New Orleans to the German Coast had been assigned to concessions, although much was not culti-vated. Darensbourg wanted more families from the German states to come to Louisiana since they made such good citizens. He thought it would be desirable for the coast to be cultivated as far as Tchoupitoulas, about eleven miles upstream from the city. During the 1720s many colonists had moved to the east bank of the river. On the coast the houses were now built on both sides of the Mississippi and marked the end of the settled area.

The Designation *Côte des Allemands*

The many complaints about the company's neglect of the German farmers in the assignment of slaves apparently finally found an ear. By 1731 there were fifteen land grants on the East Bank, all but one pos-sessing slaves. For the East Bank settlement the place name *Allemands ou Anse aux Outardes* was used. The German settlement on the West Bank had originally been named the *Village des Allemands*. Both were now referred to as the *Côte des Allemands*, which in 1731 had a total population of 267 *habitants.* This was only a few more than the original number of Germans settling a decade earlier. The west-bank settlement stretched about twelve miles along the river, while the East Bank covered approximately seven miles. Of the fifty-three concessions on the West Bank more than half had slaves. The inventory of cattle had also grown noticeably, but the German colonists still had no horses.

A report made in the spring of 1731 noted that the German settlers were very hardworking and alone furnished the market of New Orleans. With their increased resources the German farmers continued to supply the capital, now with an abundance of vegetables, herbs, butter, eggs, poultry, and other commodities in addition to the staple crops of corn and rice.

Despite the 400 concessions issued to the French nobility in 1718 and 1719 by the *Compagnie des Indes,* almost no development had taken place in Louisiana. Until 1720 there were fewer than 10 functioning concessions on the Mississippi River. Those Frenchmen who had demanded and received large concessions were motivated not by the potential wealth to be earned from developing the land but by the hope of resale profits. After ten years, in 1728, the *Compagnie des Indes* officially invalidated the old concessions between Bayou Manchac and the Gulf of Mexico. Most of the concessionaires had remained in France as absentee landlords and had done nothing to develop their land grants. However, those few concessionaires who had cultivated at least one-third of their land could retain this cultivated portion. The remaining land had to be returned to the company to be given to other settlers in the colony.

Several German families took advantage of this new land apportionment and acquired property on the East Bank below the German colony. They had to abide by the land regulations of the company, i.e., cultivate their river frontage to a depth of about thirteen acres and maintain the levee on the river. No doubt the conditions of the company were hard for the colonists to meet but, on the other hand, were necessary if the colony was to survive.

The development of Louisiana progressed slowly. One observer noted that, of all the colonies founded in America, Louisiana had the hardest beginning and the most problems to overcome. This slow pace was only partially rooted in the difficulties of taming the land. The colonists were also victimized by the trade policies of the *Compagnie des Indes.* It sold them tools and other necessities at high prices and bought their products as cheaply as possible. Much more important to

France was the profit from trade with the West Indies. So Louisiana was not supplied sufficiently either with the workers or the tools needed for development.

Since the *Compagnie des Indes* possessed a tobacco monopoly it demanded that the large concessionaires exclusively plant tobacco. The small farmers on the German Coast, however, continued to concentrate on corn and rice, crops that provided them with income and were best suited to Louisiana's climate. In 1730, however, the exportation of Louisiana tobacco to France was prohibited when the *Compagnie des Indes* released its tobacco rights. The next year the company went bankrupt after seventeen years of heavy investing in Louisiana. Although the assets of the company were sold to pay off the debt, there was a shortfall of millions of *livres,* which the French king had to assume. No doubt this heavy debt was instrumental in his later decision to transfer Louisiana to his cousin Charles III on the throne of Spain.

The loss of France as a tobacco market and the bankruptcy of the *Compagnie des Indes* did not affect the German settlers severely. They had cultivated a mixed economy based on supplying New Orleans rather than the export trade. The failure of the company actually benefited the German farmers by releasing them from all obligations. It also gave them full ownership of their land so that they could become self-sufficient farmers.

The *Côte des Allemands* under the French Crown

After the demise of the *Compagnie des Indes* in 1731, Louisiana became a crown colony. It was governed directly by France for more than thirty years. During this time France required the large concessions below the *Côte des Allemands* to cultivate indigo as the primary export crop of the colony. Tobacco was to be grown farther up in the Mississippi valley.

Under French rule the German colonists continued to cultivate mainly grain and produce. Corn was raised to feed the chickens, livestock, and slaves, while rice, fruit, and vegetables were reserved for the white population. As before, the excess was sold in the markets of the capital. A notation made in 1744 mentioned that the German colonists also brought apples, plums, pears, figs, sweet potatoes, melons, artichokes, cabbage, and various greens to New Orleans. In the travel descriptions of this period, the following observations were made (M. Bossu, *Nouveaux Voyages aux Indes orientales,* vol. 1, p. 39):

> These people are very diligent; they are regarded as the purveyors of the capital . . . Friday evenings they load their boats and travel down-stream, two to a pirogue. They offer their wares on the river bank in New Orleans from early Saturday morning on. When they finally have finished their own purchases they row back and meet again in the evening on their farms.

The years following 1731 showed growth continuing at a moderate pace on the *Côte des Allemands*. During this period, cattle raising was developed as an industry. Once again the object of this new commercial venture was to supply New Orleans, now with meat and dairy products. By 1737 the number of cattle held by the German colonists rose to more than five hundred head. The German Coast itself had increased in population to more than 12 percent of the province. It now comprised about a hundred concessions and small farms.

Within the next decade the *Côte des Allemands* developed into the second largest settlement, after New Orleans, in the province. The 1746 census counted 3,700 white colonists and 4,730 slaves in the colony, with the population center located in the capital. Although France now wanted rice also to be cultivated for export, the colony consumed the supply it produced. The excess grain crop of the small German farmers was purchased by the colonial government and stored for future needs.

Poor harvests on the *Côte des Allemands* had disastrous effects on the New Orleans market. The great floods of 1734 and 1737 resulted in a rise in the price of grain in the city. The prolonged drought two years later made the price of rice and corn again go up appreciably. The bad weather of the summer of 1750 again did considerable damage to the grain crops. The sharp decline in the food supply from the *Côte des Allemands* caused a disruption all through the delta region. The solution seemed to be to bring more Germans to Louisiana to ensure a steady supply of provisions for the capital.

The reports to France requested good (German) peasant laborers in addition to the usual demands for more slaves for field work and soldiers for protection. Forty-seven German-speaking Alsatians were recruited who were willing to go to Louisiana. These were Lutherans who chose emigration rather than the religious persecution and imprisonment threatening them in their homeland. In 1753 they sailed to Louisiana and settled in the German Coast area. More families, mostly relatives of the first group, joined the colony in 1756 and 1759. To assist these new colonists in establishing farms the French government provided them with oxen, chickens, seed grain, and farming tools. By 1754 the newcomers were able to help supply the market in New Orleans. This strengthening of the German settlement was praised by the officials in the colony. In 1754 the governor, Louis Billouart de Kerlérec, wrote (*Archives Nationales, Ministère des Colonies,* C 13 A, vol. 38, fol. 12 f):

> We have seen these new colonists satisfied with their lot, working with commendable spirit and ambition to prepare their lands for planting; and we have the daily satisfaction of seeing them furnish the city with supplies of poultry, eggs and vegetables while they easily meet their own small needs. Since they are accustomed in their own country to working to exhaustion and to a hard life, they voluntarily take on the trouble and care which tilling the land requires. Besides they are assured of receiving all the profits of their labor since they are not charged any taxes as in Europe.

The census of the German Coast taken just before the end of French rule gave the following statistics: The population had risen to 1,268 *habitants* with 535 slaves living on 186 farms. The cattle count was almost a thousand head; sheep and hogs numbered over two thousand. The small farmers' concessions had assumed extraordinary importance since their products assured the food supply for the capital of the colony.

THE SPANISH COLONIAL PERIOD

The *Côte des Allemands* under Spanish Rule

In 1756 the Seven Years War between England and France had begun, sending English warships into the gulf to blockade Louisiana. In the colony the French and Indian War, the counterpart to the European conflict, had already broken out. To protect the Louisiana Territory from English encroachment and Indian attacks Governor Kerlérec desperately needed military support. Unable to receive men or ammunition from France, the governor was forced to turn to the Spanish for assistance, a portent of things to come. When the war in Europe ended with an English victory, the two Bourbon cousins on the thrones of France and Spain had already determined the destiny of Louisiana.

France had recognized that no precious metals were to be found in the colony, and an adequate profit could not be obtained through the development of agricultural exports. At the end of French rule the colony was viewed as being of little use to France. Its main export products were less easily cultivated in Louisiana than in the West Indian colonies and, therefore, less profitable. Through the secret Treaty of Fontainebleau in 1762, France divested itself of this burden, unwanted ever since John Law's stock scheme had collapsed. Fearing the expansion of English dominance southward toward the rich mines of Mexico, Spain reluctantly agreed to accept Louisiana as a buffer zone.

When the terms of this arrangement were made public by the Treaty of Paris in the spring of 1764, the citizens of Louisiana were dismayed. Jean Jacques Blaise D'Abbadie, who had replaced Kerlérec as governor the previous year, remained as a French appointee despite Louisiana's cession to Spain. He encouraged the citizenry to appeal to the French king not to relinquish Louisiana. The delegate sent to the French court, however, was not even allowed an audience with Louis XV to discuss his mission. The next year Governor D'Abbadie died but was replaced by the ranking French officer in Louisiana, Capt. Charles Philippe Aubry. With no Spanish governor being dispatched to Louisiana, the citizenry became more and more confident that the cession was merely a political maneuver between European powers, with no consequences for Louisiana.

These convictions were shattered when a dispatch to the Superior Council arrived from Havana in July of 1765. It had been issued by Don Antonio de Ulloa, announcing his appointment as governor. However, Ulloa, an eminent scientist and captain in the Spanish navy, delayed arriving in New Orleans for another eight months, again engendering hope in the remaining French citizenry. When he did arrive with a small entourage, the populace was not impressed. Spain had underestimated the need for a large show of force, expecting the French militia in Louisiana to switch loyalties and enlist under its flag. With Ulloa in this weakened position many of his Spanish troops deserted, leaving the would-be governor virtually powerless. Ulloa, refusing to take official possession of Louisiana for fear of insurrection, sailed to Balize at the mouth of the Mississippi, where he remained for seven more months. There he waited for the arrival of his Peruvian fiancée, whom he married while still in Balize rather than returning to New Orleans for an official ceremony at St. Louis Cathedral. This act offended the people of rank in the capital, who had expected to attend an elegant wedding and become members of the governor's social circle.

Ulloa's recourse was to work through the ranking French officer, Captain Aubry, who became more or less acting governor. This was a delaying tactic for Ulloa while he waited for the arrival of sufficient Spanish troops to garrison the posts, suppress the French Superior Council, and control the seditious population.

During the turmoil of the transition from French to Spanish rule, the economy of Louisiana suffered. French paper money lost half its value, while Ulloa was chronically short of Spanish pesos. Perhaps his greatest mistake was to issue commercial edicts through Aubry, which were intended to stabilize the economy and bring Louisiana into the orbit of Spain and its colonial empire. These edicts, issued during the two years after his arrival, sowed the seeds of rebellion in the citizenry. First he refused to pay the salaries and administrative costs of the colony prior to 1766. Next he forbade trade with the neighboring English colonies and closed two of the three mouths of the Mississippi to commercial traffic. All exports from the colony had to be carried in Spanish vessels with Spanish crews. He then limited trade to selected Spanish ports and specifically banned commerce with the French West Indies. This last edict was Ulloa's undoing, for it threatened the economic viability of the colony. Trade being forbidden with Santo Domingo and Martinique jeopardized the financial survival of the merchants and plantation owners of the colony.

The O'Reilly Revolution

Open rebellion broke out in the capital in October of 1768, led by twelve conspirators, whose wealth was threatened by Ulloa's policies. Since Darensbourg was related by marriage to all but one of the conspirators, he was involved from the beginning in planning and supporting this insurrection. On the coast the French-Canadian refugees, who had recently arrived, were brought into the rebellion by the suspicion that Ulloa intended to sell them as slaves. The Germans were enlisted through the false rumor that they would not be paid for the grain Ulloa had confiscated to feed these Acadians. In the meantime Ulloa attempted to head off the German rebels by dispatching a representative to the coast with the money in question. Commandant Darensbourg, however, refused this gesture and had the representative arrested. Furthermore the German planters had been thoroughly antagonized by Ulloa's arrogance in establishing economic policies that threatened to destroy their plans to develop an export trade.

One night in late October Darensbourg ordered the mobilization of the German militia, which marched toward New Orleans and took the Tchoupitoulas gate above the city. Upon entering the capital this militia of 400 men was joined by several hundred more Germans and Acadians, other militias, and a number of residents of the city and its outskirts. This mass of almost a thousand people gathered in the city center, awaiting developments. Members of the German militia and other participants patrolled the streets to keep order while the Superior Council deliberated over the petition to oust Governor Ulloa. Under pressure from the mob and swayed by the oratory of the conspirators, the Superior Council voted for the expulsion of the Spanish governor, giving Ulloa three days to leave the city.

Ulloa and his wife, protected by a small force, boarded the Spanish frigate *Volante,* which temporarily anchored in midriver for safety. Inexplicably the vessel did not reach Havana for six months, during which time the momentum of the rebellion began to weaken. Another petition to Louis XV to return the Louisiana colony to French rule was again ignored in Paris. Assistance was also denied by the English, who now governed Pensacola. No agreement about forming an independent government with a viable economic system could be reached by the conspirators. Fear of retribution from Spain began to grow, with some of the rebellion leaders even considering flight from the city to safer havens.

These fears were realized when a Spanish armada appeared at the mouth of the river at the end of July. Gen. Alexander O'Reilly, an extremely capable officer of Irish origin, had orders to restore Spanish authority in the colony, set up a new government, and punish the conspirators who had expelled the Spanish governor. In the meantime Ulloa had reached Havana, where he reported in detail the treasonous acts of the principal rebels. Armed with this information O'Reilly, still anchored at the river mouth, received delegates sent by the revolutionaries to negotiate clemency for themselves and the citizenry.

In the city the call for armed resistance to the Spanish was answered only by the Germans. About a hundred again marched to the capital but found no support among the citizens. Once they assessed the situation, they discretely returned to the German Coast while the Spanish fleet sailed up the river to occupy New Orleans. Twenty-four ships with 2,600 armed troops landed at the port and immediately took over the main square. Without resistance Aubry, still acting governor, handed over to O'Reilly the keys to the city gates. The Spanish flag was raised, and the transfer of the colony to Spain was effected without challenge.

O'Reilly did not lose time in carrying out his orders to punish the leading insurrectionists. All twelve were tried on the evidence given by Ulloa and information collected by O'Reilly. Joseph Villeré, the leader of the German Coast militia under Darensbourg, abandoned the idea of requesting protection from the English at Bayou Manchac and decided to negotiate with O'Reilly. Upon entering the city, however, he was arrested and imprisoned on one of the Spanish frigates, where he died in a scuffle on board. Six other insurrectionists were executed by firing squad and the rest given jail sentences, which were later commuted. O'Reilly then issued a proclamation giving amnesty to all who had signed the petition to expel Ulloa.

The fate of Darensbourg was another matter. O'Reilly harbored no doubt that the commandant of the German Coast was guilty of treasonous acts. But because of his age he was treated with leniency. O'Reilly forced him to release his holdings on the German Coast and move to the city, where he could no longer wield the power and influence he had enjoyed while living among his constituents. His two sons were also removed from the coast and sent into exile in Opelousas, far from their father. This clemency toward Darensbourg was extended to the citizens of the German Coast. Although they had been the principal group involved in the rebellion, they were required only to take an oath of allegiance to the Spanish crown, as were all the citizens in the colony. No doubt O'Reilly's clemency reflected the economic importance of the German Coast to the colony, which O'Reilly did not want to disturb.

Although O'Reilly remained in the colony only seven months, he established Spanish rule with a firm hand. His reputation as "Bloody O'Reilly" was probably undeserved, for the bloodshed was limited to the execution of half a dozen conspirators. While unwavering but just in handling the aftermath of the rebellion, he ably dealt with the affairs of the colony and brought stability. What became known as the O'Reilly Revolution, although a failure, had the distinction of being the first revolution against a European colonial power on what was to become American soil.

Further evidence of O'Reilly's wisdom and goodwill as governor was shown by his assistance to the Germans from Maryland, who arrived in late 1769. Seeking to escape the persecution they faced because of their Catholic faith, this group had made inquiries of Governor Ulloa as to conditions in Louisiana. Having received the promise of religious freedom and government support, they embarked in early 1769 on an English vessel, the *Britain*, along with a group of

Acadians. Although these fifty-seven Germans and thirty-two Acadians reached the Louisiana coast without incident, they could not find the mouth of the Mississippi and mistakenly made landfall on the coast of Texas. There they were taken captive by the Spanish, their cargo of cloth and dry goods confiscated and the captain put in the stocks. The passengers were forced to work on the nearby ranches to offset the cost of their maintenance while the Spanish commandant waited for instructions from the viceroy in Mexico City. Finally freed in August, they could not reboard their vessel, which had become unseaworthy in the meantime. A trek across land to Louisiana was the only alternative. On orders from the Spanish governor they were guided to Natchitoches, the Louisiana fort closest to the Texas border. There they immediately contacted the officials in New Orleans to ask for resettlement with their compatriots on what later became known as the German-Acadian Coast.

Governor O'Reilly, who had been sent to New Orleans to quell a rebellion supported by these two ethnic groups, was not disposed to strengthen their numbers. So he assigned the wayfarers to the Iberville Post at Bayou Manchac, which marked the border with English territory. There, about eighty miles upriver from New Orleans, they were isolated in an area that frequently flooded. Nevertheless, provided with the necessary supplies for settlement as well as firearms for protection, they soon became well established and prospered. Many of these Maryland Germans later moved to higher ground on what became known as the Dutch (*Deutsch* or German) Highlands, now located just south of Baton Rouge. Others joined the German militia, moved to the coast, and married into the families there.

The census of the year 1769 gave a detailed description of the economic prosperity on the German Coast at the time the colony was taken over by Spain. The total number of inhabitants was over two thousand, the white population having doubled within the previous twenty years. The consigned land measured about sixty miles of river frontage with a depth of a mile and a half. The number of slaves in the German settlement had quadrupled since the late 1740s. Grain production predominated on the West Bank, where cypress trade with the West Indies had also developed as a lucrative business. In contrast, indigo became the main commercial product on the lower East Bank, where almost 75 percent of the concessions held slaves. The census of 1769 showed a large increase in cattle holdings in the German settlement, tripling to over 3,000 head. Almost all of the concessions had also developed dairies. Sufficient dray animals were kept for farm labor plus 2,500 hogs and almost 2,000 sheep.

In 1770 O'Reilly expropriated a plot of river frontage for the Germans, which was reserved for a church and cemetery. Two years later the citizens built a substantial structure there, staffed by Capuchin priests. Prior to this time the inhabitants on the West Bank worshiped in a small wooden building erected in 1745. Because this chapel was too rudimentary to merit a priest, the citizens conducted their own services or traveled across the river to worship at the Red Church built in 1740 on the East Bank. On the German Coast only the churches and an abandoned fort interrupted the row of farms with their houses, barns, and outbuildings. The rest was grazing land or land lying fallow or abandoned.

Expansion on the Coast

During the Spanish colonial period a significant expansion of the settled areas on the Mississippi had occurred through the influx of Acadians. These Canadian refugees of French descent began to arrive in 1765 and received land grants mainly above the *Côte des Allemands* and on the nearby tributaries of the river. The Acadians also received unsettled or abandoned river plots on the German Coast. Levees and river roads on both banks had to be extended upstream as the colonization of the Mississippi riverbanks was continued on the *Côte des Acadiens.*

From 1775 on, the *Côte des Allemands* was divided into two districts, the parish of St. Charles and the parish of St. John the Baptist, each named after the church located there. Later, at the end of Spanish rule, the *Côte des Acadiens* was similarly divided. The governor appointed a commandant for each district, who served both as head of the militia and local judge. The two new governmental entities of the German Coast were generally referred to as the *Première Côte des Allemands,* the first German Coast (St. Charles, downriver section), and the *Deuxième Côte des Allemands,* the Second German Coast (St. John, upriver section). The commandant of each area was required annually to carry out a comprehensive inspection of his parish to determine the condition of the levees, the river roads on both banks, the bridges, and the ditches. On the East Bank of the *Côte des Allemands* the Bonnet Carré bend of the river caused flooding again and again. At this spot, only four miles from Lake Pontchartrain, the river sometimes took this path to the lake rather than flowing into the gulf. In 1779 Robin de Logny, then commandant of the German Coast, reported (*Archivo General de Indias,* Seville, Seccion 11 A. Papeles de Cuba, legato 216 B):

Breaks in the Bonnet Carré levee mean the complete loss of the cattle and harvest for the larger portion of the inhabitants. Many have been forced to attempt to acquire land somewhere else on which they can live. If ways and means are not immediately found to dam the water in the Bonnet Carré area at least twenty-five miles of river frontage will no longer be cultivatable. I myself have fifty acres of grain fields under water in addition to a portion of my indigo fields. For my neighbors both upstream and downstream it is not any different. I can grab ducks from my window and fish in my backyard. That is the situation with my farm and also with my neighbors for a stretch of fifty miles upriver and at least fifteen miles downriver.

In the winter of 1783 the government finally advanced the money needed for the construction of an adequate levee at the Bonnet Carré bend. Nevertheless, severe levee breaks continued to occur. There were great floods during the next decade as well as unpredictable harvests. These conditions in the lower Mississippi delta caused numerous settlers to fail, making it even more remarkable that the small farmers of the German Coast prospered.

Weather conditions caused great swings in the grain harvests. The spring droughts adversely affected the crops. In 1784 the corn harvest was ruined but the rice crop was spared. Two years later, however, the river sank so low that salt water from the gulf came almost forty miles upriver. It destroyed the rice crop but spared the corn harvest. In August of 1779 the province was hit by a hurricane of such strength that almost all of the farms surrounding the capital suffered severe damage. Gov. François Louis Hector Carondelet reported ("Dispatches of the Spanish Governors of Louisiana, 1763-1789," *Survey of Federal Archives in Louisiana,* New Orleans, 1938):

> All the inhabitants of the Mississippi banks upriver are hard pressed because of the devastation caused by the recent hurricane, which drove water from *Lac des Allemands* toward the river. It rose up to a height of six feet above sea level behind their houses, flooded all their land, and flowed with remarkable speed toward the Mississippi. It dragged with it trees, houses, cattle, everything that it found in the way. Over a stretch of about sixty miles the land has been abandoned by the settlers who, until this point, cultivated rice of a quality exceeded nowhere. That is a terrible loss because the rice crop provided one of the staple foods for the population.

In a number of other years hurricanes caused equally great losses in the crops, equipment, buildings, and cattle. In the late summer of 1794 another vicious hurricane hit the *Côte des Allemands*. It followed the same path as the 1779 hurricane, which was also the path of the great storm of 1722. That early hurricane had wiped out the original German settlements on the coast.

In the meantime the Spanish economic policies had become more flexible, voiding the stringent decrees of Ulloa. This process had begun with O'Reilly's promotion of the cypress trade. In 1776 Spain again allowed trade with the French West Indies and later with France itself. Additionally the unrestricted importation of slaves to Louisiana was again permitted. Spain now wanted to strengthen its new colony as a bulwark against the encroaching power of the British and later the Americans. These new Spanish trade policies led to great increases in the productivity of the *Côte des Allemands*. Still grain, produce, and cattle remained the foremost products of the German farmers.

The growing prosperity of the German Coast was also made possible by a noticeable increase in slave holdings. The census taken in 1785 showed that the number of slaves in both parishes made up over half of the 3,203 inhabitants. Four years later the number of slaves on the *Côte des Allemands* had risen to more than double the white population.

The wealth of the coast was concentrated on those larger concessions in St. Charles Parish that had enough slaves to grow indigo for export. But the indigo crop varied with weather conditions. The prolonged droughts and early frosts of this period significantly depleted the harvest. But the real threat was a previously unknown insect that began to infest the indigo about this time. By 1794 it had caused so much damage that almost no indigo was harvested in either St. Charles or St. John parishes. Continuing crop failure forced the inhabitants to give up indigo completely. Most of the former indigo planters returned to cultivating corn and producing lumber. Many settlers owned their own sawmills, which operated day and night on the riverbanks during high water. The wood was transported from the cypress swamps through the canals to the river, then bound into rafts and floated downstream to New Orleans. The quantity of lumber sent from the coast to Havana and elsewhere in the West Indies was prodigious.

The *Côte des Allemands* also continued to supply the city with grain, fruit, vegetables, meat, and poultry. As from the beginning, the inhabitants transported their agricultural products by pirogue to New Orleans. When there was a shortage of food in the capital, the governor ordered the commandant of the coast to buy grain from the farmers and send it into the city. Also traders came upriver and purchased products from individual settlers for resale or export. By the end of the Spanish period the German Coast's prosperity won it the name of the *Côte d'Or,* the Gold Coast.

The river, as before, still acted as a link to New Orleans for the *Côte des Allemands.* Both the French and the Spanish colonial governments, however, set a priority on establishing roads on both banks, which the citizens were required to build and maintain. Although transportation by land became more frequent during the Spanish period, vehicles such as wagons did not exist in any great number. Additionally, these roads were often impassable because of floods, with the result that the river itself remained the only reliable traffic route.

On the German Coast the populace still remained loyal to the colony's French founders, as did the citizens in the capital, who had never adjusted to the imposition of Spanish law. There was great rejoicing on the *Côte des Allemands* when the news was received in 1800 that Napoleon was taking Louisiana back for France. His representative, the colonial prefect Pierre Clement Laussat, was highly impressed by the welcome he received from the German populace. He consequently recommended that the French government recruit a large number of German families every year for the colony. Both the French and Spanish

Pierre Laussat. *Drawing by Raymond Calvert.*

governors had also been impressed with the industriousness of this ethnic group. They, too, recognized the wisdom of acquiring more Germanic colonists.

During the French period a Swiss regiment, whose members were from various German-speaking areas, was always stationed in the colony. It was charged with the maintenance of order and protection of the colony from foreign invasion or Indian attack. Governor Bienville pointed out that these former soldiers should be settled on the *Côte des Allemands* at the end of their tour of duty instead of being sent back to Europe.

Succeeding French governors settled these Swiss soldiers on the *Côte des Allemands,* which helped to maintain the Germanic culture among the settlers. So did the "good peasant laborers" sent to the coast by Governor Kerlérec. They were reported to work with ambition and spirit to furnish the city with poultry, eggs, and vegetables. In 1769 another infusion of Germanic blood was brought into the colony by the Germans from Maryland. Both of these migrations helped to preserve the culture and traditions of the old country. The census of 1769 showed that the core of the coast's population remained Germanic although a number of French concessions were interspersed among the German holdings by that time.

Through the decades the farmers of the German Coast maintained the mentality of the original pioneers. Their orientation was toward farming for their own needs and finding profit in trade with the capital. Just as in the French period, the German Coast continued to serve as the breadbasket for the colony. During the Spanish period the livestock industry developed to such an extent that the city was supplied with meat almost exclusively by the German Coast. The export trade was also lucrative for those farmers who possessed large concessions and a number of slaves. They profited from selling grain, lumber, indigo, and later sugarcane. However, these concessionaires were the exception, not the rule. Small landholders comprised the vast majority, who supported themselves through farming and bringing their products to market in the capital. As early as 1776 Chavalier de Champigny declared (*Etat-présent de la Louisiane avec toutes les particularités de cette province d'Amerique,* The Hague: n.p., p. 17):

> The area that is still today occupied by the descendents of the Germans and the Canadians is the most cultivated and the most populous in the colony. I regard the Germans and the Canadians as the foundation upon which Louisiana has been established.

Since the German pioneers were brought into a totally French milieu, their language and culture in time were lost. No German schools or Protestant congregations were established in the colony, leaving the settlers on the *Côte des Allemands* unable to record their traditions for succeeding generations. The lack of language and religious instruction in German accelerated their assimilation, as did intermarriage with their French fellow citizens. Both men and women of German background were considered very desirable marriage partners. The males were known for their dedication to hard work and devotion to duty, while the women were considered diligent housewives and healthy, prolific mothers. Church registers showed that these intermarriages produced as many as twenty or more children.

Both sexes frequently married into the highest French social circles, where they readily adopted the language and Francophone culture.

Remnants of the culture were still readily discernible on the German Coast at the turn of the century. Some citizens remained bilingual throughout the colonial period. A few legal documents written in German script survived, as did several accounts of officials and other travelers to the coast. The reports by C. C. Robin and B. Duvallon from 1803 pointed out that the Germans still retained their language and were easy to recognize because of their accents and light complexions.

The *Côte des Allemands* under Threat

At the time of French colonization several small Indian tribes lived in the lower Mississippi delta. Governor Bienville had placed the German settlers in an area formerly cleared and cultivated by these Indians. Because of its location upriver from the fortified city, the *Côte des Allemands* was quite vulnerable to Indian attack. This problem existed for most of the century of French and Spanish rule.

The French understood how to use the Indians in reaching their military and political goals. However, their courtship of the Louisiana Indians was challenged by the British as they moved closer and closer to French-held territory. The largest Indian group in the southern part of the colony was the Choctaw tribe, which by midcentury had over three thousand Indian braves. The British became more and more successful in exerting influence over this tribe, inciting them to attack and kill the French settlers who were appropriating the Indians' land. The presence of hostile Indians, who could unexpectedly attack the colony by boat from the swamps, struck fear into the hearts of the colonists on the *Côte des Allemands.* All of the settlers owned weapons, and those able to bear arms formed their own militia. This private army was led for many years by the colony's commandant, Karl Friedrich Darensbourg, who was charged with the settlers' defense. He oversaw a militia composed of the able-bodied men of the colony, who, for the most part, were rugged pioneers and crack shots.

In 1729, shortly after the establishment of the German colony, the first Indian attack occurred. It was part of the larger massacre perpetrated by the Natchez Indians at Fort Rosalie, which had virtually annihilated the settlers there. This attack against the German villagers on the West Bank, however, was rather weak and easily repulsed. The defense put up by the settlers prevented any real damage but fed the colonists' terror of future Indian raids.

In the spring of 1748 a second Indian raid occurred. A group of Choctaws attacked the German colony on the east bank of the river, killed a colonist, and scalped his wife. The Indians took with them one of the children along with a slave, whom they expected to sell to the English. The militia members from the coast plus a contingent from New Orleans pursued the Indians, who nevertheless escaped capture. Governor Kerlérec later lamented that there were still not enough men in the colony to go into the woods to fight the Indians.

In November of the same year an even more serious Choctaw attack occurred. The Indians raided a farm on the East Bank while the residents were working in the fields. All but four settlers escaped by crossing the river to the safety of the West Bank and its militia. Learning of the raid, however, a number of other residents fled, giving the Indians the opportunity to ransack their homesteads. Because Darensbourg's militia, then 130 men strong, lacked boats to cross the river, the governor, Pierre Cavagnial de Rigaud, marquis de Vaudreuil, immediately sent three detachments from New Orleans. This time the Indians were shot or captured, their loot confiscated, and the prisoners returned to their farms.

Because fear of the Indians was already ingrained in the settlers on the coast, the aftermath of this attack was profound. The governor reported that most of the Germans abandoned their houses, left their well-cultivated land and animals, and moved to the city for safety. New Orleans had temporarily lost an essential source of supplies. As a result grain, produce, and meat from the coast became both scarce and expensive in the capital.

A year later Governor Vaudreuil promised the Germans to establish a *corps de garde* on the endangered side of the river, which reassured some of the colonists enough for them to return to their farms. In 1750 he established a small military post with thirty men on the East Bank, across from Darensbourg's homestead. There this garrison could guard the mouth of the bayou, which was often used by the Indians as a transportation waterway. Other German colonists returned only then, but settled on the safer West Bank, where they began new farms. These were at first less productive than the ones they had abandoned, which continued the temporary loss of food supplies from the German colony. Governor Kerlérec reported four years later that the settlement of the Germans had not yet recovered from the unfortunate Choctaw attack. The scarcity of well-trained soldiers in the colony resulted in fewer and fewer men being assigned to the German Coast. By the time of the Spanish take-over, the post had been abandoned.

During the Spanish period the agitation of the English caused more unrest and further Indian attacks on the white settlements. Choctaws appeared several times on the *Côte des Allemands*. A final attack in 1773, while frightening to the inhabitants, did no damage and was quickly repulsed by the coast's militia. It was general knowledge in the colony that the English were behind the Indian raids on the settlements. In revenge the citizens demanded the arrest and imprisonment of several English traders who appeared on the coast later that year.

In 1763 the Treaty of Paris ceded to England the east bank of the Mississippi from Baton Rouge upriver, so that the British sphere of influence encroached even more closely upon the main area of French settlement. The English took advantage of this proximity to continue fomenting Indian attacks on the white settlers. In 1779 Gov. Bernardo de Galvez took decisive action and marched upriver to retaliate. All of the able-bodied men of the *Côte des Allemands* joined the effort. With their help Galvez was successful by 1781 in driving the English from their military strongholds both at Bayou Manchac and Baton Rouge.

During the period of Spanish rule in Louisiana a number of assaults against British and American advances were made by the militia. In 1791 a talented military officer, Don José Pontalba, was given the command of both the German and Acadian coasts. To ward off encroachment he placed four fusilier companies on the *Côte des Allemands* and three on the *Côte des Acadiens*. Pontalba's soldiers were good scouts and riflemen and experienced in the swamps and forests. The success of Galvez's expulsion of the English from Manchac and Baton Rouge was continued by Pontalba's efficient leadership of the militia. On the *Côte des Allemands* both the Indian attacks and encroachment by the English were ended. The colony was finally in a position to enter the new century free of threats to its citizens and its territorial integrity.

The *Côte des Allemands* at the Time of the Louisiana Purchase

After the failure of the indigo crop in the 1790s the cultivation of sugarcane took over most of the lower Mississippi delta. By the turn of the century sixty sugarcane plantations had been developed on the banks of the river. The cultivation of sugarcane quickly took over in St. Charles Parish due to the number of slaves, which had increased significantly after 1782. Only a few remnants of indigo cultivation could still be found after the Louisiana Purchase. The cultivation of sugarcane was not taken up by most of the small farmers in St. John Parish. Because it demanded much more work than indigo, some farmers turned to cotton, although grain remained the main crop.

The cultivation of sugar grew steadily and spread upriver as slave holdings increased. It proved to be a great advantage for the planters, who had been badly hurt by the frequent losses of their indigo crops. The first American governor, William C. C. Claiborne, reported that there was hardly a single citizen who had not succeeded and was not solvent, even enriched. The sugarcane plantations on the banks of the Mississippi appeared to one traveler as superb beyond description. Another wrote that he had not seen such a rich and well-cultivated tract in any other part of the United States.

Farther upstream on the *Côte des Allemands* the landscape changed to a mixed economy. There sugarcane, cotton, grain, and lumber were all cultivated. Sluices in the levees were introduced to irrigate the rice fields. With high water the sawmills on the banks of the river were put to work. Also cattle raising remained important. The barnyards were reported as being full of cattle, hogs, and fowl. F. Cuming noticed that above New Orleans the river was "covered with multitudes of market boats rowing" (*Sketches of a Tour to the Western Country through the States of Ohio and Kentucky; a Voyage down the Ohio and Mississippi Territory and Part of West Florida 1807-1809,* Pittsburgh: n.p., 1810, p. 332).

The *Côte des Allemands* was pictured at the time of the Louisiana Purchase as the best-cultivated part of Louisiana. Baudry des Lozières especially emphasized the diligence of the Germans as the reason for the thriving economy (*Voyage à la Louisiane et sûr le Continent de l'Amèrique Septentrionale, fait dans les Années 1794 à 1798,* Paris: Imprimeur-Librarie, Palais du Tribunat, 1802). The French colonial prefect, Pierre Clement Laussat, made the suggestion to increase the population of Louisiana primarily by bringing in Germans. In 1803 he supported this recommendation with the following words (*Archives Nationales, Ministère des Colonies, Messidor* [June 19-July 18] 6, Col., C 13 A, vol. 52, fol. 199):

> This class of peasants, especially of this nationality, is just the kind we need and the only one that has always done well in this area, which is called the German Coast. It is the most industrious, the most populous, the most prosperous, the most upright, the most valuable population segment of this colony. I deem it essential that the French government adopt the policy of bringing to this area every year 1,000 to 1,200 families from the border states of Switzerland, the Rhine and Bavaria.

The transfer of the colony from France to Spain had not caused a great interruption in its economic development. France wished for no changes in the well-established sugarcane industry when the colony again came into its possession in 1800. The instructions to the colonial prefect early in 1802 reiterated that slavery was the basis of agriculture in Louisiana. Since this was well understood, the planters again began demanding permission to import slaves, which had been greatly curtailed under Spanish rule.

With the Louisiana Purchase the American government took over the land ordinances initiated by the French and continued by the Spanish. The area supervisor still controlled the work to be carried out by the concession owners. These regulations were retained until late in the twentieth century, when the state and the levee board took over these responsibilities.

The American government also took over the plantation system with its associated slave practices. At that time there were approximately 2,800 slaves on the coast. In 1812, when the name of the *Côte des Allemands* was officially changed to the "German Coast," the number of slaves had risen by a thousand. Every decade produced significant increases in the slave population, until there were well over 8,500 slaves laboring on the coast by 1850. Based on the increasing importation of slaves and the assurance of protective tariffs by the government, sugarcane cultivation fully matured on the German Coast. This prosperity continued until the economic and cultural development of Louisiana was suddenly ended by the Civil War.

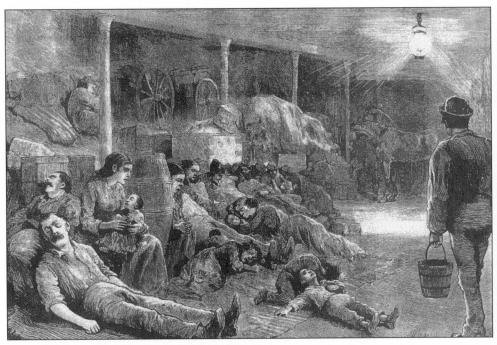

German immigrants on a Mississippi riverboat, from a German edition of *Frank Leslie's Illustrated Newspaper,* no date. *Courtesy of a private collection.*

CHAPTER TWO

German Immigration

GERMAN IMMIGRATION TO AMERICA

As far as is known, German immigration to the New Orleans region in the colonial period was limited to the German Coast and the small settlement of Maryland Germans south of Baton Rouge. Although records show Germanic names scattered in and around New Orleans there was no other significant immigration in the eighteenth century. The early years of the nineteenth century showed the same pattern. No immigration statistics were kept until 1820, when Congress began to require that port officials keep records. Before that time the number of German immigrants arriving in America had to be based on guesswork. Up to the War of 1812 between the United States and England, immigration had been quite limited. Only after the final Battle of New Orleans in January of 1815 did the number of immigrants begin to grow. In order to understand the reasons for this growth in German immigration, conditions in Europe as well as in America should be examined.

The years 1815 to 1820 saw higher German immigration levels than would follow in the next decade. Most of this immigration was from the Rhine River valley, from the provinces of Baden-Württemberg, Alsace, the Palatinate, and Hesse. Those other provinces of the Rhine that had suffered from Napoleon's continual wars for the Rhineland following the French Revolution also produced immigrants for the New World. After the fall of Napoleon, sky-high taxes were levied to pay for the damage inflicted by the wars. This was also the period of tyrannical persecution of the student societies, the *Burschenschaften,* causing the youth of the German states to seek refuge in the land of political liberty. To make matters worse, famine struck in 1817. Dutch shippers used these unfortunate circumstances to send agents along the Rhine to acquire "freight" for America. They promised riches to the poor and freedom to the oppressed. These so-called *Neulanders* went from village to village enlisting an army of emigrants who traveled up the Rhine. In 1817 alone 16,000 people traveled on barges upriver from Württemberg, and the next year almost double that number passed through Mainz on the way to Holland. There they were packed upon sailing ships bound for America, where they would work off the cost of their passage.

These immigrants were called redemptioners because they had to "redeem" their transportation costs. Once they arrived in this country they would be lined up in rows on the docks and sold to anyone who would pay the price asked by the captain. According to the laws that existed then, this constituted an actual sale, resulting in indenture for three to eight years. The redemption system was widespread in Colonial America and was practiced in most of the East Coast ports throughout the first third of the nineteenth century. Since the importation of black slaves had been made illegal in 1808, the system filled the need for cheap labor in the developing nation.

Beginning in 1820 official immigration numbers became available. Congress had passed a law requiring officials to submit reports giving the number and nationality of foreigners landing in American ports. For the decade of 1820 to 1830 these records showed somewhat over six thousand immigrants arriving from the German states. What percentage of those Germans landed in New Orleans is unknown, as is also true of the 1830s and all but the last year of the 1840s. However, New York and New Orleans were the two principal ports for the nation up to the Civil War. The choice between the two major American ports was largely a matter of chance for emigrants headed to the New World. In the era of the sailing ship, with its indefinite departure dates, the American port was chosen by the likelihood of obtaining profitable freight for the return trip.

The 1830s showed a great increase in the number of German immigrants. The official records showed almost 125,000 German arrivals nationally. These years were a stormy time in Europe, which caused emigration from the German states to increase greatly. Revolution was in the air, producing unrest in the German states of Saxony, Hanover, Nassau, and lower Hesse and outright civil war in upper Hesse.

The 1840s showed almost 400,000 German immigrants arriving in American ports, more than triple the number of the previous decade. This great exodus of the 1840s was explained by worsening conditions in the homeland, especially in Silesia, with harsh winters, bad crops, and increasing inflation. As it spread, the Industrial Revolution brought about the ruin of cottage industries, leaving thousands of artisans destitute. These factors combined to cause the failure of businesses, a loss of trade, the consequent closing of many small factories, unemployment, and finally the Revolution of 1848. Many of the most talented Germans had to go into exile as a result of the failure of this revolution. These immigrants, called forty-eighters, brought their revolutionary ideals with them and demanded that the German-Americans of the United States unite under their leadership. They wanted to drive out slavery and remodel the entire republic according to their concepts. Through bitter experience these revolutionaries gradually learned that their extreme ideas could not be carried out in their adopted country. From this point on, the leadership of the German communities in America shifted to the conservatives, many of whom were elected to nationally important and honorable positions.

German immigration reached its zenith in the 1850s. Almost one million Germans landed on the shores of America in 1857 alone. Economic and political hardship continued to drive Germans out of their homeland, as did the instability caused by the Crimean War. Emigration from the German states became common. Thousands of young men left their homeland, attracted to California by the promise of prosperity produced by the gold rush. Immigration to the West Coast increased dramatically, driving up wages and prices and creating speculation fever. At this time America also tripled the expanse of its railway system, all with borrowed money. The governmental practice of giving free land to the railroad companies accelerated the development of the Western territories of the United States, where most undertakings were also carried out with borrowed money. Bank reserves began to shrink with this new demand for loans, and lax laws allowed states to print unlimited amounts of "wild-cat paper." A crash had to come, which hit in 1857. A serious financial and industrial crisis followed, which put hundreds of thousands out of work. At this time, the anti-immigration Know-Nothing movement in the states gained great momentum because of the competition with foreigners for ever-scarcer jobs. Without this catastrophe, immigration during this period would have increased significantly instead of falling by half.

Just at this time the introduction of the oceangoing steamship made the difficult and dangerous voyage to America significantly shorter, safer, more comfortable, and cheaper. The great transatlantic steamship lines were founded during this period, forming German, French, English, Dutch, and American companies. The new steamship lines and the American railroads sent agents all over Europe to recruit passengers. These agents were joined by others from those American states that had cheap or free land to offer. Letters sent home from immigrants who had already "struck it rich" in America increased the widespread dissatisfaction with the conditions existing in Europe. There were examples of entire communities preparing to leave for America. Thousands were recruited for the developing United States, and a strong emigration movement again evolved.

New Orleans held its position as the second largest port in America not only for immigration but also for commerce. Ships bringing immigrants as ballast landed from October to May, the high season for the export of cotton. As the world's export center for cotton, New Orleans could always offer profitable freight for the return trip. Liverpool, the most important European cotton market, received hundreds of deliveries of cotton from New Orleans every year, either directly or via Hamburg and Bremen.

Those immigrants landing in New Orleans, for the most part, took Mississippi River steamboats into the interior. However, no official records were kept to trace this movement of people toward the Midwest and California. At this time these immigrants traveled via New Orleans because there was no other quicker, cheaper, or more comfortable way to reach the agricultural heartland and West Coast of the country. The advantage of the Mississippi River was that it remained free of ice, unlike the other two major waterways. The competing immigration routes from New York to Detroit and from Philadelphia to Pittsburgh were icebound for a third of the year. With the introduction of the steamboat in 1814, the strong current of the Mississippi River was conquered, causing immigration through New Orleans to rise steadily as steamboat travel improved in duration and safety. New arrivals also used the river as a quick means of traveling westward through Texas and Missouri to the Pacific Coast. Until the building of the transcontinental railroads the Mississippi River was the undisputed gateway to the West, carrying almost half of the passenger load heading inland.

The growing threat of civil war in the United States had a negative effect on the number of German immigrants going through New Orleans up the Mississippi. By 1861 the numbers had fallen to half of the previous year. With the approaching end of the war, however, German immigration rose again and soon matched the level of 1860. From this point on immigration rose steadily for the rest of the decade. This increase was caused by renewed war abroad and the annexation by Prussia of five major German states in northern Europe. After 1866 all young men in the newly enlarged Prussia were eligible for the draft, contributing heavily to the rising emigration numbers.

Unlike in the Northern areas of the United States, the Civil War had profound effects on immigration through Southern ports. The outbreak of the war resulted in a blockade of the mouth of the Mississippi River, ending immigration via New Orleans. However, during the war years, the transatlantic steamship lines in the North increased their sailings. Direct connections with Europe were also established by both the Hamburg and Bremen lines. Railroad lines linking the Eastern American ports with the interior were built farther and farther westward. The resulting change in transportation routes left New Orleans with only those immigrants heading west to and through Texas and Missouri. At the end of the Civil War transatlantic passenger steamers from Hamburg, Bremen, Liverpool, and Le Havre began to call at New Orleans. During this period the two German lines brought over fifteen thousand German immigrants to the port of New Orleans. But within ten years the city lost both German steamship lines, causing an immediate reduction in German immigration by 50 percent.

The 1870s saw the approaching demise of German immigration through the port of New Orleans but close to three-quarters of a million Germans arriving at other American ports. Nationally only the mid-decade years showed noticeably lower immigration numbers, a lull attributable to the financial crisis produced by the collapse of railroad speculation.

The next decade marked the end of German immigration through New Orleans. In 1882 the United States government improved the port of Galveston so that it could function as a shipping center. The steamship companies then found it more profitable to sail from Europe directly to Galveston, stopping in New Orleans only on the return trip to pick up freight. Ironically, German immigration on the national level reached its highest point in this same year. Over a quarter-million Germans, more than double that of any other European nationality, arrived at American ports.

Just as in the 1840s, this heavy wave of immigrants again raised severe concern in America. This time the anti-immigration movement started with the American trade unions, which complained that labor contractors were importing great numbers of cheap European workers. Under pressure Congress was forced to act in 1885, declaring illegal the importation of all contract workers.

Beginning in 1893, ship captains were required to present a detailed, notarized statement to the American consul listing all immigrants aboard before departure from any European port. There was a great rush to emigrate before these strict immigration laws took effect. European immigration totals for 1892 reached their highest point. The Germans among these immigrants came primarily from West Prussia and German-speaking Poland, the most densely populated areas of the German Empire. But that same year, bad business conditions developed in the American economy, producing more bankruptcies than in any previous year. This situation quickly lowered the number of immigrants, as did an outbreak of cholera brought from Hamburg to New York. Contributing to this decline was the gradual improvement in industrial development in Europe, particularly in Germany.

An increasingly bitter fight developed against the hundreds of thousands who were brought every year to American shores by shipping companies. At that time the persistent high unemployment was blamed on the flood of cheap European laborers. The result was pressure from all sides on Congress to pass more laws hostile to immigration. From 1890 on, the European influx began to resemble a seasonal migration. Increasingly more immigrants came in the spring to America but returned in the fall to Europe. This workforce went to the already overcrowded factories and mining operations of the East Coast, from which they could more easily return home. To combat these developments Congress passed additional laws prohibiting European laborers from returning annually to their native countries.

Immigration as a seasonal phenomenon was partially produced by the lack of a federal bureau to direct immigrants to those parts of the United States where they could settle and prosper. Nevertheless, the fertile farmlands of the Mid- and Northwest attracted hundreds of thousands of Germans. Word of mouth through family, friends, and neighbors was the main method of recruitment. Laborers and fieldworkers were also badly needed in the South and West, where there was little anti-immigrant sentiment or union agitation. Nevertheless, whatever recruitment efforts were made were largely ineffectual in bringing German immigrants where they were most needed.

GERMAN IMMIGRATION TO NEW ORLEANS

Prior to the Civil War, when New Orleans was the second most important port in the nation, international and national conditions determined immigration trends. Immigration statistics were unavailable before 1820, when Congress created the Bureau of Statistics, requiring authorities in each port city to keep records. For the first ten

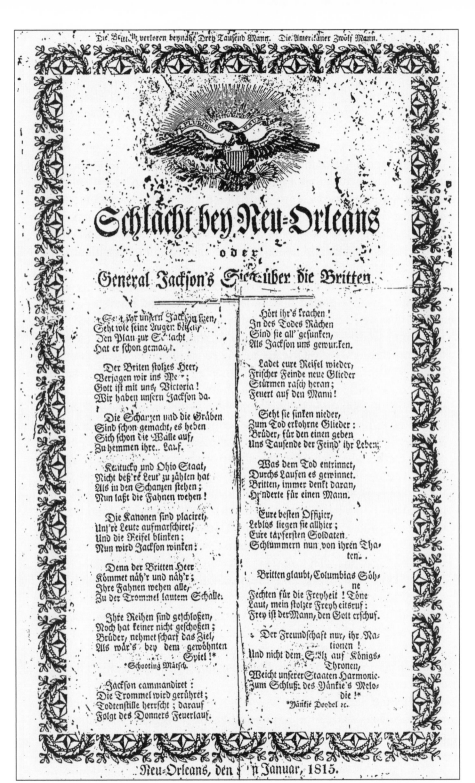

Poem in German titled "Battle of New Orleans or General Jackson's Victory over the British, New Orleans, the 8th of January, 1815." *Courtesy of the Historic New Orleans Collection.*

years, however, many of the quarterly reports never arrived in Washington. Therefore the immigration numbers for this decade had no significance.

Other sources give spotty but nevertheless important information. One estimate of German immigration for the five years between 1815 and 1820 calculated that approximately two thousand redemptioners were brought to the city. Early in 1818 a public notice documented the arrival of three Dutch ships with almost six hundred German redemptioners. These were only half of the people who had embarked in Helder, Holland. The rest had died on the voyage from sickness or starvation or had jumped overboard, driven mad by thirst.

The 1830s showed more conscientious record keeping by port authorities, who reported that almost 9,000 German immigrants had arrived in New Orleans. The last year of this decade noted 750 Lutherans among the 2,800 German arrivals. These Lutherans were traveling through New Orleans to Missouri under the leadership of Pastor Martin Stephan, a strict fundamentalist. Stephan had served in Dresden for thirty years, during which time he had developed a large following of likeminded "old" believers. After being suspended by church authorities for rejecting new scriptural interpretations, Stephan led his followers to America. The cost of passage came from a common church coffer, which enabled Stephan to bring along the church library, organ, and musicians. In Bremerhaven Stephan rented four large ships for the journey to New Orleans, which arrived safely in late 1838 and reached St. Louis early in the next year. These Lutherans founded the Missouri Synod of the True Augsburg Confession. It became one of the three governing bodies of the Lutheran Church in America, overseeing the churches of this denomination in Louisiana (see chapter 6).

The 1840s showed a great increase in official immigration numbers to more than 42,000 German newcomers. According to the statistics gathered between 1820 and 1850, German immigrants accounted for 35 percent of arrivals in New Orleans. However, records of the *Deutsche Gesellschaft* (German Society), founded in 1847 by the German community of New Orleans, presented calculations far in excess of the official numbers.

Before the founding of the *Deutsche Gesellschaft,* local officials and foreign consuls shared the responsibility for setting and implementing immigration policies in New Orleans. As long as the number of immigrants remained low, private charities provided for needy new arrivals. As immigration numbers grew, however, the German population in

New Orleans became more and more aware of the appalling conditions and illegal practices with which their countrymen were confronted. As the number of German immigrants increased, there developed an obvious need for an organization to assist these new arrivals.

The impetus to establish such an organization began in 1842. Joseph Cohn, the founder and editor of the German-language newspaper, the *Deutsche Courier,* published an appeal to help the shipwrecked passengers of the vessel *Oceana.* Approximately two hundred Germans on this ship had been stranded for more than a month south of Jamaica. To assist these passengers, the Germans of New Orleans formed the *Oceana Verein* with help from their countrymen in Philadelphia and Baltimore. The hapless wayfarers were brought to New Orleans, where they were fed, clothed, and helped on their journey west. Having successfully fulfilled its mission the Oceana Society was dissolved.

During the 1840s the great increase in German immigration via New Orleans indicated the need for a permanent organization to help these new arrivals. After several failed attempts, Cohn finally succeeded in founding such a society in 1847. The decisive instrument was a letter published in the *Courier,* which dramatically pictured the terrible conditions in Germany produced by crop failure, a harsh winter, and various other misfortunes. Everywhere, Germans were making preparations to emigrate to America. Those Germans who would be coming to New Orleans would have great need for an organization like the German Society of New York, which could give them immediate aid and protection.

The *Courier* called a meeting for this purpose, which was attended by most of the prominent German residents of the city. Of note was the famous attorney, Christian Roselius, a former redemptioner, who spoke eloquently in favor of such a society. The first general meeting was held in mid-June of 1847, during which a constitution was drafted and officers, a salaried agent, and a fundraiser were elected. The purpose of the *Deutsche Gesellschaft* was specifically to provide assistance to the many German immigrants arriving in New Orleans. This aid was to be offered by official agents, who would be supported by membership fees and fundraising activities of the society.

The German Society

On July 1, 1847, the German Society of New Orleans officially started doing business. The society's agents immediately began to board all ships bringing immigrants and to gather the Germans together in a group. Because most of these new arrivals spoke no English, the agent's first duty was to shepherd them through customs. For those traveling inland, transportation via the Mississippi River was arranged. The German Society also assisted all German immigrants choosing to remain in New Orleans. These new members of the community were provided with work, shelter, childcare, medical assistance, and funds, if necessary.

The *Deutsche Gesellschaft* kept detailed records of the Germans who landed in New Orleans as well as the number assisted in reaching St. Louis or Texas, plus those sent up the Mississippi and Ohio rivers with no predetermined destination. These records, which were published annually, gave a detailed analysis of German immigration to New Orleans over a period of fifty years. Not only did they accurately establish German immigration figures for the port of New Orleans, but they also gave interesting insights into the character of the German community and its activities in the city. Additionally, the reports traced the history and development of this remarkable organization beginning with its first year of existence until its merger with other German organizations in 1927. These reports also established much about the history and heritage of the Germans in New Orleans and other areas of Louisiana where German immigrants settled.

Society immigration records consistently showed three times the number of German immigrants when compared with the official port records. Several factors were operating to produce two sets of figures so far apart. During construction of the United States Custom House, a portion of the immigration statistics kept by the Port Authority was lost. In contrast, the *Deutsche Gesellschaft* established strict controls over all transactions. Its agents were required to record the time spent with each immigrant, the nature of the assistance given, all monetary outlays, and the eventual outcome.

Official statistics gathered by the Port Authority were partially based on the figures supplied by the ship captains, who had financial reasons for underreporting their numbers in New Orleans. Because Charity Hospital was mainly used by immigrants, all ship captains were assessed a tax for its support based on the number of foreigners onboard. To avoid payment, these ships began to land in areas neighboring the port of New Orleans. When these sections were annexed to New Orleans, ship captains simply issued false reports with low passenger figures. The Passenger Act of 1852, legislated to combat overcrowding on oceangoing vessels, also contributed to the falsification of official statistics. The ship captains continued to overcrowd their vessels but to report minimal figures, which again were taken over into the official immigration statistics. A final factor in the discrepancy was bureaucratic. Many of the Germans who landed in New Orleans came via Le Havre and were listed as French immigrants in the port records.

The formation of the German Society represented a great commitment on the part of the German community of New Orleans. The voyage to New Orleans lasted seventy to a hundred days, during which dangerous epidemics frequently broke out, often leaving children without parents. In the first year of business alone the society took over the care of thirty orphans, placing them with private families. This same year over five dozen of the passengers on the Bremen ship *Europa* died from cholera during the voyage to New Orleans. When this disease also broke out in the city, it was assumed that it had been brought by the German immigrants.

During that first summer of operation a serious yellow fever epidemic also broke out, which especially threatened foreigners. These new arrivals were already weakened from the long ocean voyage, during which they had suffered from famine and thirst. Then they had to adjust to the brutal Southern climate. The residents of New Orleans, on the other hand, had developed immunity to most of the contagious diseases that abounded. If they got sick they were nursed within their own families. In 1847, the Germans of New Orleans and neighboring Lafayette raised over twelve thousand dollars for Charity Hospital, which it received in addition to the head tax on German immigrants. With this financial clout the German Society pressed for policy changes at the hospital. Subsequently, German patients were assigned qualified German-speaking doctors, interns, and attendants. This arrangement was also continued during later yellow fever epidemics.

After five years, the Louisiana legislature more than doubled the head tax for Charity Hospital because of the heavy usage by immigrants. Of the sick who were admitted, two out of three were foreign born. These figures were used by the enemies of immigration to charge that the state was supporting an institution that its citizens did not use. Besides the head tax, the Germans of New Orleans raised thousands annually for this institution although they did not use Charity Hospital as much as other foreign groups. For example, only 43,500 Germans were treated from 1830 to 1880, a third of the number of Irish.

The great number of German immigrants arriving in New Orleans this first year required an immediate increase in funding for the society.

To raise the needed money a "poor box" was placed in every German business. Other means were found as well, such as charity dance revues, concerts in Jackson Square, and public performances by the singing organizations.

To avoid infection during the yellow fever epidemic, the agents of the society began to transfer new arrivals immediately from the ocean-going ships to Mississippi steamboats. Nonetheless yellow fever broke out on many of the overcrowded riverboats, which had neither doctors nor medicine aboard. Officials of towns along the Mississippi would not permit these steamboats to dock, so the ship officers reluctantly had to keep both well and stricken passengers onboard. Not infrequently, the gravely ill were simply put ashore in deserted places, where they died in isolation.

According to the society's annual report for 1847-48, the first year of operation, about 17,500 German immigrants landed in New Orleans. Of these, 6,000 were sent to St. Louis and almost 4,000 farther up the Mississippi and Ohio rivers, with recommendations for prospective employment in the larger cities along the way. Westward to Texas was a less popular route, with only slightly over 300 Germans choosing this direction. Most important for those deciding to remain in New Orleans was the Work Referral Bureau, which was immediately organized to supply jobs for over 1,400 of the new arrivals. This bureau could easily place skilled workers such as carpenters, wheelwrights, locksmiths, and gardeners. Unskilled workers were placed on construction sites or on the sugarcane and rice plantations around New Orleans. German women were much in demand as domestic servants.

During the next year the German Society tabulated close to 20,000 German immigrants landing in New Orleans. Over 1,500 of those Germans who chose to remain in the city were provided with employment by the Work Referral Bureau. The many thousands continuing their journey up the Mississippi were assisted in the transfer process to river steamers.

Without the help of the society's agents the immigrants often fell victim to a local scam perpetrated by so-called "translators." These men, who preyed mainly upon Germans understanding little English, were actually runners employed by the hotels, boardinghouses, and Mississippi steamers. Since they got a set price for each person they brought in, they cared little for the welfare of the immigrants. Once paid, these runners disappeared with the luggage they had agreed to deliver. To combat this practice the society advised the incoming Germans to stay aboard their ships upon arrival in New Orleans and wait for the organization's agents. The ship captains were also requested to dock right next to the Mississippi steamboats approved by the society. Passengers could then take their own suitcases directly to these steamboats once cleared through customs. However, it took seven or eight years of effort by the society before all those who profited gave up the "runner" system. Despite the warnings against such scams many German immigrants still were victimized and then turned to the German Society for financial aid. Additionally, during the year, over two hundred people arrived without funds, for whom the society covered costs of transportation from New Orleans to St. Louis or Cincinnati.

Besides assisting the victims of scams, agents of the society had to deal with cases of irresponsibility on the part of the immigrants. When husbands went ahead to get established, they sometimes neglected to leave behind addresses where their families could locate them. In these cases the money and possessions of the families were soon lost in the fruitless search. During the yellow fever epidemics, orphaned children could not be taken into the asylums, since the deaths of both parents could not be documented. The society was obligated to care for these helpless children and made every effort to place them with sympathetic private families. There were also a number of relatively minor cases of irresponsibility. Passengers would change steamboats at the last minute and leave their luggage behind. They also sometimes gave the captains their valuables for safekeeping and forgot to pick them up. Once in the city they took possessions for repair and then forgot the location of the shopkeepers. Some threw away passports and family papers because they thought such things were not required in this country.

In addition to the mounting work needed to assist new arrivals, the German Society was expected to take care of requests from clerics and bureaucrats in Germany. They wrote to the society asking for legal instruments such as death certificates needed in settling estates. During the early years of operation the society also had to contend with the criminal element in Europe. Swindlers in Antwerp were representing themselves as agents of a Mississippi steamboat line in order to sell worthless tickets for passage from New Orleans to the interior. This swindle soon spread to other European port cities. In Le Havre the thieves doubled the usual price for the trip to St. Louis and charged each traveler this extra amount as their commission. Their "contracts" entitled the immigrants to pay the other half on arrival for steamboats supposedly owned by the German Society. The society contacted

European port officials, foreign consuls, and shipping companies with appeals to combat this practice.

Forty-Eighters

The year 1848 had brought revolution in the German states, forcing thousands of well-educated and cultured Germans to emigrate. Many of these people fled to the New World to escape retribution for taking part in the uprising. New Orleans received large numbers of forty-eighters, who arrived mostly without means. They harbored the illusion that they would be welcomed with open arms. But being ardently anti-slavery, their views were not welcomed in the German community, which had little interest and no stake in the issue. These forty-eighters also aroused the animosity of the Know-Nothings, who, as antiforeign-er and anti-Catholic, were already a threat to the Germans of New Orleans. The forty-eighters, with all their high ideals and newfound freedom, had to learn to accept the status quo and go to work or starve. It was not easy to find positions that were suited to their talents and earlier status. As educated professionals they seldom accepted the menial positions that the Work Referral Bureau could offer. These intellectuals simply lacked the skills to prosper in the port-city environment of New Orleans.

Despite the German Society's best intentions it was blamed for the general dissatisfaction among these new arrivals. The society was accused of being part-owner of a number of the Mississippi steamboats, where they could profit from the overcrowding. It was held responsible for the swindles, the deaths from yellow fever, and the attempts at familiarity made by the members of the crew. In November an explosion onboard a steamer killed a number of Germans. The forty-eighters insinuated that the society was responsible for this tragedy.

The persistent overcrowding on the Mississippi steamboats leaving New Orleans finally caused the officials in St. Louis to take stringent measures. They issued an ordinance to put any overloaded riverboat into quarantine. Most steamboats continued to take as many passengers as earlier but now put off a number of them on the riverbanks below their destination. To combat this practice, agents of the German Society in New Orleans telegraphed the mayor of St. Louis when overloaded steamboats left the port. These boats were immediately quarantined upon arrival, a practice that forced them in the future to obey the ordinance. At this time the society also appealed to Congress to pass laws limiting the number of passengers allowed on the Mississippi riverboats.

After the heavy influx of forty-eighters, only about 12,000 German immigrants landed in New Orleans in 1849. Almost 2,000 were provided with work in or around the city. In 1850 over 13,000 German immigrants landed, most being forwarded upriver to or through St. Louis. However, a third of the 3,000 immigrants seeking jobs in New Orleans now could not be placed. The society could find employment only for female arrivals who would work as servants.

Providing assistance for the increasing number of immigrants seeking jobs began to tax the society's resources. Once again the German community of New Orleans rallied to the cause. Funds were raised by performances by the singer Jenny Lind, dramatic presentations by the Thielemann players, and generous contributions sent from Germany. The rules were also altered so that immigrants would be furnished with money only as a loan, which had to be repaid.

In 1851 and 1852 the number of German immigrants landing in New Orleans doubled to over 25,000. As usual about two-thirds went farther upriver through St. Louis, up the Ohio River to Cincinnati, or west to Texas. The number provided with jobs by the Work Referral Bureau rose to over 3,500. Among these new arrivals were many who sailed to New Orleans believing it was possible to travel from there to all parts of the world. A group arrived who expected that they could easily get connections from New Orleans to Venezuela. Other immigrants were assured that ships sailed every week from New Orleans to Uruguay. A firm in Hamburg sent immigrants to New Orleans who learned only upon arrival that it was 1,800 miles to their destination in Canada. Others were brought unwillingly to the city when their ships changed destinations because of assurance of a load of cotton for the return trip.

By the first half of 1853 the number of German immigrants increased to almost 33,000, with 7,000 being provided with work. Despite the increasingly large number of immigrants, the Work Referral Bureau now was able to place all those who were willing to perform unskilled labor. The major railroad companies were incorporating at this time and were beginning to build track. But the railroad lines going out from New Orleans would initially have to go through swamps. The German Society released warnings concerning the dangers of working in this disease-infested environment. The society advised immigrants to sign contracts only under the auspices of the German Society once they arrived in New Orleans. Because of the worker shortage, however, the railroads then sent agents directly to the German states. Over 3,000 workers were obtained for the Ohio &

Mississippi and the Jackson railroads through these efforts. Due to the negotiations of the society, however, these German workers were assigned only to high ground.

Lulled by the absence of yellow fever for several years, the German Society published a report describing the improved conditions in the city. Drainage activity was so widespread that New Orleans could be designated plague free. This report also pointed out the expansion of the city, the opening up of railroad lines, and the new highway connections. However, during the summer of 1853, yellow fever broke out as never before. Eight thousand residents fell victim to this plague, almost two-thirds of whom were German. The fever raged mainly among the foreign born, who had no natural immunity. The many who found work digging the canals of the city were particularly vulnerable. During the height of this epidemic the society forwarded new arrivals up the river free of charge to avoid a stopover in New Orleans.

To combat the plague the Howard Association was organized to help take care of the victims in the city. Temporary clinics and refuges for orphans were set up, and every known means was used to limit the spread of the yellow plague. But the epidemic defied all attempts to contain it. Whole families were wiped out or separated forever. Many orphans were too young to know their last names. The German Society worked in cooperation with the Howard Association, establishing four bureaus strategically located in the city. The agents of these branches were assigned to find sick Germans, report them to the Howard Association, take them to the hospital, perform the services of translator, etc. Each agent had many more cases than could be handled, even with the best intentions.

Because of the crowded conditions in the temporary clinics, the sick wanted to go to private doctors. However, those doctors were already so overloaded that they had to refuse help. Many patients died as a result. The agents also got sick, as did their replacements. At the end of September the branch bureaus were closed. All efforts to contain the spread of the disease had failed.

After this crisis the German Society concerned itself with the sanitary conditions aboard the oceangoing passenger ships. Death, usually caused by cholera, had reached a rate of almost one in five passengers. Complaints mounted that the ships charged high prices but had no separate sick quarters, no means of disinfecting the ship, insufficient ventilation, and no sanitation. The passengers were not even allowed to throw overboard the sheets and clothing of those who had died of contagion.

This and similar complaints were presented by the society to the United States Senate with appropriate recommendations, resulting in the passage of new laws applying to oceangoing vessels. Strict regulations also were enacted to protect immigrants from the dangers on the Mississippi River steamboats. Over fifty river steamers went aground each year. The new laws kept explosions, fires, collisions, etc., to a minimum.

German Immigration Peaks

The year 1853 also saw the peak of German immigration to the port of New Orleans. Over forty thousand German immigrants landed in the city, half of whom were assisted by the German Society in obtaining employment in New Orleans or on their journey upriver or west through Texas. Because of the opening of the railway from Cairo to St. Louis, low river levels were no longer a hindrance to travel. Fortunately revenue was high during the year, with donations being made by members of the society, the mayor of the city, and Germans in other parts of the state.

The year 1855, however, marked the turning point of German immigration to New Orleans, which slowed during the second half of the decade. The number of arrivals fell to 27,000 and never again approached the earlier highs. During the next four years, 1855 through 1859, about 44,000 German immigrants landed in New Orleans. Of these, almost 8,500 decided to stay in the city, because the Work Referral Bureau was able to find them jobs.

The reasons for this decline in immigration were not yellow fever or the growing threat of civil war but the construction of the transcontinental railroads. From Europe, immigrants could reach the Missouri River via New York in less than twenty days, then link up with the new railroad. In contrast, the trip to New Orleans took seventy to a hundred days, cost much more than to New York, plus required funds for the long trip up the Mississippi.

The majority of the German immigrants arriving in New Orleans were not rich but had enough money and goods to provide for their needs until established. In the early 1850s, however, a new trend in immigration developed. Church fathers in the German-speaking states of Europe began to send their unwanted poor to the New World. Five hundred poverty-stricken Germans from towns in the state of Baden arrived in New Orleans at the expense of their religious congregations. A large number of these were widows with children or never-married women. Within a few days some were lured to local houses of ill repute, necessitating legal means to obtain their release. Many died after their arrival, leaving behind helpless, underage children. Within the next few years the need for more orphanages to care for the many abandoned German children was met by the German religious congregations of the city. Later the government of Baden partially reimbursed the German Society for its expenses, but it did not prohibit further emigration initiated by its overburdened religious communities.

More than a hundred poverty-stricken immigrants expelled from the German principality of Hesse also arrived during this period. This group consisted almost entirely of sick, crippled, elderly people and single or widowed women with many underage children. When they were put out of their homeland they were told that the German Society of New Orleans would take care of them. Out of necessity a house was rented by the society for this group, a significant number of whom were later moved to Covington. Fortunately, other congregations supported their expelled members generously enough, so that, once in New Orleans, they could afford their own transportation costs and other expenses.

In addition to those groups sent to the New World by their church congregations, many sick, elderly, and unemployable immigrants continued to arrive. It was known abroad that New Orleans was the only port in the United States without laws prohibiting immigrants who were unable to work. Common opinion developed that the type of German immigrant now arriving was undesirable and would become a public burden. The society took a very positive stand against this prejudice, maintaining that, as a group, the German immigrants were people of sufficient property, if not, as in past years, of notable wealth. The upshot was a report by the U.S. secretary of state to the president that the states associated with the German Society received valuable immigrants, chiefly farmers of excellent character, industrious habits, and sufficient resources.

During this time a great number of needy German railroad workers had taken jobs in the swamps around New Orleans. Now the society had sufficient influence to have these workers transferred to high ground and healthier working conditions. Despite the warnings of the society, Germans began to be lured south of the border by the enticing promises of agents seeking workers for the railroads. Many went to Central and South America; others went to Mexico. Because of the unhealthy climate they often never returned or returned broken in body and spirit. A number of these workers returned to New Orleans from the German colony in the Yucatan, fleeing the revolution that had broken out there.

Problems were also caused by the *Mexikaners,* that is, those Germans and Austrians who served under Maximilian in Mexico and had to leave the country after his execution. The society sent some of this group on to St. Louis, as they requested. Others were brought to the state of Mississippi, and the rest were provided for by the society in New Orleans and the surrounding area.

Just before the Civil War a particularly unfortunate group of Germans and German-speaking Poles arrived unexpectedly at the port. These were the remainder of a much larger group that the railroads had lured to Venezuela, where several hundred had died of disease. With their last pennies the survivors had managed to reach the seacoast and had bought passage to New Orleans. Immediately upon arrival these foreigners were taken in by the fishmongers, bakers, and grocers of the French Market. The German Society later was able to move many of them to the western parishes for care. However, a state immigration bureaucrat intervened and took the rest to a local hotel, where an outbreak of yellow fever killed most of them. A decade later a similar situation occurred among German railroad workers returning from Nicaragua. Almost all were infected with fever or suffered from ill treatment. Once again the society took on the care of these arrivals while putting out more warnings against railroad work in the tropics.

Nevertheless a host of other unfortunate practices continued to affect the German immigrants. Pretending to offer jobs, procurers again enticed German girls into houses of prostitution. Destitute German children loitered on the docks among the cotton bales, sugar barrels, and coffee sacks, looking for a chance to "pick up" these products. The German Society interceded on their behalf with the police, who had arrested over fifty children in one day. Further difficulties arose because of the smuggling of illegal goods. At this time a ring of criminals in Europe began to board ships that were transporting large numbers of immigrants. During the trip the immigrants were persuaded to pack illegal items in their suitcases. Although individual criminals were caught by the customs officials, the ringleaders of the smuggling operation were never discovered.

After the relatively comfortable economic circumstances of 1856, a financial downturn followed in the fall of 1857. Then came the yellow fever epidemic of 1858, which killed thousands but brought a great number of people to the city looking for work. Ships from Hamburg and Bremen sailed before the epidemic was under control. One German vessel arrived at the mouth of the Mississippi at the peak of the fever. The German Society got an order from the mayor to hold the ship below New Orleans until a river steamer could be rented. The passengers were then transported upriver without stopping in New Orleans.

Although the number of German immigrants had been falling previously, 1860 seemed to mark the beginning of a new era for the German Society. Over 14,000 German immigrants landed in New Orleans. Well over a third of those remaining in the city were provided with work. After five years of lower immigration rates, the number seemed to be rising, which renewed interest in the society. This year showed the peak in membership with 509 participants, more than double the original number of 230 in 1847.

The fourteen pre-Civil War years of the German Society of New Orleans ended with great optimism for the future. By this point procedures were well established for receiving German immigrants, arranging further transportation, and providing assistance in getting established. During these fourteen years approximately 240,000 Germans had landed in New Orleans, most of whom were given help or advice by the society. German immigrants now officially made up 12 percent of the city's population, although the numbers calculated by the society were far higher. The society's agents found work for over 38,500 Germans, while almost a hundred orphans were placed in private families or public institutions. During these years the treasury took in almost $26,000 in dues and $6,000 in dividends and raised about $12,000 from balls, concerts, firework displays, civic celebrations, theater performances, and outright gifts. Direct support of about $7,000 was given to needy new arrivals. After expenses the society had a capital of almost $15,000.

Because of the decrease in immigration only a portion of the society's income was being used. It seemed that the time had come to change the organization's aims. A strong faction in the German Society believed that more effort should be expended on the Germans already settled in New Orleans rather than caring only for new arrivals. A resolution was adopted in 1860 to set up a much-needed asylum to care for needy convalescent Germans who had been discharged from other institutions such as Charity Hospital. A call went out to subscribe to this asylum fund. Two hundred new members joined the society, and contributions of over $12,500 streamed in within a month.

The Civil War

Then came the outbreak of the Civil War, during which immigration via New Orleans stopped completely. Because of the economic conditions produced by the war, the asylum fund began to decline, and the initiative had to be postponed. Within a year the society's income dropped by two-thirds. Many members did not contribute because they had nothing themselves or had to help their relatives. During these difficult war years the asylum fund, half of which was earmarked for food, was used to provide assistance to the Germans of the city. At this time the services of the society's Work Referral Bureau became extremely valuable. It was able to offer partial assistance to many and provide others with employment. During the war years over three thousand jobs were secured for the Germans of the city.

The German Society also took the lead in the city in supporting non-German families left without bread-winners. The society donated almost $7,500 from the *Volksfest* of 1861, the largest contribution made to the families of soldiers fighting for the Confederacy. Donations also came in from smaller German clubs, German theater performances, and the Swiss Benevolent Society, while the city government gave only $2,000 for the support of needy families.

Although the Germans of New Orleans recognized the dangerous political situation developing in their adopted country, they remained neutral during the Civil War. Having survived the Know-Nothing movement, they were satisfied with the status quo. The German population of the city had reasons for noninvolvement. Only a small percentage of the wealthy businessmen were slaveholders or derived income from the slavery system. The political liberals of the German community had been chiefly involved in striving for unification in Germany. The lack of a leader also contributed to the local passivity. The community's most prestigious representative, Christian Roselius, had been thoroughly Americanized and confined his interest to charitable endeavors.

Not being economically threatened, the German colony rejected the stance of their abolitionist countrymen in the North. While Democratic in their political views, they were not granted any role by the Louisiana Democratic party, since foreigners had no vote. As the decisive election of 1860 approached, the German community was castigated by its two main German-language newspapers for its political noninvolvement. As liberals by nature and nationality, they should have sympathized with the antislavery position of Lincoln and the Germans of the Northeast and Midwest. But the vast majority, who were not in competition with slave labor, simply wanted to be left in peace to carry on their trades and businesses. Breaking his usual noninvolvement, Christian Roselius publicly expressed his view that Lincoln was destroying the Union and would rob the population of its property. His views were adopted by the German community, which considered Lincoln a firebrand and a cheap politician. The Germans believed he wanted to force them into a war about an institution in which they had no economic interest. Their newspapers campaigned against the whole "Black Republican" party, but Lincoln still won the election. When the state legislature voted for secession, the German colony of New Orleans hoped that the exit from the Union would take place peacefully. Although Roselius had voted against secession, he declared himself loyal to the state and willing to fight for his honor and property, thus setting an example for his fellow Germans.

The state subsidies paid to the volunteer German militia units in the 1840s and early 1850s had been discontinued, leading to the breakup of these units. After secession the old companies were reorganized and new ones were formed. Thousands of Louisiana Germans joined military units, making up half of the thirteenth and three-quarters of the twentieth regiments of the Louisiana Infantry. The *Deutsche Zeitung* estimated that 4,000 of the 14,000 Louisiana soldiers who had left for the front were Germans. August Reichard and Leon von Zinken, both German nationals, were promoted to general and led Confederate forces in Tennessee, Kentucky, and Georgia.

As the Federal blockade of the city became more and more effective, a "German" black market was formed to bring in food from upriver. German companies of the Louisiana State Militia also performed great service to the city in keeping order during the siege. But conditions in New Orleans gradually worsened as the blockade continued. Prices rose because of a shortage of staples and the lack of governmental controls. When the city finally surrendered after a year and a half, the authorities were more afraid of riots than the occupying Union forces of General Butler.

Because Butler was well aware of the service provided by the 200,000 Yankee Germans plus the thousands of German-Americans of the Northern army, he was amicable to the German community of the city. It was able to maintain its status quo, unlike the city as a whole. The German schools and churches continued to function all through the war and Reconstruction, while the German theater thrived better in the sixties than before. The two German newspapers also continued throughout, although in a smaller format because of the shortage of paper. However, the Germans objected to Butler's rigid censorship and his blue laws closing their theaters and cafés on Sundays. Added to those ills was his requirement that all foreign residents take an oath of neutrality.

While secession and war had united the German colony, Reconstruction divided it into two violently opposed groups, the Confederate sympathizers and the Yankee sympathizers. The former outwardly conformed to the demands of the occupying forces but remained loyal conservatives. The latter, led by Michael Hahn, joined with the Federals. Christian Roselius, the natural representative of the German colony, remained disengaged. He refused the nomination by the Conservative party for governor as well as for chief justice of the Supreme Court of Louisiana, while highly criticizing Hahn for his opportunism as a federal politician.

Michael Hahn

Michael Hahn, a native of the Palatinate, was the first German-born citizen to become governor of an American state. Brought by his parents as a child to New Orleans, he had earned a law degree at Tulane University. Hahn subsequently built a political base as publisher of the newspaper, the *True Delta,* which he used to build personal support after the fall of New Orleans. Hahn was elected congressman, governor, and United States senator in the course of his political career. As governor he was in a difficult position, having to hold the radical wing of his own party in check and resist the anti-German stance of the Negro Republicans. Hahn's political views, supported by many of his German fellow citizens, were clear (see J. Hanno Deiler, *Geschichte der deutschen Presse,* p. 22): "I will tolerate the abolition of slavery; I will tolerate the education of the Negroes but I am against their political and social equalization with the white race and am opposed to giving the right to vote to the Negro."

Hahn received a letter from Lincoln on March 13, 1864 (see John R. Ficklin, *History of Reconstruction in Louisiana,* p. 42), which stated:

Michael Hahn. *Drawing by Raymond Calvert.*

I barely suggest, for your private consideration, whether some of the colored people may not be let in [to vote], for instance, the very intelligent and especially those who fought gallantly in our ranks. They would probably help, in some trying time to come, to keep the jewel of liberty in the family of freedom. But this is only a suggestion, not to the public, but to you only.

In agreement with Lincoln's wish the constitutional convention of Louisiana adopted Article XV to broaden the scope of the state constitution: "The legislature shall pass laws extending suffrage to such persons, citizens of the United States, as by military service, by taxation to support the government, or by intellectual fitness may be deemed entitled thereto."

In New Orleans the Negroes, expecting to wield political power, were alarmed at the increasing percentage of naturalizations taking place among the foreign born. Butler's successor, General Banks, encouraged the foreign element to gain citizenship and the right to vote in order to carry out Lincoln's "10 percent" plan. Civil government could be reestablished if one-tenth of the pre-secession vote could be united. With a growing population of voters, the German community saw that it could exercise political power. The Germans feared the freed slaves because of some acts of lawlessness and were especially incensed by the raids on civilians by black Federal soldiers. As Reconstruction continued, radical Republicanism veered toward the Democratic party. Eventually the entire South turned to the Democrats in reaction to the radical Republican rule during this period.

At the end of the war the German Society hoped that the large landowners would sell parcels of their land to the German immigrants. Although deprived of their Negro fieldworkers, the plantation owners wanted no foreign small farmers as neighbors. Even when their plantations fell into ruin they still would not part with their land. Only as replacements for the Negroes, as fieldworkers or farmhands, were foreigners welcome. The result was bankruptcy, with whole plantations falling into the hands of creditors.

Now political sentiment developed in favor of bringing in more European immigrants. A state immigration agency was founded by the Louisiana legislature in 1866, which was to assume the function of recruiting immigrants, now also one of the objectives of the German Society. The new commission sent agents to Europe, New York, and other cities in the Northeast to obtain immigrants for fieldwork in Louisiana. These recruiters used every means, fair and foul, to carry out this assignment. In New York harbor immigrants were transported to steamers bound for the Mississippi River before they had a chance to put a foot on land. Under the excuse that a riot was feared, these new-comers were often abducted by a military patrol. The various German societies printed thousands of warnings, which were distributed in the Eastern ports of the United States and in Germany. But, for the most part, these efforts had little effect. Almost every Mississippi steamboat from New York brought immigrants to New Orleans, where the yellow fever epidemic of that summer killed over a thousand of them.

Almost nine thousand German immigrants landed in New Orleans during the first four years of peace. Although the German Society continued its purpose of caring for these refugees, its treasury had shrunk from $24,000 to $14,000 because of the devaluation of its investments. To compound the problem most of the immigrants to New Orleans came from the poorest areas of the German states, where war and crop failure had caused great suffering. There were also a few documented cases of German criminals being sent to Louisiana.

But there was reason for optimism that this postwar negative character of immigration would change. During these years the first ocean liners began bringing immigrants directly to New Orleans from German ports. In the fall of 1867 the pioneer oceangoing steamship of the Hamburg-American Transport Association arrived, promising the long-awaited increase in German immigration figures. The next fall an ocean liner owned by the North German Lloyd Company also arrived. The two German steamship lines immediately began to lobby for freight from local and state businessmen. Louisiana businesses, however, were used to importing their goods via New York and were reluctant to give their business directly to the steamship lines. Jealousy between the Bremen and the Hamburg lines compounded the problem. In New Orleans the competition between the two lines, the lack of freight, and a decline in immigration from the German states ended the steamship connections. By 1883 both steamship lines had cancelled their sailings.

From 1870 to 1873 almost twelve thousand German immigrants landed in New Orleans, half of whom remained in the city. The outlook for German immigration began to look favorable at this time for new reasons. Plantation owners had gradually come to the conclusion that white workers would have to be handled and compensated differently from the slaves. So the former slave cabins were remodeled into residences, a well-balanced diet was offered, and wages were paid in cash. In many parishes these immigrants also had the opportunity to purchase farmland.

At this point the German Society decided to use the asylum fund to set up a depot for new arrivals similar to New York's Castle Garden. Circulars inviting Germans to emigrate to Louisiana were then sent to the main cities in Germany. However, the new recruitment attempts by both the society and the Louisiana immigration commission failed. So the society's first priority, to build a "Castle Garden" to attract immigrants, had to be abandoned.

In contrast, requests for migrant German workers increased. The railroad construction, which had been interrupted by the Civil War, now began again. Railroad workers got good wages plus room and board. The planters finally began to make contracts with immigrant families, offering them a place to live, the necessities to begin farming, half the harvest, and twenty-five acres as a gift. In return the immigrant only had to agree to work during planting and harvesting. This system offered great advantages to the new arrivals, who could learn the art of farming under the expert guidance of the planters. But there were few takers; the best opportunities in Louisiana were passed up. To compound matters, the Supreme Court declared the head tax on immigrants illegal, wiping out this source of funds used by the state bureau. The bureau then limited its efforts to sending brochures to Europe, which were useless since there were no resident agents in German ports to distribute them. From this point on the German Society of New Orleans became the only effective force in the state promoting German immigration.

The national press, which was politically opposed to the South during Reconstruction, continued to print horror stories, which were either fabricated or greatly exaggerated. These stories were calculated to give the impression that, "down South," shameful acts were regularly committed against blacks and "whites with Northern ideas." The view was widespread that the South, especially Louisiana, was truly a hell where no one could protect his family, possessions, or earnings. The German Society could have combated the critics of the South by altering its tactics and giving publicity to the prosperity of the German colonies already existing in Louisiana. German settlements were thriving in Acadia and East Feliciana parishes. Additionally the new Southern Pacific Railroad line running through Louisiana to Houston was attracting German colonists from the Midwest.

In the North and West, however, a financial crisis developed during the 1870s. Since many factories had to close, a mass migration of those without work came to the South. In Louisiana, laborers could work on the sugar plantations from October until March and then return home, where they could benefit from a second agricultural cycle. These migrant workers were needed to fill the shortage of field hands since few immigrants from abroad were available.

Statistics for the next sixteen years (1873-89) showed that over twenty-two thousand Germans landed in New Orleans. Of these about fourteen thousand were sent to Texas. However, the number sent up the Mississippi fell to almost zero. The rest remained in New Orleans and were cared for by the German Society. The society quietly continued its work although the general public believed that it was no longer needed. The membership fell drastically until, by the end of the 1870s, the total stood at only seventy-four, while the capital fund was just over thirteen thousand dollars. The 1870s saw the decline of a number of once-promising German activities: the German community schools, the German theater, the many events sponsored by the *Turnverein,* the military companies, the men's singing societies, the *Harmonie Club,* etc.

Careful financial control and limits on activities were necessary for the survival of the society. The salaries of the agents were voluntarily reduced as were the business costs and travel funds. Monetary support could be offered to immigrants only in cases of extreme need. This policy of "standing pat" won the society few friends, but the officers continued this course, convinced that it was necessary for the future of the society. These monetary limitations caused conflict with the state bureau, which had access to public funds. When the society proposed that the legislature dissolve this organization as a wasteful bureaucracy, nothing was done other than offer the society a small monthly stipend.

The year 1883 brought to New Orleans the Cotton Centennial and World's Industrial Exposition. It lasted through two winters and a summer and attracted many visitors from the North and West as well as from Europe and Central and South America. The society did not want to let this opportunity go by without having an exhibition worthy of the German community. J. Hanno Deiler made a proposal to the other German societies in the country to create an exhibit that would showcase the influence of German immigration on the development of the United States. But most of the societies did not approve of the plan, noting that no money was available for such purposes. Although this effort collapsed, Deiler organized a group in New Orleans known as the United Singers and pushed for holding a "German Day" at the fair.

This was carried out successfully with the enthusiastic cooperation of the German community.

Seven years later Deiler was able to greatly surpass this low-profile effort by persuading the North American Singers Association to hold its annual convention in New Orleans. Over a period of several years he raised the funds to build a large, ornate hall at Lee Circle for the *Sängerbund*'s three-day songfest. The hall housed 1,700 singers from sixty-four different German singing societies, a hundred-piece orchestra, and 6,400 spectators. Every performance was a sellout, with the event attracting the largest audiences the city had ever known.

At the end of 1886 the German Society of Milwaukee appealed to its sister societies to vigorously support a law allowing voting rights for foreigners after five years in the country. The New Orleans society declined to offer its support, explaining that it had always tried to stay away from political issues. Two years later the Milwaukee German Society again turned to its sister organizations with the request for a convention of all the German societies of North America. Almost all of the chapters, including the New Orleans society, replied positively. But the German-American press criticized these societies for setting themselves up as representatives of the entire German population, causing the Milwaukee convention to be cancelled. So ended the society's involvement in the controversy over giving the vote to foreigners.

At this time many German farmers from the Northwest came to the offices of the society to ask for advice in choosing land in Louisiana for settlement. These were usually people of mature years who had migrated to the North and Northwest decades earlier and had become discouraged after long years of fighting the harsh winters. They had given up their homesteads out of fear of a helpless, infirm old age and the lack of a promising future for their children. They wanted to start a new life in the South under better conditions. However, only a slight increase in the German population of the state could be attributed to those moving South in search of better farming conditions. The 1890 census listed only 14,627 German settlers in Louisiana.

The German Society After Forty Years

On May 31, 1887, the German Society of New Orleans ended its fortieth business year. On this occasion the secretary reviewed the activities of the society since its founding on the first of June in 1847. Almost 285,000 German immigrants had landed in the city. The society's agents had taken care of customs procedures for every German immigrant needing assistance and had been available to advise all. Over half of those who arrived took advantage of the society's help in traveling to other parts of the country. About 118,000 immigrants had been assisted in reaching St. Louis, while almost 40,000 had been helped on the way to destinations on the Ohio River. The society had also forwarded approximately 22,000 immigrants to Texas. The treasury had expended $17,500 in assisting needy immigrants by providing free passage and provisions for continued travel. Through the efforts of the society's Work Referral Bureau almost 70,000 immigrants had obtained employment or went into domestic service either in the city or in the vicinity. The conditions aboard ship, on the Mississippi steamers, and in inns and other lodgings had improved through continued lobbying by the German Society. People who were guilty of unconscionable acts against the immigrants either in Louisiana or in Europe had been brought to justice. Many orphans, whose parents were lost either during the Atlantic crossing or after arrival in the port, had been placed by the society's agents in private families or public institutions.

German immigration to New Orleans fell to practically zero by the end of the 1880s. At the beginning of the decade the Southern Pacific Railroad had begun operations, which opened the way to the great Southwest prairie region. The immigration patterns that developed with this new access route circumvented New Orleans and led to a steady decline in German immigration to and through the port. The loss of a direct steamship line from Germany also contributed to the fall in immigration numbers. Consequently the society no longer kept books on immigration through the port.

From this point on the German Society kept statistics only of those assisted in getting work. Between 1888 and 1896 only about twelve thousand Germans obtained employment through the Work Referral Bureau. Its efforts had become more and more difficult because of an annual influx of several thousand Italians. This competition for unskilled labor cut back the number of jobs available and significantly lowered pay. For the most part, the Italians settled in the countryside, where they became fruit and vegetable growers. To make a little extra money they could work for low wages on the neighboring sugar plantations because their basic income was derived from truck farming. Beginning in 1890 the need for German workers steadily fell, with the number declining each year along with wages.

At the end of the 1880s the capital fund of the German Society had reached almost $19,500. Once again the time had come to think about widening the purposes of the society. J. Hanno Deiler proposed that a German archive and library be founded, which was approved by the society. Nevertheless there was active opposition and considerable head shaking. By the turn of the century the total appropriated for this invaluable activity was only $250. Deiler also proposed that the society contribute to the German Protestant Home for the Aged and Infirm. Since the society had collected money in the past for such an asylum, it began to donate funds to this institution.

At this time the suggestion was also accepted to widen the purposes of the society. In the future the society would extend its services to all Germans, that is, German immigrants, Germans who lived in New Orleans, and recuperating Germans who had been released from the hospital before they were strong enough to work. Chits would be sold to the German population at one dollar each so that those who could not afford the society's annual dues could participate in these endeavors.

The year 1894 marked an important turning point in the German Society's policies. It was agreed that the society should support the current efforts being made by the state immigration bureau and other organizations. The period that followed brought about a modest revival in the society's activities. The new directions adopted by the society created greater interest in the public, which resulted in doubling the membership. The society was redefined and expanded to act as an agency dedicated to attracting German immigrants. Only stable settlers were desired, i.e., only those who had funds of at least five hundred dollars. Appropriate advice and the right to acquire land in the state of Louisiana were to be offered to potential settlers.

The society decided to publish a realistic brochure so that only those who had a chance of succeeding would emigrate. A new booklet would be printed in German with accurate and appropriate information for potential German settlers. It would be widely distributed in this country and in Germany. Members of the German community who knew nothing about their German heritage would be informed of the monumental work of the German people, the accomplishments of the German Society, and the success of the many German institutions and businesses of the state.

J. Hanno Deiler chaired the committee that produced the desired booklet, called *Louisiana, ein Heim für deutsche Ansiedler* ("Louisiana, a Home for German Settlers"). Over a hundred thousand copies were printed and sent abroad as well as to all parts of the United States. The new brochure corrected the many false impressions that had been spread about the state of Louisiana. Until the outbreak of World War I the German Society continued its efforts to recruit German immigrants for settlement in Louisiana. Although innumerable inquiries resulted from the distribution of these brochures, only a few hundred German families immigrated to the state despite the society's efforts.

A review made in 1897 of the past fifty years of activities of the New Orleans German Society showed that about 290,000 German immigrants had landed in the city. The cash position of the society was over $15,500 and membership on April 1, 1897, was 138. Over 82,000 immigrants had found work through the efforts of the society's Work Referral Bureau. Since it had become increasingly difficult to find work for those Germans who turned to it, the society began offering direct financial assistance to the poor, the unemployed, and those institutions caring for the sick and the aged. In recent years the amount of direct aid given was almost $12,500. The German Society had become a philanthropic organization dedicated to helping Germans and their institutions. The society also began to give large contributions to other charitable institutions in the city, such as the German Protestant Home for the Aged and Infirm and the Parker Convalescent Home.

In 1895 J. Hanno Deiler had been elected president of the German Society, a position that he held until 1909, giving fourteen years of dedication. It could be said that he was the driving force behind the society at the turn of the century. During his tenure the society made a number of attempts to attract colonists to Louisiana in cooperation with the Louisiana Commission of Agriculture and Immigration. Although Deiler had brought new life and vigor to the society, there was no longer a pressing need for its services. By the turn of the century German immigration had fallen to a trickle. The German population of New Orleans had essentially become Americanized and lost interest in its heritage. The previous "German" areas of the city had been assimilated into the general economic and political landscape. All of these factors made the German Society's existence no longer as meaningful as before.

World War I

When World War I broke out in Europe, the German Society's membership was greatly concerned. Ironically, the war in Europe had a unifying effect on the German population in New Orleans. The German-Americans of the city rallied together in defense of their homeland. They eagerly responded to fundraising drives for the

German and Austrian Red Cross, raising $7,000 in two evening bazaars attended by over 6,500 residents. The German Society even held a big celebration in honor of Bismarck's hundredth birthday in April of 1915. But when the United States entered the war, the society halted all activities and maintained a very low profile.

After the war, the society partially revived and in 1924 again became involved in relief efforts by raising funds for the German Red Cross. The social functions of the society were also rejuvenated. In 1927 a huge affair was arranged for the visiting German ambassador, Baron Hugo von Maltzan. Although an effort to reestablish a German steamship link to New Orleans failed, four lines already calling at the port agreed to the appointment of a German-speaking doctor for their passengers and crew.

The remaining years of the existence of the German Society showed a period of decline. Nevertheless, in its last years, the society gave thousands of dollars to groups aiding Germany's poor, its undernourished children, and its liberated prisoners of war. One of its last charitable acts was to send food, clothing, and financial aid to Florida for those Germans who had fallen victim to the great hurricane of 1926.

Early in 1928 the *Deutsche Gesellschaft von New Orleans* gave up its independent existence to merge with the *Turnverein* and several of the German singing societies of the city. Together, they formed the *Deutsches Haus,* an institution that still exists today and continues to be an active force in the community.

CHAPTER THREE

Settlement Patterns

GERMAN SETTLEMENTS AND PLACE NAMES

The German Coast. In 1722 the first German settlement in Louisiana was established about twenty-five miles upriver from New Orleans, on what became known as the *Côte des Allemands,* the German Coast. This settlement, the fourth oldest in the United States, was largely unknown to the historians of German immigration until recent years.

At the beginning of the eighteenth century thousands of Germans were recruited from the German-speaking lands of Europe to settle the French colony of Louisiana. This enterprise was undertaken by John Law and his *Compagnie des Indes.* Only through settling the land could the English encroachment from the northeast and the Spanish threat from the Floridas be countered.

It is estimated that only half of those recruited ever reached the French port of Lorient, where these immigrants were to be loaded onto ships sailing to Louisiana. Port records show about four thousand arrivals, half of whom died during an outbreak of disease, probably cholera, while waiting for embarkation. Four hundred were sent back home after John Law's business venture failed, and no more ships were available for transportation. Six hundred remain unaccounted for but probably settled somewhere in the region around Lorient. Less than fifteen hundred emigrants actually embarked on the journey across the Atlantic. Again half of this number perished at sea due to starvation and disease, were captured by pirates, or were washed overboard during tropical storms. Of those who did reach Louisiana, more than half died on the beaches of the Mississippi Gulf Coast from overexposure and tainted seafood. This ever-dwindling band was finally transported by Governor Bienville to the banks of the Mississippi River and settled on land that had been partially cleared by Indian tribes. A hurricane in 1722 dispatched almost a hundred of the remaining settlers. The census of 1724 set the number at 169, all that were left of the original recruits, estimated to be as many as eight thousand.

Nevertheless this number was significant in view of the sparse population of the area. New Orleans, then the only other settlement in the Louisiana Territory, had only about eight hundred residents and fewer than one hundred structures. Against all odds these Germans survived and provided the breadbasket for New Orleans, assuring the survival of the French colony during the colonial period (see chapter 1, "The *Côte des Allemands* under the *Compagnie des Indes*").

Baton Rouge/Dutch Highlands. In Baton Rouge street names still mark the original location of this German settlement known as the Dutch (*Deutsch* or German) Highlands, originally settled by Germans from Maryland. Street names such as Siegen and Essen are remnants of this early German presence. These Germans, who arrived in late 1769, were seeking to escape the persecution of Catholics in Maryland. Having received the promise of religious freedom and government support from Governor Ulloa, they embarked with a group of Acadians in early 1769. Although these colonists reached the Louisiana coast without incident, they could not find the mouth of the Mississippi and made landfall on the coast of Texas. A trek across land to Natchitoches, the Louisiana fort closest to the Texas border, was the only route open to them. Once in Louisiana they contacted Gen. Alexander O'Reilly, then acting head of the colony. He assigned the wayfarers to the Iberville Post at Bayou Manchac, which marked the border with English territory. Provided with the necessary supplies for settlement and protection, they soon became well established and prospered. Many of these Maryland Germans later moved to higher ground on what became known as the Dutch (*Deutsch* or German) Highlands now located in South Baton Rouge (see chapter 1, "The *Côte des Allemands* under Spanish Rule").

The Third District, New Orleans. During the second decade of the nineteenth century the first Germans to disembark at the port of New Orleans were called redemptioners. The redemption system had come about as a result of the law passed in 1808 forbidding the further importation of Negro slaves into the developing states of the Union. Since field hands and domestic workers were badly needed in the South, Dutch shippers brought in thousands of destitute Europeans who were searching for a better life in the New World. These immigrants were called redemptioners because they had to "redeem" their passage by indenturing themselves for a period of years. Redemptioners were brought primarily to the port of New Orleans, which, until the Civil War, was second in importance only to the port of New York. Upon arrival at the dock they were sold by their ship captains to plantation owners, merchants, and shopkeepers.

Because of the disintegration of the social and economic systems in the German-speaking states of Europe during this period, a steady stream of immigrants began to arrive at the port of New Orleans. While records show over two thousand German redemptioners arriving between 1817 and 1820, it is believed that the number was double that amount. By 1830 there were an estimated seven thousand Germans dispersed throughout Louisiana, a large percentage of whom had been brought in as redemptioners. This stream of immigrants reached flood proportions by the early 1850s and receded only when the transcontinental railroads and northern waterway routes offered safer passage into the interior of the developing nation. German immigration through the port of New Orleans stopped during the Civil War and, unlike in the Northern ports, never again reached the antebellum numbers (see chapter 2).

Because of high costs and overcrowding in the central city, most German immigrants sought cheap land and working opportunities in the developing suburbs. This migration was markedly increased due to a head tax levied against ship captains for each immigrant brought to the New Orleans port. To avoid these costs, the ships dumped their cargo of German newcomers above, below, and across from the port itself. Soon three distinctly German communities developed, which preserved the language, culture, and way of life of the *Vaterland* (fatherland).

Until 1852 New Orleans was divided into three independent municipalities. The First District, which was predominately French, was located in the area from the river to the lake between Canal and Esplanade. The Second District comprised the American Sector, which also ran from the river to the lake between Canal and Felicity streets. The river end of these districts comprised the central city.

The Third District occupied the entire city below Esplanade Avenue. The portion above Franklin Avenue was called Faubourg Marigny, with the lower portion originally being named "the Brewery" after a structure built there in the eighteenth century. This section, the former plantation of Nicholas Daunois, was cut off from Marigny by a ropewalk along a portion of Franklin Avenue. In the mid-nineteenth century it became known as "Little Saxony" or the *Faubourg des Allemands* (German Suburb) because of its almost exclusively German population. The lower border was Press Street, named for the cotton press built there in 1832. St. Paul's Lutheran Church and Holy Trinity Catholic Church remain as a legacy of the German heritage of the area.

The City of Lafayette. Another heavily German area formed along the river, extending to St. Charles Avenue and bounded by Felicity Street and Louisiana Avenue. This area, then known as the City of Lafayette, is now called the Lower Garden District. It was established as an entity in 1833, which a local newspaper, the *Louisiana Advertiser,* described as an "asylum of rogues" with a fair share of "swindlers, peddlers, and other violators of the law." By midcentury the settlement included a large working-class population with a concentration of German immigrants, listed by the census of 1850 as 40 percent of the city's population. Lafayette had become a meat-processing center, made possible by the delivery of cattle from the west bank of the Mississippi River by the St. Mary Market Steam Ferry Company. This ferry line linked the end of the Texas cattle trail to Grand Cours Wiltz, now called Louisiana Avenue. In 1852, the City of Lafayette was incorporated into New Orleans as the Fourth District. It was known for its foul odors resulting from the slaughterhouses on the riverfront with their associated tanneries, tallow renderers, and soap and lubricant manufacturers. Magazine Street became a commercial strip with iron

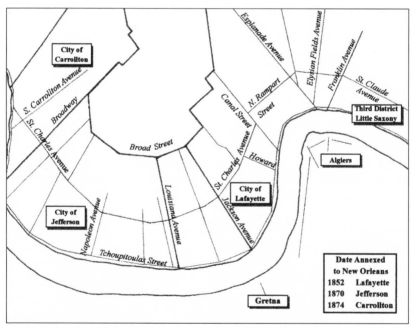

German settlements in regional New Orleans, ca. 1850. *Map by Raymond Calvert.*

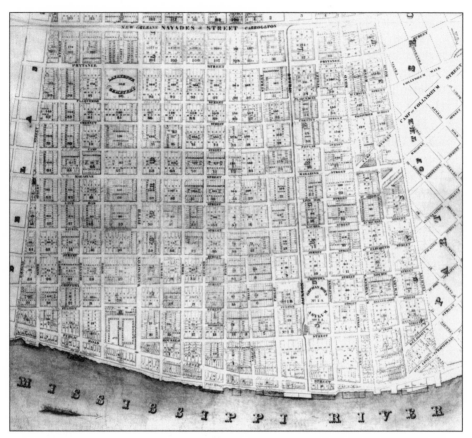

Street plan of the City of Lafayette, 1842. *Courtesy of the Historic New Orleans Collection.*

foundries, tobacco warehouses, millwork plants, ice manufacturers, breweries, and cotton presses. St. Mary's Assumption Catholic Church, the German-Jewish Gates of Prayer Synagogue, and the Jackson Avenue Evangelical Church remain landmarks built by the Germans of the area.

Jefferson City. Neighboring the City of Lafayette was Jefferson City, into which the German population of Lafayette spilled as more and more immigrants settled in the area. Originally incorporated in 1846 as the Borough of Freeport it was annexed by New Orleans in 1870 as the Sixth District. The boundaries of Jefferson City began at Toledano Street downriver and extended upriver to Joseph Street. According to the census of 1860 almost half of the population was German. By that time these German immigrants had established eighty-four slaughterhouses, continuing the butchering industry of Lafayette. Others wanted to escape the urban character of Lafayette and established forty dairy and truck farms farther upriver. The large German population soon formed a congregation, which built the First German Evangelical-Lutheran Church in 1866, now named the Salem United Church of Christ, and St. Henry's Catholic Church.

The City of Carrollton. The third major German suburb to develop was in Carrollton at the bend of the river, where land was plentiful and cheap labor was needed. Carrollton had been established in the 1830s as a summer resort for wealthy New Orleanians and was granted a charter as a city in 1845. Even today the old city hall stands, and the community retains an honorary mayor. The center of Carrollton was at the river bend, where the Carrollton Railway depot stood. The main attraction was the Carrollton Hotel, a two-story plantation house surrounded by gardens and walkways. Railway and riverboat passengers could disembark at the Carrollton levee to enjoy a day of relaxation in the hotel and gardens. One of the city's founders was Samuel Kohn, born in Bavaria. A young Prussian immigrant, Karl Zimpel, became deputy city surveyor in 1833. Economically dependent on the lumber industry, the City of Carrollton grew slowly and was eventually incorporated into New Orleans in 1872 as the Seventh District. The churches Mater Dolorosa and St. Matthew's, both having a large percentage of members of German heritage, still serve the community.

Mechanikham. German immigrants, many of them mechanics, began settling on the west bank of the Mississippi River in the village of Mechanikham (Mechanics' Home), laid out in 1836 directly across from the emerging City of Lafayette. Hired to dig a canal in exchange for land, the laborers and their families created a close-knit community, which remained distinctly German well into the twentieth century. The village was laid out by Nicholas Destrehan with a commons facing the river and two streets on each side. Destrehan allowed the settlers to have their own local government, which he came to regret when he himself was fined $10,000 for flogging one of the villagers. According to the 1850 census, approximately one-third of the population there was German.

Two years after Mechanikham was established, an adjacent community, Gretna, was planned by the St. Mary's Market Steam Ferry Company, which operated service across the river to Lafayette. This part of the Mississippi's west bank developed at the end of the Texas cattle trail. Because of Gretna's ordinances forbidding slaughtering operations, the St. Mary's ferry company transported live cattle across the Mississippi to Lafayette's riverfront with easy access to St. Mary's Market. Thanks to its anti-slaughtering ordinances Gretna was able to preserve its rural quality.

A third village, McDonoghville, also developed in this vicinity on the West Bank, by then known as the First District of Jefferson Parish. These three villages grew into towns with industrial and residential neighborhoods. By the turn of the century it became apparent that all three would benefit by combining into an entity separate from Jefferson Parish. In 1913 the first, second, and third wards were incorporated as the City of Gretna, an independent municipality with its own mayor and aldermen appointed by the governor. It retained its early German element, with the city's first five mayors, serving from 1913 to 1985, being of German descent.

Algiers. Adjacent to the area that became Gretna was Slaughterhouse Point, now Algiers, which obviously did not adopt the anti-slaughtering policies of its neighbor. Because the Texas cattle trail ended in this area, the town developed as a major railroad and freight center. Newly arriving German immigrants could find cheap accommodations on the West Bank and work as laborers on the docks or in the slaughterhouses. In time a number of Germans who settled in Algiers acquired land, where they dairy farmed and grew produce for the French Market, directly across the river. In 1870 Algiers was annexed to New Orleans as the Fifth District.

Germantown. A significant German colony developed near Minden, halfway between Ruston and Shreveport in North Louisiana, before the Civil War. Germantown was founded in 1835 by German settlers seeking religious freedom in the pietistic tradition of German communities established in America during the previous century. The Quaker, Shaker, Amish, Mennonite, and Pennsylvania Dutch settlements were all part of this pietistic movement of the eighteenth century.

The religious dissidents who formed Germantown were forced to leave their homeland because of the seditious political activities of their leader, Maximilian Ludwig Proli, who was seen as the Messiah by his followers. Proli, who then called himself Count Leon von Proli, was an alchemist and visionary who claimed direct ancestry from Christ. He saw himself as the prophet of the Second Coming, the judge of mankind, and the chosen instrument of God, destined to establish a new order on earth. In 1829 he issued a proclamation to the pope in Rome as well as to the kings and princes of Europe, demanding abdication of their worldly powers in deference to the imminent approach of the last judgment, with Proli as its instrument. Understandably, he was arrested and exiled.

This man was actually a peasant, born as Bernhard Müller, in Kostheim in 1788. Because of the poverty of his family, as a boy he was put into a cloister, where his religious fanaticism developed. At fourteen he was sent out by the brothers to work as a servant, a position from which he ran away. He then wandered for several years in the Taunus Mountains wearing a chain and hair shirt and recording his religious visions. Luckily he found a protector, Landgrave Karl of Frankfurt, a nobleman convinced of Proli's God-given ability to change base metal into gold. Landgrave Karl soon introduced Proli to his powerful and wealthy circle of friends, among whom Proli soon developed a significant following.

In 1831 he left Frankfurt with fifty-six followers and eventually settled in Louisiana, at Grand Ecore, just outside of Nachitoches. Proli chose this location because it was on the same geographical latitude as Jerusalem. However, yellow fever broke out in the new colony, killing a number of the settlers, including Proli himself. The houses, which they had built on a bluff over the Red River, were undercut and washed away by spring floods. Proli's valiant common-law wife, the wealthy and visionary daughter of a Frankfurt merchant, then led the colonists along a branch of the river to what was called Corianna Allen's Landing. Here the countess purchased a large tract of government land.

In this colony, now named Germantown, twenty-five log cabins were built to house the basic industries that were to make the settlement self-sufficient. In addition to the necessary living quarters, the colonists built a communal kitchen; school; cotton gin; mill; smokehouse; tannery; shops for the shoemaker, blacksmith, candle-maker, and tinsmith; plus the all-important Germantown store. The store handled the products of the above industries, farm and dairy produce, and cotton, wool, and silk cloth woven by the women. No church, however, was built, as worship was held outside on benches under the shade of a group of live-oak trees.

Since the colony itself was set up on a communal basis, there was no private ownership. Alchemy was to be pursued, and the gold thus produced was to finance the settlement so that all members could live the spiritual life of peace and harmony in this Proli-decreed new order. When alchemy failed to produce the gold needed to support the colony, good German thrift, industry, and business sense prevailed. The

Germantown store flourished, supplying not only the needs of the colony but also those of the surrounding vicinity. The colony prospered until the ravages of the Civil War reached North Louisiana. The German colonists willingly shared the food and clothing offered for sale in the Germantown store with all those in need during the war years. As a result, the economic underpinnings of their settlement were destabilized. When the debt was not repaid, the commune was forced into bankruptcy. Only then, in 1871, was the colony dissolved, the land divided, and the members dispersed.

Outside of New Orleans a number of other settlements were formed by German immigrants, many of whom had come to Louisiana as redemptioners in the earlier part of the century. These colonies were scattered throughout the state, at first along waterways and then clustered near railroad stops. After the Civil War the *Deutsche Gesellschaft* (German Society), which had chapters in a number of American cities, began to act as a conduit of information through which Germans across the nation learned of the rich resources, mild climate, and favorable agricultural conditions in Louisiana. German farmers were recruited from the Midwestern states of Iowa, Kansas, and Nebraska and from the Northern states of Wisconsin and North and South Dakota. Through the society these recruits were put in touch with Louisiana German families, which assisted them in getting established. By the turn of the century the Louisiana Department of Agriculture and Immigration took over this function and began actively advertising for German farmers.

Pine Grove. Before the Civil War a number of German settlements were established in Louisiana in addition to Germantown. In the 1830s Father Finley of the German Presbyterian Church congregation established a church and German school at Pine Grove in West St. Tammany Parish. This German-language school was the first to be established in Louisiana.

Schlosser/Frenier. A year after the founding of Germantown this colony was established by Martin Schlösser, who came from the vicinity around Mainz. The settlers established what was later named Frenier, an area between the Mississippi River and Lake Pontchartrain. Together these Germans cleared the forest, loaded the lumber on barges, and sent it to New Orleans. Logging and barging became their principal means of support. When Adam Schlösser, Martin's brother, arrived in 1849, the colony, which had grown to twenty-five German families, changed directions. Adam realized that there was no hope of continued profit from logging and introduced the settlers to farming. On the rich alluvial land they specialized in growing cabbage, which was marketed as Frenier sauerkraut. The vegetable dealers from the French Market in New Orleans came every year and bought the crop right out of the fields. When the Frenier station of the Illinois Central Railroad line was established in 1854, the Chicago market was opened to Louisiana farmers. The railroad introduced refrigeration and express freight trains that could cover the distance between New Orleans and Chicago in forty hours. This meant that Louisiana fruit and vegetables could reach the Chicago market before the produce from Florida and California and could bring double the money. Prosperity came to Schlosser, which grew to 4,000 acres of cabbage, planted in December and harvested from March to May. In the summer and fall the Schlosser farmers could grow other crops for their personal needs and for profit.

Unfortunately this German settlement was doomed by its location on the narrow stretch of land between the Mississippi River and Lake Pontchartrain. Serious crevasses occurred, causing the settlers to lose their homes three times. Of note was the Rita Crevasse, which flooded all the land between Frenier and Manchac in 1890. But within nine months the enterprising German farmers of the area had filled in the crevasse.

In 1895 a German Catholic church named Holy Cross was built by the colonists under the leadership of Archbishop Francis Janssens. A German- and English-language school had been established years earlier. However, the colony began to lose its German heritage around the turn of the century when the Italians took over many of the old sugar plantations and turned them into truck farms. The Schlosser farmers could not compete in price on the open market with the Italians, so the settlers moved into other businesses. The hurricane of 1915, however, wiped out the entire area.

Talisheek. In 1848 another German congregation established a church and school at Talisheek. The founder of this settlement was Helmut Voss from Mecklenburg, Germany. Most of these colonists settled on the free government land available at that time in St. Tammany Parish. The settlers were each allotted the usual 160 acres, on which they planted crops for their own use plus sugarcane and castor beans for profit. In 1859 they built a large schoolhouse in which studies were offered in both German and English, and no tuition was charged for half the year. By 1875 the colony had grown to the point where a

Southern Methodist congregation led by Rev. Friedrich Matthies could establish another church. Sunday services alternated between German and English each month.

Franklin. In 1859, just before the Civil War broke out, a German colony was established in Franklin (St. Mary Parish) by the congregation of the German Methodist Episcopal Church of the South. Since no German immigration took place during the Civil War years, and far fewer newcomers arrived thereafter, no further settlements were established until the 1870s.

Liberty Settlement. Near Talisheek another German colony was established in 1876. It was founded by Ludwig Geissler, a political agitator who attempted to set up the colony as a socialistic commune. Geissler was a writer who had begun the publication in New Orleans of a radical worker's newspaper called *Der Hammer.* He was also a novelist and dramaturge, who produced theater pieces that were performed in a log cabin he himself built in the woods of St. Tammany Parish. After the failure of the communal organization of the settlement, the Germans turned to farming for personal profit, which attracted other German farmers to the colony. It soon grew to encompass seven miles of acreage along the road from Madisonville to Ponchatoula, where approximately thirty German families settled down to raising sugarcane, rice, and cattle. The farmers of this area brought in the latest equipment, including their own steam-driven sugar press. In 1891 they established a Catholic church led by Rev. Joseph Kögerl, who ministered to this congregation as well as the Catholics of Covington.

Fabacher. Rev. Peter Leonard Thevis, pastor of Holy Trinity Catholic Church in the Third District of New Orleans, had a great interest in promoting German Catholic immigration to Louisiana. He inspired Joseph Fabacher, a wealthy businessman and parishioner, to purchase 14,000 acres for settlement in Acadia Parish. Fabacher chose this location for the new German community because of the fertility of the marshland and the proximity to a projected railroad line. About sixty Germans from New Orleans along with other newly arrived immigrants moved there in 1870. By the next year the settlers had built a chapel and school and had planted orchards and vineyards. With the encouragement of Joseph Fabacher they introduced the culture of rice to this part of the state and produced the first large rice crop ever grown in Southwest Louisiana. Ten years later Anton Frey, a prominent businessman in New Orleans and a relative of the Frey family in

Fabacher, donated forty acres for the establishment of another German colony, which became Roberts Cove. The town of Fabacher, now called Ritchie, continued to thrive economically but gradually began to lose its German roots around the turn of the century.

Roberts/German Cove. The year 1881 saw the development of what later was named Roberts Cove, also located in Acadia Parish, near Rayne with its just-completed Southern Pacific Railroad line. This colony was founded by German immigrants, also brought by Father Thevis of Holy Trinity Catholic Church in New Orleans. These new arrivals were seeking freedom from the officially decreed Lutheranism of North Germany and conscription under Otto von Bismarck. Within the next two years the colony increased from forty-nine to eighty-five, with Father Thevis and the original settlers bringing over relatives and their families as well as other new colonists.

Just at this time the Benedictines of the St. Boniface Monastery in Munich were preparing to leave the country. Bismarck had already expelled the Jesuits from Germany, and the Benedictines of Bavaria, in fear of a similar fate, wanted to establish themselves in a country where religious freedom was guaranteed. Rev. Aegidius Hennemann, one of the monks from St. Boniface, was sent to the United States to prepare the way. In 1883 he made contact with Father Thevis in New Orleans, who directed him to the German community of Roberts Cove. There he purchased 640 acres for a monastery, high school, and college. Father Hennemann's first act was to convert several wooden structures on this property to a chapel and rectory. A schoolhouse had already been built on the forty acres donated by Anton Frey. Father Hennemann served as the first priest but, weakened by tuberculosis, died during his first year of service. Through Father Thevis the Abbey of St. Meinrad in Indiana agreed to purchase the land, locally referred to as German Cove, and put it at the disposal of the settlers. The property and its buildings were to serve as the foundation of a new parish, for which the abbey agreed to provide the clerics. The old schoolhouse was moved to the temporary church property, where it could also serve as a church for the growing congregation. In 1894 the congregation erected a new schoolhouse and church, a frame structure with a tower supporting a six-foot cross. This structure survived until 1954, when the present-day brick church was built.

For these very devout Catholics the church was the center of their lives. They named it St. Leo after the contemporary Pope Leo XIII, an ardent opponent of Bismarck, and were true to the Catholic ritual of the old country. The church school educated the children in their *Platt Deutsch* (Low German) dialect as well as in High German. The German language was used exclusively by the settlers in their homes, religious services, and the school. German customs and traditions were retained in their cooking, clothing, social interactions, and holiday celebrations.

These hardy, industrious Germans settled down to rice farming. Up to this point only "providence rice" had been produced, so named because sufficient rain to produce a crop was left to providence. The scientific bent of the German mind soon enabled them to develop a new irrigation system of dams, levees, and pumps based on the technology of their former Dutch neighbors. In the hands of the Germans, the cultivation of rice, which their Acadian neighbors had grown only in small plots, became a stable and profitable Louisiana industry. The German rice farmers prospered, bought more land, and spread throughout the surrounding area.

As the anti-German feeling surrounding World War I increased, members of the settlement suffered public beatings and other humiliations. Three residents were arrested for expressing their natural sympathies for the German kaiser and one was killed in an argument. It became illegal for the colonists to use their native tongue. Only in their church rituals could they maintain their unique German heritage. Prayers and hymns were continued in German, but German for the rest of the service was dropped. Since they could no longer teach their children in German, they temporarily turned them over to the Sisters of the Most Holy Sacrament in Lafayette. Later, however, they were forced to close their school and to cease calling their colony German Cove.

However, even today, some remnants of the German heritage of this colony are retained. Baptisms are performed on the day of birth, and German hymns are sung for nuptial and requiem masses at St. Leo. Visitors also find the Roberts Cove German Heritage Museum of interest. The observance of St. Nicholas Eve is perhaps the most authentically German of all the customs retained in the Cove. On the night of December fifth St. Nicholas appears in his cardinal's miter and long red robe with his companion *Knecht* (servant) Ruprecht, also called Black Peter. Depending on their behavior during the year, the children are either rewarded with trinkets by St. Nick or punished with switches and lumps of coal by Black Peter.

Other German settlements of Acadia Parish: Crowley, Trilby, Cartville, Jennings. Crowley's German population was located close to Roberts Cove, six miles west of Rayne on the Southern Pacific Railroad line. It had its own German Evangelical Lutheran Church of the Missouri Synod, founded in 1895 by Rev. J. W. F. Kossmann of Lake Charles. There were about thirty German families living in Crowley at that time. Another small German colony was located near Fabacher at the Southern Pacific Railroad station of **Trilby.** The site was selected by Adolph Baumann and J. I. Daughenbaugh in 1893. Records show that a German Catholic church was erected by the settlers. On the same railroad line another small German community known as **Cartville** developed near the railroad station of Iota. There the settlers built their own German Lutheran church. Nineteen miles farther along the Southern Pacific Railroad line, west of Crowley, the German settlement of **Jennings** was established in Calcasieu Parish. It was founded in 1879 and named after the man who served as contractor for the railroad line. There the first German farmers settled who were to come to Louisiana from the state of Iowa. Eight years prior to this Pastor H. Gellert led a number of families from Schleswig, Germany, to this area, where they settled on both sides of Bayou Nezpique. In 1871, Pastor Gellert held the first religious service in the open air for his German followers. On the anniversary of this service in 1895 the community celebrated the opening of their own German Evangelical Lutheran church, built with three steeples like St. Louis Cathedral in New Orleans.

Lake Charles. In 1887 the Zion Lutheran Church in New Orleans sent Rev. Samuel Hoernicke to Lake Charles as resident missionary to the German Lutheran settlers located there. These colonists had been brought by Capt. Daniel Goos, a resident of Lake Charles for fifty years and owner of the first local sawmill. They came as experienced mill workers and shipbuilders from the Island of Föhr in the North Sea. With the opening of the Southern Pacific Railroad line another influx of Germans arrived in Lake Charles. They formed the First German Evangelical Lutheran St. Johannes Congregation, which established a church and its own school in 1888. Rev. J. W. F. Kossmann served as pastor; he also headed the Lutheran church in Crowley. Their parochial school was the first school to be established in Lake Charles and, for a period, was the only school, which was attended by children of all faiths.

Clinton/Buetoville. In 1871 a German settlement was founded near Clinton in East Feliciana Parish, established by the German priest Rev. Friedrich Bueto. A number of his followers joined him and founded the colony of Buetoville. Other Germans from the Northern and Western states were attracted to the rich soil and good farming conditions in this area of Louisiana. Eleven years after a German Methodist church had been founded in 1881 to serve the Germans on the west bank of the Comite River, a German Evangelical Lutheran church and school were founded on the east bank. A newspaper article in the *New Orleans Deutsche Zeitung* in 1895 mentioned these two German churches and the good German-English school and capable teaching staff. The German farmers rented their land at first, raised cattle, and grew crops for their own needs and cotton for profit. They were known for their thrift and hard labor, which they performed without the help of Negro field hands. Within ten years their land was completely debt free. The German heritage of these colonists was retained longer than in most settlements of the time, as evidenced by the continuation of the German-English school until the onset of World War I.

Keatchie/Carmel. About twenty miles from Shreveport in De Soto Parish a German farming community called **Keatchie** was established around 1860. Wilhelm G. Spilker, who became postmaster, and several other German families were the original settlers. In 1871 Charles Schuler from Mühringen, Württemberg, purchased 960 acres of land there. During the Civil War Schuler had joined the Chalmette Regiment of the Confederate Army and was stationed in Shreveport, where he served as commandant of the western district of Louisiana. After the war he settled in Keatchie and prospered as a farmer, gradually acquiring 2,300 acres, most of which he rented out to other German farmers. The respect accorded the German immigrants in North Louisiana was illustrated by Schuler's election to the state legislature representing De Soto Parish. **Carmel** was established in De Soto Parish in 1888 by German Carmelites from Marienfeld, Texas. They founded a college, which attracted a number of German families to settle there.

German settlements were developing in the 1880s as new towns in many sections throughout Louisiana. Typical among them were those listed above. There were also thriving German settlements in the parishes of St. Helena, Webster, and Washington, all of which had their own German church congregations, schools, and industries. Soon after the turn of the century, however, the populations of these towns became more diversified, losing interest in their German heritage as well as the need for the German language.

The widespread presence of Germans in the state can be seen in the many villages and towns with German place names. Students of the German heritage of Louisiana owe a great debt to J. Hanno Deiler, whose research into the state's German past was done around the turn of the century. Much of the knowledge he preserved would have been lost had he not recorded his findings in a number of publications, which he personally financed.

The following town listing is in alphabetical order. The date of founding or incorporation, the parish, and the origin of the name are provided. Notes and the source(s) are given in italics.

Date	Name of Town	Parish	Origin of Name

1870 **Algiers**   Orleans   Arab word meaning "peninsula"
Annexed to New Orleans; St. Bartholomew Church (now Holy Name of Mary) had many German parishioners
Leeper; Dixon

1722 **Augsburg**   St. Charles   German imperial city
One of three original German Coast villages
Leeper, 1976; Blume

1817 **Baton Rouge**   East Baton Rouge French translation of Indian name meaning "red stick"
Large German community in southern portion originally called Dutch Highlands
Deiler, Ansiedler

?   **Bayou Teche** (waterway)   Named for Germans who settled on bayou; Teche is corruption of *Deutsche* (Germans)
Bayou flows through parishes of St. Landry, St. Martin, Iberville, and St. Mary
Deiler, Presse

?   **Bayou Thunder** Lafourche   Thunder-ten-Tronckh, town in
     von Trank   Westphalia on German/Dutch border popularized by Voltaire's *Candide*
Whitbread, Jeff. Parish

1875 **Boniface**   St. Tammany   Named by Rev. J. B. A. Ahrens for St. Boniface, apostle to Germans
Later renamed Talisheek
Leeper, 1976

1740s **Bonnet Carré**   St. John the Baptist Right-angle bend in river; land
looks like "square bonnet"
Later renamed Laplace; many Germans migrated from Karlstein on German
Coast to east bank of river after 1722 hurricane
Leeper, 1977

1840s **Buehler's**   East Baton Rouge   John Christian Buehler
   Plains
Louisiana and Lower Mississippi Valley Collection (LLMVC); Deiler, Presse;
River Road

1895 **Buetoville**   East Feliciana   German pioneer Friedrich
Bueto, founder
German Methodist and Evangelical Lutheran congregations established here
Deiler, Ansiedler

1882 **Bunkie**   Avoyelles   Mispronunciation of "monkey"
Formerly called Irion; named after toy monkey (Kletteraffe) *of Mary Mackie*
Haas, daughter of A. M. Haas, German planter
La. Bio.; Leeper; La. Guide

1888 **Carmel**   De Soto   Named by Rev. Anastasius
Peters, German Carmelite priest
Anton Frey gave German Carmelites migrating from Marienfeld, Texas, ten
acres of land seven miles northeast of Mansfield
Leeper, 1976

1852 **Clinton**   East Feliciana   Named by John Bostick for
DeWitt Clinton (1769-1828)
Germans in Clinton and nearby Buetoville
Leeper, 1976; Deiler, Presse, Ansiedler

1900s **Crowley**   Acadia
Germans brought here through advertising by Duson brothers to till rice
fields
Deiler, Presse; Leeper, 1976

?   **Des Allemands** St. Charles   *Lac des Allemands* (Lake of the
Germans)
Downriver from first German settlements
Leeper, 1976; Deiler, Presse

1780s **Destrehan**   St. Charles   Plantation owner
One of early settlements of Germans on east bank of Mississippi River
Leeper, 1976; River Road

| ? | **Donner** | Terrebonne | German word meaning "thunder" |
Deiler, Presse

1784 **Dutch Highlands**   East Baton Rouge   Dutch is corruption of *Deutsch* (German)

Germans from Hagerstown, Maryland, settled here after flooded out at Hackett's Point, near Manchac; J. B. Kleinpeter was first successful sugar-cane planter on highlands
Deiler, Presse

? **Dutchtown**   Ascension   Dutch is corruption of *Deutsch*
Deiler, Presse

1893 **Erath**   Vermilion   August Erath, native of Switzerland, mayor of New Iberia

Leeper, 1976

1870s **Fabacher**   St. Landry   German founder, Joseph Fabacher

Deiler, Presse

1848 **Fisher**   Sabine   German postmaster
Deiler, Presse; Leeper, 1976

1892 **Fisher**   Jefferson   Jules and Isadore Fisher, Alsatian proprietors of general store

Now Lafitte
Swanson, Jeff. Parish

1836 **Frenier**   St. John the Baptist
Formerly named Schlosser after founder of German settlement on 700 acres between Mississippi and Lake Pontchartrain; settlement destroyed by hurricane in fall 1915
Deiler, Presse; Leeper, 1976; Borel

? **Frey**   Acadia   Anton Frey, German pioneer
Deiler, Presse

1780s **Galveztown**   St. John the Baptist Bernardo de Galvez
Set up in colonial period as fort for protection from British; large German population, second in size to Spanish (Isleños) settlers; town had church called St. Bernard whose mission church was at St. Gabriel; town abandoned, fell into ruin
Leeper; River Road

1876 **Geismar**   Ascension   Louis Geismar, settler from
                                           Alsace
Deiler, Presse

1722 **German Coast**   St. Charles and St.   *La Côte des Allemands,* for
                          John the Baptist   Germans who settled there,
                                             1722
Leeper

1835 **Germantown**   Webster   Nationality of settlers
Second Louisiana settlement established by followers of Count Leon von Proli
Leeper; Deiler, Presse; Krouse

1890 **Gessen**   Tangipahoa   Named by Rev. Luke Gruwe,
                                           O.S.B.
Now called Rosaryville; Gessen (Goshen) was land Joseph gave father Jacob
and brothers (Gen. 47:5-6); Brother Luke wanted to call settlement St. Joseph,
but name already taken in another parish; German-speaking monks settled
here before relocating to St. Benedict
Leeper

1834 **Grand Ecore**   Natchitoches
First Louisiana settlement of Count Leon von Proli and his followers; Proli
died here from yellow fever; location chosen because on same geographical
latitude as Jerusalem
Leeper; Deiler, Ansiedler

1813 **Gretna**   Jefferson   Part originally called Mechanik-
                                           ham (mechanics' home)
German settlement on west bank of Mississippi River
Curry

1906 **Grosse Tete**   Iberville   German-French
Deiler, Presse

?   Haasville   Ascension   German-French
Deiler, Presse

1871 **Hahnville**   St. Charles   Michael Hahn, governor of
                                           Louisiana
Hahn laid out town; site was portion of his sugarcane plantation
Deiler, Presse; Biog. and Hist. Memoirs; Leeper, 1976

?   **Hamburg**   Ascension   German port on Baltic
Deiler, Presse

1870s **Helvetia**   St. James   Helvetia Plantation with co-op
                                            sugar mill
Helvetia was Latin name for Switzerland (two-thirds of country was/is
German speaking)
Leeper, 1976; River Road

1903 **Hessmer**   Avoyelles   Named by William Edenborn
                                            for sister-in-law, Hester
La. & Ark. Railroad built by Edenborn
Leeper, 1976

1722 **Hoffen**   St. John the Baptist Hoffenheim, near Sinsheim,
                                            Germany
One of three original villages on German Coast; 1724 census listed Hoffen
with 25 men, 30 women, 26 children
Leeper; Blume

?   **Hofpower Bayou** Ascension   *Hofbauer* means "courtyard
                                            planter/builder"
Deiler, Presse

1880s **Hohen Solms**   Ascension   Named by John B. Reuss;
                                            corruption of Hohenzollern,
                                            German royal house
Germania Plantation in this town
Leeper, 1976; River Road

1888 **Husser**   Tangipahoa   Hypolyte Husser, first postmaster
Husser's father was blacksmith from Alsace
Leeper, 1976

1902 **Iota**   Acadia   Greek word meaning "very
                                            small quantity"
C. C. Duson, area rice developer, refused to exclude settlement from link to
Southern Pacific Railroad: "Not by one iota will I cut out this area"; site
selected by Adolph Baumann and J. I. Daughenbaugh in 1893
Leeper, 1976

1879 **Jennings**   Jefferson Davis   Southern Pacific Railroad
                                            contractor, Jennings McComb
Deiler, Presse, Ansiedler

?   **Kaplan**   Vermilion   Leopold Kaplan, German rice
                                            planter who reclaimed marshland
La. Biog.

1722 **Karlstein**   St. John the Baptist Captain of German Coast, Karl
                                            Friedrich Darensbourg
Now called Lucy; one of original settlements on German Coast
Leeper; Blume

1887 **Killona**   St. Charles   Killona Plantation (demolished)
First church built by Germans in Louisiana located here; in Gaelic Kilona
means "Church of John" (St. John the Baptist)
Leeper

1830s **Kleinpeter**   East Baton Rouge   J. B. Kleinpeter
Kleinpeter was German; first successful sugarcane planter on Dutch
Highlands
Deiler, Presse; River Road

?   **Kleinwood**   Ascension   *klein* means "little" in German
Deiler, Presse

1860s **Klotzville**   Assumption   German founder Abe Klotz,
                                            postmaster
Six miles north of Napoleonville on Bayou Lafourche
Leeper, 1976; Jews of La.

1834 **Kraemer**   St. John the Baptist First postmaster, Lawrence
                                            Kraemer, from Waldkirch,
                                            Germany
Kraemer owned general store with post office; member of one of three families
living there (all German); land later donated for Catholic church and school
Leeper; Robichaux

1917 **Krotz Springs**   St. Landry   C. W. Krotz, from Defiance,
                                            Ohio; of German heritage
Leeper; Deiler, Presse

1867 **Lake Charles**   Calcasieu
German settlement with German church
Deiler, Presse

?   **Lehmann**   Concordia   First postmaster, German pioneer
Deiler, Presse

?   **Lieber**   Ouachita   First postmaster, German pioneer
Deiler, Presse

1876 **Liberty**   St. Tammany   Named by German founder for
     Settlement   political/economic views
*Established as socialistic commune by radical publisher and writer Ludwig
Geissler*
Deiler, Ansiedler

1876 **Lucy**   St. John the Baptist Named by Charles Huget for
                               his fiancée, Lucy Trudeau
Later name for Karlstein
Leeper; Blume

1880s **Lutcher**   St. James   L. J. Lutcher
*Lutcher was pioneer German lumberman; had one of world's largest cypress
sawmills*
Leeper, 1977; River Road

1722 **Mariental**   St. Charles   Alsatian village near Hagenau,
                               Germany
One of three original villages on German Coast
Leeper, 1976; Blume

?   **Mayer**   St. Helena   First postmaster; name means
                               "mayor/large-farm owner"
Deiler, Presse

1836 **Minden**   Webster   Named by Charles Veeder for
                               hometown Minden, in
                               Westphalia, Germany
Incorporated in 1850
Leeper, 1976

1895 **Mowata**   Acadia
*German Baptist church located here; named by landowner who needed more
water for his rice fields*
Jackson

1883 **Nesser**   East Baton Rouge Ludwig ("Louis") Nesser,
                               native of Trier, Germany; first
                               postmaster
Leeper, 1977

1718 **New Orleans**   Orleans   Named for duc d'Orleans,
                               regent to French king Louis XV
Largest German settlement in Louisiana as well as in South before Civil War
Gardner, 1860

1890s **Oldenburg**   Vermilion   Named after hometown of
Baron von Bastrop, who brought
Germans to Ouachita River

Near Abbeville
Deiler, Presse

1830s **Pine Grove**   St. Tammany   Known for piney woods
German congregation established Presbyterian church with first German-
language school in Louisiana
Deiler, Ansiedler

1861 **Ponchatoula**   Tangipahoa   Choctaw word meaning
"hanging hair" (Spanish moss)

Site of German settlement
Leeper, 1976; Deiler, Presse

1804 **Red Church**   St. Charles   Named for color of church
Little Red Church, now St. Charles Borromeo, replaced 1740 red log church,
which, in turn, was replaced in 1921 by present white brick structure
Leeper, 1977

?   **Rhinehart**   Catahoula   German pioneer; established
post office

Deiler, Presse

?   **Ringgold**   Bienville   German pioneer; established
post office

Deiler, Presse

1881 **Roberts Cove**   Acadia   Local farmer
Originally called Hennemann, then St. Leo's; also German Cove; German
settlers came from Geilenkirchen, near Aachen; Fr. P. Leonhard Thevis was
main force in bringing family and friends there
Kondert, Acadia Parish; Deiler, Ansiedler; McCord

1850 **Ruddock**   St. John the Baptist C. H. Ruddock, co-owner of
(ca.)   Ruddock Cypress Co., Ltd.
German settlement destroyed by hurricane of September 1915
Deiler, Presse

1907 **St. Benedict**   St. Tammany   Patron saint of the order
Was estate owned by Hosmer family; originally named Cedar Hill for cedar
trees; renamed for patron of German-speaking Benedictine monks from
Gessen
Leeper, 1977

1767 **St. Gabriel**   Iberville
Site where original Acadians from Nova Scotia landed along with Germans
from Maryland; records from church kept in Galveztown
Leeper, 1976; River Road

?   **Schleh**   Ouachita   German pioneer; established
post office
Deiler, Presse

1836 **Schlosser**   East Baton Rouge   Martin Schlösser from
Rhineland
Destroyed by hurricane of September 1915
Deiler, Presse

?   **Schriever**   Terrebonne   German pioneer; established
post office
Deiler, Presse

1905 **Sondheimer**   East Carroll   Emanuel Sondheimer
Sondheimer was developer of lumber mill for bandsawed southern cypress
Leeper, 1976

1909 **Sorrento**   Ascension   Named by German, William
Edenborn, after Sorrento, Italy
German immigrant who built railroad here in 1902; spent honeymoon in
Sorrento
Leeper, 1976

1890 **Swarts**   Ouachita   Named for German Ed George
Swartz of Swartz Lumber
Company; postmaster
Leeper, 1976; Deiler, Presse

1883 **Talisheek**   St. Tammany   Nearby stream, a Choctaw word
meaning "gravel"
Formerly called Boniface (named by German Benedictine monks for patron
saint); station on gulf for Mobile & Ohio Railroad; town recorded on
Ludlow's map, 1873
Leeper, 1977; Deiler, Presse

?   **Waggaman**   Jefferson   U.S. senator, postmaster George
Augustus Waggaman
Waggaman was of German descent, owner of Avondale Plantation; settlement
originally railroad stop
Swanson; Deiler, Presse

1907 **Waldheim**   St. Tammany   German word meaning "forest home"

Originally named St. Boniface by Rev. J. Ahrens for church located there
Leeper, 1976

1899 **Weiss**   Livingston   Settler Friedrich Weiss

Other families with German surnames in area: Hess, Hunstock, Kyzar,
Reininger; Weiss established post office in 1899, discontinued in 1949
Leeper, 1976; Deiler, Presse, Ansiedler

1930 **Wisner**   Franklin   German settler Edward Wisner, first postmaster

Hope Estate site of first settlement
Leeper, 1976; Deiler, Presse

?   **Zimmerman**   Rapides   German pioneer; established post office

Deiler, Presse

1848 **Zwolle**   Sabine   Hometown of postmaster Jan de Goenjen of Zwolle, Holland (then German state)

Leeper, 1976

STREET NAMES, MONUMENTS, AND HISTORICAL MARKERS

Street Names

As the German immigrants assimilated and climbed into the middle class in the New Orleans area, a number of them became involved in suburban land development. Examples were Joseph Wiltz in the City of Lafayette, Solomon Cohn, Samuel Kohn and Karl Zimpel in Carrollton, and Charles Wirth in the university section. The streets of New Orleans and its suburbs that bear German names attest to the role of the Germans in the development of the area.

As happened in other cities, all things German became suspect when the world wars broke out. Three streets crossing St. Charles Avenue had originally been named after Napoleon's battles, all of them located in German-held territory. During World War I, Berlin Street was renamed General Pershing, although the city fathers failed to recognize Jena and Austerlitz as Germanic cities. Alterations to common nouns were made as well. Both the frankfurter (named after street food eaten in Frankfurt, Germany) and wiener-wurst (Vienna sausage) were renamed "hot dogs," while sauerkraut became "victory cabbage."

A number of streets in the New Orleans area were named after/by prominent Germans or German-Americans (see chapter 9). The names of cities/regions in the former German states or in present-day Germany also were used.

Alsace. This street was named after the province of Alsace, which has been under either German or French control during its history. Residents of Alsace, now part of France, are historically bilingual. A group of German-speaking Alsatians came to Louisiana in the mid-colonial period and settled on the German Coast.

Austerlitz Street. This street was named after Napoleon I's victory over Austria at Austerlitz. Then part of the Austro-Hungarian Empire, Austerlitz is now in the Moravian province of the Czech Republic.

Behrman Avenue, Behrman Highway, and **Behrman Place.** These are all located in Algiers (the Fifth District of New Orleans, on the west bank of the Mississippi River). They were named after the German-American Martin Behrman (1864-1925), mayor of New Orleans for sixteen years (1904-20).

Breslau Street. Renamed in 1894, it is now a section of South Robertson. This street was originally named after the German city of Breslau, once Prussian, now part of Poland.

Charlmarx Street. Karl Heinrich Marx (1818-83), a German philosopher, revolutionary, and economist, was the author of *Das Kapital* and, along with Friedrich Engels, the *Communist Manifesto.* Curiously the French form of Karl Marx was used for the street name.

Cohn Street. Solomon Cohn, a German native, moved to Carrollton in 1836. He was one of the developers of Carrollton and was elected to its first city council in 1845. He established Carrollton's first industry, a ropewalk between Levee and Second streets. Along with Millaudon and Zimpel he developed the New Orleans and Carrollton Railway.

Copernicus Street. Nicolaus Copernicus (1473-1543), an astronomer, was the first to maintain that the earth revolved around the sun. His work influenced that of Galileo, Newton, and Kepler. "Copernicus" was the Latinized form of *Köper,* meaning twill-cloth maker. Copernicus was from East Prussia and spoke German as his native language. The street in Gretna was renamed Rupp Street but today is Huey P. Long Avenue.

Darensburg Court, Algiers. During the early colonial period in Louisiana, Karl Friedrich Darensbourg was commandant of the German Coast settlement for forty-eight years. He and his militia played an important role in the O'Reilly Revolution of 1768.

Donner Drive; Donner Canal. Charles J. Donner was secretary of the New Orleans Levee Board in the 1930s when Martin Behrman was mayor of the city. The street runs along the Donner Canal, separating Algiers from Gretna. William R. Donner was a railroad engineer connected with the Huey P. Long Bridge. His name derives from the German word for "thunder."

Dreyfous Avenue. Felix J. Dreyfous, of German-Jewish heritage, was president of the board of City Park and one of its founding members.

Earhart Boulevard. Frederick A. Earhart, a German-American, was appointed chairman of the Civil Service Commission by Mayor Martin Behrman. He also served as commissioner of public utilities in 1930. One of his major achievements was the consolidation of the city's five railroad stations into Union Passenger Terminal. He taught pharmacology at Loyola University and established a chain of drugstores in the city. He also served two terms in the Louisiana Senate.

Frankfort. This street was named after Frankfurt, Germany. Frankfurt originally got its name from its use as the "ford for the Franks." It was located near a shallow area of the Rhine River, which the Germanic tribe, the Franks, used as a crossing point into the territory that today is France.

Friedrichs Avenue. George C. Friedrichs was a real-estate developer who was responsible for creating a racetrack, open for only three years (1905-8), that today is the site of Metairie Cemetery. His forebear Mathias Friedrichs, from Weilersheim, Alsace, was listed in the 1724 census of the German Coast.

General Meyer Avenue. This street in Algiers was named after the German-American general Adolph Meyer, who successfully lobbied Congress for the establishment of the Algiers Navy Yard during World War II.

Grand Cours/Route Wiltz. Now Louisiana Avenue, this street was originally named after Joseph Wiltz, a plantation owner in Faubourg Plaisance (later part of the City of Lafayette). He divided the land into forty-two plots, with Grand Cours Wiltz as the main thoroughfare. Wiltz dedicated the riverfront portion to public use, which resulted in many legal actions by his heirs trying to regain title. Three-quarters of a mile downriver was the plantation of his sister Margarethe, called the

Widow Wiltz. It was also later subdivided, with the main street becoming Jackson Avenue, named after Andrew Jackson to celebrate his victory in the Battle of New Orleans, 1812. Joseph Wiltz was one of the early German immigrants who settled on the German Coast.

Hamburg Street. This street was named after Hamburg, Germany, by the developer of the area, Alexander Milne. Hamburg was one of the most important city-states of the medieval trade association, the Hanseatic League. The American hamburger is named after the popular street food in Hamburg called *Bouletten*. A *Boulette* resembles a large meatball served with sauce and a bun, similar in concept to the American hamburger.

Haydel Street. Adam Haydel sold land in New Orleans East to the government for Interstate 10 and then purchased other land farther east for a subdivision. He named one of the streets after himself. His ancestor Hans Jacob Heidel (Haydel) was one of the original German pioneers who settled the German Coast. Heidel was the progenitor of a very large family, with female descendents of the first five generations marrying into seventy-four different families.

Jahncke Road. Fritz Jahncke was one of the most important Germans of the city in the late 1800s and early 1900s. He came to New Orleans in 1872 to execute a contract for John Schillinger of New York, who had developed a cement paving process. From 1876 to 1880 Jahncke paved the sidewalks and streets of the city, then branched out into general contracting. He owned and operated a barge and dredging company and was active in the establishment of the Jackson Brewery complex and the development of the riverfront, lakeshore area, and New Basin Canal. He and his three sons went into the shipbuilding business during World War I. His sons continued the family business, Jahncke Services.

Jena Street. This street, along with Austerlitz, was named after one of Napoleon's famous victories on German territory. Jena is a thriving university town in what was East Germany.

Law Street. This street was named by Bernard Xavier Marigny, along with other streets such as Abundance, Hope, Virtue, Force, and Genius. Some researchers attribute the name to John Law, the notorious financier for the duc d'Orleans, after whom the city of New Orleans was named. Law was instrumental in bringing Germans to colonial Louisiana (see chapter 1).

Linhuber Street. Josef Linhuber immigrated to New Orleans from Germany and acquired property in New Orleans East in 1940, which he developed into a subdivision. His surname appears erroneously on many maps as Lyn Huber.

Lowerline Street. This street was named by the surveyor of the City of Carrollton, the Prussian Karl Frederick Zimpel. It marked the lower boundary of the city, an independent entity until its annexation to New Orleans in 1872.

Norman Mayer Street. Norman Mayer (1874-1937) was a cotton broker (Norman Mayer & Co.) who served as director of the New Orleans Cotton Exchange and the Canal Bank & Trust Co. As a philanthropist he served as a trustee of the Jewish Widows and Orphans Asylum.

Press Street. This street marked the site of the largest cotton press in the city. It was designed and built in 1832 by German architect, surveyor, and contractor Karl Frederick Zimpel. The street was originally named Cotton Press Street.

Pressburg Street. This street was named after the capital of Slovakia (now called Bratislava) by the area's developer, Alexander Milne. It was the scene of Napoleon's treaty with Austria after his victory in the Battle of Austerlitz, formerly a Germanic area located within the Austro-Hungarian Empire.

Rhine Drive. This street in Algiers was named for the Rhine River, the only river in Europe flowing from south to north. It forms most of Germany's border with France and flows into the North Sea through the Netherlands.

Roman, North Roman, and **South Roman** streets. These streets were named after the governor of Louisiana, André Bienvenu Roman, who served from 1831 to 1835 and again from 1839 to 1843. He was a descendent of the German pioneer Johann Rommel (also spelled Rome, Roman, Romelle), who was listed in the 1724 census of the German Coast.

St. Nick Drive. This street in Holiday Park subdivision on the west bank of the river was named after St. Nicholas. "Santa Claus" is a corruption of the name of this Germanic figure. A portion of Rampart Street was originally also called St. Nicholas Street.

St. Roch Avenue. St. Roch cemetery and mortuary chapel were named after this saint by the German priest Fr. Peter Leonhard Thevis. Thevis was born in Cologne and came to New Orleans as assistant pastor of Holy Trinity Catholic Church. To fulfill his promise to St. Roch for saving the congregation of Holy Trinity during the yellow-fever epidemic of 1867, he later built St. Roch Campo Santo mortuary chapel with his own hands. After his death in 1893, he was buried under the floor of the chapel, where a memorial to him still stands. The cemetery, located in the once heavily German Third District, has many monuments with German inscriptions.

Samuel Place. This public square on Napoleon Avenue in Faubourg Bouligny was named after one of the German associates in the New Orleans and Carrollton railroad enterprise, Samuel Kohn.

Strasbourg Court. This street in New Orleans East is named after the German-French city in Alsace.

Teche Street. There are contradictory opinions concerning the derivation of this name. One view is that it is a corruption of the word *Deutsche,* so named because of the many German settlers originally living in Algiers. This street was formerly called Monroe Avenue but was renamed in 1894.

Vienna Street; Vienna Court. These two streets, which run through the subdivisions of the reclaimed land on the south shore of Lake Pontchartrain, were named after the capital of Austria.

Warsaw Street. Now renamed Republic Street, this street was originally named by the area developer, Alexander Milne, after the present capital of Poland. Warsaw (*Warschau*) was Prussian territory during the partitioning of Poland.

Weiblen Street. This street was named after Albert Weiblen (1857-1957), born in the German state of Württemberg. He came to New Orleans in 1885 as a stonecutter. By 1887 he had established his own business, the Weiblen Marble and Granite Company on City Park Avenue. Many of the marble memorials in Metairie Cemetery were produced by his company, including his own, a red marble tomb.

Wiltz Lane. This street was named after Louis Alfred Wiltz, a descendent of Joseph Wiltz, an original German Coast pioneer from Thuringia. Louis was born in Algiers in 1843. He developed a mercantile business, was elected alderman, then mayor of New Orleans in 1872. At age twenty-nine he became a state legislator, then speaker of the Louisiana House of Representatives. He was elected governor of Louisiana in 1879 but died of tuberculosis in 1881 while still in office.

Wirth Place. This street in the uptown section between Freret and Magnolia was named after the merchant and landowner Charles Wirth (1851-1936), who developed

Louis Wiltz. *Drawing by Raymond Calvert.*

the surrounding area. Wirth, who was born in Freudenstadt, Württemberg, came to New Orleans in 1864 and later married Josephine Hauck, also of German origin. He founded Wirth's Grocery Store on Magazine Street in 1872. Later he became president and largest stockholder of the Standard Brewing Company, which produced *Wirthbräu* (Wirth Brew). He also served as a member of the city council and president of the German Protestant Orphan Asylum.

Zimple Street. This street in Carrollton was named after Karl Frederick Zimpel, surveyor, architect, engineer, mapmaker, and contractor. He was born in 1801 in Prussia, then came to New Orleans as an engineer for the New Orleans and Carrollton Railway. In 1833 Zimpel became the city surveyor, engineer, and developer of the City of Carrollton, located on the site of the Macarty Plantation. He designed and built a number of New Orleans' important public buildings, after which he returned to Germany.

Other streets in the New Orleans area with German names:

Street Name	Section/Suburb	Street Name	Section/Suburb
Berg	Lakeshore	Kuebel	N.O. East
Berger	Marrero	Lang	Algiers
Bodenger	Algiers	Levy	N.O. East
Brodtmann	Algiers	Muller	Algiers
Deckbar	Jefferson	Philander (Burmaster)	Gretna
Doerr	Arabi	Ruck	Algiers
Eiseman	Marrero	Stahl	Gretna
Eisenhower	Metairie	Strehle	Gretna
Fried	Gretna	Stumpf	Gretna
Gelbke	Gretna	Wagner	Algiers
Herschel (Wiedman)	Gretna	Weigel	Marrero
Hyman	Algiers	Werner	Marigny
Jung	Westwego	Weyer	Gretna
Kabel	Algiers	Wiegand	Bridge City
Klein	Westwego	Wilty	Metairie
Kraft	Algiers	Wuerpel	Lakeview

New Orleans Monuments

Monument to the Immigrant. This monument, designed by Franco Alessandrini, was erected in 1995 in Woldenberg Park. It is an eighteen-foot white Carrara marble statue depicting a family disembarking after a long ocean crossing. The four figures are placed on a triangular base, which depicts the prow of their ship. The inscription reads: *Dedicated to the Courageous Men and Women Who Left Their Homeland Seeking Freedom, Opportunity and a Better Life in a New Country.* This sculpture represents all immigrant groups, including the Germans. It stands in the old Indian Market, which was located on the riverbanks adjacent to the original city. There the Germans of the *Côte des Allemands* sold their farm products, which were essential to the survival of the city throughout the colonial period. In the nineteenth century this area developed into the port of New Orleans.

War Memorial Arches. Located in the upper Ninth Ward at 3800 Burgundy Street in the once heavily German Third District is the **World War I Veterans' Memorial Arch.** Its inscription reads: *Erected A.D. 1919 by the People of This, the Ninth Ward, in Honor of Its Citizens Who Were Enlisted in the Combative Service. In Memory of Those Who Made the Supreme Sacrifice for the Triumph of Right over Might in the Great World War.* The **Jefferson Memorial Arch,** located on the Gretna City Commons, was erected in 1923. A Gretna engineer, Jacob Huber, formed the Jefferson Memorial Organization in 1918 to raise funds for a World War I memorial. It was later dedicated to all of Jefferson Parish's veterans and contains the names of Confederate and World War I soldiers. The engraver was Anthony Adams Huber, the stonecutter for St. Roch cemetery.

Berlin Bear. The three-foot bronze sculpture of the Berlin Bear, symbol of that city, was given to New Orleans in 1968 to commemorate the visit of the mayor of Berlin, Willi Brandt. It symbolized the friendship between the cities of Berlin and New Orleans. The membership of the *Deutsches Haus* claimed the statue when the Rivergate Convention Center was demolished in 1995. It is now located in the foyer of the *Deutsches Haus,* 200 South Galvez Street.

Audubon Park Monuments. The neoclassical **Entrance Gate** to the park on St. Charles Avenue was commissioned in 1921 by Mrs. Maurice Stern in honor of her husband. The gate was executed by Moise Goldstein, while Weiblen Marble and Granite Company created the design. The **Sophie and Simon Gumbel Fountain** was installed in 1918 directly behind the entrance. It was designed and cast in bronze by the Austrian sculptor Isidore Konti (1862-1938). The **Newman Bandstand** was given in 1921 by Rebecca Kiefer Newman in memory of her husband, Isidore Newman. The architect was Emile Weil. The inscription reads: *Dedicated to music in memory of Isidore Newman, Rebecca Kiefer Newman.* The **Merz Memorial Zoo** was endowed in 1938 by Valentine

World War I Veteran's Memorial Arch, 3800 Burgundy Street. *Photograph by Raymond Calvert.*

Merz, president of New Orleans Brewing Company. The architect was Moise Goldstein. The **Odenheimer Aquarium** and **Odenheimer Sea Lion Pool** were erected in the 1920s. They were given by Sigmund Odenheimer, first president of the *Deutsches Haus*. The neoclassical designs were created by Favrot & Livaudais and Samuel Stone.

City Park Monuments. The **Stern Auditorium** addition to the New Orleans Museum of Art was built in the late 1960s by Edith Rosenwald Stern. The **Jahncke Fountain** formerly in front of the museum was commissioned by the family in memory of Fritz Jahncke. It was erected shortly after his death in 1911. The **Hyams Wading Pool** is embellished with a bronze sculpture by Isidore Konti. Crossing the lagoon, leading to the casino, is the **Dreyfous Bridge,** given by the Dreyfous family in memory of Felix J. Dreyfous, president of the board of City Park and one of its founders. German designers were also responsible for several other structures in the park. The **Bandstand** was designed by Emile Weil as a replica of the Temple of Love at Trianon Palace, Versailles. Andry & Bendernagel designed the **Peristyle Pavilion,** while the **conservatories** were conceived of and executed by Julius Koch.

The **Newcomb College Entrance Gates** were erected in 1934 at 1229 Broadway. Richard Koch was the architect.

Historical Markers

The historical markers listed in this section designate the sites where the Germans of Louisiana settled, built their homes and churches, or participated in important historical events. The location of each marker and the wording on each sign are given, followed by the German connection if not explained on the marker. The Louisiana Highway Commission oversees the historical marker project. Other unofficial markers placed by various groups and organizations do not have the distinctive format of the commission markers.

Ascension Parish. The historical marker designating **Galveztown** is inscribed with the following:

> Old Spanish town at junction of Amite River and Bayou Manchac. Settled by Anglo-Americans, 1776-78, seeking Spanish refuge from American Revolution, and by Canary Islanders (Islenos). Named for Spanish Governor Bernardo de Galvez. Town was abandoned by 1810. Set up in colonial period as fort to protect from British; large German population, second in size to Spanish (Islenos) settlers; town had church called St. Bernard, whose mission church was at St. Gabriel.

This marker is located in Galvez, on Louisiana Highway 42, near Port Vincent.

East Baton Rouge Parish. About 1880 the German immigrant Georg Kleinpeter established the **Dutch Highlands.** The historical marker reads:

Ben Hur Road to Siegen Lane first area settled under Spain by Germans, upon signing of treaty with England and Spain. Where road began was the Georg Kleinpeter site, original claimant. Leader in agriculture who grew sugar cane with success, first time on high land; built first cotton gin, 1790. His son, John Baptiste, erected first steam sugar mill on high land, 1832.

The marker is located on Highland Road, Louisiana Highway 42, just east of Gardere Lane, in Baton Rouge.

Iberville Parish.

[**Bayou Teche**'s] name comes from Indian legend that writhing snake (*Tenche*) made stream bed, or from *Deutsch* after German settlers. Approximately 80 miles long, bayou starts near Port Barre, converges with Atchafalaya near Morgan City. Important waterway in Louisiana history for Indians, traders, settlers.

It is located in New Iberia on U.S. Highway 90. Also in Iberville Parish is **St. Gabriel,** dating back to 1761-63. Its historical marker reads:

Church of the Iberville Coast built by Acadian exiles in 1769. It was located in 1773 in Spanish Manchac on a land grant given by that government. German settlers came from Maryland in 1784.

It is located in St. Gabriel, Louisiana Highway 23.

Jefferson Parish. In Jefferson Parish is located **Mechanikham,** now part of Gretna. Its historical marker states:

Incorporated 20 August 1913. John Ehret, First Mayor. Seat of Jefferson Parish government since 1884. German settlement laid out in 1836 by Benjamin Buisson for Nicolas Noel Destrehan as Village of Mechanikham.

It is located on Huey P. Long Avenue Commons between Tenth and Eleventh streets. A historical marker for the town of **Carrollton** reads:

Laid out by Charles Zimpel in 1833. Jefferson Parish seat 1851-1874. Annexed 1874 by New Orleans. 1854 Courthouse, located at 719 South Carrollton Avenue, designed by Henry Howard.

Zimpel was a Prussian surveyor and cartographer. Carrollton is located on the site of the Macarty Plantation, formerly the uppermost part of Bienville's 1719 land grant.

Livingston Parish. Located in Lake Maurepas is **Maurepas Island.** Its historical marker reads:

> Near Lake Maurepas named by d'Iberville, 1699, for Maurepas, French Marine Minister. Villages: Maurepas, Bear Island; head of island settled by Germans, French, Spanish. Civil War Gunboat Bonnet Carré sank here.

Orleans Parish. Now part of New Orleans, located at 200 Magazine Street, is the **Bienville's Plantation** marker, which reads: *Here, on a plantation granted to him on March 27, 1719, by the Company of the Indies, stood the residence of Jean Baptiste Lemoyne de Bienville, founder of New Orleans. This plantation was sold by Bienville in April 1726 to the Jesuit Fathers from whom it was confiscated in 1763.* About a dozen of the original German pioneers settled here after the 1722 hurricane destroyed their homesteads on the German Coast. The **Dufour-Baldwin House,** located at 1707 Esplanade Avenue, bears a historical marker reading:

> A classical example of the Greek Revival-Italianate style. Designed by noted architects, Henry Howard and Albert Diettel, constructed in 1859 by Wing and Muir for Louise Donnet and Cyprian Dufour, a prominent attorney, author and state senator. Dufour sold the home in 1870 to Arthemise Bouligny and Albert Baldwin, a leading businessman and philanthropist, who retained the property until 1912. Prior to 1859 the frontage was owned by free persons of color, Auguste Reynal and Bernard Crokin. The remainder was owned by the illustrious Creole, Basilice Pedesclaux-Duchamp.

Diettel was from Dresden, Germany. **Shangarai-Chasset/Gates of Mercy** is inscribed: *Site of the first permanent [German] Jewish house of worship in state of Louisiana. Gates of Mercy synagogue, 1845: located at 410-20 North Rampart Street, Gates of Mercy, chartered by the state in 1827, confirmed the abolition of the Code Noir, which had denied Jews the right to live and worship in Louisiana and by so doing affirmed American freedoms of religion and assembly.*

Plaquemines Parish. Located on Louisiana Highway 23 is a marker noting the following about **Venice:**

> Near this site on April 9, 1682, LaSalle claimed Louisiana for France. Father Zenobius Membre, a member of the expedition, sang the Te Deum. On March 3, 1699, Father Anastase Douay, member of Iberville's expedition, celebrated the first Mass of record in French Louisiana.

The first German (Hans or Heinz) to come to Louisiana was a member of this expedition. He avenged La Salle's murder by killing the murderer.

St. Charles Parish. The historical marker denoting the **Battle of Des Allemands** has the following inscription: *Le district des Allemands, settled by Germans about 1720, the scene of numerous skirmishes between Confederate guerillas and Union forces, 1862-1863. Most famous skirmish resulted in capture of an entire detachment of Union soldiers on September 4, 1862.* It is located in Des Allemands on U.S. Highway 90. The marker for **Home Place,** located in Luling, Louisiana, reads: *Built in 1790s this French Colonial raised cottage is of West Indies bousillage construction. Owners included La Branche, Fortier, Gaillaire, Keller family ownership since 1885.* La Branche (Zweig) was a German pioneer. **Les Allemands'** marker reads:

> German immigrants, led by Karl D'Arensbourg, joined other Germans from John Law's Arkansas concession to settle here in 1722. Chapel erected by 1724. These industrious German farmers saved New Orleans from famine.

It is located in Killona, five miles above Hahnville on the west bank of the Mississippi River. **St. Charles Borromeo,** the "Little Red Church," bears the inscription:

Louisiana state historical marker. *Photograph by Anthony Tassin.*

First constructed of logs about 1740. Burned and rebuilt, 1806. Famous river boat landmark twenty-five miles from New Orleans where boat captains traditionally paid off their crews. Again burned and rebuilt 1921.

The Little Red Church was located in Destrehan on Louisiana Highway 48; its congregation was originally German. The historical marker for **L'Anse aux Autardes** is to be found in New Sarpy on Louisiana Highway 48. It reads:

Bustard's Cove 1722. Settled by Canadians, French. Bienville came here in 1699 from Lake Pontchartrain using small waterways, portage. LeSieur and Canadians used the route and were met here by Iberville and Tonti Feb. 24, 1700. It became part of the 'Second German Coast' about 1730.

St. James Parish. On Louisiana Highway 18 is located **Vacherie.** Its marker reads:

Bayougoula Village, 1713. Settled by Canadians and French; later by Germans, Acadians, Spaniards. Here in 1730 Governor Perrier organized expedition against Natchez Indians. Early cattle raising center. French records referred to area as Tabiscana.

St. John the Baptist Parish. Located in Edgard, on Louisiana Highway 18, is **St. John the Baptist Catholic Church.** Its marker is inscribed:

1770; From which civil parish was named. First church on second German Coast when Louisiana was colony of Spain. Served west and east banks of river until 1864. Old cemetery contains grave of wife of Gen. P. G. T. Beauregard and John Slidell family tomb.

Webster Parish. Located near Minden is **Germantown:** *About 7 miles northeast on Route 186 are remnants of a colony founded in 1835 by followers of Count Leon who came from Germany to America for a religious belief. There they operated a communal village until 1871.*

Chapter Four

Buildings

PUBLIC AND COMMERCIAL BUILDINGS, LODGES, AND HALLS

New Orleans has always been noted for its architecture. As a major city and principal port of the South, its architecture reflects the diversity of styles and influences found only in a few other major centers of commerce, like New York and Chicago. The architectural trends of the times were reflected in the public buildings of the city. New Orleans also had its own indigenous architecture, which expressed itself in small shops and in individual residences. Not all styles seen in the great Northern cities were represented in New Orleans during the years following the Civil War. Reconstruction had impoverished the city, crippling the development of commerce and eliminating the construction of new public buildings. But during the decades before the Civil War, New Orleans had experienced a building boom.

In the 1830s, several well-trained German architects and builders had come to New Orleans, including Karl Frederick Zimpel, Henry Moellhausen, and Jacob Rothass. They had to adjust their European training to the conservative tastes that prevailed in the city. However, their work was distinguished by the rigorous training and lengthy apprenticeships they had received in the German system of education.

Zimpel was a young Prussian aristocrat who soon established a lucrative career in the city as a surveyor, engineer, and architect. His tastes were mainly classical, in keeping with the style then in vogue in both Europe and America. He was highly successful in those areas in which he was trained and, in a short time, became deputy surveyor and chief engineer for the city. In 1833 he laid out and developed the City of Carrollton. Perhaps his most important achievement was the detailed map of New Orleans he produced in 1834. Dissatisfied with the quality produced by the lithographers in New Orleans, he sent his original drawing back to Germany. On the return trip the lithographic stone and reproductions were lost at sea, making the Zimpel map a collector's item. As chief engineer of the New Orleans and Carrollton Railway, which ran from Canal Street to Carrollton Avenue along Nayades Street (now St. Charles Avenue), he got involved in land speculation. Having little experience in this area, he soon fell into debt and fled the city. After only seven years of working in New Orleans, he returned to his native Prussia.

Henry Moellhausen, another Prussian architect, also came to New Orleans in the 1830s. His principal contribution to the city was through his skillful architectural renderings, but few buildings of his design were constructed. Perhaps his most important achievement was the influence he exerted on the noted architect Henry Howard, who had been his student. Another German teacher of architecture was Jacob Rothass, who specialized in classical and Gothic design. Trained in Munich in the fine arts, he was an adept architect and surveyor. Like Moellhausen, his main contribution was his renderings and surveys.

The 1840s saw revolution in the German states and an influx of German immigrants to New Orleans, called the forty-eighters. Among these were artisans and building tradesmen as well as educated professionals. At this time in New Orleans, prosperity was encouraging the development of new areas, where construction of all types created a need for skilled craftsmen and architects. In the German communities of the day there was a growing need for churches, schools, and other institutions, creating a demand for German-trained architects and journeymen. Many settled in the City of Lafayette because of the cheap land and urban environment. More than half the population of the city center along the waterfront was German.

Edward Gottheil, who also arrived in the 1840s, established an elite architectural business in Lafayette. To escape his German-Jewish background, he married a Creole and adopted the lifestyle she represented. With the wealth he had acquired as a successful architect he left his profession and went into the building-materials business. Here he failed miserably and lost everything, including his wife and daughter, who moved to Paris. Gottheil subsequently left the city and, with the outbreak of the Civil War, joined the Confederate army. After the war he secured the position of Louisiana commissioner for the European expositions in Paris and Hamburg. His last years produced no architectural work although he had designed over a dozen residential and commercial buildings before the war. He died in Charity Hospital, abandoned by the family and friends of his prosperous and productive period.

Other notable German architects of the prewar period were Charles Lewis Hillger and William Drews. Hillger and Drews settled together in the City of Lafayette until Hillger's marriage to Emelie Fitzner, a Prussian of Polish heritage. Hillger and Drews first established a carpentry business, which they developed into a successful building firm. Their clients were primarily Germans, who appreciated the craftsmanship of their work. Before war broke out the two had constructed more than a dozen houses, stores, and churches in the Lafayette area. In the German tradition they acted both as designers and builders for their residential, business, and institutional clients. However, the partners ignored the architectural styles of Europe, designing primarily in the traditions popular in America. Hillger also worked alone for the downtown German community, where he designed several buildings.

With the onset of the Civil War, however, Hillger separated from his wife for a time and moved to Baltimore. Nevertheless the pair had seven children within the next fifteen years. Drews remained in New Orleans during the war but lost his young wife to disease. He soon fell into debt, sold his property, and left the city. At the same time, just as the Civil War ended, Hillger returned to New Orleans. He built a new residence for his large family in a rural setting, upriver from Lafayette, away from the semi-urban German community. Professionally he joined forces with his former apprentice Ferdinand Reusch, who had become a successful builder. His clients remained the wealthy Germans for whom he had designed before the war. However, Hillger's style had changed, influenced by the eclectic styles of Europe, which he had experienced during his years in Baltimore. His prosperous clients preferred designs fitting their personal tastes rather than the Greek Revival style dictated by fashion. The German churches, which he designed in the Gothic and Romanesque styles, established his reputation as an innovative church architect. Several non-German congregations commissioned him to design and build new churches as New Orleans recovered during Reconstruction. Perhaps Hillger's greatest accomplishment, however, was the palatial Grunewald Hall, which he designed in Bavarian Baroque style. Fronting on Canal Street, the hall's ground floor contained a music store and showrooms, while an ornate concert hall graced the upper floors.

At age fourteen, William Fitzner had emigrated from Prussian Pomerania the year his sister Emelie married Charles Hillger. Once in New Orleans he was intensively trained in architecture and construction by his brother-in-law's business partner, William Drews. Further training as a draftsman came from a stint in the office of the city surveyor. As a full-fledged master builder he received his first contract at age twenty-four. The Italianate style, with which he embellished his residential and commercial designs, appealed to him more than other newly introduced European architectural modes. However, he adopted the High Victorian Gothic preferred by Hillger for church design. Like Hillger, Fitzner remained loyal to the German community of Lafayette. His clients were almost exclusively German, as were the builders with whom he worked. He even married three successive German women while residing in Lafayette: Solomea Schutterle, who died in childbirth; then, within a year, Caroline Hoppemeyer; and, finally, Anna Blattner.

Albert Diettel came to New Orleans as a forty-eighter after having trained and worked in Dresden. His experience as a railroad engineer enabled him to gain a position as a construction engineer for the expanding American railroads. In the 1850s he settled near the City of Lafayette, where he worked with a wealthy local builder, E. W. Sewell. In 1856 he returned to Dresden to marry Eliza Müller, then came back

to New Orleans to enter into a partnership with the well-known Henry Howard. Diettel was the subordinate partner, managing the business and supervising construction during Howard's prolonged absences in spring and summer. However, his designs had a marked influence on the architectural style of the firm, introducing elements of German Romanticism. This German Baroque style was most evident in the imposing landmarks, St. Mary's Assumption and St. John the Baptist churches. When the Civil War broke out, Diettel ended his partnership with Howard and joined forces for a year with another German architect, William Thiel. He then left for Dresden for the remaining years of the war, returning in 1867. Diettel took up his architectural practice once again, winning contracts from German

St. John the Baptist Catholic Church, 1872, 1139 Dryades Street. *Courtesy of the Historic New Orleans Collection.*

real-estate speculators and church and synagogue congregations. The German Baroque style still predominated in his designs, into which he later introduced elements of the French Empire style. Diettel spent the rest of his career in New Orleans, living modestly and working primarily with his fellow countrymen.

William Thiel, the architect of the famous Turners' Hall on Lafayette Street, lost his partnership with Diettel for reasons of bad faith. Although Thiel's architectural accomplishments were outstanding, his business and personal ethics left much to be desired. Before coming to New Orleans he had been involved in several real-estate swindles and had absconded to Nicaragua with sizeable embezzled funds. After a few years in New Orleans he suddenly left for Cincinnati with his German wife and children. There he is thought to have staged his own death from cholera. Whatever happened, he returned alone to New Orleans in 1856 and married another German woman, Pauline Sirjacques. He first began a lumbering business in the swamps above New Orleans with another German, Edward Würzberger. After a falling-out he turned to practicing architecture and built a dozen residential and commercial buildings for his German clients in New Orleans. He also obtained contracts for important institutional structures besides Turners' Hall, such as the German National Theatre, Odd Fellows Hall, and several syn-agogues. Apparently he returned to respectability, join-ing the *Deutsche Gesellschaf* (German Society) and culti-vating relationships with the wealthy and influential Germans of the city. His death in 1870 kept him from participating further in the architectural renaissance that New Orleans enjoyed after Reconstruction. It was during this period that most of the great public buildings of the city were erected in Greek Revival style, a number of which were designed by German architects.

These outstanding German

Odd Fellows Hall, which replaced the original building (burned 1866), from *Jewell's Crescent City Illustrated,* 1873. *Courtesy of a private collection.*

architects left their imprints on the city of New Orleans. But others played important roles, such as Julius Koch and Dietrich Einsiedel, both of whom brought to New Orleans the expertise they had acquired while working in America's Northeast. German master builders who plied their trade in New Orleans included David Sigle, Valentine von Werner, Otto Walther, and W. H. Krone. Fritz Jahncke, who first came to New Orleans as a cement contractor, paved the streets and sidewalks of the city and expanded into a number of other businesses. Albert Weiblen and Victor Huber established important granite and marble industries, producing the remarkable grave monuments for which New Orleans is noted (see chapter 9).

Other German architects were: Albert Bendernagel (New Orleans Stock Exchange; Norman Mayer Memorial Building; Howard Tilton Memorial Hall and Richardson Memorial Building, Tulane University), Theodore Brune (St. Joseph's Abbey, Covington), Hans Diettel (Sixth District Building & Loan), Charles and Diedrich Einsiedel (Jackson Brewery, Security Brewing Company, Lane Cotton Mill No. 3), Moise Goldstein (National American Bank, 145 Carondelet), Eugene Hymel (Jackson Homestead, 5600 block of

Residence of Fritz Jahncke, Howard Avenue, from *City of New Orleans*, 1894. *Courtesy of the Louisiana Collection, Earl K. Long Library, University of New Orleans.*

Annunciation), E. E. Seghers (Customhouse on Marais Street, demolished), Emile Weil (Saenger Theater; Whitney National Bank, 228 St. Charles; New Orleans Canal and Banking Building, 210 Baronne). The German builders with whom the architects worked included Henry Bensel, Joseph Fromherz, John R. Eichelberger, Adam Graner, Henry Hellwig, W. H. Krone, Arthur Liebe, Christian D. Rodick, and Louis Schermann (see also "Private Residences" below).

The following list gives native German architects, alphabetically, with a chronology of the public buildings each designed. These architects were trained in the exacting standards of their homeland. Many of these buildings were financed and built by the German community for its own use. However, other public buildings had no German connection except the nationality of the architect. The locations and architectural styles, when known, are also noted. The second listing gives the lodges and halls dedicated to the use of the German community and its societies.

Major German Architects and Their Buildings

Theodore Brune (birth date unknown; died 1932)
1908   **Mater Dolorosa Catholic Church**
        1238 South Carrollton Avenue
        Romanesque Revival style
        Also extension, Mater Dolorosa Hall, corner Plum Street
1908   **Saint Joseph Abbey Church**
        Saint Benedict, Louisiana
        Romanesque Revival style

Albert Diettel (born 1824 in Dresden; died 1896)
1857   **Medical School Building**
        Tulane Avenue
        (Howard and Diettel partnership)
1859   **Third Presbyterian Church**
        Royal Street between Elysian Fields and Frenchmen Street
        Became Holy Redeemer Catholic Church; destroyed by Hurricane
        Betsy in September 1965
1859   **425, 429, 431 Carondelet Street**
        Three three-story Italianate buildings with stores below and residences above
1860   **St. Mary's Assumption Church**
        Josephine and Constance streets
        German Baroque style; attributed to Diettel
1860   **Saints Peter and Paul Church**
        Burgundy Street

1861   **Hebrew Rest Cemetery** (brick wall surrounding cemetery)
        Elysian Fields Avenue
1869   **St. John the Baptist Church** (completed 1872)
        1139 Dryades Street; with associated Dominican convent school
        and academy. Church was built to serve the thousands of immi-
        grants settling in this area when digging the New Basin Canal in the
        1830s. Most were living around the turning basin at Howard
        Avenue and Hercules Street. Designed by Diettel after church in his
        birthplace, Dresden.
1872   **Southwestern Exposition Building**
        St. Charles Avenue and Carondelet Street
1873   **Gates of Mercy, Congregation Shangari Chassed** (demolished)
        North Rampart Street
1882   **Southern Brewing Company** (demolished)
        North Villere and Toulouse streets
1883   **St. Elizabeth's Children's Home** (enlarged, remodeled, wing
        added)
        1314 Napoleon Avenue

William Drews (born 1825 in East Prussia; worked in New Orleans in 1850s;
        death date unknown)
1854   **St. Joseph Orphan Asylum** (demolished)
        Laurel and Josephine streets
1855   **First Street Presbyterian Church**
        First Street, City of Lafayette
        Builder: Drews; architect: Adam Graner
        Greek Revival style
1857   **Redemptorist Fathers Seminary,** St. Joseph complex (with
        Hillger)
        Bouligny, Jefferson City
1860   **First German Lutheran Church** (with Hillger)
        Third District
        Burned in 1889, rebuilt in same style

William Fitzner (born 1845 in East Prussia; died 1914)
1800s   **Rice, Birn & Co. Hardware Store** (demolished)
        Lower Camp Street
1881   **Lane Cotton Mill No. 2**
        Napoleon Avenue
        Romanesque Revival style
        Four-story brick addition to mill no. 1 built in 1883 at 4610
        Tchoupitoulas Street
1882   **St. Mary's Dominican Convent**

7214 St. Charles Avenue
1882   **Louisiana Brewing Company**
Jackson Avenue corner Tchoupitoulas Street
1883   **Louisiana Avenue Methodist Church**
Louisiana Avenue
High Victorian Gothic style
1883   **Crescent Jute Manufacturing Company**
2800 Chartres Street
1888   **Weckerling Brewing Company** (demolished)
Magazine Street and Delord (now Howard Avenue)
1889   **Lafayette Brewing Company** (demolished)
Lafayette and Tchoupitoulas streets
1890s   **Standard Brewing Company** (demolished)
Johnson Street
1900   **Security Building & Loan**
1335 Calhoun Street; 604-6 State Street

Charles Lewis Hillger (born 1830 in East Prussia; died 1879)
1849   **Grunewald Hall**
Canal Street
German Baroque style
Destroyed by fire in 1892; Hotel Grunewald built in 1908, originally conceived as rear extension to hall
1855   **St. Joseph Church** (demolished)
1032 Carondelet Street
Mixture of Baroque, Byzantine, Gothic, and Romanesque styles
1869   **German Protestant Orphan Asylum**
State, Camp, Webster, Chestnut streets
Builder: Henry Friedrich
Two three-story brick dormitories (demolished, 1976); stable
1870   **Temple Sinai**
1032 Carondelet Street between Howard Avenue and Caliope Street
Builder: Peter Mittlemass
Mixture of Romanesque and Byzantine styles
Adapted to become New Orleans Repertory Theater, 1969 (demolished)
1871   **Zion Lutheran Church**
1924 St. Charles Avenue, corner St. Mary Street
Carpenter Gothic style
1872   **Jackson Avenue Evangelical Church**
Jackson Avenue corner Chippewa Street
1873   **Trinity Episcopal Church** (new facade)
1329 Jackson Avenue

1874   **Thalia Street Presbyterian Church** (demolished)
       Thalia Street
       Modified Victorian Gothic style
1875   **Rayne Memorial Methodist Church**
       St. Charles Avenue
       High Victorian Gothic style
1875   **Canal Street Presbyterian Church** (demolished)
       Canal Street
       Modified Victorian Gothic style
1877   **Lafayette Fire Insurance Building**
       2123 Magazine Street
       Builder: Henry Bensel, Jr.
       "Flamboyant" Italianate style

William Thiel (1821-70)
1865   **Gates of Prayer** (Shangarai Tefiloh)
       Jackson Avenue
1866   **Werlein Concert Hall**
       Baronne and Perdido streets
       Remodeled as German National Theatre in 1881; destroyed by fire
       in 1891; site of former De Soto Hotel, now remodeled as Le
       Pavillon Hotel
1868   **Turners' Hall**
       Lafayette and O'Keefe streets
       Italianate style

Karl Frederick Zimpel (born 1801 in Prussia; worked in New Orleans 1830-
       37; returned to Europe; death date unknown)
1831   **Bishop's City Hotel** (demolished)
       Camp and Common streets
       Neoclassical style
1832   **Bank of Orleans** (demolished)
       Canal Street and Exchange Alley
       Greek Revival style
1833   **Banks Arcade** (partially demolished)
       Now part of Board of Trade Plaza, 316 Magazine
       Neoclassical style
       Four units remain of original block-long row built for Thomas
       Banks; Hotel Vonderbank (formerly St. James Hotel), part of
       original arcade
1833   **Orleans Cotton Press**
       Roufignac and New Levee streets
       Utilitarian design
       Compressed 150,000 bales per annum

1835   **Carrollton Hotel and Gardens**
At Canal & Carrollton Railway station, Carrollton Avenue and levee
Antebellum plantation style; attributed to Zimpel

Lodges and Halls Dedicated to the Use of the German Community and Its Societies

1836   **Kaiser (Kayser) Hall**
Josephine and Chippewa streets
Ballroom served as general meeting hall for Germans during week; Saturday nights used for German dances, Sunday mornings for Mass before St. Mary's Assumption Church built
Nau; Samuels; Deiler, Presse, Churches

1849   **Grunewald Hall**
Canal Street
German Baroque style
Destroyed by fire in 1892; in 1908 Hotel Grunewald (now Roosevelt/Fairmont) built as rear extension to hall
Nau

1849   **Schumann Hall**
32 Orleans Street
First named Sacramento House, later Louis Stein's; oldest German meeting hall in New Orleans
Deiler, Presse

1850   **Helvetia Hall (Lodge No. 44)**
(ca.)   Louisiana Avenue and Magazine Street
Edwards 1870

1850   **Teutonia Hall (Lodge No. 10)**
(ca.)   Iberville Street and Exchange Alley
Newspaper File, New Orleans Public Library (NOPL); Edwards 1870

1853   **Germania Lodge No. 29**
Jefferson City
Nau

1855   **Odd Fellows Hall**
Camp and Lafayette streets
Nau

1859   **David Crockett Fire Hall**
205 Lafayette Street, Gretna
Jeff. Review 1937; Swanson

1860   **Union Hall**
Jackson Avenue between Annunciation and Chippewa streets
Used for services by German Lutherans
Deiler, Churches

1865 **Deutsche Companie Halle**
(forerunner of Harmonie Club)
112 Common Street, then
Camp Street near Julia Street
In 1872 moved to Exchange
Alley and Bienville Street
Nau; NOPL; Jews of La.

1865 **Deutsches National Theater und Halle**
City of Lafayette
Nau

1866 **Werlein Concert Hall**
Baronne and Perdido streets
Remodeled as German National
Theatre in 1881; destroyed by
fire in 1891

Werlein Concert Hall/German National Theatre, Baronne and Perdido, from *Jewell's Crescent City Illustrated,* 1873. *Courtesy of a private collection.*

1866 **Steinbrunn Hall**
Gretna
Edwards 1870

1884 **Mechanics' Hall** (William Tell Fire Hall)
Newton and Third streets, Gretna
Property purchased by Michael Flesch and John Kaiser from
Louisa Destrehan for William Tell Hook and Ladder Co. No. 1; site
of annual Grand German Ball
Swanson

1885 **Germania Hall (Lodge No. 46)**
(ca.) 4415 Bienville Street
NOPL

1890 **Sängerhalle**
Adjacent to Lee Circle, site of former Katz and Besthoff building
Built to house 1890 *Sängerfest* (singing festival) of North American
Sängerbund
Nau; Deiler, Presse

1896 **Athenaeum (auditorium)**
Clio Street and St. Charles Avenue
Built by Young Men's Hebrew Association
Engelhardt; Jews of La.

1896 **Young Men's Hebrew Association Hall**
St. Charles Avenue and Clio Street
Jews of La.

1897 **Harmonie Club Hall**
Canal Street, site of present Boston Club
Jews of La.; Soards 1916

SAENGER-HALLE, LEE CIRCLE NEW ORLEANS, LA.

Sängerhalle, built at Lee Circle for the 1890 convention of the North American Singers Association, from program for the *1890 Sängerfest. Courtesy of the Historic New Orleans Collection.*

1922	**William D. White Masonic Lodge, F. & A.M.**
	501 Amelia Street, Gretna
	La. Directory
1928	**Deutsches Haus**
	200 South Galvez Street
	Nau
?	**Masonic Temple of the Mystic Shrine**
	St. Charles Avenue and Perdido Street
	Zacharie; Nau

PRIVATE RESIDENCES

The earliest private structures for which records exist are those of the thirteen German families who left the German Coast after the hurricane of 1722. These settlers were offered small plots by Governor Bienville on the upper portion of his original land grant. In return for farming the land Bienville gave them provisions for a year, farming and building tools, a cow, two hogs, four hens, and a rooster. These Germans were to repay Bienville for their land after getting established, but most left within a few years to resettle with their countrymen on the German Coast. Their houses were no doubt primitive, as were the first homesteads in the original three German villages.

An indigenous architecture developed early along the River Road, upstream from New Orleans. Elements of West Indian styles suited to the semitropical weather were adopted, producing raised cottages with hip roofs, galleries, and rooms opening into each other to avoid breeze-blocking hallways. Styles varied according to the finances available, from small farmhouses in Creole cottage style to palatial residences. The smaller plantation homes were usually planned by the property owners working with local builders. The gracious antebellum mansions, however, were for the most part designed by trained architects. These wealthy farmers, whose primary residences were located on their rice and sugarcane plantations, also commissioned smart townhouses for the social season in New Orleans.

Later, in-town residences also developed in indigenous architectural styles, for example, the numerous cottages, shotgun houses, and camelbacks found throughout the city. Most neighborhoods contained a mix of substantial single houses, single and double cottages, and multiple units, all in a similar style, along with small shops, family-run enterprises, and commercial strips. Most of the residential areas of the city became semi-urban, in contrast to strictly urban or suburban.

When the great influx of German immigrants came to New Orleans in the nineteenth century, they settled in the suburbs of the city, where they could purchase land cheaply and avoid the overcrowding and high prices of the city center. By the 1850s, however, those German and German-Americans who had become successful businessmen wanted imposing residences like those of the French Creoles and Americans. They demanded homes in the finer New Orleans neighborhoods, designed in a grand manner by architects of note.

Since the choice of architects and builders was a personal matter, not all of the prosperous Germans stayed within the German community when seeking designers and craftsmen for constructing their new homes. Conversely, non-German men of wealth frequently chose noted German architects. Most of the well-known German architects listed earlier in this chapter were commissioned by their wealthier countrymen to design impressive residences. The architectural partnership of Hillger and Drews was particularly popular. Before the Civil War it designed and constructed notable homes for Henry Baum, a successful German boot and shoemaker, Carl Kohn, a wealthy Bavarian Jewish banker, A. W. C. Manouvrier, the owner of a wholesale grocery company, and Nels Anderson, a successful dairyman in Lafayette. After the war Hillger created grand villas for successful Germans such as John Auguste Blaffer, founder of two banks, and

Julius Weis, a Bavarian Jew who had begun as a country peddler. Through hard work and impeccable honesty, Weis had established a cotton factorage and a comfortable fortune. Albert Diettel also built a number of stylish homes before the Civil War, while William Fitzner was active in residential construction in the 1870s and 1880s. Both of these architects worked outside the German community as well as with their countrymen.

Other mansions were built in fashionable locations, for example, those on St. Charles Avenue. Although designed by non-German architects they were commissioned by highly successful Germans to display their newly acquired wealth. Among the most impressive in New Orleans were the mansion of the cigar king, Simon Hernsheim, now the Columns Hotel, and the Fabacher residence, demolished in the 1940s, which took up a whole city block. Lawrence Fabacher had founded and developed the Jax Brewery, the largest producer of beer in the South. Also noteworthy was Fannie Kiefer Newman's huge Romanesque stone mansion built on "the Avenue," the Swiss chalet of Cuthbert Bullit, which was moved from St. Charles to Carondelet Street, and the Van Benthuysen residence (now The Elms), which housed the German consulate prior to World War II.

Other residential architects and builders with German backgrounds were Michael Zeringue (Zehringer), Julius Weis, Charles Bier, Edward Sporl, Moise Goldstein, Emile Weil, Richard Koch, and John Baehr, as well as most of the German architects who designed public buildings.

Residence of Laurence Fabacher, Prytania Street, from *City of New Orleans, 1894. Courtesy of the Louisiana Collection, Earl K. Long Library, University of New Orleans.*

The notable residences listed below are divided according to those designed by German architects and those built/owned by Germans and German-Americans. The second listing is divided between city and country homes. Residences are listed by dates of construction. Building styles and architects, when known, are also given.

New Orleans Homes Designed by German Architects

1830s   **Sigle Residence**
          826 Frenchmen Street
          Early Greek Revival style
          Architect: David Sigle
          Guide to New Orleans Architecture (Guide)

1852   **Maddox-Brennan House**
          2507 Prytania Street
          Architect: John Barnett; supervising architect: Edward Gottheil; builder: John R. Eichelberger
          Guide

1852-60   **Nels Anderson Residence**
          2705 and 2715 Magazine Street
          Early Italianate style
          Architect: Charles Lewis Hillger
          Irvin

1855   **Carl Kohn Residence**
          1855 St. Charles Avenue, across from Lafayette Square
          Three-story home on site of former residence
          Architects: Hillger and Drews; builder: Drews
          Architecture II

1858   **Residence** (now used as commercial building)
          1612 St. Charles Avenue
          Architect: Albert Diettel
          Guide

1858   **Residence**
          1411 Canal Street
          Italianate style; three-story townhouse with attached coach house and two-story stable
          Architects: Howard and Diettel
          Architecture II

1858   **Mansion** (demolished 1896 to build Esplanade Girls' High School)
          2438 Esplanade Avenue
          Architects: Howard and Diettel
          Architecture V

1859-60   **Dufour-Baldwin House**
          1707 Esplanade Avenue

Late Classic style
Architect: Albert Diettel; builders: Wing and Muir
Guide

1859   **Weber House**
1912 Bienville Street
Classic style; three-bay townhouse
Architect: Charles Lewis Hillger; builder: Henry Saenger
Architecture VI

1860-61   **Residence**
Conti Street near Derbigny Street
Architect: Albert Diettel
Wilson

1868   **Cuthbert Bullit Residence**
3627 Carondelet Street
Swiss chalet originally located on St. Charles Avenue; moved in
1883 by Samuel Hernsheim to make way for new mansion
Architect: Edward Gottheil
Irvin; Guide; Architecture VII

1869   **Residence**
2127 Dauphine Street
Late Classic style
Architect: William Thiel; builder: Lewis Schermann
Architecture IV

1869   **Blaffer House**
1328 Felicity Street
Italianate style; built for John Auguste Blaffer
Architect: Charles Lewis Hillger; builder: F. Reusch
Irvin; Guide; Architecture I

1870s   **Residence**
3005 St. Charles Avenue
Architect: attributed to Albert Diettel
Guide

1870s   **Two Double Residences**
1608-10, 1612 St. Charles Avenue
Single Residence
1618 St Charles Avenue
Now converted into shops
Architects: Howard and Diettel; builder: Elijah Cox
Architecture I

1872   **Harmony Street Row**
1223-41 Harmony Street
Originally four identical Italianate camelbacks
Architect: William Fitzner; builder: Louis G. Wilkins
Guide

1872   **Leech Home**
2122 and 2124 Magazine Street, between Josephine Street and Jackson Avenue
Architect: Charles Lewis Hillger; builder: Louis Sherman
Architecture I

1879   **Lanaux House**
547 Esplanade Avenue
Italianate townhouse with Second Empire detailing
Architect: William Fitzner
Guide

1883   **Thorn House**
1435 Jackson Avenue
Architect: William Fitzner; builder: Conrad Wundenberg
Irvin; Guide; Architecture I

1883   **Simon Gumbel**
Prytania Street between Philip and First streets
Architect: William Fitzner
Irvin

1883   **Julius Weis Home**
Jackson Avenue and Chestnut Street
Architect: Charles Lewis Hillger
Irvin

New Orleans Homes Built/Owned by Germans and German-Americans

1819   **Vincent Nolte House**
541 Royal Street
Architect: Benjamin Latrobe
Guide

1830   **Richard Koch House**
2627 Coliseum Street
German-Swiss Chalet style; residence of French ambassador 1886-1903
Guide

1832   **Hermann-Grima House**
820 St. Louis Street
Georgian style; residence of Samuel Hermann, merchant banker from Frankfurt, Germany
Architect: William Brand
Guide; Architecture VI

1838   **Miltenberger House**
900-910 Royal Street
Originally three identical Georgian-style townhouses
Guide

1840   **La Branche Buildings**
621-38 St. Peter Street, 708 Royal Street
Eight three-story brick row houses facing St. Peter, Royal, Orleans
Alley; St. Peter houses have exquisite cast-iron balconies, added ca.
1850
Guide; Wilson; Deiler, Creoles

1840s   **Joseph Solomon House**
1572 North Broad Street
Gabled and dormered cottage with Doric columns; one of most historic buildings in area
Architecture VI

1850s   **William Schmidt Residence**
Coliseum Street
City of New Orleans

1850s   **F. M. Ziegler Home**
Seventh Street
City of New Orleans

1852   **Christian Roselius Residence**
515 Broadway
House and gardens once occupied entire square
Architecture VIII

Residence of William Schmidt, Coliseum Street, from *Jewell's Crescent City Illustrated*, 1873. *Courtesy of a private collection.*

1857   **Bultmann House**
1525 Louisiana Avenue
Fashionable funeral home, oldest in New Orleans; expanded (ca. 1885) by Anthony Fritz Bultmann, son of German immigrants; includes home on Louisiana and St. Charles avenues
Architect: William Freret, originally built as his private residence
Guide

1859   **Del Bondio House**
1456 Camp Street facing Coliseum Square
Italianate style; mansion built for Emile Ferdinand Del Bondio of Mainz, Germany
Architect: Thomas Wharton
Guide

1860s   **J. H. Keller Mansion**
Magazine Street, adjoining his large soap-manufacturing complex
City of New Orleans

1865   **Luling Mansion**
1438 Leda Street, formerly 704 Esplanade Avenue
Italianate style; originally on eighty acres; residence of cotton factor Florenz A. Luling, who left German state as forty-eighter; became Louisiana Jockey Club, 1880
Architects: Gallier and Esterbrook
Architecture V

Residence of Florenz A. Luling, 1438 Leda Street, from *Jewell's Crescent City Illustrated,* 1873. *Courtesy of a private collection.*

1868   **La Branche House**
        1217 Kerlerec Street
        Greek Revival style
        Architect: Eugene Surgi
        Guide; Deiler, Creoles

1868-69 **Van Benthuysen Residence** (now The Elms)
        3029 St. Charles Avenue
        Remodeled between 1883 and 1896; housed German consulate
        prior to World War II; at outbreak of war Consul Baron E. von
        Spiegel forced to leave city
        Guide

1870s   **Henry Lochte Home**
        Carrollton Avenue
        City of New Orleans

1870-71 **Werlein House**
        5800 St. Charles Avenue
        Italianate villa style
        Guide

1872   **Simon Hernsheim Mansion** (now Columns Hotel)
        3811 St. Charles Avenue
        Italianate style with Second Empire motifs
        Guide

1880s   **Lucien Napoleon Brunswig Residence**
        Prytania Street
        Home of wholesale pharmaceutical and manufacturing magnate
        City of New Orleans

1880s   **Frederick Loeber Mansion**
        Coliseum Street
        City of New Orleans; Nau

1880s   **Charles Wirth Residence**
        Wirth Place, Freret and Magnolia streets
        Wirth developed this area
        Architecture VIII; Fortier; Nau

1883   **Westfeldt House**
        2340 Prytania Street
        Greek Revival style
        Carpenter: J. H. Behan
        Guide

1890   **Isidore Newman Home** (demolished)
        3607 St. Charles Avenue
        Architects: Sully and Toledano
        Architecture VII

1890s   **Lawrence Fabacher Mansion** (demolished 1941)
        5705 St. Charles Avenue

Residence of Frederick Loeber, Coliseum Street, from *City of New Orleans,* 1894. *Courtesy of the Louisiana Collection, Earl K. Long Library, University of New Orleans.*

Owner of Fabacher's Restaurant; founded Jackson Brewery
City of New Orleans; Nau

1892   **(Lawrence) Fabacher's Row**
Prytania Street between Marengo and Milan streets
Row of modern flats
City of New Orleans; Architecture VII

1905   **Fannie Kieffer Newman Home** (sister-in-law of Isidore Newman)
3804 St. Charles Avenue
Romanesque style
City of New Orleans

?   **F. G. Ernst Residence**
Second Street
Home of rice baron, president of Board of Trade
City of New Orleans

?   **Marx Isaacs Residence** (now Latter Library)
5120 St. Charles, originally whole block bounded by Soniat and Dufossat streets
Guide

New Orleans Area Homes Built/Owned by Germans and German-Americans

1752   **Ambrose Heidel (Haydel) House** (demolished)
(ca.)   River Road near Fifty Mile Point

One of oldest documented colonial dwellings; Heidel arrived 1721 on *La Garonne*
River Road; Deiler, Creoles

1786 **Waguespack House** (Bourg House)
River Road, Vacherie
Joseph Wagensbach settled on German Coast 1722
River Road; Deiler, Creoles

1787-91 **Homeplace Plantation** (Keller House)
Hahnville
Owned since 1889 by descendents of German Coast pioneer Hans Peter Keller, arrived 1721 on *La Garonne;*
Wilson; Deiler, Creoles

1790 **Laura (Waguespack) Plantation** (originally Whitney
(ca.) Plantation)
River Road at Fifty Mile Point
Johann Jakob Heidel House and numerous outbuildings; Ambrose Heidel arrived 1721 on *La Garonne*
River Road; Deiler, Creoles

1792 **La Branche Plantation House** (burned during Civil War)
East Bank, near Jefferson/St. Charles parish line
German Coast pioneer Johann von Zweig arrived 1721 on *La Garonne* (*Zweig* is German for "branch"); given French name by cleric marrying him to Susanna Marchand
River Road; Deiler, Creoles; Swanson

1796 **Kleinpeter-Knox House**
Baton Rouge
Dutch (corruption of *Deutsch* [German]) Highlands pioneer Johann Georg Kleinpeter arrived ca. 1785
LLMVC; Deiler, Creoles

1800 **Lucien La Branche Plantation**
(ca.) River Road, West Bank, just above Westwego
Sugarhouse only remaining building; German-American La Branche (Zweig) one of eleven original commissioners of Jefferson Parish (1825)
Swanson

1805 **Zeringue House**
(ca.) River Road, Hahnville
Acadian-style cottage, hip roof
Michael Zehringer settled on German Coast 1722; purchased 1815 by owner of Homeplace, Louis E. Fortier; property has original Lucy schoolhouse; Lucy was site of original German Coast
River Road; Deiler, Creoles; Swanson

1830 **Trosclair Plantation House**

(ca.)   River Road, Hahnville
         Raised Creole cottage
         Johann Georg Troxler settled on German Coast 1722
         River Road; Deiler, Creoles

1835   **Helvetia Plantation House** (destroyed by Hurricane Betsy 1965)
         Community of Central, River Road, East Bank
         Named Helvetia in 1870s, Latin for Switzerland; purchased in 1908
         by Louis Hymel; German Coast pioneer Peter Himmel arrived a
         century earlier
         Guide; Deiler, Creoles

1840   **Hymel (Crescent) Plantation House**
         River Road, Vacherie
         Raised Creole cottage, hip roof
         Owned by descendents of German Coast pioneer Peter Himmel
         River Road; Deiler, Creoles

1840   **La Branche Plantation Dependency** (renamed Idle Hour Farms
         1940s)
         River Road, East Bank, near Jefferson/St. Charles parish line
         Creole *garçonnière* in Federal style (only remaining building)
         River Road; Deiler, Creoles

1840   **Seven Oaks (Zeringue) Plantation** (demolished 1977)
         Westwego
         Louisiana plantation style surrounded with Doric colonnade
         Architect: Valentine von Werner
         Cable; Wilson

1840s   **Schexnaydre House**
         Donaldsonville; moved to Ascension Parish Cajun Village, La.
         Hwy. 70
         Hans Reinhardt Schekschneider arrived 1721 on *La Garonne*
         River Road; Deiler, Creoles

1840s   **Schexnaydre House**
         Community of Wallace, River Road
         Creole cottage
         Hans Reinhardt Schekschneider arrived 1721 on *La Garonne*
         River Road; Deiler, Creoles

1856   **Delhommer-Hermitage Plantation Houses** (demolished)
         River Road, at Bonnet Carré Spillway
         Raised Creole cottages with outbuildings
         Delhommer was part of Darensbourg concession; Widow
         Delhomme was Darensbourg's granddaughter (née Louise
         Destrehan); married owner of Hermitage, P. Rost; sold in 1906 by
         Rost family to overseer George Kugler
         River Road

1856   **San Francisco Plantation**
        River Road, Garyville
        Steamboat Gothic style
        Built for Edmund Marmillion, died shortly after completion; inher-
        ited by son Valsin, whose Bavarian wife redecorated plantation;
        sold by her as widow 1879; now house museum owned by
        Marathon Oil Company
        River Road

1857   **Nottoway Plantation**
        White Castle
        Neoclassical and Italianate-style plantation home
        Architects: Howard and Diettel

1858   **Salsburg Plantation House** (demolished)
        River Road, West Bank, adjacent to Sunshine Bridge
        Three-story house on landscaped terrace built for Jacob Lebermuth
        River Road

1880s- **Elfer House**
90s   River Road, East Bank, near Jefferson/St. Charles parish line
        Creole cottage
        Original Helfer from German states, settled in 1760s
        River Road; Deiler, Creoles

1883   **Allemania Plantation House** (burned 1930s)
        River Road, West Bank, South Baton Rouge
        Called Hard Times Plantation until purchased by Johann Reuss,
        native of Hohenzollern (German royal house); renamed Allemania
        (Latinized French for "Germany")
        River Road

1884   **Germania Plantation**
        River Road, West Bank, near Hohen Solms, south of Baton Rouge
        Victorian bungalow with number of outbuildings including a sec-
        ond house, school, church, store
        Property purchased 1867 by Johann Reuss, native of Hohenzollern
        (German royal house) who combined Mulberry Grove, Elsie, and
        Cuba plantations; son later purchased Ashland Plantation, renamed
        it Belle Helene
        River Road

1885   **Darensbourg House**
        River Road, Lucy, on Bonnet Carré Point
        Creole cottage
        Karl Frederick Darensbourg commandant of German Coast forty-
        eight years
        River Road; Deiler, Creoles

1939   **Avondale Plantation**

West Bank, Waggaman
Built for George Augustus Waggaman, U.S. senator, federal judge, La. secretary of state, Va. native, descendent of German pioneer (né Wagoner); established railroad stop, post office, giving name to town
Architect: William Brand; builder: Francis Gott
Guide; Deiler, Creoles; Swanson

CHAPTER FIVE

Work

TRADES, BUSINESSES, AND PROFESSIONS

Most of the early German immigrants settling in the New Orleans area came without financial resources. These newcomers, who knew little or no English, took whatever work they could find, usually as unskilled laborers, draymen, or gardeners, until they could accumulate or borrow enough capital to begin their own business ventures. The typical German immigrant was agriculturally oriented but was also endowed with inherent business acumen. Upon immigration he was anxious to learn the language and adopt the way of life of his new country so that he could successfully enter into business.

A number of German immigrants went into dairy farming and the nursery business on the outskirts of the city. Most of the nurseries in the New Orleans area began as German family businesses, for example, the Eichling, Eble, Farley, Kraak, Holst, and Scheinuk nurseries. These Germans are said to have introduced to New Orleans the concept of colorful planting as an alternative to the all-white Creole garden based on smell.

Many immigrants moved beyond the city to undeveloped land, where they could cultivate large tracts. Just as the earlier pioneers had done on the German Coast, they cleared and drained the cypress swamps on the western shore of Lake Pontchartrain. Here they began vegetable farming (primarily cabbages), which developed into an industry supplying New Orleans, as their countrymen had done earlier. With the building of the Illinois Central Railroad their markets expanded to the Midwest, where they could supply markets a month earlier than local farmers. Unfortunately this whole enterprise was wiped out by the vicious hurricane of 1915.

It is interesting to note that the German draymen of New Orleans had a virtual monopoly, which the more enterprising developed by furnishing horse-drawn burial conveyances. New Orleans today has a number of German-founded mortuaries, reflecting the immigrant roots of this business. Well-known names are Bultmann, Schoen, Leitz-Egan, and Muhleisen.

A number of the newly arrived Germans were skilled handworkers, trained in the German guild system. They worked as gold- and silver-smiths (Adler, Hausmann, Weinfurter), stonemasons (Huber, Weiblen), and ironmongers. By 1800 German foundries had developed cast iron, which offered lighter weight at a cheaper cost than wrought iron. German artisans skilled in this process, such as Froehlich, Koretke, and Hinderer, established businesses, which set the standards for the trade. The lengthy apprenticeships required of those entering the building trades made German journeymen sought-after cabinetmakers and builders. Christian Lindauer, for example, traveled over much of Europe to absorb the styles and methods used in other countries before immigrating to New Orleans. Other noted German cabinetmakers and carpenters were Kohlmaier and Freiburg. Also of importance was the Lotz family from Darmstadt, whose four sons became carpenters/builders active in the Third District in the 1850s.

Another area dominated by the Germans was the restaurant, small-hotel, and coffeehouse/beer-parlor business. These establishments were run in the German *Gasthaus* tradition, where good food and drink, comfort and comradeship were cultivated. Best known was Merz's Café (later Kolb's), which became the longest-surviving German restaurant in the city. Other popular spots were Stevedores' Exchange and Coffee House ("coffee house" was a euphemism for "tavern"), Fabacher's Restaurant, and Krost's Beer Parlor (see chapter 8). The wholesale and retail food business also attracted many Germans. In the French Market, German butchers had a virtual monopoly. Well known were the breakfasts cooked for these butchers by Elizabeth Kettenring, the German widow of Hypolite Begué. The Schwegmann supermarkets were a reminder of the first small store in the Third District, established in the late 1860s. The names of other German grocers are familiar to residents, for example, Eicke, Frey, Schott, and Wirth. Germans also gravitated to the baking business, establishing bakeries that catered to the German preference for hard-crusted, heavier breads rather than the French bread popular among the Creoles. The German *Brötchen,* a round breakfast roll with a hard crust, had to be freshly baked each day in the Old World tradition. The proper German housewife visited the local bakery every morning to bring fresh *Brötchen* to her family. Still today a number of German bakeries serve the community. Hubig, Ledner, Leidenheimer, and Reising are all well-known names in the business.

The German character, which valued honesty, hard work, high standards, and thrift, soon lifted a number of first- and second-generation German immigrants into the moneyed classes. Examples of successful entrepreneurship were Hernsheim's tobacco factory, the import-export businesses of Vincent Nolte, who traded with European markets as early as the 1830s, and Schmidt & Ziegler, who imported foodstuffs to New Orleans from the Caribbean. Many of these successful businessmen entered the world of finance in the city, establishing banks and insurance companies such as the Metropolitan, formerly the Deutsche Bank, and the Germania, which later merged with the Whitney and the Teutonia Bank. Of particular note was the New Orleans Canal and Banking Company, which funded the building of the New Basin Canal. Perhaps the German entrepreneur who left the most lasting mark on the city was Fritz Jahncke. In 1875 he established Jahncke Services, which produced the cement for the city's streets and public buildings.

The German Revolution of 1848 brought an educated class of Germans to the New Orleans area. These Germans took an active part in the professional life of the area as doctors, lawyers, journalists, musicians, engineers, and architects. Prominent among the doctors were Karl von Poellnitz, who organized a union of German physicians, setting the medical standards of the city, and Karl Luzenberg, who established his own hospital. German physicians worked with barbers, who practiced bloodletting and tooth extractions. Together they formed a network with the German apothecaries of the city, who specialized in European herbal remedies. The Pharmacy Museum in the French Quarter was a functioning business at the turn of the last century, operated by the Frantz family. Other familiar pharmaceutical names were Earhart, Otto, and Stumpf.

Among the successful professionals were the attorneys Christian Roselius, who was offered (but refused) a partnership with Daniel Webster, and Michael Hahn, newspaper editor, plantation owner (Hahnville), and state governor. Music establishments were well represented by Germans, among them the firms of Philip Werlein, Louis Grunewald, and Emile Johns & C. P. Manouvrier, as were musicians such as Theodore von La Hache, Victor Huber, and the German scholar, choirmaster, and organist, J. Hanno Deiler. The many German clergymen who led their congregations are identified in chapter 6. One of the most notable was the Presbyterian minister Louis Voss, who, like Deiler, was a scholar and historian of the German heritage of Louisiana (see chapter 9).

The establishment of consulates to facilitate enterprise and promote trade became necessary as the Germans of the city founded successful businesses. Trade with the German states before unification was active in New Orleans. One example was the cotton trade between New Orleans and the port city of Bremen on the North Sea. Cotton from all over the South was sent down the Mississippi River to be baled in New Orleans and then exported. The city-state of Bremen had developed a large merchant fleet, which sailed to New Orleans to transport this American product to Europe and then England for milling. These boats offered cheap transportation for the return trip to New Orleans and filled their holds with German immigrants as ballast. Thus the cotton trade was responsible for bringing a large number of Germans to the port of New Orleans.

Those German-speaking sovereign cities and states doing business with New Orleans needed consulates in the city to promote trade as well as to deal with immigration problems. In the heyday of commerce with the ports of Hamburg, Bremen, and Lübeck, the arrival of their ships was celebrated by the German community with parades to the docks and festivities on shipboard followed by lavish parties in the city for the officers. This custom is continued today by the German honorary consuls in New Orleans.

Consulates representing the German states were active during the period before the Civil War. After 1857 only a few German states established or continued consulates in New Orleans. Once the transcontinental railroads had linked the East Coast to the West, a direct Northern route was opened via the port of New York. For immigrants heading to the Midwest, alternate routes via water were developed from several East Coast ports. From then on, only those immigrants bound for the lower Mississippi and Texas came through the port of New Orleans.

It was not until 1879 that Congress commissioned the engineer James Eads to resolve the complexities of dredging and deepening the mouth of the Mississippi. Although the port of New Orleans could then accommodate the largest oceangoing ships of the time, German immigration to the port had already peaked. With the establishment of a unified German nation by Otto von Bismarck in 1870-71, economic conditions improved steadily. The developing opportunities in Germany, the adverse climate of New Orleans where yellow fever was still rampant, the establishment of alternate immigration routes, and the channel problems of the mouth of the Mississippi all worked together to sharply reduce the number of German immigrants arriving in the area.

In 1882 the United States government deepened Galveston's shipping channel to accommodate large vessels. Consequently the two main German shipping companies, the Northern Lloyd and the Hamburg-American lines, no longer called at the port of New Orleans. This left the city without major German trade connections to Hamburg and Bremen and severed the direct passenger connection. With fewer German passenger and commercial ships coming to the port, the need for consulates from the German states lessened, and a number of them closed their offices in New Orleans.

The *Deutsche Gesellschaft* took over much of the work that the discontinued consulates had performed. Since the mission of the society was to assist German immigrants arriving at the port, its agents handled problems with passports, visas, and other legal matters. They also helped newcomers communicate with relatives and friends through the national network of German Societies. Monetary assistance for transportation and other costs was supplied when needed. For those choosing to remain in New Orleans, the society's Work Referral Bureau found employment and gave advice on getting settled.

Legal and trade issues became the responsibility of the German Consulate when it was established in 1873 to represent the newly unified country. The first consul general was the Honorable John Kruttschnitt. A residence on St. Charles Avenue (now The Elms) housed the German Consulate prior to World War II. At the outbreak of the war the consulate was closed and the consul general, Baron E. von Spiegel, was forced to leave the city. Six years after the war ended a consular office was reestablished, which was upgraded a few years later to consulate general. It functioned until 1953, when it was designated simply as a consulate. Twenty years later it was given responsibility only for Louisiana rather than for a five-state area. When it was closed in 1989 its duties were taken over by the Houston German Consulate General. At this time the German business community formed the Louisiana German-American Chamber of Commerce to take over the public relations function of the consulate. Educational institutions of the city and state worked with the Houston and Atlanta Goethe Institutes, financed by the German government with the purpose of promoting the German language and culture. From 1990 on, honorary consuls were appointed by the German government to represent Louisiana.

This section lists a sampling of the German trades and businesses that served both the German community and the area in general before the world wars. Noteworthy were the two natural German monopolies, the brewing industry and the printing of German-language newspapers. Because of the number and diversity of the German business establishments, only those that advertised and/or were well known have been listed. The type of business, date of establishment or citation in an article or advertisement, location, owner/proprietor, and sources are given, when known. Businesses are arranged alphabetically under each heading. This section also lists the German states represented by consulates, the dates of their establishment, their locations, and the names of the consuls. After unification, the German nation, like other foreign countries, was represented by one consulate. The 1861 city directory, printed just after the outbreak of the Civil War, lists thirty consulates, eleven of which represented German states. These figures dramatically show the commercial interdependence of New Orleans and the German-speaking states of Europe.

date = date of establishment
cited = date cited in an article, advertisement, etc.

Bakeries

date	*cited*	
	1916	**Joseph Binder, Inc.**
		2615 St. Claude Avenue, branch at 901 Independence Street
		Diamond
1890 (ca.)		**Heebe's Union Steam Bakery** (Tasty Bread)
		501 Lafayette Avenue, Gretna
		George Heebe
		Jeff. Parish Review, 1937
1916 (ca.)		**Simon Hubig's Honey Fruit Pies**
		2417 Dauphine Street
		Gardner 1916
	1909	**Klotz Cracker Factory**
		615 Tchoupitoulas Street
		Soards 1909
1860		**Thomas Kron & Bro.**
		4 South Market Street, St. Mary's Market
		Gardner 1860
1870		**Ledner Bakery**
		3501 Hessmer Avenue, Metairie
		Albert Ledner
		Guide
1896		**G. H. Leidenheimer Baking Co., Ltd.**
		Melpomene Street and Loyola Avenue

1916 1501 South Franklin Street
President: G. H. Leidenheimer; secretary-treasurer: J. C. Beals
Festschrift

1888 **Wilhelm Losch Steam Bakery**
2715 Rampart Street
Specialty: *Deutsche Eier Nudeln* (German egg noodles)
Altenheimbote

1908 **Otto R. Meyer Hygienic Steam Bakery**
3400 Dauphine Street, corner Desire Street
Otto R. Meyer
Prim

1866 **Miller & Diuelmann Wholesale Confectionery Co.**
50-75 South Peters Street
Christopher H. Miller
Biog. & Hist. Memoirs

1913 **H. P. Schwartz Bakery and Confectionery**
1826 Camp Place
Fresh pumpernickel Tuesday and Friday
Festschrift

1904 **Staehle Baking Company**
406-8 South Rampart Street
F. Staehle
Engelhardt

1920 (ca.) **Sunrise Bakery, Inc.**
6117 St. Claude Avenue
1947 5020 Orleans Street
Joseph H., Andreas F., Paul A. Reising
Polk 1947

1908 **Susslin Bakers & Millers**
2475-77 Dauphine Street near St. Roch Avenue
Adolph Susslin
Prim

Banks/Financial Institutions

1865 **City National Bank** (changed to Germania, 1869)
620 Canal Street
Nau; City of New Orleans

1880 (ca.) **German-American Homestead Association**
1918 Changed name to Liberty Homestead Association
Berchtold

1866 **Germania Life Insurance Company**
810 Gravier Street
Manager: Cartwright Eustis

1881		Reorganized as Commercial-Germania Trust & Savings Bank 311-15 Camp Street President: Jacob Hassinger; cashier: Gustav Adolph Blaffer
1918		Dropped "Germania" from name 811 Common Street *Festschrift; Berchtold; Engelhardt; Nau; City of New Orleans*
1869		**Germania National Bank of New Orleans** 620 Canal Street
	1903	Germania National Bank and Central Trust and Savings Bank merged with Whitney National Bank; became Whitney Central Bank & Trust Company President: George Q. Whitney *Nau; City of New Orleans; Engelhardt; Zacharie*
1920 (ca.)		**Hecht & Co., Investment Bakers** Founder: Rudolf H. Hecht *La. Biog.*
?		**Kohn, Weil & Company, Merchant Bankers** 500-514 Canal Street *Nau; City of New Orleans; Korn*
1869		**Lafayette Fire Insurance Company** 2123 Magazine Street President: John X. Wegmann *Diamond; Festschrift*
1878		**Hermann Meister Insurance Agency, Inc.** 211 Camp Street, Room 601 *Diamond*
1870		**Metropolitan Bank** (former Deutsche Bank) 410-12 Camp Street President: P. W. Dielmann; vice-president: A. G. Ricks; cashier: A. C. Wuerpel *Nau; Altenheimbote, 1888; Engelhardt*
1831	1861	**New Orleans Canal and Banking, Inc.** Camp and Gravier streets Organized with $4 million in capital to construct New Basin Canal *Gardner 1861; Nau; Huber*
1904		**Provident Building & Loan Association** 413 Whitney Central Bank Building President: Nicholas Nutter; secretary-treasurer: Jay R. Schoen *Diamond*
1847		**M. Shumard & Co.** Southern Department of German Insurance Co. of Freeport, Illinois

626-30 Common Street
City of New Orleans

1893 **Teutonia Bank & Trust Company/Teutonia Loan and Building Company**
327 St. Charles Avenue
President: Eugene F. Buhler
Nau; City of New Orleans; Engelhardt; Zwelling

1871 **Teutonia Insurance Company of New Orleans**
217 Camp Street
Presidents: Albert P. Noll, William B. Schmidt
Agents: Frank Langbehn, Ed. J. Heintz

1913 405 Camp Street
Nau; Engelhardt; Festschrift; Altenheimbote

1890 (ca.) **Third District Homestead**
Founder: William Franz
Nau

1908 **Third District Savings, Banking & Trust Co.**
Dauphine and Piety streets
Officers: Ernest J. Leonhard, Louis Kuentz
Prim

1865 **Julius Weis & Son, Exchange Brokers & Merchant Bankers**
817 Gravier Street
Officers: Simon, Samuel, and Marion Weis
Jews of La; Gardner 1860; Korn

1847 **Gustav Westfeldt Versicherung; *Feuer, Blitz, Windsturm, u. Profit Versicherung*** (fire, lightning, windstorm, profit insurance)
Corner Carondelet and Common streets
Local director for Liverpool & London Globe Insurance Co.
Festschrift

Breweries

See below under "Breweries and Beer Gardens"

Dairies

1902 **Joseph Kohler**
Nelson and Fern streets
Soards 1902

1902 **Mrs. Nicholas Rauch**
8018 Hickory Street
Soards 1902

1902 (ca.) **Bernard Schoendorf Dairy**
3203 Bienville Street

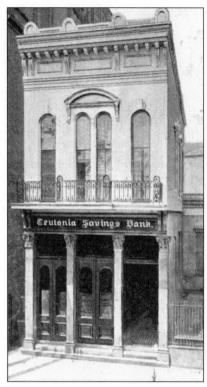

Teutonia Insurance Company, 217 Camp Street, from *The City of New Orleans*, 1894. *Courtesy of the Louisiana Collection, Earl K. Long Library, University of New Orleans.*

Schoendorf Dairy making deliveries, from the Library of Congress. *Courtesy of a private collection.*

1916 3539 Havana Street
Soards 1902, 1916
1902 **Henry Schroeder**
337 Burdette Street
Soards 1902
1853 **Henry Ziegler Dairy**
St. Patrick and Seventh streets
Gardner 1860

Drugstores/Pharmacists/Chemists

1888 **H. Dannenmann's Cut-Rate Drug Store**
Magazine and State streets
Altenheimbote
1888 **J. Engelbach's Homöpathische Apotheke**
154 Canal Street
Altenheimbote
1894 **Finlay & Brunswig, Wholesale Pharmaceutical Manufacturers**
Lucien N. Brunswig
City of New Orleans
1870s **Louis S. Metz's Pharmacy**
Beinville and Prieur streets
Huber
1890 **Charles Oplatek Drugstore**
Front Street, Gretna
Proprietor/owner Austrian pharmacist and optician; closed at his death 1925
Gretna Diamond Jubilee Coll.
1911 **Louis R. Otto Pharmacy**
Magazine and Josephine streets
1913 Later Louis R. & J. S. Otto Pharmacy
8320 Oak Street
Festschrift; Gardner1860; Gretna Diamond Jubilee Coll.
1870 **Stumpf's Drug Store**
Founded in New Orleans; moved to Gretna
1876 **John Stumpf's Son(s)**
Front and Lavoisier streets, Gretna
Manufactured Magic Hoodoo arsenic-based insecticides, Rust-A-Way; sold disinfectants, repellants, waxes, pine oils, soaps, sanitary supplies; exported to the Caribbean
Jeff. Parish Review, 1947; Story of La.

Grocers (Wholesale)/Butchers

1867 **Ferdinand del Bondio, Wholesale Grocer**

		54-56 Lafayette Street
		Soards 1867
1863		**Hermann Eicke** (chief competitor to Schwegmann's)
		Louisa and Dauphine streets
		Diamond; Schwegmann
1888		**B. H. Flaspoller's Sons, Wholesale Grocers**
		322 Tchoupitoulas and 421 St. Peter streets
		Altenheimbote
1908		**Georg Flick, Butcher**
		Stalls 72-80, Zengel Market
		Prim
	1908	**L. A. Frey & Sons**
		Anton Frey, Butcher
		Stalls 38-39, French Market
		Xavier Frey
		Stalls 15-19, Zengel Market
	1928	Jos. Frey Choice Meats
		Stalls 40-41, French Market
		Later moved to Burgundy Street
		Prim; Diamond
1910 (ca.)		**Konrad Kolb, Grocery and Delicatessen**
		Gentilly Road
		Also owned Kolb's Restaurant, St. Charles Avenue
		Voss; Stall; Laguaite
1890		**Langhof Brothers, Molasses, Syrup, Sugar Brokers**
		216-18 Fulton Street
		Engelhardt
1872		**Henry Lochte & Co., Limited**
		319-25 Tchoupitoulas Street
		City of New Orleans; Engelhardt
?		**Jacob Röhm**; *Kalbfleisch, Schwienefleisch* (veal, pork)
		Stalls 35-41, Poydras Market
		Echo
1845		**Schmidt & Ziegler, Ltd.**
		428-36 South Peters Street
		Founders: William Schmidt, F. M. Ziegler
	1928	232 Canal Street
1890 (ca.)		Developed Willowood Plantation, Jefferson Parish (sugar
		plantation, mill)
		Diamond; City of New Orleans; Engelhardt

Schmidt & Ziegler, Ltd., wholesale grocers, 400 block South Peters, established 1845, from Engelhardt, 1904. *Courtesy of the Historic New Orleans Collection.*

1894	**Schneider & Zuberier**
	Tchoupitoulas and Common streets
	Hermann Zuberier
	City of New Orleans; Dixon

1894   **Schneider & Zuberier**
Tchoupitoulas and Common streets
Hermann Zuberier
City of New Orleans; Dixon

?   **Bernard Schott, Butcher**
Gretna (butcher shop)
Became owner of Bernard Schott Meat Packers; developed national meatpacking business, first located in Upper Ninth Ward
Zwelling

1881   **Schwegmann Supermarkets, Inc.**
Piety and Burgundy streets
Began as G. A. Schwegmann Grocery Store
Garret Schwegmann
Diamond

1888   **Charles Wirth Grocery Company, Ltd.**
3302 Magazine Street
Altenheimbote

Jewelers/Silversmiths/Watchmakers

1870   **D. H. Adler**
Exchange Place
Edward's 1870

1898   Coleman Adler & Sons
722 Canal Street
Soards 1898

1888   **Rudolph P. Baurhenn, Watchmaker and Jeweler**
1806 Dryades Street, near Erato Street
Formerly with Frantz & Opitz
Altenheimbote

1888   **Christian Fischer, Watchmaker & Jeweler**
751 Rampart Street, near Julia Street
Altenheimbote

1867   **Frantz and Sander, Manufacturing Jeweler & Diamond Setter**
William Frantz and A. H. Sander

1880   Became Frantz & Opitz, *Goldarbeiter und Diamanten Fässer* (goldsmiths and diamond setters)
Royal and Bienville streets
William Frantz; Henry Opitz
Altenheimbote

1898   Became Frantz Brothers & Co.
William and Henry Frantz, George A. Hoffman, Leopold Jansen

1903   Became William Frantz & Co., Jewelers & Opticians
142 Carondelet Street
Festschrift; Berchtold

1865   **A. B. Griswold & Co.**
610 Frenchmen Street
Arthur Breeze Griswold, former partner to Heyde & Goodrich; Henry Thomas

    1924   Bought out by Hausmann's, Inc.
Diamond

1870   **Henry Hausmann, Jeweler and Silversmith**

    1881   Theresa Rosenbuch Hausmann and children Louis and Gabriel
186 Poydras Street; later 135 Baronne Street
Soards 1916; Altenheimbote

    1860   **Heyde & Goodrich**
Canal and Royal streets
Gardner 1860

1861   **H. Hoppensitz & Bros., Watchmakers & Jewelers**
2109 Magazine Street
Watch inspectors for N.O. Railway & Light Co.
Festschrift

1852   **Küchler & Himmel**
Christopf Küchler, Augustus Jansen, Adolphe Himmel, Bernard Terfloth

1853   **J. C. Meyer & Son, Jewelers**
1233 Decatur Street
Prim

1888   **H. Schmidt, Watchmaker & Jeweler**
130 Exchange Place
Altenheimbote

1861   **Thomas, Griswold & Co.**
Successors of Heyde and Goodrich
Henry Thomas, Jr., A. B. Griswold, William Goodrich

1903   **Weinfurter's Jewelry Palace**
Royal and Bienville streets
Motto: "Good German Economy"

1916   339 St. Charles Avenue
Engelhardt; Festschrift; Gardner1860

1888   **Jakob Young;** *Diamanten, Uhren u. Schmuckladen* (diamond, watch and jewelry store)
632 Magazine Street
Altenheimbote

Lumber/Wood/Cabinetmakers

1916   **Freiburg Mahogany Company**
Harahan
Sawmill and veneer plant
Harry Freiburg
Jeff. Parish Review 1937

1923   **Kohlmeyer & Kohlmeyer Company**
1018 Harmony Street
Soards 1923

1832   **Christian Lindauer**
Gormley's Canal, former City of Lafayette
Irvin

1913   **F. Salmen Brick & Lumber Co.**
Office: 716 Common Street; sawmill: Slidell
Festschrift

Metalworks/Iron Foundries/Blacksmiths

1891   **L. Eichhorn**
Banks and Gayoso streets
Soards 1891; Festschrift

1908   **Frohlich's Iron Works**
Alvar and Chartres streets
Prim

1880 (ca.)   **Hinderer's Iron Works**
Frederick Hinderer began as iron-furniture maker with Frederick Daimler

1889   Became partner with William Spitz, then co-owner with Charles Pike (Pike Fences) of Novelty Iron & Fence Works
Third District

Later moved to Camp Street; exported to Gulf States, Mexico, Central America
Festschrift; Architecture III

1871   **R. G. Holzer Manufactory & Sheet Metal Works**
317-23 Burgundy Street
Holzer (1844-1906) was German-Swiss; business still in operation
Festschrift

1903   **F. H. Koretke Brass & Mfg. Co., Ltd.**
922-24 Magazine Street
Engelhardt

1867   **Mithoff & Geenen, Cooper, Tin and Sheet Iron Workers**
226 Magazine Street
Soards 1867

1825   **Moses Schwartz Foundry Co., Ltd.**
451 Howard Avenue, corner Constance Street
Engelhardt

1890s   **William J. White (Witte), Blacksmith**
200 Lafayette Street, Gretna
Gretna Diamond Jubilee Coll.

1860   **Wood & Miltenberger Foundry**
57 Camp Street
Also agent for cast iron from Philadelphia firm
Architecture III; Gardner 1860

Mortuaries

1883   **Bultmann Mortuary Service**
80 Magazine Street
Owner: Anthony Friedman Bultmann

1888   A. F. Bultmann; *Leichenbestatter und Einbalmierer* (body enhancer and embalmer)
2917 Magazine Street
Purchased Fellman's undertaking buiness; also offered livery service; later moved to St. Charles and Louisiana avenues
Soards 1884; Engelhardt; Altenheimbote

1874   **Frantz & Schoen**
155 North Peters Street
Soards 1884; Altenheimbote

1884   **Ambrose Leitz**
461 Magazine Street
Soards 1884

1884   Louisa Leitz
825 Tchoupitoulas Street
Soards 1884

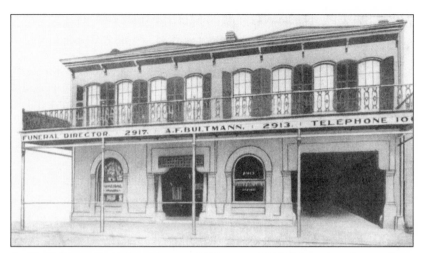

A. F. Bultmann's undertaking establishment, 2917 Magazine Street, from Engelhardt, 1904. *Courtesy of the Historic New Orleans Collection.*

	1904	Jacob Leitz
		2347 Annunciation Street
		Engelhardt
	1909	Mrs. Ambrose Leitz, Sr.
		2409 Tchoupitoulas Street
		Soards 1909
1885		**Louis A. Muhleisen**
		1833 Dryades Street
		Soards 1909
	1847	**Orleans Manufacturing Company**
		Caskets and coffins
		H. L. Frantz
		Voss
	1908	**Jacob Schoen & Son**
		535 Elysian Fields Avenue
		Engelhardt
	1908	W. Jacob Schoen
		3135-37 Burgundy Street between Clouet and Louisa streets
		Manager: Geo. C. Rademacher
	1908	Bernard A. Schoen, Funeral Director & Embalmer
		632 Marigny Street
		Prim
	1909	**S. Sontheimer & Sons**
		1030 Louisiana Avenue
		Soards 1909

Music Stores/Publishers/Pianos & Musical Instruments

1856   **Louis Grunewald & Co., Ltd., Piano & Music Store**
735 Canal Street
Also music publisher; moved to ground floor of Grunewald Concert Hall, corner St. Charles Avenue and University Place·
City of New Orleans; Engelhardt; Gardner 1861

      1903   **Junius Hart Piano House**
1001 Canal Street
Engelhardt

      1888   **Victor Huber, Music Teacher**
930 Poydras Street
Expert on Tyrolean zither
Altenheimbote

1830   **Emil Johns & C. P. Manouvrier Co.**
113 Chartres Street between Conti and St. Louis streets
Published *Album Louisianais,* first music with New Orleans imprint
Deiler, Presse

1853   **Werlein's Music Store**
614 Canal Street
Philip Werlein Southern Music House
329-35 Baronne Street
Also music publisher; published "Dixie," Confederate marching song

      1861   365 Camp Street
Gardner 1861; City of New Orleans; Engelhardt

Nurseries/Florists

1887   **Charles Eble, Florist & Nursery**
106 Baronne Street

      1913   121 Baronne Street; nursery: 1503 Upperline Street
Festschrift; Nau

1880   **Eichling's Avenue Floral Company**
4320 Canal Street

      1902   Richard Eichling Seed & Nursery Co., Ltd.
3453 Magazine Street

      1923   129 Camp Street
Nau

1880 (ca.)   **E. A. Farley**
1733 Touro Street, Gentilly
Catherine Farley
Nau; Gardner

1886		**Holst Garden and Greenhouses**
		City Park Avenue
		Christ Holst
1880 (ca.)		**Henry Kraak**
		Head gardener for Fabacher estate on St. Charles Avenue
1900 (ca.)		Established own flower shop and nursery (Kraak's)
		Eleonore Street between Garfield and Pitt streets
		Architecture IV
	1916	**Frank Rieth Family Florist**
		1401 St. Charles Avenue
		Later 1 Metairie Road
1919		**Scheinuk Florist**
		2600 St. Charles Avenue
	1923	2042 Broadway
		Gardner 1916
1920 (ca.)		**Voelker Florist**
		St. Claude Avenue and Congress Street
		Soards 1923

Publishers

See below under "The German-Language Press"

Other

1880 (ca.)		**Gumbel & Co.**
		Cotton brokerage
		Founder: Simon Gumbel
		Jews of La.
	1882	**Simon Hernsheim & Bros.** (La Belle Creole Tobacco Factory)
		755 Magazine Street
		Employed 1,000 workers; largest cigar manufacturer in America; acquired by Liggett & Myers
		Architecture II; Biog. & Hist. Memoirs; Reinders
1906		**Victor Huber & Sons**
		Gretna
		Established Victor Huber Memorials, makers of granite and marble cemetery headstones and decorative grave markers
	1920s	Bought St. John Cemetery
		4800 Canal Street
		With sons Leonard, Albert, Elmer; developed Hope Mausoleum
		Zwelling; Metairie Cemetery; Architecture III

La Belle Creole Cigar Factory, from *Biographical and Historical Memoirs of Louisiana. Courtesy of a private collection.*

1875	**Jahncke Services, Inc.**
	814 Howard Avenue
	President: Fritz Jahncke; officers: three sons Paul, Walter, Ernest Lee
	Business also included subsidiaries:
1903	Jahncke Navigation & Improvement Company
1918 (ca.)	Jahncke Shipbuilding Company, Inc.
	Madisonville
	Engelhardt; Jahncke
1849	**J. H. Keller Soap Works**
	St. Andrew and Howard streets; office: 110 Gravier
	John H. Keller
	City of New Orleans; Engelhardt
1900 (ca.)	**Lane Cotton Mills**
	President: Sigmund Odenheimer
	Jews of La.
?	**Menge Patent Pumps**
	631 Tchoupitoulas Street
	Developed the "Great Menge Patent Pump and Improved Elevator Dredge," specially designed for canal and levee building

J. H. Keller's Southern Soap Factory, St. Andrew and Howard streets, from *Gardner's New Orleans Directory,* 1869. *Courtesy of the Louisiana Collection, Earl K. Long Library, University of New Orleans.*

	Owner: John Menge
	Young
1890 (ca.)	**Mente Bag Factory**
	Two factories, world's largest importer of jute
	Owner: Eugene Mente; president: E. B. Benjamin
	City of New Orleans
1860s	**Rodewald Brothers, Tobacco Manufacturers**
	National leaders in field in mid-1800s
	Clark
1890 (ca.)	**Gustav Seeger**
	"New Home" sewing machine
	916-18 Canal Street
	Developed monopoly on sewing machines at turn of century
	Echo
1890 (ca.)	**Union Sulfur Co.**
	Sulfur, Louisiana
	Frasch process made U.S. world leader in sulfur production
	Founder: Herman Frasch
	La. Biog.
1887	**Albert Weiblen Steam Marble & Granite Works**
	824 Baronne Street
1906	Plant on City Park Avenue at St. Louis Street
	Engelhardt; Metairie Cemetery

Consulates

YEAR CONSULATE	CONSUL	ADDRESS
1838		
Bremen	Frederick Frey	Royal Street
Prussia and Hamburg	F. W. Schmidt	Bienville Street
1842		
Baden and Bremen	Frederick Frey	Royal Street
Prussia	F. W. Schmidt	Bienville Street
Saxony (and Denmark)	J. F. C. Vles	47 Chartres Street
1850		
Baden	F. H. Eimer	Row A, Exchange Alley
Bremen	Frederick Rodenwald	23 Blank Place
Hamburg	William Voegel	88 Bienville Street
Hanover	James Behm	88 Bienville Street
Mecklenburg	William Prehm	94 Conti Street
Prussia	William Voegel	88 Bienville Street
Saxony	J. F. C. Vles	108 Common Street
Württemburg	F. Honold	54 Royal Street
1851		
Oldenburg	William Voegel	88 Bienville Street
1854		
Hanover	A. Reichard	57 St. Charles Avenue
Nassau	F. V. Freudenthal	31 Gravier Street
1857		
Bavaria, Baden, Austria	F. H. Eimer	17 Carondelet Street
1860		
Hesse Cassel	Richard Thiele	20 Union Street
1861		
Braunschweig	F. W. Freudenthal	17 Carondelet Street
Hamburg	Charles Koch	20 Canal Street
Hanover	A. Reichard	12 Carondelet Street
Oldenburg	Richard Thiele	20 Union Street
1868		
Lübeck	E. Stockmeyer	41 Union Street, second floor
1873		
German Empire	John Kruttschnitt	42 Perdido Street
1899		
German Empire	Baron von Mysenburg	
1916		

German Empire	Paul Roh	510 Whitney Building
1923		
German Republic	Baron Hans von Ungelter	503 Whitney Building
1930		
German Republic	Rolf Jaeger	
1938		
German Empire	Baron E. von Spiegel	3029 St. Charles Avenue

BREWERIES AND BEER GARDENS

The German community of New Orleans is credited with the introduction of beer to the city as an everyday beverage and substitute for the more expensive wine preferred by the French. Before the 1850s a beverage called "city beer" was consumed by the common man in the saloons and restaurants of New Orleans. This concoction was made according to a secret formula from fermented molasses and vermouth but contained no preservatives. Consequently it would spoil during transportation and had to be drunk soon after it was brewed. Beer drinkers added syrup to mitigate the herbal taste and were known to suffer violent hangovers if they overindulged. It was the custom for the oldest boy in German families to fetch a bucket of beer at the end of the day to be drunk with dinner. A number of breweries sprang up, supplying the demand for this beverage. In 1845 the first city brewery appeared in New Orleans, on Philip and Royal streets, owned by Wirth and Fischer. A local German newspaper described the product of this *Stadtsbreuerei* (city brewery) as made of magic and big barrels of sugarcane syrup mixed with Mississippi River water. Despite the popularity of city beer in the German community, the brewing business was hampered by the necessity of drinking the beer on the day it was brewed.

In 1851 the first lager beer was imported from the Schenk Brewery in Pittsburgh by the local saloon keeper Christian Krost. This shipment initiated a change in the daily habits of the populace. The superior stability and taste of lager beer were immediately recognized, and a regular supply line from the Lemp Brewery in St. Louis was set up. As demand grew, Lemp could not fill the orders received from New Orleans, so lager beer made in Philadelphia and Milwaukee was also brought to New Orleans. Its success, however, was impeded by several factors. In the winter the barrels froze en route; in the summer they exploded on the docks. Newspaper accounts reported Germans running to the river front with vessels to scoop up the beer as it drained out of the barrels. Another negative factor was the cost of transportation, which ran up the price so that the popular demand for a five-cent beer could not be met. As a result, some enterprising German saloons served a local beer product out of Milwaukee barrels, which went unnoticed by tipsy drinkers.

Krost's example found imitators, and soon lager beer was successfully extended beyond Orleans Street, the "beer center" of the city. For a long time the main area for lager beer remained below Canal Street in German taverns in today's French Quarter. When the Americans, who at first were quite skeptical about lager beer, began to give up their prejudices, the German tavern keepers made a break with tradition. They established locations above Canal Street in the American sector and in St. Mary's Market on the river front.

In 1852 bock beer was introduced by Krost, who also imported and popularized bottled beer from Germany. The more initiated and experienced clientele preferred this imported ale and "Bremen" beer. The "bottle art" (broken green and brown beer bottles cemented along the tops of patio walls as a security device) seen in the French Quarter stems from this period.

In 1864 Georg Merz was successful in brewing the first lager beer in the city, which he introduced to open his tavern, *Erster Felsenkeller.* Merz developed this process just before the Civil War broke out, which suspended the importation of beer to New Orleans. Since cooling was essential to producing lager beer, Merz attempted to ship in "natural" ice from the state of Maine. Because of time and distance, however, the ice melted before it arrived at the docks. Such difficulties prevented the industry from developing until the invention of the Windhausen Refrigerating Machine in 1879 and the establishment of insulated ice-houses for storage. Merz immediately installed one of these new machines in his brewery on Robertson Street, which actually became the first attempt at air-conditioning in the city. These developments made it possible for lager beer breweries to be established in the 1880s. The first was the Southern Brewery, located in the French Quarter on the site of the former Merz tavern and restaurant.

Perhaps the most successful of all the New Orleans German "beer barons" was Lawrence Fabacher, who established the famous Jax Brewery on Decatur Street. The brewery still stands today but has been converted into an amusement/shopping center, one of the most popular tourist attractions of the French Quarter. Fabacher began his career in the food and beverage business with the highly successful Fabacher's Restaurant and Oyster Bar, first located below Canal Street and then in the American sector. Realizing the financial potential of lager beer, he sold the restaurant to his brothers Anthony and Peter and founded Jax Brewery in 1890.

Despite the competition from other breweries established a decade earlier, Fabacher's entrepreneurial acumen prevailed. He soon established Jax as the most widely drunk beer in New Orleans and developed the brewery into the largest in the South. With his newly acquired wealth he built a mansion on the most fashionable street of the American sector, St. Charles Avenue. Designed by the New York society architect Stanford White, it sprawled over five acres, taking up an entire city block. In addition to the huge main house, expansive enough for his German-American wife and growing family, Fabacher had White put in a summerhouse with a marble saltwater swimming pool and gymnasium, stables, a greenhouse, a large garage, and quarters for thirteen live-in servants. The grounds featured wide lawns with sunken gardens and mosaic patios complete with fish ponds, all shielded from onlookers by thickly planted shrubbery.

Not surprisingly, Fabacher's castle seemed out of place amid the other homes on the Avenue, which were Victorian-style houses, quite conservative by comparison. In addition, the life-style that Fabacher provided for his family aroused considerable comment among the old guard. He flaunted his money with sports and town cars, a chauffeur-driven limousine, wardrobes imported from Paris, a yacht for Caribbean cruises, and summers in Europe. Fabacher's ostentation was considered garish by the elite of the city, who excluded him and his family from their guest lists and private clubs. The Fabachers, however, ignored these insults and focused on the arts, charity work, and their own close family circle. In typical German fashion, they turned to birthdays, anniversaries, and weddings for socializing, events that they celebrated in elegant style. By the late 1930s, however, the depression, prohibition, and estate taxes combined to destroy the fabled largesse of the Fabachers. The staff of servants had to be let go, the grounds became overgrown, and the mansion and outbuildings began to decay. Reluctantly, the seven Fabacher children decided to sell. Because no buyers came forward, the only solution was to demolish the structures on the property and divide it into lots for real-estate development. However, the legacy of the brewery was continued by the son and, in turn, the grandson of the founder. With the return of prosperity after World War II the brewing business again became profitable. Once more the Fabachers and their heirs acquired wealth, now as shareholders in the Jackson Brewing Company. The family continued to own and control the business until the late 1970s, when the brewery complex on Decatur Street was sold to make way for the municipal river-front development project.

The city directories list almost thirty breweries during the period from 1850 to the turn of the century. The larger breweries owned and operated beer gardens, where the local populace could sample the beverages produced. These gardens were more like parks than drinking spots and were attended by the whole family, usually on Sunday nights. In good weather a picnic supper was eaten on benches under the trees and dancing commenced in the pavilions with twilight. *Familienbälle* (family dancing/balls) were widely advertised in the German newspapers and were always well attended.

The National and the more elegant Tivoli Gardens were the most popular of the German *Biergärten*. The Tivoli was located on Bayou St. John, then on the outskirts of the city, which also served as New Orleans' first park. In addition to a lush setting it offered tables under the trees for *Kaffee und Kuchen* (coffee and cake) as well as pavilions for dancing and drinking.

The following description of the Tivoli Gardens appeared in 1853 in Stahl's *New Orleans Sketch Book* (p. 35):

> A large yard shaded by trees, under which are numerous tables and benches separated by short intervals, and capable of accommodating two couples each; lampposts interspersed with shell walks, a bar with strong liquors and warm water at one extremity; beer men with large baskets filled with beer jugs, which pop like champagne bottles and emit a frothy, yellow fluid that will make you sleep before it makes you tipsy; and in the center, the dance house, a circular building, the flooring surrounded by a balustrade with a single door, and elevated on a platform, an orchestra of a dozen brazen instruments. The Stars and Stripes float in the breeze above the whole. Five cents is paid by each male partner for the privilege of one waltz, which occupies nearly ten minutes. The *Frauen* [ladies] pay nothing, heaven bless them! Often as many as twenty couples are whirling around at one time. Strangers and mere spectators crowd outside of the balustrade, gazing upon the waltzers. The proper Germans not engaged in the dance are seated upon the diminutive benches under the trees, gargling gutturals and beer.

A general description of the German beer gardens appeared in the *New Orleans Picayune* on October 30, 1849:

Conducted on a scale not often seen, the beer gardens of New Orleans [began on Bayou St. John] a few blocks beyond the [ship turning] basin of the Old Canal in Faubourg Tremé. Nearest the city was the Vauxhall Garden, across the street, the largest, the Tivoli Garden, and several squares of unnamed establishments, which charged a dime, but gave a glass of refreshment to each guest. The gardens were thickly planted with choice trees and shrubbery beneath which were benches and tables, and amid which were latticed bowers and arbors. There were buildings for barrooms, ice cream, cakes, coffee, etc. The capacious ballrooms, bare of furniture, were almost entirely open at the sides. In galleries far above musicians poured forth German waltzes, to which couples danced for a half-dime each ten minutes. The gentlemen dancers mostly wore their hats; the ladies' attire was plain and modest. Chilly winters did not eliminate attendance. German beer, quite bitter and strongly flavored with hops, was the favorite beverage, accompanied by a curious German doughnut and ginger cakes. Good order, a spirit of mutual accommodation and intense vivacity prevailed. Sunday afternoons and evenings drew the largest crowds of old, young and middle-aged Germans, [but also] French, English, Irish, Spanish and Italians in race or extraction.

Today beer remains the favored alcoholic beverage of the common man in the New Orleans area. It is said that more beer is drunk in New Orleans per capita than in any other American city, with the exception of Milwaukee, a city well known for its German population.

This section gives a chronological list of the breweries of the New Orleans region, the dates they were established (*date*) and/or referenced (*cited*) in an article, advertisement, etc., their original locations, the owners and associates, pertinent notes, and sources.

Breweries

date   *cited*

1845   **Stadtsbreuerei** (City Brewery)
              Philip and Royal streets
              Owner: Wirth and Fischer
              City beer
              Deiler, Presse
1850s   **J. Christen**
              Moreau and Spain streets
              J. Christen

City beer
Deiler, Presse

1850s   **Fassnacht Brothers**
Annunciation and Poeyfarre streets
Louis and Samuel Fassnacht
City beer
Gardner 1860; Deiler, Presse

1850s   **Georg Guth**
72 Conti Street
G. Guth
City beer
Gardner 1861; Deiler, Presse

1850s   **George Merz**
Villere and Toulouse streets
City beer; also tavern and restaurant; later site of Southern
Brewery
Deiler, Presse; Nau

Merz Brewery, Toulouse Street, from *Graham's Crescent City Directory*, 1867. *Courtesy of the Louisiana Collection, Earl K. Long Library, University of New Orleans.*

1850s		**Jacob Zoelln City Brewery & Beer Saloon**

1850s **Jacob Zoelln City Brewery & Beer Saloon**
Magazine and Delord streets (Howard Avenue)
Gardner 1860; Deiler, Presse; Mygott

1855 **Old Canal Steam Brewery**
Canal Street
Georg Merz
1864 Robertson Street
Lager beer
New Orleans Times, Dec. 29, 1865, p. 6, c. 2; Daily Picayune, May 16, 1872, p. 2, c. 6

1860 **Carl Krost**
49-51 Conti Street
Gardner 1860

1860 **Nicholas Schmidt**
Philip and Annunciation streets
Gardner 1860

1864 **Louisiana Brewery**
Jackson Avenue and Tchoupitoulas Street
John Boeler, P. Dielmann, J. Hassinger, H. Engelhardt, F. Fehr
Deutsche Zeitung, July 2, 1864, p. 3, c. 4

1875 **Eagle Brewery**
540-47 Tchoupitoulas Street
George Auer
Festschrift; Edwards 1870

1875 **Hope Brewery**
South Prieur Street
Peter Blaise
Nau

1880 **Lafayette Brewing Company**
Lafayette and Tchoupitoulas streets
H. Bassmeier
Nau

1880 **Pelican Brewing Company**
282 Villere Street
1890 North Peters between Montegut and Louisa streets
Owner: Eugene Erath; officers: J. Langles, Charles Schumacher, Albert Erath
Nau

1882 **Southern Brewery**
North Villere and Toulouse streets
President: Peter Blaise; vice-president: G. Faehnle; secretary: E. Pragst; board member: H. H. Bierhorst; brewmaster: Fritz Gund
Nau

Southern Brewery, North Villere and Toulouse streets, from Engelhardt, 1904. *Courtesy of the Historic New Orleans Collection.*

1888   **Crescent Brewing Company**
              Canal Street and Claiborne Avenue
              Daily States, August 16, 1888, p. 8, c. 2
1888   **Weckerling Brewing Company**
              Magazine and Delord streets (Howard Avenue)
              President: J. J. Weckerling; vice-president: Theodore
              Brummer; brewmaster: Thomas Hofer
              Nau
1889   **Belgian Brewery**
              Montegut Street
              Nau
1890   **Jax Brewery**
              Decatur (formerly Levee) and St. Peter streets
              President: Lawrence Fabacher; secretary-treasurer: Gustav
              Oertling; officer: Tom Hofer; brewmaster: Michael Jacob
              Named after Andrew Jackson; Romanesque Revival castle-
              like building with warehouses and bottling plants; beer
              originally called Jackson Bohemian Beer
        1974 Closed
        1984 Main building reopened as shopping/entertainment center
              by Jackson Brewery Development Corp. of Berger, Blitch
              and Friedman
              Designer: Steven Bingler, after London's Crystal Palace;
              concept copied from San Francisco's Ghirardelli Chocolate
              Factory's conversion
              "Charles Einsiedel, architect," Daily Picayune, June 7,

1891, c. 5; Engelhardt; Soards 1916; Laborde, Errol,
"What's Happening at the Jax Brewery?" Gambit 4, no. 29
(July 23-29, 1983): 19-21

1891   **Algiers Home Brewing Company**
Brooklyn Avenue, Algiers
Officer: Z. W. Tinker; brewmaster: Henry Reinsinger
Produced 25,000 barrels lager beer annually
"Plant destroyed by fire," D. C. Item, June 4, 1893, p. 3, c.
6; Engelhardt; Dixon

1891   **American Brewing Company**
Conti Street between Royal and Bourbon streets
President: Edward G. Schliedler; vice-president: U. Koen;
brewmaster: William Breisacher; bottler: John Blank
Engelhardt; Nau

1896   **Security Brewing Company** (St. Joseph Street Depot)
341-45 North Diamond Street, Algiers
Vice-president: A. M. & J. Solari; secretary-treasurer: T. L.
Macon; brewmaster: Henry Reinsinger
Continued operation of Algiers Home Brewing Co. after its
1893 fire
Dixon

1898   **Columbia Brewing Company**
Elysian Fields Avenue and Chartres Street
President: Charles Karst (father of Edward Karst, mayor of
Alexandria); officers: Gustav Paul, Charles Rieder, C. W.
Scheurer, Andrew Schloesser; brewmaster: John Rettenmeier
Nau; Festschrift

1898   **Standard Brewery**
514-32 South Johnson and South Prieur streets
President: Charles Wirth; vice-president: Harry
Armbruster; officer: Charles H. Schenck
Nau; Engelhardt; Soards 1916

1904   **Consumers Brewing Company**
Clio and South Liberty streets
President: J. Weiler; vice-president: J. Egloff; treasurer/
superintendent: H. Reinniger
Festschrift; Engelhardt; Soards 1916

1907   **Dixie Brewing Company**
Tulane Avenue
President: Gustav Oertling
Survived prohibition by selling ice, ice cream, and "near
beer"; still in operation
Daily Picayune, Nov. 1, 1907, p. 8, c. 1-3

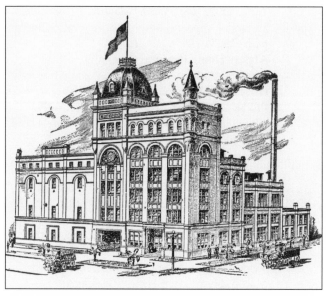

Dixie Brewing Company, Tulane Avenue, from *Deutsche Tage Festschrift,* 1913. *Courtesy of a private collection.*

1911		**National Bräuerei**
		Gravier and Dorgenois streets
		President: Charles A. Wagner; vice-president: Albert Werner
		"National sold to Falstaff," Times-Picayune, Dec. 15, 1936, sec. 2, p. 16, c. 1; Engelhardt
1912 (ca.)		**Union Brewing Company**
		2809 North Robertson and Press streets
		Festschrift
	1916	**Falstaff Manufacturing & Mercantile Company**
		Vice-president: E. Buernemann; manager: J. L. Schulz
		Distributor for Lemp Brewery of St. Louis
		Soards 1916
	1978	Closed
	1920	**Anheuser-Busch Brewery**
		Gravier and South Front streets
		Cable

Beer Gardens

date   cited

	1840s	**National Beer Garden**
		St. Peter Street at Bayou St. John

Stall; Deiler, Presse

1840s **Old German Union**
Orleans Street
Schuman, Stein and Krost
Deiler, Presse

1843 **Tivoli Gardens**
Bayou St. John
H. Rolling
Deiler, Presse; Stall

1848 **Schleuter's Beer Garden**
St. Charles and Gravier streets
Nau

1850s **Casino Beer Garden**
Carondelet Street
Abel & Rochow
Deiler, Presse; Nau

1850s **Lafayette Gardens**
City of Lafayette
Deiler, Presse

1850s **Punecky's Beer Garden**
Prieur Street
Deiler, Presse; Stall

Tivoli Gardens, Basin Street and Bayou St. John. *Courtesy of the Historic New Orleans Collection.*

1850s		**Schroeder's Beer Garden**
		Levee and Short streets
		Mahe
	1850s	**Zum Grünen Garten**
		Levee and Josephine streets
		Matthias Thomann
		Deiler, Presse
1851		**Krost Beer Garden**
	1856	Conti Street
	1857	1863 Common Street
		Christian Krost
		Deiler, Presse; Nau
1853		**Louis Stein's**
		Bienville Street
		Deiler, Presse
	1870s	**Bensel and Dirks**
		Deiler, Presse; Nau
	1880	**Carrollton Garten**
		Deutsche Zeitung, Apr. 20, 1880
	1895	**Over the Rhine Beer Garden/Restaurant**
		Spanish Fort
		Huber
1890s		**Court Exchange**
		Rousseau and Philip streets
		NOPL
1890s		**Doerr's Beer Garden**
		Live Oak and Acht streets
		NOPL
	1910	**Heidelberg Family Garden**
		419-23 St. Charles Street
		Charles Schutten
		Soards 1909
	1937	**E. Klaus's New Beer Garden**
		Westwego
		Jeff. Parish Review, 1937

THE GERMAN-LANGUAGE PRESS

The history of the German press in the New Orleans region started with the development of separate German communities in and around New Orleans. Its beginnings can be traced to the late 1830s, a time when only a very few Germans lived in the central city. The newly arriving German immigrants did not stay in the densely populated and expensive "downtown" area. As in most port cities, these newcomers were drawn to the suburbs, which offered inexpensive accommodations and cheap land. Several German communities soon formed in the areas surrounding New Orleans. Once established, these suburbs attracted the new arrivals, who joined their families and friends. Most had been recruited by letters from these residents extolling the opportunities available to German newcomers. From them the newly recruited immigrants could expect their first helping hand.

Three major communities developed as German immigration to the city grew. One was located in the Third District below Esplanade Avenue, then an independent entity. The heavily German core was known as Little Saxony. A second community developed about a mile and a half above Canal Street in the City of Lafayette. It was also an independent city, extending from Felicity to Toledano streets, but was incorporated into New Orleans in 1852 as the Fourth District. The third major German community was located in the City of Carrollton, four miles farther upstream at the bend in the river, today the Seventh District. In these areas the first German institutions were established: churches, schools, theaters, restaurants, clubs, dancehalls, family-oriented beer gardens, trades, and businesses.

New Orleans at that time had only one streetcar line, running from Canal to the City of Carrollton, along present-day St. Charles Avenue. Because it was expensive and time consuming to travel back and forth among these far-flung areas, the German communities remained isolated from each other. Most of the Germans stayed where they had originally put down roots, that is, within their church parishes in one of the separate German communities.

Germans were inclined by nature toward narrow local loyalties, stemming from their allegiance to the province of their origin in the *Vaterland* (fatherland). At this time in Europe, there was no united Germany but rather a series of principalities organized along feudal lines. Because of the diverse dialects and cultural practices of these principalities, they remained independent and isolated from one another. This provincial mentality, typical of the German nationality, predominated in the communities around New Orleans. The German reading public of each was interested primarily in local news and events. This promoted the founding of separate newspapers for the Third District, Lafayette, and Carrollton.

The founding of the first German paper in the New Orleans area took place late in 1839. It was called *Der Deutsche* (*The German*), a well-presented, attractive weekly publication put out in the City of

Lafayette. In addition to printing the local news, the editor of the newspaper had a higher purpose. He wanted to arouse interest among the German public in national politics. At this time the anti-immigrant Know-Nothing movement was wielding great political influence upon national elections. The object of *Der Deutsche* was to present independent and neutral views of the political positions of both the Democratic and Whig parties.

The natives of New Orleans at this time expressed widespread hostility to all things foreign, especially to the increase in German immigration. The following memorandum put out in 1839 reflected the views of the common man of the city (broadside, quoted in *Der Deutsche,* Nov. 16):

> Hordes of foreign workers have taken over jobs in the United States, almost all trade and banking opportunities, branches of science, the law, preaching positions, most of the established honorable professions, teaching posts in the high schools and universities. Likewise, the press has fallen into the hands of those foreigners. It is the duty of the American people to limit the opportunities of foreigners to common labor, the one job that they are suited to.

Der Deutsche countered with the following pledge to its constituents: "We will monitor those politicians who are prejudiced against immigration, especially against Germans. We always will make known to the German immigrants their rights, their position and the law."

After a half-year of appearing only in the German language, the paper changed its format to increase circulation. Beginning in mid-June of 1840 an English-language edition entitled the *German-American* was also published. The two editors had different political allegiances, resulting in *Der Deutsche* becoming a vehicle of the Whig party rather than an independent publication. After the defeat of the Democratic nominee, the Whig party candidate, William Henry Harrison, was elected president of the United States. No longer needing to raise support for the Whigs after the election, *Der Deutsche* came to an end.

At the beginning of 1842 *Der Deutsche Courier* (*German Courier*) appeared in Lafayette, published twice a week by the firm of Joseph Cohn & Co. Cohn complained that the switch in political positions of *Der Deutsche* had caused distrust among the Germans of a similar undertaking. However, with the *Courier,* he intended to offer an organ that would unify public opinion in the separate German communities. Beginning the next year Cohn served as editor as well as proprietor. The *Courier,* like all

New Orleans papers of that period, contained the local news, business and entertainment advertisements, reprints from European newspapers, but additionally political articles. As proprietor and editor, Cohn could present his own views, which reflected the platform of the Democratic Party. Four years later, on August 1, 1847, he sold the *Courier* to Karl Medicus, who moved the office of the newspaper.

When Cohn sold the *Courier,* he was required to sign a contract prohibiting him for one year from taking part in any other German newspaper enterprise. Cohn respected the contract to the day, but on August 1, 1848, he returned to the newspaper business, founding the *New Orleanser Deutsche Zeitung* (*New Orleans German Gazette*) in his original location on Poydras and Tchoupitoulas streets. It became the longest-running German newspaper (until 1907) in the history of the New Orleans German press.

Cohn sold the paper in 1853 to Peter Pfeiffer and Jacob Hassinger and started a German bookstore in Jackson Square. At the same time he studied notarial work and, by the following year, became a qualified notary. For the next twenty-five years, until his death at age sixty-five, he occupied this position and earned the general respect of the community. Cohn was a quiet, shy man who never strove for attention. Although he had come to New Orleans as a lowly typesetter he had established his own general printing business by age twenty-five. In the course of his career in publishing he amassed a small fortune through his entrepreneurial efforts. Over the years Joseph Cohn became perhaps the most outstanding and respected person associated with the German press of New Orleans.

As immigration numbers grew during the 1840s the German population in New Orleans became more and more aware of the many problems that confronted their immigrant countrymen. The need for an organization to assist those German immigrants was made known in January 1842, when Joseph Cohn published an appeal in *Der Deutsche Courier* to establish an immigrant aid society. Although Cohn continued to call attention to this need, his pleas to the German community had no immediate effect. It was not until five years later that Cohn finally was successful in galvanizing the German community to action. The Germans in the City of Lafayette led the other German communities in establishing a citywide association to provide aid and protection to the newly arriving German immigrants. This was the first major undertaking in which the Germans of the entire area cooperated, for which Joseph Cohn alone was responsible.

On July 1, 1847, the *Deutsche Gesellschaft von New Orleans* (German Society of New Orleans) officially began its work. Operating as a volunteer charitable association, it developed a long and illustrious history (see chapter 2, "German Immigration to New Orleans"). Through the *Deutsche Gesellschaft* and his newspaper endeavors, Cohn achieved wide recognition in the German community. His efforts never flagged in elevating the standing of the Germans in the city and in defending their rights as foreign-born citizens.

In the 1848 election, both the *Courier* and the *Deutsche Zeitung* represented the Democratic Party. Therefore there was a great need for a Whig-oriented newspaper. When the *Courier* failed a month after the appearance of Cohn's *Deutsche Zeitung,* a consortium was formed, whose president was the secretary of the Whig council. This consortium acquired the *Courier*'s type   (*Fraktur*) and published a new German paper named *Die Glocke* (*The Bell*). Karl Schlüter, who ran a nursery and beer garden on Gravier and St. Charles Avenue, was the driving force behind this daily publication. It gave extended coverage to Gen. Zachary Taylor's victorious return from Mexico and his later candidacy for president. After Schlüter came five other editors, including Dr. S. Wiener, the first editor of Cohn's *Deutsche Zeitung.* However, a fire that summer forced the paper to stop publishing.

Even though critically weakened, the *German Gazette* was reactivated later in the year by a new editor, Franz Beuter. Under the excuse of wanting to publish a religious brochure he was able to acquire German type from a rival. Although the Whigs already had an organ in *Die Glocke,* he published *Der Wahre Republikaner* just before the presidential election of 1852. After the election, in which the Whigs lost, Beuter demanded repayment from the party for the type he had purchased.

The 1850 census recorded 11,500 German-born residents already in New Orleans. The next five years showed the largest growth in German immigration in the city. It was thought that this flood of refugees would only increase, creating a greater need for German newspapers. The many political refugees who came to the New Orleans area after the German Revolution of 1848 awakened local German interest in the homeland. Potentially this increased the need for another newspaper since most of the immigrants could read their mother tongue. There were many well-educated, well-off men among the political refugees, who were willing to take a financial interest in a newspaper endeavor. Since they could not find work that was comparable to their experience and abilities they wanted to convince the public of the need for an expanded German press.

Der Louisiana Zuschauer (the *Louisiana Spectator*), *Official for the City and Jefferson Parish,* had its beginnings in Jefferson City, an area adjacent to Lafayette that was heavily populated by Germans. Ever since the presidential election in 1848, an English-language Whig paper, the *Louisiana Spectator,* had existed there. The German lawyer Christian Roselius, a prominent Whig who lived in the area, took part in writing and editing this paper. On the first of June in 1850 a German edition of the *Spectator* appeared with the name *Der Louisiana Zuschauer.* It was much praised in the press. The following was quoted in J. Hanno Deiler, *Geschichte der New Orleanser deutschen Presse* (p. 12):

> The *Louisiana Spectator* is a sterling Whig paper and is published partly in the German language. It is written in the best German that has ever been published in the two cities of Lafayette and Carrollton. The paper is well established, now far advanced in the second year, and in the hands of a man who knows how to use it for the advancement of the Whig cause.

A number of other local newspapers appeared at this time, but no issues have been preserved. Of them only *Die Louisiana Staatszeitung* (the *Louisiana State Newspaper*) had an extended run as the first newspaper to appear in the Third District. Founded by Ewald Hermann Boelitz & Co. in the early 1850s, the *States* was supposed to be politically independent. It appeared at first three times a week, then daily, except Mondays, like the other papers of the time. Boelitz soon recognized that this undertaking had no chance of success as a municipal newspaper and decided to move to the central part of the city. At the end of the first year he set up an office in Exchange Alley. Two years later the *Staatszeitung* was acquired by other newspaper people, who enlarged the format. But within a few months Boelitz once again took over, now in partnership with Moritz Hoffmann, the former publisher of the *Boston Merkur (Boston Mercury)*. The main articles were written in an inferior manner during the whole period when Boelitz was in control of the editing. He allowed his five capable reporters only to write supplements, never lead articles. This produced a paper in which the non-editorialized parts generally were far better than the main articles.

The tastelessness of the *Staatszeitung* was exemplified by its coverage of Lola Montez, the "Spanish" dancer born in Scotland who had danced her way into the heart of King Ludwig I of Bavaria. At the end of 1852 the paper reviewed *Lola Montez in Bavaria,* which she had choreographed and produced at the Placide Theater in New Orleans. The newspaper ludicrously characterized Lola as a true republican, using her influence with the king for the betterment of the people of Bavaria. After her performance she claimed to have been cheated of her share of the entry fees by the business manager, who subsequently sued her for libel. Additionally, Ludwig von Reizenstein, an employee of the *Staatszeitung,* openly claimed to have been intimate with Ms. Montez in Munich. He had been a member of a radical student group named *Alemania,* which her admirers had formed for her support and protection.

To escape the scandals she had created in the city, she surreptitiously left New Orleans on a Mississippi steamboat. On board she demanded that a place be reserved for her dog next to her at the dining table. When the captain did not comply, she attacked him viciously. He then picked up the puppy and threw it into the river. When the captain came to the next stop he put the enraged Lola off the boat.

In 1854 the lack of taste typical of the *Staatszeitung* was again reflected in its serialized printing of von Reizenstein's controversial *Geheimnisse von New Orleans* (*Secrets of New Orleans*). Although this type of scurrilous literature was popular at the time, Reizenstein attempted to outdo all other efforts in this genre and, indeed, was successful. Many well-known and respected New Orleans Germans were satirized in this work, which subsequently caused a general scandal. The turmoil, however, did not stop the *Staatszeitung* from bringing out daily continuations of the novel for over a year. Later Reizenstein attempted to atone for his youthful literary sins by confiscating whatever editions of the *Geheimnisse* he could find.

In 1856 Boelitz dissolved his partnership with Moritz Hoffmann and became the sole owner of the *Louisiana Staatszeitung.* No longer accountable to a partner, he increased his attacks on the rival German newspaper, the *Deutsche Zeitung.* One of his vengeful acts was to hire away Prof. Theodore Boesche, a native of Hanover, from his editorial position with the *Deutsche Zeitung.* Boesche was a very capable and well-traveled man. On the third day of his new employment, however, he was arrested for drunkenness and thrown into prison, where he died of a heart attack. This situation caused another outbreak of hostilities between the two newspapers.

During the Civil War all independent political discussion in the *Staatszeitung* ended. The editorializing was either in a radical Republican tone or limited to publishing and praising the reports of the military authorities. When New Orleans fell in 1862, the *Louisiana Staatszeitung* suddenly became the enthusiastic supporter of Gen.

Benjamin Butler and his administration. The rival *Deutsche Zeitung,* however, maintained a conservative but still Unionist stance, while sympathizers with the Confederacy had no organ at all. The *Staatszeitung* pilloried the composition of the existing military and put out a call to the young Germans of the city to join the Federal army. Its articles in particular demanded competent officers rather than socially prominent fops. In backing the Union the *Staatszeitung* created continued turmoil by spreading rumors of intrigues planned by the Confederacy against New Orleans.

In 1864 the Federal government required that delegates be elected to a convention to give the state of Louisiana a new constitution. The *Staatszeitung* supported the governor's candidate, Michael Hahn of the *Freistaatspartei* (Free State Party). Boelitz even gave campaign speeches for Hahn, expecting in return to get the sole right to print the constitution in the German language. But the *Deutsche Zeitung* also had supported Hahn's party. The two adversarial papers came up with the idea of "tossing a coin." Whoever lost had to provide the translation and the typesetting, which both would print, and profits would be divided. The *Deutsche Zeitung* won the toss. Another rare example of cooperation between the two rivals occurred in the presidential election of this period. Both the *Staatszeitung* and the *Deutsche Zeitung* gave up their independent positions and supported the entire Democratic slate of candidates.

After the Louisiana constitutional convention, Boelitz's career with the *Louisiana Staatszeitung* rapidly came to an end. He decided to separate from his wife and return to his homeland to live on a large inheritance he had received from his father. In the fall of 1865 he gave his wife full power-of-attorney over his New Orleans property and placed the *Staatszeitung* at her disposal. Frau Boelitz then sold two-thirds of the newspaper to its employees. In 1866, Peter Pfeiffer and Jacob Hassinger acquired the *Staatszeitung* for the price of $5,000.

In early January of 1865 Fritz Ehren, a longtime employee of both the *Deutsche Zeitung* and the *Louisiana Staatszeitung,* celebrated the founding of the *Staatszeitung* by publishing a literary weekly, to which he gave the name *Louisiana Staatszeitung No. 2.* Since neither the *Deutsche Zeitung* nor the *Staatszeitung* had a weekly publication, Ehren truly believed he was performing a service with this undertaking. However, the public did not show enough interest, and four months later the publication had to be ended.

With the final collapse of the *Louisiana Staatszeitung,* the *Deutsche Zeitung* of Pfeiffer and Hassinger became the only German journalistic

Jacob Hassinger, proprietor and owner, *German Gazette/Deutsche Zeitung,* from *Program of the 26th North American Sängerbund,* 1890. *Courtesy of the Historic New Orleans Collection.*

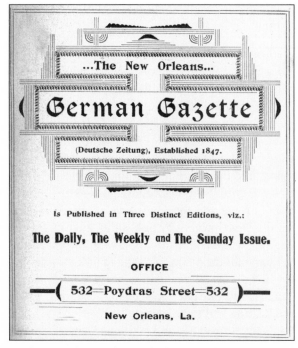

German Gazette/Deutsche Zeitung, from *Soards City Directory,* 1901. *Courtesy of the Louisiana Collection, Earl K. Long Library, University of New Orleans.*

undertaking in New Orleans. But the monopoly did not last long, for differences soon developed between Pfeiffer and Kredell, the local editor. Hassinger, who was tired of all the quarrels, suggested to Pfeiffer that one or the other of them sell out. He hoped that, if his partner withdrew, he would be able to keep Kredell as editor and prevent the founding of a new opposition newspaper. In the spring of 1866, Hassinger acquired Pfeiffer's interest. But Kredell was successful in convincing a number of well-off and influential Germans of the dangers of the monopoly then enjoyed by the *Deutsche Zeitung*. This group then formed the New Orleans Journal Association to found a second German newspaper and put up capital of $25,000. That summer Kredell went to Cincinnati and New York to get equipment and experienced prsonnel. He returned with M. F. Sibilski of the *New Yorker Staatszeitung* and the publisher Georg Müller. In September of 1866 the first edition of the *Tägliche New Orleans Journal* (*New Orleans Daily Journal*) appeared.

The *Daily Journal* was conceived as a newspaper for the central city, with Leon Toll von Zinken put in charge by the directors. Von Zinken was a war hero celebrated in those circles sympathetic to democracy after the fall of the Confederacy. But despite the important names and capital involved, the *Daily Journal* collapsed in 1867 after only six months. The equipment and type were acquired by the book publisher Louis Schwarz and the printer Georg Müller. From this point on Müller ran a general printing business.

In the fall of 1860 Sebastian Seiler began the publication of a weekly paper called the *New Orleans Journal*. He had been the chief editor of the *Deutsche Zeitung* from early 1859 to mid-1860. The main purpose of this publication was to make life impossible for Georg Foerster, Seiler's replacement as editor of the *Deutsche Zeitung*. Before his move to New Orleans, Foerster had been an itinerant correspondent for a New York newspaper and had sent pro-Union correspondence to New Orleans during his travels. This correspondence was published by Seiler, forcing Foerster to flee the city by the end of the year. How long the *New Orleans Journal* existed after this act of revenge is not known. Ironically, after the fall of New Orleans, Seiler himself became a radical Republican and worked tirelessly for the cause of the Negro's right to vote.

The personnel of the *New Orleans Journal* then began a weekly newspaper, the *New Orleans Montagspost* (*New Orleans Monday Post*), a humorous gossip-filled weekly published by S. N. Lehmann, Georg Müller, and M. F. Sibilski. It survived for only thirteen editions, from March to July in 1867. Then Sibilski was hired as editor of the *Deutsche Zeitung*.

Die Tägliche Deutsche Zeitung

New Orleans Deutsche Presse.

Mastheads. *Courtesy of a private collection.*

By the winter of 1867-68, the monopoly of the *Deutsche Zeitung* was again challenged by pressure to found an opposition newspaper. Sibilski, the editor at that time, was frequently seen with the book dealer Louis Schwarz, who had bought the *New Orleans Journal*'s equipment and type when it went under. In mid-March of 1868 the daily *New Orleans Deutsche Presse* appeared with M. F. Sibilski as publisher, behind which was a new corporation, the New Orleans German Press Association, with $25,000 in capital. At the end of the month an official agreement was drafted, the signers of which were all Democrats, mostly prominent Catholics of Jefferson City. To protect themselves, these men insisted on a provision that forbade attacks on any religious denomination. Georg Foerster became chief editor of the *Presse.* He had held this position at the *Deutsche Zeitung* twice and had also edited the Catholic *Cincinnati Volksfreund* (*Cincinnati People's Friend*). The staff was soon joined by John P. Weichardt as treasurer and press agent. He was a dramatist by trade, who had come to New Orleans with Ostermann's theater group.

Foerster, Sibilski, and Weichardt were the three men who took up the fight against Hassinger's *Deutsche Zeitung.* The editor of the *Deutsche Zeitung* at that time was a Northerner and a radical Republican. He supported the nominees for the state constitutional convention and Warmoth for governor. The *Presse,* however, ridiculed these convention nominees and supported the opposition candidates. The election battle waged by these two editors exceeded in bitterness everything that had transpired between the two German newspapers up to then. Since the *Deutsche Zeitung* now represented the Republican Party, it had to support the nominated (Union) candidates, considered turncoats by the German community. The *Presse,* as an organ of the Democratic Party, had the advantage of supporting a number of established, well-known German citizens. Of the *Deutsche Zeitung*'s candidates, the *Presse* called one "a candidate for the penitentiary or gallows," another "that infamous creature." Ex-governor Hahn was labeled "our countryman who has deserted" and that "short rascal with a mouth that talks big."

When the *Deutsche Zeitung,* now the only German Republican paper, received the contract for publishing the convention business, it was accused by the *Presse* of bribing the convention delegates with whiskey "by the gallon." The *Deutsche Zeitung* was also accused of making villainous statements, of using indecent language, and of provoking controversy. Indeed, during the first two years of Reconstruction, the paper did support whichever party guaranteed it printing contracts. Its politics ranged from supporting the unreconstructed Democrats to promoting the radical Republicans. Thereafter it returned to its former Democratic policies for the remainder of its existence.

The *Presse* did not last long despite its capital and its controversial articles. In 1868 the stockholders decided in a general meeting to sell the entire business to Georg Müller and Peter Pfeiffer, the part owner and former business manager for Hassinger's *Deutsche Zeitung.* The sale value was $4,000 plus a contract to take over the debts of the New Orleans German Press Association.

Heinrich Heidenhain answered this purchase by publishing a new paper, *Die Tägliche Abendpresse* (the *Daily Evening Paper*). When the Pfeiffer-Müller *Presse* began publishing in January of 1869, Heidenhain's *Abendpresse* ended. Four months later Pfeiffer sold his interest in the business to Müller. From that point, Müller carried on his general printing business under the name of the Press Job Printing Office. Foerster, Sibilski, and Weichardt were given a release and again became employed by the *Deutsche Zeitung.*

The failure of the *Presse* was a devastating defeat for Georg Müller. It was the second newspaper venture for which he had acted as both printer and publisher. The first had been the *New Orleans Montagspost,* which also had failed. Müller's hate for the *Deutsche Zeitung* was directed particularly against Georg Foerster, the man who was again sitting in the editor's chair. When the *Deutsche Zeitung* was destroyed by fire in 1897, Müller could not bring himself to offer it his German type, which he almost never used.

Müller's greatest wish was to see a German newspaper in New Orleans to rival the *Deutsche Zeitung.* His first newspaper undertaking after the collapse of the *Presse* was *Die Laterne* (*The Lantern*), a humorous, satirical weekly paper, which was printed by his press in the spring of 1872. Rather than taking on the responsibility of being the owner or editor, Müller contented himself with writing short editorials and other offerings for the new paper. But *Die Laterne* aroused little enthusiasm in the German community and soon failed.

With the approach of the presidential election of 1876, Müller decided to put out a Democratic weekly newspaper. Because of the rapid disappearance of the founding capital of both the *Journal* and the *Presse,* he took no financial risks. He himself acted as publisher, editor, and printer in creating the *Louisiana Deutsches Journal.* But Müller's journal had no object of attack and therefore no justification for its existence. The *Deutsche Zeitung* already supported the Democratic ticket, so the *Journal* could only repeat on Sundays what the *Deutsche Zeitung* had been printing all week. When the German community did not immediately recognize his attempt to give them a second German newspaper, he became enraged. Out of bitterness Müller allowed the journal to die, but after a couple of years he took up the work again, only to drop it for a second time.

In early 1884 a men's singing club, the *Frohsinn,* was founded by the Bärenklub (Bear's Club) on St. Charles Avenue. Georg Müller became secretary of this singing society and an active participant in the *Bärenklub.* The *Frohsinn* members also used the location for carnival-like presentations, comic speeches, and orations and gave thought to expanding into a drama as well as a singing society. For Müller, this type of entertainment offered journalistic material, while the new society offered him potential subscribers. Müller thought it was again time for him to launch a German newspaper. At his own expense he decided to publish a humorous, satirical German newspaper, the *Narrhalla* (*Madhouse,* a play on *Valhalla*), as an organ of the Bear's Club. Only a few issues appeared, however, because of desertions in the ranks of the organization.

Another eight years went by until Georg Müller again introduced a newspaper to the German public, the *New Orleans Deutsches Familienjournal mit dem Beilage, Unser Lustigen Blätter* (*New Orleans Family Journal with the Supplement, Our Funny Papers*). The *Familienjournal* was a local chronicle, which made unkind remarks about the *Deutsche Zeitung,* gave its own view of the world, offered reports from the fatherland, and had a women's section, jokes, general news, a house-and-garden section, and eight pages of printed cartoons. Because of Müller's repeated failures, the German public had no faith in this new undertaking and did not meet the necessary subscription level. The *Familienjournal* along with its funny papers failed with its twenty-first issue. Müller mourned the collapse of his mission to establish a second German newspaper in New Orleans. In the last issue of the *Familienjournal* he published a black-bordered death notice decorated with widow's weeds and a flower-bedecked burial plaque, on which were the names and dates of his numerous newspaper undertakings.

In May of 1893 Hugo Lehmann developed a plan for publishing a monthly newspaper to encourage German immigration to Louisiana. Since many farmers from the Northwestern part of the United States had settled along the Southern Pacific Railroad line between Rayne and the Texas border, a "land boom" had been generated there. Lehmann succeeded in interesting the Duson brothers, large landholders in this area, in such a newspaper. This publication was to be distributed both in the United States and Germany. Twenty thousand copies of the *Südliche Pionier* (*Southern Pioneer*) were printed by Georg Müller, who strongly supported Lehmann's undertaking.

After the first edition, which received the desired subscription level in Acadia Parish, the interest of the Duson brothers and their associates slacked off. At the same time Lehmann wanted to become independent of Müller. In August of 1893 he applied to the German Society of New Orleans for a loan to assure the continued publication of his newspaper. The directors, who were dedicated to helping German immigrants, agreed to the request and bought a set of *Fraktur* type, which was rented to Lehmann. Several months later a second edition of the *Südliche Pionier* appeared. Two thousand copies of this edition plus 10,000 of the first edition were deposited with the North German Lloyd steamship line for distribution in Germany. Unfortunately the entire venture failed, so the German Society took back its type to protect its investment. The book printer Müller would gladly have seen a second German newspaper in New Orleans but not a second general printer. So he bought the type from the German Society to avoid its falling into the hands of someone else.

After he had given notice of the death of his own enterprises, Müller had another chance to attack the *Deutsche Zeitung*. In the spring of 1896 it had published an article titled "Fritz Roelling's Work," accusing this life-insurance agent of unethical practices. Roelling answered with a scurrilous handout, which he distributed on the street and in public bars. It not only attacked the reporters of the *Deutsche Zeitung* who were responsible for the article but also Jacob Hassinger, the owner, who was totally uninvolved. A fistfight resulted between Roelling and Hassinger, with the case being turned over to the criminal court. Roelling, while free on bail, put out a monthly paper, *Unser*

Käseblatt (*Our Local Rag*), but changed its name to the *German Kritiker,* with the subtitle *Lokalanzeiger für jeden wackern Deutschen in New Orleans und umliegenden Dörfern* (*Local News for Those Good Germans in New Orleans and Surrounding Towns*). The first sixteen issues were printed by Paul J. Sendker, a young book publisher who had just established himself in the central city. Then Roelling moved his paper to Georg Müller, who took it on both as guarantor and printer.

At the beginning, Roelling's energetic agitation and delight in scandal brought the *Kritiker* many readers. The paper openly expressed Roelling's hostility toward the *Deutsche Zeitung* and jealousy of the Hassinger family. But soon Roelling took a more circumspect approach in order to convince Hassinger to drop the charges pending against him. As a result, public interest in the *Kritiker* began to cool. After a last-ditch attempt failed to attract stockholders, it closed in 1897.

In the fall of that year Georg Müller sold his printing business, which he had run for exactly thirty years. At the end of 1897 he moved to California, where he made an unsuccessful marriage to a widow but died after only a year. On reading his will it was discovered that his name was not Müller but Gumbel. No reason other than fear of anti-Semitism was ever established for Müller's name change as a young man just arriving in America.

As this history shows, the German press of the New Orleans region tells a lengthy tale. As an industry it was fraught with financial difficulties, inconsistent publication runs, frequent alteration of editorial viewpoints, changes in ownership, etc. Conflicts among editors and publishers resulted in numerous resignations and new startups. Only the *Deutsche Zeitung* had a continuous run, lasting from 1848 until April of 1907. However, the last ten years were unprofitable for the paper. By this time the German community had largely become assimilated, resulting in most patrons preferring to read and advertise in the mainstream English-language papers. Three months after the appearance of the last issue of the *Deutsche Zeitung,* Oscar Grillo, editor of the discontinued paper, tried to salvage the German press by publishing the *Neue Deutsche Zeitung.* At first it appeared twice a week, but after a year it became a weekly. By 1917 the newspaper only comprised eight pages. With the onset of World War I and the subsequent anti-German acts passed by the Louisiana legislature, the German press of New Orleans disintegrated. One last effort was made by the *Deutsche Gesellschaft* in 1925 to publish a German-language newspaper. However, the endeavor failed, causing a number of the society's members financial losses and ending the history of the German press of New Orleans.

The following is a listing of New Orleans German-language newspapers by date of their establishment. The name, publisher, and editor(s) of the newspapers are given, followed by the dates published, pertinent notes, available copies, and sources. Listings from the Louisiana Newspaper Project Printout, Online Computer Library Center (OCLC) and the National Bibliographic Database are listed by their OCLC codes: LHC = Historic New Orleans Collection; LNC = New Orleans Public Library; LRU = Tulane University; LUUJ = Louisiana State University, Louisiana and Lower Mississippi Valley Collection; LXO = Louisiana State Museum Historical Center.

German-Language Newspapers

1839   ***Der Deutsche*** (*The German*)
      Publs.: Emil Johns and Co., R. A. I. Richter; eds.: Ainsworth & Schücking, F. Zerland
      Nov. 16, 1839-July 8, 1840, weekly; July 15-Nov. 1840; semiweekly in German and English, entitled *The German-American;* published with an additional masthead in German as *Der Deutsch-Amerikaner*
      Vehicle of the Whig party; purpose: to interest readers in the politics of the U.S. and its anti-immigrant and anti-German sentiment; advised Germans of their rights and the law; continued by the German-American Press, 1890
      Copies: LRU
      Louisiana Newspapers, 1965; Arndt, Zeitungen

1842   ***Der Deutsche Courier*** (*German Courier*), subtitled *Eine Zeitschrift für Politik, Literatur und Leben* (*A Magazine for Politics, Literature and Life*)
      Publs.: Joseph Cohn and Co., Buschmann; ed.: Alfred Schücking, E. Liebe
      Jan. 8, 1842-Sept. 1848; sold to Karl Medicus, Aug. 1, 1847-1848
      Democratic paper, semiweekly, Oct. 14, 1850-?; name came from the *Louisiana Courier,* the most important newspaper of its day; organ to unify the Germans
      Copies: LRU
      Deiler, Presse; Louisiana Newspapers, 1965, 1990; Arndt, Zeitungen

1848   ***Die Deutsche Zeitung*** (*The German Gazette*); title varies: *Die Deutsche Zeitung* (1858-55); *Tägliche Deutsche Zeitung* (1856-72, 1877-89); *New Orleanser Tägliche Deutsche Zeitung* (1872-77)
      Publs.: Joseph Cohn, *Gesellschaft Buchdrucker;* Pfeiffer & Hassinger, Pfeiffer & Co. (Pfeiffer, Hassinger, Gabain), Jacob Hassinger, *Aktien-Gesellschaft* (Hassinger, Albert Heim, Valentin Merz, Chas. F. Buck, who formed directorate), thereafter known as New Orleans German Gazette Publishing Co.

Eds.: Joseph Cohn, Dr. S. Weiner, Eduard Doerk, Rev. Heintz, Eduard von Gabain, Georg Foerster, Sebastian Seiler, Louis Constant, M. F. Sibilski, Ferdinand Seinecke, Hugo Möller, J. Hanno Deiler, Bartels, Lesse, Wichers von Gogh

Aug. 1, 1848-Apr. 13, 1907

Absorbed *Louisiana Staatszeitung,* 1866; followed by *Neue Deutsche Zeitung;* daily, except Monday; weekly on Thursdays (1858-70) as *Die Wöchentliche Deutsche Zeitung;* Sunday edition (1866-1907): *Sonntags-Blatt der New Orleans Deutschen Zeitung;* also as *New Orleans Deutsche Zeitung: Sontags-Ausgabe;* Cohn sold it March 1, 1853, to Peter Pfeiffer and Jacob Hassinger; issues from 1865 to Apr. 15, 1897; destroyed by fire

Copies: LHC, LNC, LXO

Deiler, Presse; Louisiana Newspapers, 1965, 1990; Arndt, Zeitungen

1848 **Die Glocke** (*The Bell*)

Publs.: Consortium president: R. R Southmayd, secretary of Whig Council

Eds.: Karl Schlüter, Dr. Langenbecker, Klaus Schlotte, August Schneider, Dr. S. Weiner, Dr. Kiekbach, Witte & Co.

July 1, 1848-Feb. 16, 1850; publication ceased due to fire

Whig daily; published in English and German

No copies available

Deiler, Presse; Arndt, Zeitungen

1849 **Louisiana Zuschauer,** *Officiell für die Stadt von Lafayette* (*Louisiana Spectator, Official for the City of Lafayette*); also published under the title *Louisiana Spectator, Dorfzeitung* (*Village Newspaper*)

Eds.: Christian Roselius, Johann Eduard Kopp

March, 1849-?; published in English and German in 1850

Whig weekly

No copies available

Deiler, Presse; Arndt, Zeitungen

1850 **Der Wahre Republikaner** (*The True Republican*)

Ed.: A. Elfeld

March 19, 1850-?

Die Glocke reactivated under this new name

No copies available

Deiler, Presse; Arndt, Zeitungen

1850 **Louisiana Staatszeitung** (*Louisiana State News*), subtitled *Louisiana State Gazette,* 1864-66

Publs.: Ewald Hermann Boelitz, Johann Eduard Kopp, Georg Lugenbühl, H. Cohen; eds.: E. H. Boelitz, J. G. Brasch, Carl Friedrich Heunisch, H. Cohen, Theodor Boesche; printer: *Gesellschaft Buchdrucker*

July 9, 1850-March 1, 1866; tri-weekly July 9-Aug. 5, 1850; then daily except Monday
Published in the Third District; survived longer than other *Dorfzeitungen;* published Ludwig von Reizenstein's *Geheimnisse von [Secrets of] New Orleans* in installments, 1854-55; merged with *Tägliche/Wöchentliche Deutsche Zeitung*
Copies: LHC, LNC, LRU
Deiler, Presse; Louisiana Newspapers, 1941, 1965; Arndt, Zeitungen

1850 *Das Arbeiterblatt* (*The Worker's Paper*); *Dorfzeitung* (*Village Newspaper*)
Ed.: August Kathmann
Oct. 14, 1850-51; weekly
Founded by the *Allgemeiner Arbeiterverein* (General Workers Union), also known as *Stadtmännischer Allgemeine Arbeiterverein* (City Man's General Union); purpose: to advise and protect German immigrant workers from competition of slaves, intolerable conditions, climate
No copies available
Deiler, Presse; Arndt, Zeitungen, Presse

1850 *Deutsche Courier No. 2* (*German Courier No. 2*); also listed as *Der Deutsche Courier Dorfzeitung* (*Village Newspaper*)
Publ.: *Vereinigte Arbiter* (United Workers); ed.: E. Liebe
Oct. 14, 1850-?
Copies: LRU
Deiler, Presse; Louisiana Newspapers, 1965; Arndt, Presse

1851 *Der Alligator* (*The Alligator*)
Publ.: Mississippi Delta-Amphibien; ed.: Ludwig von Reizenstein
May 12, 1851-?
Weekly (on Mondays)
No copies available
Deiler, Presse; Louisiana Newspapers, 1965; Arndt, Zeitungen

1851 *Lafayetter Zeitung* (*Lafayette Newspaper*); *Dorfzeitung* (*Village Newspaper*)
Ed.: J. E. Kopp
June 1, 1851-?
Published three times a week
Copies: LNC
Deiler, Presse; Louisiana Newspapers, 1965; Arndt, Zeitungen

1851 *New Orleanser Tageblatt* (*New Orleans Daily Paper*); *Dorfzeitung* (*Village Newspaper*)
Ed.: Ludwig von Reizenstein
June 1, 1851-?
No copies available
Deiler, Presse; Arndt, Zeitungen

1852 **Der Pekin Demokrat** (*The Peking Democrat*)
Ed.: Ludwig von Reizenstein
Vehicle to publish his novel, *Geheimnisse von New Orleans*
No copies available
Arndt, Zeitungen

1852 **Der Wahre Republikaner** (*The True Republican*)
Whig campaign organ, Oct.-Nov. 1852
No copies available
Arndt, Zeitungen

1853 **Der Communist** (*The Communist*); *Dorfzeitung* (*Village Newspaper*)
Publ. & ed.: E. Cabet
1853-?
Weekly organ of the *Communisten-Verein* (Communist Union)
No copies available
Deiler, Presse; Arndt, Zeitungen

1854 **Deutsche-Englische Wöchenzeitung** (*German-English Weekly Newspaper*); *Dorfzeitung* (*Village Newspaper*)
Publs.: Central Committee of the *Deutsche Verein* [German Union] of the First, Second, Third and Fourth Districts, the Turners' and the Barbers' unions
1854-?
No copies available
Deiler, Presse

1855 **Louisiana**
Publs.: Lugenbuhl & Boelitz; ed.: Dr. Gussmann
March 26, 1855-?
Arndt, Zeitungen

1856 **Carrollton Journal;** *Dorfzeitung* (*Village Newspaper*)
Publ.: Friederich Fischer and Co.
May 1, 1856-Jan. 6, 1857
German-English weekly
No copies available
Deiler, Presse; Arndt, Zeitungen

1859 **Jefferson Parish Wächter** (*Jefferson Parish Guardian*); *Dorfzeitung* (*Village Newspaper*)
Ed.: Pastor Ludwig P. Heintz
Nov. 20, 1859-60; ceased publication after one year
No copies available
Deiler, Presse; Arndt, Zeitungen

1866 **New Orleans Journal/Tägliche New Orleans Journal** (*[Daily] New Orleans Journal*)
Publ.: Leon von Zinken; eds.: Kredell, M. F. Sibilski, Georg Müller
Sept. 1, 1866-March 18, 1867

Daily; included weekly edition, *Das Wöchenblatt [Weekly] der New Orleans Journal,* Jan. 31-March 1867 (5 issues)
Founded after demise of *Louisiana Staatszeitung* to counter *Deutsche Zeitung*
Copies: LNC
Deiler, Presse; Louisiana Newspapers, 1990; Arndt, Zeitungen

1867   **New Orleans Montagspost** (*New Orleans Monday Post*)
Publs. & eds.: S. N. Lehmann, Georg Müller, M. F. Sibilski
March 6-July 29, 1867
Literary and humorous weekly (13 issues); founded by personnel from the *Tägliche New Orleans Journal*
No copies available
Deiler, Presse

1868   **Tägliche New Orleans Deutsche Presse** (*Daily New Orleans German Press*)
Publs. & eds.: M. F. Sibilski, Georg Foerster; treasurer and press agent: John Weichardt
March 15, 1868-May 26, 1869 (59 issues)
Supported by New Orleans German Press Association; weekly edition entitled *Wöchentliche New Orleans Deutsche Presse,* March 19-Aug. 27, 1868; Sunday edition entitled *Sonntags-Blatt der New Orleans Deutschen Presse,* Sept. 1868-Apr. 1869; conservative Democratic daily, except Mondays; merged with the *Tägliche Deutsche Zeitung* in May 1869
Copies: LNC
Deiler, Presse; Louisiana Newspapers, 1941, 1965, 1990; Arndt, Zeitungen

1868   **Die Tägliche Abendpresse** (*The Daily Evening Paper*)
Publ. & ed.: Heinrich Heidenhain
Dec. 24, 1868-Jan. 12, 1869
No copies available
Deiler, Presse

1869   **Der Familienfreund** (*The Family Friend*)
Ed.: Rev. J. B. A. Ahrens, D.D.
Apr. 2, 1869-1903
Biweekly until 1892; semimonthly 1893-95; monthly 1896-1903; 4 pages; organ of the German Methodist Church of the South
Copies: LUUJ
Louisiana Newspapers, 1990; Arndt, Zeitungen

1870   **Echo von New Orleans** (*Echo of New Orleans*), subtitled *Wochenblatt für die Deutschen im Süden der Vereinigten Staaten* (*Weekly for the Germans in the Southern United States*)
Publ. & ed.: Rev. Peter Leonhard Thevis

May 1-Sept. 11, 1870
Roman Catholic weekly (appeared on Sundays) put out by Father
Thevis, pastor of Holy Trinity Church, with approbation of the arch-
bishop; ceased under pressure from Chancery for his stance on the
Franco-Prussian War
Copies: LUUJ
Louisiana Newspapers, 1941, 1965; Arndt, Zeitungen

1872   **Der Kinderfreund** (*The Children's Friend*)
Ed.: Rev. J. B. A. Ahrens
1872-74
Monthly; organ of the German Methodist Church, South Louisiana
Conference
Arndt, Zeitungen

1872   **Die Laterne** (*The Lantern*), subtitled *Humoristisches satyrisches
Wochenblatt* (*Humorous Satirical Weekly*)
Publ.: E. Buhlert & A. Hertzberg; ed.: E. Buhlert; printer: Georg
Müller
Apr. 13, 1872-?
4 pages
No copies available
Deiler, Presse; Louisiana Newspapers, 1965; Arndt, Zeitungen

1875   **Louisiana Staatszeitung No. 2** (*Louisiana State Newspaper No. 2*)
Ed.: Gawrzyjelski
Jan.-Apr. 1875
Monthly literary paper
No copies available
Deiler, Presse; Louisiana Newspapers, 1965

1876   **Der Hammer** (*The Hammer*)
Publs.: Ludwig Geissler, Jacob Mueller
March-Oct. 1876
Radical socialist workers' paper
No copies available
Deiler, Presse; Arndt, Zeitungen

1876   **Louisiana Deutsches Journal** (*Louisiana German Journal*)
Publs.: Georg Müller, Peter Krämer; ed.: Georg Müller
Aug. 20, 1876-March 4, 1877
Democratic political weekly
No copies available
Deiler, Presse; Louisiana Newspapers, 1965; Arndt, Zeitungen

1879   **Deutscher Hausfreund** (*German Home Friend*)
Aug. 1879-?
No copies available
Louisiana Newspapers, 1965

1882   *Neue Welt* (*New World*)
       Publs. & eds.: Henry A. Schwebe, Franz Schumacher
       1882-92
       Weekly
       Arndt, Zeitungen
1883   **Evangelisch-Lutherische Blätter** (*Evangelical-Lutheran Paper*), sub-
       titled *Zum Besten des Bethlehem-Waisenhauses* (*The Best from the
       Bethlehem Orphan Asylum*)
       Publs.: Rev. P. Roesener, G. J. Wegener
       June 1883-May 1891
       Organ of Evangelical-Lutheran Conference of New Orleans, part of
       Evangelical-Lutheran Synod of Missouri; monthly; 4 pages
       Arndt, Zeitungen
1884   **Narrhalla** (*Madhouse*)
       Publ. & ed.: Georg Müller
       Feb. 1884 (1 issue)
       Satirical-humorous organ of the *Bärenklub,* German song and drama
       club begun by singing society *Frohsinn*
       No copies available
       Deiler, Presse; Arndt, Zeitungen
1889   **Der Christenbote** (*The Christian Messenger*)
       Feb. 1889-Nov. 1890
       Newsletter of Second German Presbyterian Church
       Copies: LHC
1891   **New Orleans Deutsche Familienjournal,** *mit dem Beilage, Unsere
       Lustigen Blätter* (*New Orleans German Family Journal, with the
       Supplement, Our Funny Papers*)
       Ed.: Georg Müller
       May 9-Sept. 26, 1891 (21 issues)
       No copies available
       Deiler, Presse; Arndt, Zeitungen
1892   **Der Altenheimbote** (*Old Folks Home Messenger*)
       Eds.: Louis Voss, Henry Dietz, A. H. Becker, D. Mathaei, J.
       Pluermeke; Mores Leifeste
       Jan. 1892-Apr. 1918; May-July 1918 as *The Home Messenger*
       Published monthly for the Protestant Home for the Aged and Infirm
       Copies: LHC
       Arndt, Zeitungen
1893   **Der Südliche Pionier** (*The Southern Pioneer*), subtitled *Organ zur
       Förderung der deutschen Einwanderung im Süden* (*Organ to
       Encourage German Immigration to the South*)
       Ed.: Hugo Lehmann
       May 31, 1893 & July 15, 1893 (2 issues)

Sponsored by large landowners in Louisiana prairie (Duson brothers of Crowley); 4 pages
Copies: LNC
Deiler, Presse; Louisiana Newspapers, 1941; Arndt, Zeitungen

1896   **Unser Käseblättchen** (*Our Local Rag*); *Dorfzeitung* (*Village Newspaper*)
Ed.: Fritz Roelling
June 22, 1896 (1 issue)
Succeeded by *Der Deutsche Kritiker*
Copies: LNC
Deiler, Presse; Louisiana Newspapers, 1941, 1965

1896   **Der Deutsche Kritiker** (*The German Critic*)
Publs.: Paul Sendker Publishing Co. Ltd., German Kritiker Publishing Association; eds.: Fritz Roelling & Seeman
July 6, 1896-June 14, 1897
Weekly, appeared on Monday; 4 pages
Copies: LNC
Deiler, Presse; Louisiana Newspapers, 1941, 1965; Arndt, Zeitungen

1897   **Der Negerfreund** (*The Negro Friend*)
Publs.: L. Keller, Rev. H. J. Patzelt
1897-1947
Quarterly; 16 pages; religious illustrations; purpose: religious and industrial education of Negro children in Lafayette, La. and Galveston, Tex.
No copies available
Deiler, Presse; Louisiana Newspapers, 1965; Arndt, Zeitungen

1901   **New Orleans Journal,** also known as *Das Deutsch-Englische Wochenblatt* (*The German-English Weekly*), subtitled *Unabhängige Zeitung für den Humor, die Satyre und den Ernst des Lebens* (*Independent Newspaper for the Humor, Satire and Seriousness of Life*), also subtitled *Unabhängiger Anzeiger* (*Independent Advisor*)
Publ.: New Orleans Journal Publishing Co. (Otto Wichers von Gogh, C. Schertz, Georg Müller, Rob. J. Maloney, M. R. Neuhauser, J. T. Wolfe); ed.: von Gogh
Aug. 18-Dec. 15, 1901 (18 issues)
Weekly; German and English; 4 pages
Copies: LNC
Louisiana Newspapers, 1990; Arndt, Zeitungen

1902   **Salem Echo**
Eds.: Rev. F. Frankenfeld, Ewald Kockritz, Rev. Paul M. Schroeder, E. G. Kuenzler, Rev. F. C. Schweinfurth, Robert Lincks
June 1902-Dec. 1939
Monthly; 8 pages; organ of Salem Evangelical Church; German until

1899; English and German 1899-1911; English 1911 on as *Milan Street Echo*
Copies: LNC
Louisiana Newspapers, 1941, 1965; Arndt, Zeitungen

1903 **The Southern Lutheran**
Jan. 1903-Dec. 1917
Monthly; published in New Orleans and Gretna in German and English; merged with *Evangelische-Lutherische Blätter*
Copies: LNC
Arndt, Zeitungen

1907 **Neue Deutsche Zeitung** (*New German Gazette*)
Publs. & eds.: Oscar Grillo, Oswald Thau, George Schanzback & Co.
June 23, 1907-March 1, 1908
Weekly and on Sundays as *Neue Deutsche Zeitung: Sontags-Ausgabe,* June 23, 1907-Aug. 5, 1917 (37 issues); March 4, 1908-Jan. 27, 1909, appeared on Wednesdays as *Wöchentliche Rundschau (Weekly Panorama)*, independent weekly, 8 pages (48 issues); semiweekly: 1907-March 1, 1908; weekly on Sundays, March 8, 1908-1917; succeeded *Wöchenliche Deutsche Zeitung, Sonntags-Ausgabe (Sunday Edition)*; followed *Tägliche Deutsche Zeitung*
Copies: LHC, LNC, LRU
Louisiana Newspapers, 1941, 1965; Arndt, Zeitungen

1916 **Südliche Rundschau** (*Southern Panorama*)
Publ.: Universal Publishing Co.; ed.: Emila Brunnier
1916-17
Weekly
No copies available
Louisiana Newspapers, 1965; Arndt, Zeitungen

1922 **Our Church Visitor**
Ed.: Rev. Louis Schweickhardt
Jan. 1922-Aug. 4, 1929
From 1926 titled *St. Matthew's Church Visitor;* organ of St. Matthew Evangelical Church; monthly
Copies: church
Louisiana Newspapers, 1941

1925 **Wöchenblatt des Südens** (*Southern Weekly*)
Publ.: D. N. Van Geldern
June 21-Sept. 27, 1925
Louisiana Newspapers, 1965

1945 **Der Rundblick, Lagerzeitung der deutschen Kriegsgefangenen** (*The Review, Camp News of the German POWs*)
Publ.: Camp Plauche, New Orleans; ed.: Gustav Baumann
June 1945-46

In German; bimonthly
Copies: Library of Congress
Arndt, Zeitungen; Deiler, Presse

1945   **Das Echo**
Publs.: German POWs, Camp Livingston, La.; eds.: Paul M. Oietzsch, Erich Gerdes
Sept. 1945-Jan. 1946
In German and English
Copies: Library of Congress
Arndt, Zeitungen; Deiler, Presse

1945   **Freiheit** (*Freedom*), subtitled *Camp Claiborne Prison Camp News*
Publ.: *die deutschen Kriegsgefangene der Lager Claiborne* (German POWs of Camp Claiborne); ed.: Otto Meitzler
Oct.-Dec. 1945
Biweekly in German and English
Copies: Library of Congress
Arndt, Zeitungen; Deiler, Presse

1945   **Lagerzeitung** (*Prison Camp News*)
Publ.: Camp Polk German POWs; ed.: Fritz Brzoska
Nov. 25, 1945-46
In German with English translations
Copies: Library of Congress
Arndt, Zeitungen; Deiler, Presse

CHAPTER SIX

Religion and Education

CHURCHES AND SYNAGOGUES

One of the first acts of the German immigrants in the New Orleans region was to establish religious congregations. It was important to them to be able to worship in their native tongue in their newly formed communities. Three principal German areas emerged. One was located in the Third District below Canal Street, the second above Canal Street in the independent City of Lafayette, which spilled over into neighboring Jefferson City, and the third at the bend of the river in the City of Carrollton. Each area developed houses of worship to serve its large German-speaking population.

Since Louisiana was entirely Catholic from its beginnings as a French colony, there was little evidence of Protestantism. It was only after the Louisiana Purchase that the German immigrants of the early nineteenth century established a foothold in New Orleans. These Protestants initially attended Christ Church, founded by an Episcopal congregation in 1805. It was 1825, two decades later, before they could establish their own unified German Protestant congregation and another decade and a half before they could build their first church (1839).

It is interesting that the first German church founded in New Orleans was Protestant rather than Catholic. In the German states, Protestants had long been divided among the dominant creeds of Reformed, Lutheran, and Evangelical. But the Prussian Union of 1817 had forced the northern Germans to merge into a state church with a common liturgy and governance controlled by the reigning monarch. This model was adopted in New Orleans. However, the old doctrinal differences brought from Germany soon emerged, causing division and rancor. As other Protestant congregations formed, they established Lutheran and Evangelical churches that were independent units, many of which did not affiliate with a synod for years. Their affairs were administered by a body of representatives from the membership, which held regular meetings and reported to the congregation. They were empowered to hire and fire pastors, buy property, and direct the financial structure of the church. This independence explains to a large extent why so many Protestant congregations in the New Orleans region formed and disbanded over the years. It also explains the difficulties in obtaining preachers, since synodical pastors would not accept calls to independent churches. Although the result was a lack of leadership and frequent changes of pastors, the congregations still feared to apply to a synod. They were afraid of spiritual bondage and a loss of religious freedom and their privilege of self-government. However, most of the Evangelical and Lutheran churches that survived eventually did affiliate with a synod.

Clio Street Church (First Evangelical Church). The first Protestant congregation was established by the redemptioners who had landed at the port of New Orleans in 1818. Because they had no church they met on Sundays wherever they could. However, they were warned not to sing, so as to keep their Catholic neighbors from becoming aware of their gatherings. Soon this Protestant congregation found a schoolhouse in which to meet, then a makeshift church building, and finally in 1839 a new structure, called simply the Clio Street Church. Nine years before building their church, the congregation had received a charter, signed by the governor, under the name of the First German Protestant Church and Congregation of New Orleans. In the beginning it was simply a Protestant church attended by all denominations. In 1880 it joined the Evangelical Synod of North America, but that same year the church burned down. Although a new structure was immediately built on the same site, it was again destroyed by fire in 1905 and rebuilt on Carondelet Street. Long before this, in 1889, English was introduced into the confirmation classes for the young, who had little interest in maintaining the language of their parents. Services were also held in English every other Sunday night. From 1900 until 1918, services were conducted in both English and German. Between the two world wars, German services were offered only on a few special occasions.

St. Paul's German Evangelical-Lutheran Church. From the very beginning, the Clio Street Protestant congregation suffered from dissention over doctrine and leadership, resulting in several other German Evangelical/Lutheran congregations soon being formed. One congregation, which eventually developed into the leading Protestant force below Canal Street, first met in a fire-engine house, then a private home. Finally, in 1840, the members used flatboat boards to build a modest church, the *Deutsche Evangelische Orthodoxe Kirche,* on the corner of Port and Burgundy streets. In 1848, it adopted a more conservative doctrine and renamed itself St. Paul's German Evangelical-Lutheran

Church. In 1860 the church burned but was rebuilt and continued as an all-German congregation until 1883, when English was introduced into the services. The next year a second pastor was appointed for the English-speaking members, which caused a split in the congregation. Out of necessity, the English group withdrew from St. Paul's in 1888 and formed its own Lutheran church. In 1893 English services were introduced at St. Paul's, and the word "German" was taken out of the name of the church. The hurricane of 1915 blew off the steeple and severely damaged the church, which was later repaired with a lower steeple added. By 1918 German services were held only twice a month and then completely eliminated except for a brief period between the world wars.

Jackson Avenue German Evangelical Church. German Protestants in the City of Lafayette above Canal Street were primarily served by the Lafayette German Evangelical Church, which had its beginnings in 1846 in a private home. That same year the congregation built a church on the corner of Philip and Chippewa streets. Here again the doctrinal differences within German Protestantism manifested themselves, causing dissention in the congregation. The first pastor was soon dismissed, followed by seven others, each of whom lasted only a year or two. One was actually driven out of the church by the women of the congregation wielding buggy whips and umbrellas. Peace was not restored until 1864 by Rev. Ludwig P. Heintz. Upon his arrival, he recognized that the most pressing need in the area was for an institution to care for the many children orphaned by the yellow-fever epidemics. He first established the German Protestant Orphan Asylum, which served the community well into the next century. He then turned his energies to building a new church, which he accomplished within a decade, by 1876. It was located on the corner of Jackson Avenue and Chippewa Street and named the Jackson Avenue German Evangelical Church. By 1902 English was the language used in all services, as a result of the church's affiliation with the Evangelical Synod of North America. The use of English also helped retain the congregation.

St. Matthew German Evangelical Church. Rev. Ludwig P. Heintz went from Lafayette to the City of Carrollton, where, in 1847, he eventually established a church on Zimple Street to serve the Protestants of that city. There doctrinal differences once again caused a split, with a number of members following a newly arrived Swiss-German pastor, Martin Otto. This congregation built a church just a few blocks away from Heintz's structure. It was known as the Otto Church to differentiate it from Heintz's Rooster Church, so called because of the weathercock on its steeple. Neither congregation could survive independently, but attempts to reunite in 1878 failed because the two congregations could not agree on which building to use. In 1884 the differences were settled and the Otto Church became the meeting place, while the Rooster Church building was sold. In 1890 the reunited Protestants of Carrollton built a new church at Carrollton and Willow Street named St. Matthew German Evangelical Church. Within the next decade English services were introduced and both languages were used until 1922. Today a Sunday service in German is still held once a month in the church, conducted by the pastor of the German Seamen's Mission.

Zion German Evangelical-Lutheran Church. Rev. Henry Kleinhagen, one of the later pastors of the Clio Street Church, left that first German Protestant congregation in 1848. He established the Zion German Evangelical-Lutheran Church on Euterpe Street, just below the City of Lafayette. No regular English services were held until 1892 except for those confirmed in that language. Within two years, however, the main services were given in English. Both languages were used until World War I and again between the world wars. Thereafter German was used only occasionally as a favor to the older members of the congregation.

St. John's German Evangelical-Lutheran Church. In 1852 still another group split off from the Clio Street Church and founded St. John's Evangelical-Lutheran Church at Iberville and Prieur streets, just upriver from the heavily German Third District. German was used exclusively until 1882, when the introduction of English split the congregation. The German adherents remained within the church and successfully resisted the use of English until 1893. At that time English was introduced into the evening services and confirmation classes since the young people already preferred English to their parents' native tongue. From then on the use of English increased while German declined. When the church was sold in 1917, the congregation met in a schoolhouse until a chapel at Pierce and Canal streets could be erected. In 1924 the present church was built on this site to serve the Germans who had moved beyond the former City of Carrollton toward Lake Pontchartrain. As was the case with the other German churches, the use of the language was discontinued during World War I. By 1926, however, there were not enough German-speaking members to justify the continued use of the language.

Bethlehem German Evangelical-Lutheran Church; Milan Street German Evangelical-Lutheran Church. Two noteworthy German Evangelical-Lutheran churches of the Missouri Synod were formed in the second half of the nineteenth century. One was the church established by the Bethlehem Congregation in 1887, which

St. John's German Evangelical-Lutheran Church, 1871, Iberville and Prieur streets. *Courtesy of Special Collections, Tulane University.*

took over a church on Felicity Street and Claiborne Avenue. This church had been built much earlier (1854) by Rev. Henry Kleinhagen, who served as pastor until his death in 1885. The second was the German Evangelical-Lutheran church established in 1862 at Milan and Camp streets, formerly known as the First German Evangelical Church of the Sixth District (Jefferson City). Within both of these congregations, German was used only for a short time because assimilation of the German element of the city accelerated toward the end of the century.

German Lutherans who had settled in Algiers and Gretna on the west bank of the Mississippi crossed the river for years to attend services at St. Paul's or St. John's. In the nineteenth century both Algiers and Gretna were self-contained villages, isolated from the mainstream of life in New Orleans. Consequently German remained the common language there long after it had been abandoned by the Germans of the city. It was important for the children of these pioneers to learn to read and write the language that they already spoke and understood. So these German congregations also founded German-language schools associated with their churches (see "German-Language Schools," below).

German Evangelical-Lutheran Trinity Church in Algiers; **Salem German Evangelical-Lutheran Church** in Gretna. In 1875 a group formed the German Evangelical-Lutheran Trinity Church in Algiers, which affiliated with the Missouri Synod. This congregation established a church at Eliza and Olivier streets together with a school to retain the German language spoken by its members. In Gretna a German Protestant congregation was organized in 1866, first as a mission and, after considerable arguments over affiliations, finally as the Salem German Evangelical-Lutheran Church.

In addition to the predominant German Evangelical-Lutheran churches, German Presbyterian and Methodist churches were also established in the New Orleans region.

First Street German Presbyterian Church. The first German Presbyterian church was established at Laurel and First streets in 1854. German was used exclusively until 1892. However, by the turn of the century, it became apparent that English services were far better attended than those in German. Finally, in 1912, when only three old ladies appeared for the German service, the language was dropped, and in 1918 the word "German" was taken from the name of the church.

Second German Presbyterian Church. The second German Presbyterian church was established in 1864 on St. Roch Avenue (then Poet Street) between St. Claude and North Rampart streets. Three years later it moved to North Claiborne and was renamed the Claiborne Avenue German Presbyterian Church. The fate of the German language followed the pattern of the First Presbyterian Church. By 1900 German services were limited to afternoon sessions, and by 1915 the word "German" was eliminated from the name.

Emmanuel German Presbyterian Church of the North. The third Presbyterian church was established in 1877 by a splinter group from the Milan Street German Evangelical-Lutheran Church. It joined the Presbyterian Church of the North in 1880, taking the name of the Emmanuel German Presbyterian Church. That year the property it had acquired at Camp and Soniat streets was mysteriously transferred to the pastor, Owen Riedy, whom the congregation then accused of fraud. In a judgment of the court in 1891 the congregation reacquired the property but was forced to sell it in 1902 to pay its debts.

The poor of these Presbyterian churches were assisted by a legacy of $100,000 left by the former redemptioner Caspar Auch in 1886.

In and around the City of Lafayette a number of Methodist congregations and churches were formed to serve the German population of the area. The first was appropriately named the **First German Methodist Episcopal Church.** German Methodists from Cincinnati established a small mission chapel on rented ground on Melicerte (now Erato) Street in 1840. The first Methodist church moved in 1858 to Dryades Street, just below the City of Lafayette. German was used until 1887, when the younger generation demanded the use of English. The church functioned until 1906, when the building was sold. In 1846 another Methodist congregation was formed by Rev. Carl Bremer, the pastor of this first Methodist congregation. It became known as the **Piety Street German Methodist Episcopal Church of the South.** In 1871 the congregation of the first Methodist church united with another Methodist group in the Third District to found the **Felicity Street German Methodist Episcopal Church.** A new church was built on Loyola and St. Andrew, which used both German and English until World War I. In 1923 it united with the Napoleon Avenue Methodist Church. Nearby the **Soraparu Street German Methodist Episcopal Church** had been founded in 1853 as the fourth German Methodist church in the New Orleans region. A split in the congregation in 1870 led to the formation of still another Methodist church at Eighth and Laurel streets. German was used in all of these churches until the turn of the century, when English was introduced. Because of World War I and the anti-German acts passed by the Louisiana legislature, all services in German were banned by 1917-18.

German Methodist Episcopal Church of the South. In Carrollton a Methodist congregation was organized in 1845 as a mission by Methodists from Mobile. Until a church was built it met in a shed on the levee, but eventually it built a church in 1859 at Plum and Joliet streets. Because the congregation did not grow, the church went out of existence in 1883.

Third German Methodist Episcopal Church of the North. The Third District German Protestants were first served by a Methodist church established below Canal on Burgundy Street. German was used until 1870, when English was introduced. Both languages were used until the turn of the century, when the congregation united with the English-speaking Moreau Street Church. Before this, in 1874, a split in the congregation had led to the formation of another German Methodist congregation, which built a church on Rampart between Ferdinand and Press streets, known as the Third German Methodist Episcopal Church of the North. The property was sold to an individual in 1900, dissolving the congregation.

Germans of the Catholic faith who immigrated to New Orleans became part of the dominant religion of the area, with allegiance to the pope in Rome. Because the German Catholic churches were all organized under the guidance and supervision of a bishop, they did not experience as much administrative strife as did the Protestant churches. The German Catholic churches shared a common doctrine and liturgy, thus avoiding the disputes and divisions over dogma that plagued the Protestant congregations. Since Catholic churches worldwide held their masses in Latin, the use of German in the liturgy was restricted. In most cases the congregations listened to their homilies and sang their familiar hymns in their native language until the turn of the century. With the reforms of the Second Vatican Council in the 1960s English was introduced as the language of the mass.

St. Mary's Assumption German Catholic Church. Perhaps the most widely known German Catholic church was located in the City of Lafayette. Its charter dated back to 1836, but only eight years later, in 1843, did a priest from the German Redemptorist order arrive to minister to the many German-speaking Catholic immigrants who had settled there. In the beginning, on Sundays Fr. Peter Tschackert (Czackert) rented *Kaiserhalle,* a popular dancehall, which his followers converted late each Saturday night into a makeshift chapel. There he could offer

St. Mary's Assumption German Catholic Church, 1860, Constance and Josephine streets. *Courtesy of a private collection.*

catechism classes and religious instruction in German and gradually built a German Catholic congregation. In 1844 the first German Catholic church in the state of Louisiana was built, a modest frame structure, which was named St. Mary's Assumption Church. It served the congregation for a decade and a half until a much more pretentious church was built on Josephine Street next to the original church. The entire congregation of St. Mary's worked alongside the Redemptorist fathers in building the new church. A plaque today describes how the women parishioners carried bricks in their aprons to the building site. The church was built in modified baroque style with a gilded, domed bell tower that can still be seen throughout the area. The four great bells, together weighing 4,000 pounds, still fill the neighborhood with their melodious sounds. Through the years the interior was embellished to match the graceful exterior. Still today one can view the beautiful stained-glass windows, great organ, and high altar made in Munich, Germany, one of the finest examples of woodcarving in the country. The Redemptorist fathers of St. Mary's continued its German heritage throughout the decades, offering at least one sermon in German on Sundays until 1917 and the advent of World War I.

Holy Trinity German Catholic Church. The Catholics in the Third District below Canal Street were served by Holy Trinity German Catholic Church, a small frame structure erected in 1847 on the corner of St. Ferdinand and Dauphine streets. Within three years, however, it burned to the ground, a victim of a rancorous dispute over ownership and authority among the priest, archbishop, and congregation. A new church was built the next year, and the parish soon developed into one of the most important in the city. Much of this success could be credited to the initiative of a young German priest, Fr. Peter Leonhard Thevis from Cologne. He arrived in 1867 and became pastor the next year, serving the parish for twenty-five years. Holy Trinity held regular German services up to 1917 and thereafter on high-feast days, with the exception of the war years.

St. Boniface German Catholic Church. Through the years Holy Trinity had seen its congregation spread toward Lake Pontchartrain. Since the distances had become great and the roads were bad, it became increasingly hard for the Germans in the outlying sections to attend services. In 1869 St. Boniface German Catholic Church was established at Galvez and LaHarpe streets for those Germans in what became a separate parish. Sermons were given in German until 1917, when the parish was discontinued. The congregation moved to St. Bernard Avenue, where it established the Church of Our Lady of the Sacred Heart.

Mater Dolorosa German Catholic Church. The first Catholic congregation that formed in Carrollton in 1847 at first met in a private home. The next year a parish was formed and a church built, called Nativity of the Blessed Virgin Mary or St. Mary's Nativity. Because the preaching was offered only in German, the French- and English-speaking parishioners became so agitated that they threatened to burn down the church. This resulted in masses being said in all three languages until 1870, when the Franco-Prussian War broke out in Europe. Filled with patriotic loyalty, the Germans of Carrollton turned against their French neighbors and demanded a separate church, which was built across Cambronne Street from the original structure. It received its own German priest and a new name, Mater Dolorosa German Catholic Church. This left the old church to the French, and both existed side by side until 1898, when the archbishop appointed Fr. Francis Prim to unite the two churches. From that time on services were offered in English only. The present church was built in 1909 at Carrollton Avenue and Plum Street.

St. Henry's German Catholic Church. In 1856 St. Henry's Church was established by the Lazarist Fathers on Berlin Street (now General Pershing) between Magazine and Constance streets. This church served the Germans of Jefferson City, an area that developed as an upriver expansion of the City of Lafayette. Lacking a priest, the church was closed in 1871 for a brief period until a secular German-speaking pastor was obtained, Rev. J. B. Bogaerts. In 1911 the national character of the parish was cancelled by Archbishop Blenk, opening the congregation to all Catholics, not just those of German stock.

Gates of Mercy Synagogue. Through the years a number of congregations and synagogues were formed by German-Jewish immigrants in addition to the many Catholic and Protestant congregations and churches. In the 1840s heavy immigration from the German states included a number of Jews, many of whom settled among their compatriots. Within that decade over two hundred German Jews had affiliated with the Gates of Mercy Synagogue, established in 1828 on Rampart Street. A large number of Jewish immigrants from South America and the Caribbean necessitated a second congregation, the Dispersed of Judah, which was formed in 1846. It followed the Portuguese ritual and was given its own synagogue at Bourbon and Canal streets by Judah Touro. In 1882 these congregations finally merged to form Touro Synagogue, first located on Carondelet Street. A decade later a beautiful structure on St. Charles Avenue was built under the leadership of Rabbi J. L Leucht from Darmstadt, Germany.

Gates of Prayer Synagogue. In the City of Lafayette the German Jews formed a congregation in 1847 known as the Gates of Prayer. After being located in a rented house on Jackson Avenue and later a two-room structure purchased in 1855, the congregation acquired a building site at Jackson and Chippewa streets. There a synagogue was erected in 1867 by the congregation, which later moved to a temple on Napoleon Avenue and finally, in 1975, built a large synagogue in Metairie.

Temple Sinai. The Reform movement in Judaism of the 1860s was soon embraced by a part of the Gates of Prayer congregation, which broke away in 1870. It then built its own synagogue, Temple Sinai, located on the corner of Calhoun Street and St. Charles Avenue. This congregation was led by a German rabbi, James K. Gutheim, who had come from Westphalia in 1849 to serve the German-Jewish congregation in the downtown area.

By the mid-1870s second-generation German-Americans were exerting their influence in the various houses of worship. These more acculturated young people saw no reason to continue the German language in services. Every German church had to introduce English, although German remained the official language. Those that were slow to do so saw a noticeable decline in attendance or suffered a split in the congregation.

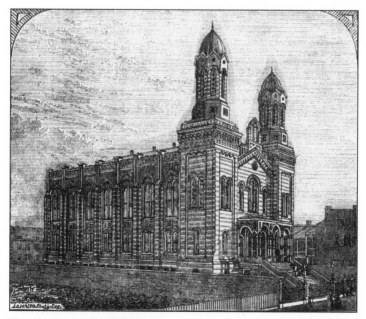

Temple Sinai, ca. 1870 (now demolished), from *Waldo's New Orleans Illustrated Visitor's Guide. Courtesy of Touro Infirmary Archives.*

By 1914 half of the German churches had discontinued their German services altogether, while the other half had become bilingual. It was not until World War I and the draconian laws forbidding all things German that the language completely disappeared from the former German churches of the city. The many churches that had retained German in their official designations changed their names to denote their new, nonethnic nature. Today German can be heard only in the monthly services held in the former St. Matthew German Evangelical Church in Carrollton, now the St. Matthew United Church of Christ.

The following section presents a compilation of information on the German churches, congregations, and synagogues in the New Orleans region. The dates 1818 through 1961 mark the beginning and end of the period of their establishment in this area. Historically these churches maintained their ethnic identity, if not the German language, and continued to function until 1970. The criteria used to determine the Germanic origin of each church were historical and linguistic. However brief their existence, the churches listed were known to be have been founded by Germans or to have used the German language in their services or instruction. Most also had German-language schools that taught the children in their native tongue for most subjects or for part of the day.

Many more German congregations are listed in the first section than are mentioned in the preceding essay, which lists only the most important. The second section lists German congregations and their houses of worship in Louisiana outside the New Orleans region. The next section lists New Orleans area churches and synagogues that were originally German and are currently still in use. Most are well known in the area for their historic and aesthetic value. The table is arranged chronologically by the founding date (*estab.*) of each congregation and/or the original building, followed by the date of the present structure (*struct.*). The name, address, architect and/or contractor, notes, and sources follow. Finally the convents built specifically for German nuns, and their locations, are listed by date of founding.

German Churches, Synagogues, and Congregations Established in the New Orleans Area from 1818 to 1961

Date	Church	Location	Denomination
1818	**First Protestant Church**	Clio between	Evangelical
1825	**Congregation;** became First	Carondelet and	
	Evangelical Church (Clio Street	St. Charles	
	Church); later became First Trinity	119 N. Murat Street	United Church
	Evangelical United Church of Christ		of Christ

1828 Gates of Mercy Synagogue;	Rampart Street	Jewish
1882 Merged with Touro Synagogue	Carondelet Street and St. Charles	
1840 First German Methodist	Erato Street between	Methodist
1906 **Episcopal Church;** renamed Franklin Street Methodist Church	Camp and Magazine	
1840 German Orthodox Congregation of Lafayette	Constance and Race	Evangelical
1846 Disbanded		
1842 German Orthodox Evangelical Church of New Orleans	Burgundy and Port	Evangelical
1848 Renamed St. Paul's German Lutheran Evangelical Church		
1842 United Christian Church	Dumaine Street	Independent
? No church was ever built; congregation met in engine house of (German) Louisiana Fire Co. #10		
1843 St. Mary's Assumption German Catholic Church	Josephine between Constance and Laurel	Catholic
1845 German Methodist Episcopal Mission of the South in Carrollton	Levee Street	Methodist
1859 Built church	Plum and Joliet	
1923 Became Napoleon Avenue Church	Napoleon Avenue	
1846 Craps/Piety Street German Methodist Episcopal Church Established as Second German	Craps, formerly Piety Street Union Street	Methodist
1858 Methodist Mission; burned down Rejoined Piety Street Church		
1985 Became Trinity United Methodist Church	2221 Filmore Street	
1846 German Evangelical Church and	Philip and Chippewa	Evangelical
1876 Congregation in Lafayette; became Jackson Avenue Evangelical Church	Jackson and Chippewa	
1846 St. Matthew German Evangelical Church and Congregation in Carrollton	Zimple between Monroe and Leonidas	Evangelical

1847	**Holy Trinity German Catholic**	St. Ferdinand	Catholic
1997	**Church;** closed; congregation	between Dauphine	
	joined St. Vincent de Paul Church	and Royal	

1848	**Mater Dolorosa German Catholic**	Cambronne between	Catholic
	Church; estab. as Holy Trinity	Maple and Burthe	
	German Catholic Church		
1871	German congregation left and built	South Carrollton	
1899	present church; renamed Mater	and Plum	
	Dolorosa Church		

1848	**Zion German Evangelical-**	Euterpe between	Evangelical-
	Lutheran Church	Baronne and Dryades	Lutheran
1871	Renamed Zion Lutheran Church	1924 St. Charles Ave.	

1850	**Gates of Prayer Synagogue**	Jackson Avenue	Jewish
1975		400 West Esplanade	
		Metairie	

1850	**Danish-German Evangelical-**	Elmira, Chestnut,	Lutheran-
	Lutheran Church of Algiers	Alix, and Eliza	Evangelical
1865	Church and land sold at sheriff's sale		

1852	**St. John's German Evangelical-**	Iberville and	Evangelical-
	Lutheran Church	Prieur	Lutheran
	Renamed St. John Lutheran Church	3937 Canal Street	Lutheran

| 1853 | **Free Evangelical Congregation** | Front/Levee between | Evangelical |
| | Disbanded same year | Port and St. Ferdinand | |

1853	**Soraparu Street German**	Soraparu between	Methodist
	Methodist Episcopal Church	Chippewa and	
	of the South	Annunciation	
1893	Disbanded		

| 1853 | **United Disciples of Christ** | Sixth between Laurel | Presbyterian |
| 1867 | Disbanded | and Annunciation | |

1854	**Bethlehem German Evangelical-**	Felicity Street	Evangelical
	Lutheran Church		
	(Kleinhagen's Church)		
1889	Disbanded		

| 1854 | **First German Presbyterian** | First and Laurel | Presbyterian |

Church of New Orleans; became
First Street Presbyterian Church
1983 Disbanded

1855	**German-English Baptist Church**	Coliseum Place	Baptist
1866	Disbanded		

1855	**Otto's Church** and Congregation	Madison near Third	Evangelical
	Became St. Matthew's	1333 S. Carrollton	United Church of Christ

1855	**Pastor Enrat Berger's**	Odd Fellows Hall	?
	Humanity Congregation	Camp and Lafayette	
1857	Disbanded		

1856	**St. Henry's Church**	Gen. Pershing between Magazine and Constance	Catholic

1857	**German Emmanuel Mission**	Rampart and	Episcopal
	of the Episcopal Church	Bienville	
1862	Disbanded		

1858	**Marais Street Mission** of the	Marais between	Methodist
	Methodist Church of New Orleans	Conti and St. Claude	
	Disbanded same year		

1859	**St. Joseph Church**	Lavoisier and Sixth	Catholic
	(German-English Parish)	Gretna	

1864	**Second German Presbyterian**	St. Roch between N.	Presbyterian
	Church of New Orleans	Claiborne and N. Rampart	
1867	Became Claiborne Avenue	Morrison Road	
	Presbyterian Church		

1866	**Milan Street German**	Milan and Camp	Evangelical
	Evangelical-Lutheran Church		
	Formerly First German Evangelical		
	Church of the Sixth District		United Church
1903	Renamed Salem United Church of Christ		of Christ

1866	**Salem German Evangelical-**		Lutheran
	Lutheran Congregation in		
	Gretna		
1871	Affiliated with German Evangelical	?	Presbyterian

	Presbyterian Church of the North		
1872	Church erected	418 Fourth Street	
1867	**St. Thomas Church**	Rampart and	Catholic
1871	Disbanded	Bienville streets	
1868	**Felicity Street German Methodist Episcopal Congregation** of the North	Loyola and St. Andrew	Methodist
1871	Church built		
	Became Felicity United Methodist Church	1816 Chestnut	
1869	**St. Boniface German Catholic Church**	Lapeyrouse and Galvez	Catholic
1917	Merged with Our Lady of Sacred Heart		
1963	Closed; congregation joined Corpus Christi Church		
1870	**German Northern Presbyterian Church** of Algiers	?	Presbyterian
1871	Disbanded		
1870	**Second German Methodist Episcopal Church** of the North	Eighth and Laurel	Methodist
1870	**Temple Sinai**	6227 St. Charles Avenue	Jewish
1872	**Touro Synagogue**	4238 St. Charles Avenue	Jewish
1874	**Third German Methodist Episcopal Church** of the North	Rampart between St. Ferdinand and Press	Methodist
1900	Disbanded		
1875	**German Evangelical-Lutheran Trinity Church**	Olivier and Eliza	Evangelical
	Became Trinity Lutheran Church of Algiers	624 Eliza Street	Lutheran
1877	**Emmanuel German Presbyterian Church** of the North	Camp and Soniat	Presbyterian
1880	Sold to German Presbyterian Immanuel Congregation		
1900 ca.	Disbanded		

1879 Pastor Perpeet's Protestant Congregation 1887 Disbanded	N. Derbigny between Iberville and Bienville	Evangelical
1881 Emmanuel German Evangelical-Lutheran Church Became Emmanuel Lutheran Church 1990 Merged with Grace Lutheran Evangelical Church (daughter church)	St. Louis and Prieur N. Broad and Iberville Canal Boulevard	Evangelical
1897 St. Cecilia Catholic Church	N. Rampart	Catholic
1926 Trinity Evangelical United Church of Christ; merged with First Evangelical United Church of Christ to form First Trinity Evangelical United Church of Christ	N. Pierce 119 N. Murat	Evangelical United Church of Christ
1961 St. John Evangelical Church 1970 Disbanded	Joliet Street	Evangelical

German Churches Outside of the New Orleans Area

Date	Church	Location	Denomination	Parish
1859	**German Methodist Episcopal Church** of the South	Franklin	Methodist-Episcopal	St. Mary
1874	**German Methodist Episcopal Church** of the South United with English congregation in 1884	Lake Charles	Methodist-Episcopal	Calcasieu
1880	**St. Leo German Catholic Church** Colony settled through efforts of Father Thevis of Holy Trinity Church in New Orleans	Roberts Cove	Catholic	Acadia
1881	**German Methodist Episcopal Church** of the South Area settled by Father Bueto; depending on language of pastor services fluctuated between English and German	Buetoville near Clinton	Methodist-Episcopal	East Feliciana
1887	**First German Evangelical Lutheran St. John Congregation** Pastored by Rev. Paul Roesner from Zion Lutheran Church in New Orleans	Lake Charles	Evangelical-Lutheran	Calcasieu

1887 German Evangelical-   Clinton   Evangelical-   East
        Lutheran Church   Lutheran   Feliciana
Carl Nierman was first pastor; in 1893 Lutheran missions proposed for Ponchatoula
in Tangipahoa Parish

1888 German Catholic   Carmel   Catholic   De Soto
        Carmelite Order
Order purchased land in Tangipahoa Parish; Fr. Athanasius Peters from Marienfeld,
Tex., became prior; later Benedictines of St. Meinrad Abbey purchased same land;
rock chapel at Carmel completed in 1891, giving evidence of success of Carmelite
mission

1889 German Benedictine   Gessen   Catholic   Tangipahoa
        St. Joseph Priory
Fr. Luke Gruwe of St. Meinrad Abbey first prior; others included Brother Kilian
Gessner, Brother Thaddeus Hoelzle, Brother Mathaeus Stamm, and Ludwig Lex,
relative of Father Koegerl of St. Boniface Church in New Orleans; moved near
Covington to place named St. Benedict

1894 First Lutheran Church   Crowley   Lutheran   Acadia

1895 Holy Cross Catholic Church Frenier   Catholic   Tangipahoa
Church begun by Benedictine monk, Fr. Leander Roth

1927 St. John Lutheran Church   Iota   Lutheran   Acadia

German Churches and Synagogues Today

estab. struct.

1840 1889 **St. Paul's Lutheran Church**
            Burgundy and Port streets
            Architects and builders: Charles Lewis Hillger and William Drews
            Earliest building lost to fire in 1860; second building erected same
            year, lost to another fire; third building erected, currently in use
            Architecture IV

1844 1999 **St. Mary's Chapel**
            Jackson Avenue between St. Charles Avenue and Prytania Street
            Originally named Church of Our Lady of the Assumption; later called
            St. Mary's Assumption
            Calvert; Gurtner

1844 1860 **St. Mary's Assumption Church**
            Josephine between Constance and Laurel streets

Architect: attributed to Albert Diettel
Finest example of German baroque architecture in New Orleans
Calvert; Gurtner

1847 1853 **Holy Trinity Church**
721 St. Ferdinand between Dauphine and Royal streets
Architects: T. E. Giraud and Larr (or Loisy)
Last national Catholic church to survive; closed March 29, 1997;
congregation transferred to St. Vincent de Paul Church on
Dauphine Street
Calvert; Gurtner

1847 1908 **Mater Dolorosa Church**
South Carrollton Avenue and Plum Street
Architect: Theodore Brune
Originally called St. Mary's Nativity Church
Calvert; Gurtner

1847 1909 **St. Matthew United Church of Christ**
South Carrollton Avenue and Willow Street
Architect: William Drago; builder: J. A. Petty
German-language church service held on first Sunday of month
Deiler, Churches; Calvert

1848 1871 **Zion Lutheran Church**
1924 St. Charles Avenue and St. Mary Street
Architect: Charles Lewis Hillger
Irvin

1853 1924 **St. John Evangelical-Lutheran Church**
Iberville and Prieur streets
Architect: Samuel Stone, Jr.
Deiler, Churches

1855 1925 **St. Henry Church**
General Pershing and Constance streets
Architects: Diboll and Owens; contractor: Lionel Favret
Originally German national Catholic church; became parochial
in early twentieth century
Architecture VII; Calvert; Gurtner

1857 1926 **St. Joseph Church**
610 Sixth Street, Gretna

Architect: William Richard Burk; contractor: Joseph Fromherz
Spanish baroque style
Calvert; Swanson; Gurtner

1858 1876 **Jackson Avenue Evangelical Church**
Jackson Avenue and Chippewa Street
Architect: Charles Lewis Hillger
Irvin

1862 1906 **Salem United Church of Christ**
4212 Camp Street, corner of Milan Street
Architects: Diboll and Owens; contractor and builder: James
Petty
Architecture VII

1872   **Salem German Evangelical-Lutheran Church**
418 Fourth Street, Gretna
Originally the German Evangelical Presbyterian Church of the
North; formed Evangelical Protestant German Congregation in
1866
Deiler, Churches

1872 1909 **Touro Synagogue**
St. Charles Avenue and General Pershing Street
Architect: Emile Weil; contractor: Jacob K. Newman
Established as Gates of Mercy (Shangarai Chassed) using
Ashkenazi (German) rite; in 1881 amalgamated with Sephardic
(Spanish and Portuguese) congregation, the Dispersed of Judah
(Linfuzoth Yehudah); became the Gates of Mercy of the
Dispersed of Judah; renamed Touro Synagogue by Rabbi Isaac
Leucht in 1937
Architecture VII

1874 1876 **St. Roch's Shrine (Chapel)**
1725 St. Roch Avenue
Built by Fr. P. Leonhard Thevis of Holy Trinity Church
Calvert

1875 1911 **Evangelical-Lutheran Trinity Church**
624 Eliza Street, Algiers
Affiliate of St. John's Church, Iberville Street, New Orleans
Deiler, Churches

1889 1932 **St. Joseph Abbey Church**
St. Benedict, La.
Architect: Theodore Brune
Founded by Benedictines from St. Meinrad Abbey, Indiana
Calvert

Convents Built for German Nuns

1856 **Convent of the School Sisters of Notre Dame**
Josephine and Constance streets
Fr. Thaddeus Anwander, Redemptorist rector, purchased two-story building

1873 **Convent of St. Boniface**
Lapeyrouse Street between North Miro and North Tonti streets

1870s **Convent of the Sisters of Christian Charity**
Constance Street between General Pershing and Milan streets
Now Stella Maris Maritime Center

1870s **Convent of the Benedictine Nuns**
Dauphine Street between St. Ferdinand and Press streets

1881 **Convent of the Redemptorists** (and rectory for the priests)
Constance between St. Andrew and Josephine streets

1899 **Convent of the Sisters of Perpetual Adoration**
2321 Marais Street
Later called Convent of the Most Holy Sacrament; nuns operated St. Agnes Academy, the last wing of which was built in 1907; these nuns also served at Infant Jesus College, 614 Seventh Street, Gretna; they also took over school at Roberts Cove

1902 **Convent of Mater Dolorosa**
Cambronne Street

GERMAN-LANGUAGE SCHOOLS

The first institutions formed by the developing Louisiana German communities were churches, where Sunday school classes were immediately established to teach religion to the children in their own tongue. Soon the churches formed schools where all subjects were taught in the German language. In the New Orleans area German schools were first

Schoolchildren giving a German May Day performance, from *Harper's Weekly*, 1866. *Courtesy of a private collection.*

Schoolchildren's Mardi Gras float, "Coming of the Germans," ca. 1930, from the Frank Collection. *Courtesy of the Historic New Orleans Collection.*

established in the Third District. The heavily German cities of Lafayette and Carrollton, several smaller sections of New Orleans, plus Gretna and Algiers on the West Bank soon followed suit. German schools continued in operation throughout the Civil War and Reconstruction. After the war there was an increase in enrollment in all parochial and private schools, including those teaching only in the German language. This increase was due to Negroes being admitted to the public schools, resulting in white families sending their children elsewhere.

For years the German communities of New Orleans had lobbied to replace French with German in the public schools. It was not until 1910 that their efforts to introduce German were successful. The New Orleans school board mandated that German be taught in all public high schools, while elementary schools were required to offer German as an afternoon option. Only in 1917, with the onset of World War I and the passage of laws prohibiting the use of the language, did German disappear from Louisiana schools. From 1931 through 1938, German was reinstated but banned again during World War II. After the war German was once again introduced into many of the public, private, and parochial high schools in the state. German is still taught in several public, private, and parochial secondary schools in New Orleans, in a number of public high schools in the larger cities, and in most of the colleges of the state.

In New Orleans the first German elementary school, St. Paul's Lutheran School, was founded in 1840 in the Third District, a suburb also known as *Faubourg des Allemands* (the German suburb). This was a year before the establishment of the free public school system in New Orleans. Soon German-language high schools were formed, not only as part of the parochial system but also as private, nonsectarian institutions. Perhaps the best known of these was the Ueber School, operated by Johann and Jacob Ueber, two brothers from the Rhineland. This private school functioned in the Third District for over fifty years. In higher education German was introduced as early as the 1850s. The University of Louisiana, later renamed Tulane University, was the first to offer instruction in the German language, two years of which were required for all graduates.

In 1880 J. Hanno Deiler took a census of the German-language schools of New Orleans, counting 3,005 children in attendance. Deiler estimated that an additional 1,300 children were studying German in the parochial and private elementary schools, high schools, and colleges.

These numbers did not include the German Methodist and Presbyterian Sunday schools in the city where religious instruction was given in German.

In the 1880s, the same time period when Deiler took his census, new towns were developing in many areas throughout Louisiana. A number of these towns were established by German immigrants, becoming thriving communities with their own churches, schools, and industries. Soon after the turn of the century, however, the population of these towns became more diversified, losing the need for the German language. The first German-language school in Louisiana, however, was established fifty years earlier than these new towns. In the 1830s the German Presbyterian Church established a German-language school at Pine Grove in West St. Tammany Parish. This school also predated the first German-language school established in New Orleans, the population center of the state.

German Education in the New Orleans Parochial Schools

The first German-language schools to be established were the parochial schools. These parochial schools of the past furnished an alternative to the public school system and enjoyed a larger attendance. They differed from their counterparts in requiring a knowledge of German as well as adherence to the faith of the churches that established them. Their founders were German immigrants who had little opportunity to learn the English language. They conversed in German at home, their pastors and teachers were German born, and they expected their children and children's children to continue to use the German tongue. They struggled mightily to maintain their parochial schools in order to preserve their language and culture. Between the years 1840 and 1856 almost all denominations had succeeded in establishing at least one school.

Lutheran Schools

The Lutheran parochial schools were the most numerous of the German-language schools, even exceeding the number of Catholic schools. Most of the textbooks used in these schools were recommended by the Missouri Synod and published by the Concordia Press located in that state. Since these books corresponded to those being used in the public schools in New Orleans, students from the Lutheran elementary schools could enter the public school system at any point.

Qualified teachers, most of whom were trained in Northern synodical schools, were reluctant to accept positions in New Orleans because of the climate and the yellow-fever epidemics. A second difficulty resulted from individual Lutheran churches and their schools not being affiliated with a synod. These independent churches and schools cherished their self-government but offered prospective teachers no retention guarantees. Difficulties in securing teachers from other cities were shared by all of the parochial schools.

St. Paul's German Evangelical-Lutheran School. The oldest German parochial school in New Orleans, a Christian day school, was sponsored by the congregation of St. Paul's Lutheran Church. St. Paul's was established in 1840 by Pastor Christian Sans, who first began German services and school instruction in an empty fire-engine house in the Third District. At the same time he established a congregation and school at Race and Constance streets for the many German families in the City of Lafayette. When the engine house in the Third District was sold in 1843, the congregation built a church and school on the corner of Port and Burgundy. They hired Johann and Jacob Ueber as the first teachers. Including the pupils from both of these Lutheran schools, attendance grew rapidly to over three hundred children. When the Ueber brothers resigned to begin their own school, however, the community had great difficulty in finding qualified replacements. Nevertheless the school in the Third District continued to thrive despite many subsequent changes in pastors and teachers. After the church joined the Missouri Synod in 1870, it could then obtain teachers from the Lutheran teacher-training seminaries in the North and Midwest. The use of the German language in the school continued until 1893, when German became limited to religious instruction. The school was closed in 1900, and, within a few years, the church limited German services to Sundays and church holidays. By 1917 services were held in German only twice a month and on special occasions. With the outbreak of World War I, these were discontinued.

Zion German Evangelical-Lutheran School. In mid-June of 1853 the board of the Lutheran Zion Church decided to establish a Christian day school for the children of the City of Lafayette. After failing to persuade the congregation of St. John's Lutheran Church to join in the effort, Zion established its own school in 1854, initially located in an addition to the church on Euterpe Street. The sudden death of the rector at this time required the appointment of a new pastor, who had to take charge of the school until a teacher could be found. Attendance soon reached almost 100 children, requiring a two-room school, built in 1866 on Loyola near Jackson Avenue. Because the congregation was spread over a wide area, an additional school nearer the river was needed. In 1869 a building was erected at Chippewa and Fourth streets and two teachers were hired. By 1870 the schools of the Zion congregation were fully attended and much constructive work was done. The Chippewa school enrollment grew so rapidly that several increases in the teaching staff were needed. By 1886 it had an enrollment of 145 students and had outgrown its quarters. A school society was organized by the Zion members to maintain and enlarge the two schools and to begin kindergartens in each. However, the overcrowding along with a shortage of funds forced the abandonment of this very successful kindergarten system within a few years. By 1890 the attendance at both schools had begun to decrease, so the congregation decided to build a central school, thus eliminating the need for some of the teachers. A new school on Carondelet Street was built in 1894, and both of the older schools were closed. By the end of that school year 138 children were in attendance. Financial difficulties, which had begun earlier, grew worse so that the board could afford to pay only three teachers. The result was a drop in attendance, as many of the children entered public schools to avoid the overcrowding. The pastor then took charge of the lower grades but found that he was unable to do both school and pastoral work. Consequently the congregation reduced the school to two rooms. Due to the lack of teachers and crowded conditions, the enrollment by 1898 dropped to 60 pupils. In 1901 the school was closed but reopened in 1909. However, no German instruction was offered.

St. John's Evangelical-Lutheran School. This became the third German-language school organized by a Louisiana Lutheran church congregation. After refusing to join in Zion's educational efforts, it founded its own Christian day school in 1854 in a cottage at Iberville and Prieur streets. It proved to be impossible to get a competent teacher until the congregation joined the Missouri Synod in early 1857. The capable leadership of the teacher hired, a Mr. Koehnke, caused such an increase in attendance that the school cottage soon became inadequate. A lot on Johnson Street between Iberville and Bienville streets was purchased, where a new and larger school was constructed. From 1858 until 1870 there was a continuous, almost yearly change of teachers while the enrollment increased so much that another room had to be added to the school. By the end of the 1870s, however, financial difficulties developed. Only one teacher could be afforded, who had to take

Children of St. John's Evangelical-Lutheran School, 1903. *Courtesy of the Historic New Orleans Collection.*

over the instruction of all grades, together over a hundred pupils. Until 1903 religious instruction in the school as well as some schoolwork was given in the German language. This continued until the 1917-18 term, when all teaching in German was discontinued.

The Emmanuel German Lutheran School. This school was established by the Evangelical-Lutheran Church of the Ohio Synod. In 1883 it built a school with three large rooms at St. Louis and Prieur streets. The enrollment was about 120 students, who were taught by two synod-trained teachers. A third was soon added, but the school was forced to close in 1892 because of low enrollment. It was reopened by demand in 1899 but closed again two years later because of poor attendance.

The Evangelical-Lutheran Trinity School. The Algiers Evangelical-Lutheran Trinity congregation hired a teacher for its Christian day school before it engaged a resident pastor. Upon its founding in 1875 a teacher was sought who would also be able to conduct services in the church. Although the enrollment was small throughout the history of the school, it steadily increased until two teachers had to be secured. The school was closed sometime before 1917. When it reopened with four grades in 1925, no German was taught.

The Salem German Evangelical-Lutheran School. The Salem German Evangelical-Lutheran Congregation in Gretna was established in 1866, but it had no special school building until 1877, when a German-English school was founded. The pastor taught in German in the morning; subjects were taught in English in the afternoon. German teaching lasted at least through 1897, German catechism instruction was continued through 1898, and some German services were held in the church until 1917.

Other Evangelical Schools

The German-American Elementary School (Rooster Church); **the Otto German Evangelical Protestant School.** Two Protestant schools emerged in Carrollton to serve the many German children of the community. In 1846 the first German Protestant church in Carrollton was organized by the congregation of St. Matthew German Evangelical Church. It was commonly known as the Rooster Church because of the weathercock on its roof. As early as 1856 children of the congregation were instructed in German either by the pastor or German-speaking teachers. In 1873, a new school building was erected at Madison and Third streets. At first the supervision of the schoolwork was left to the pastor, but because frequent disputes arose between him and the teacher, a board was created to manage the school. Almost twenty years earlier, in 1854, there had been a division in the church congregation, and a second church had been established, named the Otto Church after its first pastor, Martin Otto. In 1871 this church established a second Protestant school, the Otto School, located on Burthe Street between Dublin and Madison. Only one teacher was hired for an enrollment of over a hundred students. In 1884 the two Protestant congregations reunited and retained the Rooster Church school, while the Otto school building was sold. The school board set up ten years earlier was also retained and charged with preserving "the precious inheritance of the German language . . . for future generations." German was used for all religious instruction, while academic subjects were taught in English. The school flourished until 1892, when it was closed and the seventy-five pupils transferred to the public schools.

The Evangelical Protestant German-American School. The German Evangelical Protestant Church on Jackson Avenue was founded in 1846 to serve the Germans of the City of Lafayette. Ten years later the congregation established a parochial school, which flourished from 1856 until 1892 on property adjoining the church. The school hired four teachers, each having two or three classes in one room. Sometimes the pastor also had to undertake teaching within the school. Most of the German students did not go any further than elementary school, but those who entered public high school were well prepared. The use of the German language was continued for the congregation until the death of the last German-speaking pastor in 1901.

First Evangelical Church School. Little is known about this school on Clio Street other than it was established by Rev A. H. Becker in 1859. The congregation of the Clio Street church was the first Protestant religious group to be founded in New Orleans, dating back to 1818. Like the Evangelical church on Milan Street it eventually joined the Evangelical Synod of North America. J. Hanno Deiler listed it as having a student population of eighty-seven in his census of the German schools of New Orleans in 1880. In 1896 the school was discontinued for financial reasons.

The First German Evangelical School of the Sixth District. The First Evangelical Church on Milan Street in Jefferson City was established in 1866. It was not until five years later that a parochial school was needed to serve the German immigrants who continued to settle upriver from the City of Lafayette. In 1872 the congregation decided to build a schoolhouse, which used German as the language of instruction until 1886. At this time the pastor of the church introduced English into the school as well as the church services. By 1900 German was no longer used in either the grade school or the Sunday school.

Presbyterian Schools

The First Street German Presbyterian School of New Orleans. This school was established in 1854 in the former City of Lafayette at First and Laurel streets on the same property as the church. In 1866 the congregation erected a spacious new school building on Sixth Street between Laurel and Annunciation streets. There classes were conducted in German and English until 1883. The last teachers, who later married, were Rev. Louis Voss and Miss Irene Gaschen. This school was the first of all the German-language schools to close its doors.

The Claiborne Avenue Presbyterian School. This school built in 1868 was also used for worship for two years until the congregation erected the Second German Presbyterian Church of New Orleans as an addition to the school. From this point until 1890 German was used in the school in the morning and English in the afternoon. The textbooks were similar to those used in the Lutheran schools. The attendance per year ranged between fifty and sixty children until the school closed in 1896.

Catholic Schools

St. Mary's School for the Germans. To serve the heavily German Catholic community of the City of Lafayette, a parochial school was started in 1848 at Constance and St. Andrew streets. Fr. Peter Tschackert (Czackert), the Redemptorist priest of St. Mary's Assumption German Catholic Church, rented a room for the school in the residence of one of the church's trustees. In 1854 a three-story brick building adjoining the church was completed and opened as a German schoolhouse. Initially it was used as a girls' school but later expanded to include a school for boys. The rector of St. Mary's applied to the School Sisters of Notre Dame in Wisconsin for nuns to take charge of the *St. Marien Schule fuer die Deutschen* (St. Mary's School for the Germans). One hundred and fifty girls attended on the first day, who were classified by grades that corresponded to the public school system. In 1869 the Brothers of Mary sent a corps of Marist teachers to New Orleans to take charge of the German boys' upper school, assisted by the Redemptorist fathers of the church. The Notre Dame sisters then took over the grammar school. There were seven levels, usually completed when the students were about fifteen years old. The use of the German language was encouraged at all times on the playground and in the classroom. Merits were given to those who went through the day without speaking a word of English. Those possessing the most merits went to the head of the class. A final examination was held each year for the students before an audience of parents and teachers. By 1880 St. Mary's School had 850 students enrolled and was a great source of pride for the fathers, brothers, and sisters teaching there. The use of German for instruction was discontinued around 1910, and the school was demolished in 1923.

Holy Trinity German Catholic School. Another parochial school using the German language was established in 1871 by Rev. Peter

Leonhard Thevis, pastor of Holy Trinity Church. Lay teachers served in this school in the Third District until Benedictine Sisters took charge. German was used until World War I .

St. Henry's German Catholic School. In 1873 St. Henry's Church organized a small parochial German-language school. The teachers belonged to the Sisters of Christian Charity, an order founded in the German states in 1849. German was used in teaching nearly all subjects from 1873 until 1900, after which German reading was taught as an elective subject for about five years.

German Catholic School. There is very little known about this school in Carrollton, which was established in 1872. The first teacher was Alois Deiler, who had immigrated to New Orleans with his brother, J. Hanno Deiler. In 1882 the schoolhouse was uprooted and flung across the street by a tornado. Fortunately, the school was not in operation at the time, and there were no casualties. It was closed in 1895.

St. Boniface German Catholic School. In 1869 St. Boniface Church was completed as a filial church of Holy Trinity Parish. From the beginning it also served as a school. On weekdays the sanctuary was closed off and the nave was partitioned into classrooms. The pews were used as school benches with writing boards attached by hinges. Two years later a separate schoolhouse was built. J. Hanno Deiler was brought from Munich to teach the upper classes and to act as church organist. The next year Benedictine brothers took over the lower grades. The teaching in German was not discontinued until 1917 with the approach of World War I.

St. Joseph's Catholic School in Gretna was established in 1864 as a German-English school located within the church itself. A teacher from Luxembourg was hired for the twenty-five children who initially enrolled from the heavily German parish. In 1868 a separate schoolhouse was built, which soon required two teachers for an enrollment of 130 children. Lay teachers served in the school until about 1875.

German Education in the New Orleans Orphan Asylums

There was a great need for institutions to take care of the many German children orphaned by the yellow-fever epidemics in New Orleans. Church congregations stepped into this void and established three orphanages specifically for the German children of New Orleans. In these asylums, schools were conducted, which were attended by children in the neighborhood as well as by the inmates. The three asylums were the German Catholic St. Joseph's Orphan Asylum, the

German Protestant Orphan Asylum, and the Bethlehem Orphan Asylum (see chapter 7, "Orphanages and Homes for the Aged").

German Education in the New Orleans Private Schools

A perusal of the city directories of New Orleans and the surrounding suburbs reveals a surprisingly large number of private schools that gave instruction in German. Virtually nothing is known about these schools or the large number of private German teachers not attached to any particular school. Several of these private German-language schools, however, were outstanding and well attended in their day.

The Turnschule. This private school was sponsored by the *Turngemeinde* (Turner's Society), a German men's organization founded in 1849 as a local branch of the national *Turnverein*. As the name implies (turners were gymnasts), the society was dedicated to the development of the body as well as the mind. It provided a well-respected school for the children of its members. During the summer only gymnastics were offered, but during the winter a full range of courses was taught. The use of the German language was fostered in the curriculum, which included history, mathematics, singing, and other foreign languages. The *Turngemeinde* was housed in an impressive building on Lafayette Street, where it could serve the Germans of both the Third and Fourth districts.

The Ueber School. This private, nonsectarian school was established in the Third District by Johann and Jacob Ueber specifically as a German-language school. It continued for over sixty years in the same one-room schoolhouse, gaining renown as far away as New York City. The Ueber brothers, who were from the Rhineland, began their teaching careers in 1840 at St. Paul's German Evangelical-Lutheran School. After a decade they started their own school on North Rampart Street between St. Ferdinand and Port streets. Students of all faiths were admitted, although the principal text used was the Bible. The Ueber School continued year round without summer holidays, with attendance during the winter of about 150 and during the summer of about half that number. School fees were adjusted to the circumstances of the family. Those worthy children who were unable to pay the tuition were offered an education free of charge. By 1890, their fiftieth year as educators, the Ueber brothers had taught more than 3,000 pupils, many of whom later became prominent residents of New Orleans. The brothers continued their school until 1901, which marked the death of Jacob. Johann, however, continued teaching for four more years until he closed the school to enjoy a well-earned retirement.

Mrs. Chapman's (and Mrs. Blake's) **School.** The oldest still-surviving school offering the German language, now known as the Louise S. McGehee School, was first called Mrs. Chapman's School. Then it was conducted as an upper school in a private mansion located in the Garden District at Second and Prytania streets. This school was the only private high school recognized by Newcomb College, which admitted its graduates without examination.

Mrs. E. Matthew's Private Academy; the **Locquet-Leroy New Orleans Female Collegiate Institute.** Several smaller private schools offered German, among them Mrs. E. Matthew's Private Academy for Girls on Josephine Street and the Locquet-Leroy Institute on Camp Street. Both were established in 1872.

German Education in the New Orleans Public Schools

In the early 1850s the German community attempted to establish a public school in the Third District called the German High School. It was administered by a school board as nonsectarian, with no religious instruction offered whatsoever. The school was disbanded during the great yellow-fever epidemic of 1853.

Soon after this attempt, the German community began a drive to replace French with German in the public school curriculum. An editorial in *Die Tägliche Deutsche Zeitung* from 1868 read:

> The Board of School Directors [should] decide to end the teaching of French in the public schools in order to break the influence of the Creole element which has long limited the development of Louisiana. New Orleans is no longer a French colony but rather a part of the American Republic. Hundreds of thousands of local Creoles can no longer speak or understand French. German should be learned, for the knowledge of the German language is at least of equal value for the educated as is French.

It was not until 1910 that German was added to the curriculum of the New Orleans public school system. That year Joseph Reuther, president of the German Society of New Orleans, was elected to the school board. He and Dr. John C. Ransmeier, professor of German at Tulane University, succeeded in establishing German as a regular subject in the public high schools and as an afternoon elective in the grade schools. When German was added as a subject of study, the large public high schools reported up to 10 percent of the student population electing German. Some upper schools offered four levels of German-language training and an extracurricular German Club. Through Dr. Ransmeier's influence the German Society donated suitable German libraries to the various high schools and offered prizes each year for the best work produced by these young German scholars. German was not only taught in the high schools but was also added to the curriculum in the evening schools established for adult learners. Unfortunately, only eight years after German had been introduced in the public schools and was beginning to gain a foothold, anti-German propaganda leading up to World War I caused it to be discontinued.

Just as the introduction of German in the public schools in 1910 was largely due to the efforts of the German Society, so was its reinstatement in 1931 made possible chiefly through the efforts of the *Deutsches Haus,* the successor organization to the German Society. Sigmund Odenheimer, first president of the *Haus,* contributed several thousand dollars to provide teachers of German for two public high schools. The membership of the *Haus* continued to lobby the school board to restore German to the public school curriculum. One member, Rev. Louis Voss, pastor of the First Street German Presbyterian Church, was able to persuade the many German clergymen of the city to support this issue from the pulpit. Pastor Voss also circulated an essay entitled "Why German Should Be Studied" for posting or printing in church bulletins.

With the opening of the Alcée Fortier Boys' High School in 1931, German courses were again offered as a result of pressure from the German community. Approximately 150 students elected the language until the subject was discontinued in 1938. In 1932 German classes sponsored by the *Deutscher Schulverein* (German School Society) were added in several grammar schools as an extracurricular subject. German was also offered to adults in the evening at Warren Easton High School. Again, after being taught for only seven years in various New Orleans schools, German was dropped from the public school curriculum in 1938 with the approach of World War II.

Other German-Language Schools in Louisiana

The Pine Grove German Presbyterian School. The first German-language school in Louisiana was established in the 1830s by the German Presbyterian Church of Pine Grove, West St. Tammany Parish. This school was founded so that the children could continue speaking and learning in their native tongue. A second German language school was established in the same parish at Talisheek in 1848, eleven years after the founding of the colony. There both German and English instruction were given. By 1895 no tuition was charged for half the year. German-English schools had also existed for years in Frenier (Tangipahoa Parish) and Keatchie (De Soto Parish).

The Clinton German-English Lutheran School. In 1871 the town of Clinton in East Feliciana Parish was established by a German pioneer, Friedrich Bueto. An article in the *New Orleans Deutsche Zeitung* in 1895 mentioned Clinton's good German-English school, its capable teachers, and its two churches. The school was organized by a Lutheran congregation about 1878 but discontinued shortly before World War I.

St. Leo's Catholic School. In 1881 a German colony was established in Acadia Parish at what is now called Roberts Cove, known as German Cove until World War I. A wooden schoolhouse was erected in 1883 where the German language was used exclusively. For some time Benedictine Sisters served as teachers in the school, but at the end of their service three lay teachers from a teachers seminary in Germany were brought in. With the onset of World War I the children could no longer be taught in their native tongue. So the school was closed during the war years and the children turned over to the Sisters of the Most Holy Sacrament in Lafayette. The original school was the size of most small-town schools, about fifty children, who were given instruction through the seventh grade. The pupils then attended the public high schools in either Rayne or Crowley. At the turn of the century Crowley also housed a German elementary school, but it ceased to function in 1914 because of insufficient attendance.

St. John's German Evangelical-Lutheran School. In 1887 the Zion Lutheran Church in New Orleans sent a resident missionary to Lake Charles to minister to the large number of German Lutheran settlers there. In 1888 this missionary, Rev. Samuel Hörnicke, was made pastor of St. John's First German Evangelical-Lutheran Congregation. A church was soon built where he could hold services and give religious instruction in German. The church's Sunday school was attended by about forty children. Two years later the congregation built a Lutheran parochial school next to the church. As the first school to be established in Lake Charles, it was attended by children of all faiths. The pastor of the church acted as the teacher in the school and educated the children through the sixth grade. Between 1890 and 1905 the enrollment ran over fifty students, but it later dwindled with the establishment of a public school system in the city. The pupils attending the parochial school could then enter the public high school, where they were able to continue the study of German. As was the case everywhere else, all German teaching was discontinued with the onset of World War I.

German Education at Louisiana Colleges and Universities

The infamous acts passed by the Louisiana legislature in 1918 not only forbade the teaching and speaking of German but also the possession of anything written in German. Such prohibitions were particularly galling at the college level, where academic freedom had always been so highly prized.

Tulane University. The University of Louisiana, which opened in 1847, became known as Tulane University in 1884. As early as 1852, German was included as one of the twelve courses of study offered for the freshman, sophomore, and junior years. J. Hanno Deiler, trained at the Royal Normal College of Munich, was appointed for the 1878-79 term. Professor Deiler taught at Tulane University until 1907 while concurrently teaching at Tulane High School until 1890, when German was discontinued. A graduate course of study was first offered in 1894 and was continued until 1919, when the Acts of the Louisiana Legislature forced the suspension of all German offerings. Courses in German were not resumed until the 1927-28 term.

Newcomb College. This college, opened as the women's college of Tulane University in 1886, offered four years of German instruction from the beginning. Professor Deiler and Rev. Louis Voss both served as instructors until the 1918 term, when German was discontinued. German was not resumed until 1922. Offerings were steadily increased until 1931, when sufficient courses for a major in German literature were available for the first time. The professors and teachers of German at Newcomb College also gave German instruction at Newcomb High School from its opening in 1898 until it closed in 1913.

Louisiana State University. The state university was founded by the legislature in 1855 on land granted by the federal government for the establishment of "a seminary of learning" in Louisiana. Classes were begun in 1860 but were suspended until 1865 because of the Civil War. The university received its present charter in 1871 as the Louisiana State University and Agricultural and Medical College. German instruction was offered from this time on and was required for the bachelor of science, bachelor of philosophy, and master of arts degrees.

Loyola University of New Orleans. This university was established in 1911. German was offered each semester until it was discontinued in 1918. It was not resumed until the 1933-34 term. Students could select German as a major or minor for the bachelor of arts degree.

The draconian acts of the Louisiana legislature in 1918 outlawing all things German doomed the teaching of German in any Louisiana school. Since possession of written German was also illegal, the valuable German library collections of the public high schools and colleges were confiscated. The restoration of German at the college level was not begun until the 1922-23 term at Newcomb College. The legislative acts prohibiting the teaching of German had been repealed only the year before. Tulane followed in 1927, the public schools in 1931, and Loyola in 1933. Only seven years passed, however, before the legislature again prohibited all things German with the onset of World War II.

Nevertheless, the teaching of German in Louisiana survived all of these setbacks. St. Mary's Dominican College offered German until it closed in the 1980s. Delgado Community College also offered German sporadically, but it discontinued the offering in the 1990s when a foreign-language requirement was dropped for students seeking a degree.

Today there is a large number of students of German at Tulane, Loyola, the University of New Orleans, and Louisiana State University, its branches, and other affiliated state educational institutions. German is also offered at Xavier and Dillard universities, two private, church-affiliated schools. Because of the wide recognition of the value of the language, German will continue to be included in the curriculum of Louisiana institutions of higher learning.

There were many other schools in addition to those described above. Over the years nearly thirty German-language private and parochial schools developed in the German communities of the New Orleans region. These are enumerated by date of founding in the first section below. If known, the first teachers are also listed; often the pastor served in this capacity. Those private and parochial schools of the New Orleans region that offered German as a subject for study are listed with pertinent data in the second section. The next section lists the New Orleans public high schools in which German was taught. More than ten other German-language schools were located around the state in communities established by German immigrants. In the last listing their locations are given, as are the dates when they were founded. When known, the headmasters/principals and teachers are also noted.

New Orleans Region Private/Parochial German-Language Schools

1840 St. Paul's German Evangelical-Lutheran School
    Established by Rev. Christian Sans in engine house on Chartres Street
    First teachers: Johann and Jacob Ueber
1843 Port and Burgundy streets, Third District

1900   Closed
       Hoffman; Deiler, Churches
1840   St. Paul's German Evangelical-Lutheran School
       Race and Constance streets, Fourth District
       Lafayette City Advertiser, Jan. 29, 1842; Nau; Hoffman
1848   Mater Dolorosa School
       Original school called St. Mary's Nativity Catholic School on
       Cambronne Street
       First teachers: Benedictine Sisters
1872   Mater Dolorosa School built; South Carrollton, corner Plum Street
       First teacher: Alois Deiler
1895   Closed
       Hoffman; Deiler, Schools; Soards 1880
1848   St. Mary's (Assumption) **Catholic School**
       Begun in private home (Staub residence) by Fr. P. Tschackert
       (Czackert)
       First teacher: Brother Louis Kenning
1854   *St. Marien Schule für die Deutschen* (St. Mary's School for the Germans)
       three-story brick schoolhouse adjoining church; began as girls' school
       Constance and St. Andrew streets
       First teachers: Sisters of Notre Dame
1869   Boys' school established
       First teachers: Marist Brothers
1875   Year of highest attendance (1,136 children)
1923   Demolished
       Hoffman; Laguaite; Deiler, Schools; Calvert
1849   Turnschule (Turngemeinde)
       Lafayette Street; for children of members of the Turnverein
       Laguaite
1850   Ueber School
       Year-round school for 51 years on North Rampart between St.
       Ferdinand and Port streets, Third District
       First teachers: Johann and Jacob Ueber
       Hoffman; Deiler, Schools
1853   Independent German High School
       Third District
       First teacher: W. Helfer
       Hoffman
1853   St. Joseph Orphan Asylum School
       Temporary asylum at First and Annunciation streets; established by St.
       Mary's Assumption Parish Association
1854   Three-story brick building at Josephine and Laurel streets
       Hoffman

1854 St. John's German Evangelical-Lutheran School
Established by Pastor Schieferdecker at Iberville and Prieur streets
1858 Elementary school on Johnson between Loyola and Bienville streets
First Teacher: Mr. Koehnke
Hoffman; Laguaite

1854 First Street German Presbyterian School
First Street between Laurel and Annunciation streets
1866 Larger schoolhouse built on Sixth between Laurel and Annunciation streets
First teachers: Rev. Louis Voss (also pastor); G. M. Zinser; Miss Irene Gaschen
1883 Closed
Deiler, Schools; Laguaite; Hoffman

1854 The Zion German Evangelical-Lutheran School(s)
Elementary school attached to church, on Euterpe between Baronne and Dryades streets
First teacher: Theodore Bünger
1866 Second elementary school, on block bordered by Jackson, White, Loyola, and Josephine streets, City of Lafayette
1869 Additional elementary school, on Chippewa and Fourth streets, City of Lafayette
1887 Building became pre-theological seminary, established by Albert F. Hoppe
1894 Elementary schools consolidated into new school built on Carondelet Street
1901 Closed
Deiler, Schools; Hoffman

1856 St. Matthew's German-American Elementary School
Established by Rooster Church
1873 Madison and Third streets, City of Carrollton
First teachers: Pastor Geller; Mr. Pfeiffer
1884 Reunited with Otto School; used building on Madison and Third streets
1892 Closed
LLMVC; Hoffman

1856 Evangelical Protestant German-American School
Jackson Avenue; established by Jackson Avenue Evangelical Church
First teacher: G. M. Zinser
1892 Closed
Laguaite; Hoffman

1858 First German Lutheran Church School
Fourth and Port streets, Third District
Deiler, Churches, Schools

1859 First German Methodist Episcopal School

Melicerte (now Erato) Street
First teacher: L. A. Frech
Laguaite; Deiler, Churches, Schools

1859 First German Protestant Evangelical Church School
Clio Street between St. Charles Avenue and Carondelet Street
First teachers: Rev. A. H. Becker; G. M. Zinser
1896 Closed for financial reasons
Deiler, Churches, Schools

1864 St. Joseph's Catholic School
Lavoisier and Sixth streets, Gretna (located within church)
First teachers: Father Bogaerts, Herr Bruch
1868 Separate schoolhouse built
Deiler, Churches; Soards 1880; Hoffman

1866 German Protestant Orphan Asylum School
State and Camp streets; established by Pastor Heintz of Jackson Avenue
German Evangelical Church
First teacher: P. Schuman
Hoffman; Soards 1880

1868 Second Presbyterian Church and School
St. Bernard and North Claiborne avenues
First teacher: Rev. F. O. Koelle
1896 Closed
Hoffman; Deiler, Churches, Schools

1869 St. Boniface German Catholic School
North Galvez and Lapeyrouse streets
First teachers: Rev. J. Koegerl, J. Hanno Deiler (principal until 1879)
1917 Closed
Soards 1880; Hoffman

1871 First German Evangelical Protestant School (Otto School)
Burthe between Dublin and Madison streets, City of Carrollton
First teachers: Rev. Martin Otto, Julia Oswald
1884 Closed; reunited with Rooster School
Konrad; Soards 1890; Hoffman

1871 Holy Trinity Catholic School
Royal between St. Ferdinand and Press streets; originally on Dauphine
Street behind Bruser residence
First teacher: Rev. P. Leonhard Thevis
1910 Became free parochial school under Fr. J. V. Prim
Soards 1880; Deiler, Schools; Hoffman

1873 St. Henry's Catholic School
Berlin (now General Pershing) and Constance streets
First teachers: Rev. J. Koegerl; Sisters of Christian Charity, head-
mistress Sister Xaveria

1970s Closed
> *Soards 1880; Hoffman; Historic Churches*

1875 Evangelical-Lutheran Trinity School
Olivier and Eliza streets, Algiers
First teacher: Rev. G. Buchschacher
1916 German discontinued
ca. *Deiler, Churches; Hoffman*

1877 Salem German Evangelical-Lutheran School
Gretna
First teachers: Rev. John Gruber, Mrs. Hildebrand
> *Soards 1880; Hoffman*

1883 Bethlehem Evangelical Lutheran Orphan Asylum School
Andry and North Peters streets; established by group of Lutheran churches led by St. Paul's
First teacher: Herr Mäsch (also superintendent)
> *Deutches Haus Coll., Historic New Orleans Collection (HNOC); Hoffman; Deiler, Schools*

1883 Emmanuel German Lutheran School
Established by the Ohio Synod on Prieur and St. Louis streets
First teachers: Rev. John. F. Doescher, Mrs. Metz, Mr. Nicholas (also principal)
1892 Closed because of low attendance
1899 Reopened by popular demand
1901 Closed again because of low attendance
> *Hoffman; Deiler, Schools*

New Orleans Region Private/Parochial Schools Offering German

1842 United Christian Church School (trilingual)
116 North Rampart Street
Teacher: J. A. Fischer
> *Deiler, Churches*

1872 English, French and German School
North Robertson, corner St. Ann Street
> *Laguaite*

1872 German-American School
Royal Street; later moved to 346-48 Common Street
> *Laguaite*

1872 German Catholic School
Carrollton
First teacher: Alois Deiler
1895 Closed
> *Deiler, Churches*

1872 Locquet-Leroy New Orleans Female Collegiate Institute

280 Camp Street
Laguaite

1872   Mrs. E. Matthew's Private Academy for Girls
349 Josephine Street
Laguaite

1872   The Salem German Evangelical School
Founding church formerly called First German Evangelical Lutheran
Church, Milan and Camp streets, Sixth District
First teachers: Pastor Quintius, Mr. Meier, Mr. Speicher
1900   German discontinued
Soards 1880, 1890; Deiler, Schools; Hoffman

?   Mrs. Chapman's (and Mrs. Blake's) **School** (later **Louise S. McGehee
School**)
Second and Prytania streets
Laguaite

1884   Lesch German School
Kendall

1891   St. Joseph Priory
Gessen, La.; established by German-speaking Benedictine monks from
St. Meinrad Abbey in Indiana
Prior and director of seminary: Fr. Luke Gruwe
1902   Moved to St. Benedict; secondary education as well as college-level
studies offered until 1960s
Deiler, Churches; Deutsches Haus Coll., HNOC

New Orleans Public High Schools Offering German

1850   German High School
Third District
1853   Closed because of yellow-fever epidemic

1910   McDonogh High School No. 1
1532 Calliope Street
Hoffman

1910   McDonogh High School No. 3
740 Esplanade Avenue
Hoffman

1913   Esplanade Girls' High School
2426 Esplanade Avenue
Hoffman

1913   Sophie Wright Girls' High School
1413 Napoleon Avenue
Hoffman

1926   Warren Easton High School
3019 Canal Street

1932 German offered in evening for adults
Hoffman

1931 Alcée Fortier Boys' High School
Freret Street, corner Nashville Avenue
Laguaite

German-Language Schools Outside the New Orleans Region

1830s German Presbyterian School
Pine Grove, West St. Tammany Parish
Pastor Finley
Hoffman

1859 German-English School
Talisheek, St. Tammany Parish
Hoffman

1859 German Methodist Episcopal School
Franklin, St. Mary Parish
School and church disbanded after Rev. John E. Rengdoff departed
Deiler, Churches

1871 Clinton German-English School
East Feliciana Parish
Hoffman

1883 St. Leo's Catholic School
Roberts Cove, Acadia Parish
First teacher: Johann Kögl of Bregenz (Voralberg)

1891 Began German-English school
Teachers: Benedictine nuns, followed by Sisters of the Most Holy
Sacrament, Lafayette
Hoffman; Deiler, Churches

1889 German Catholic Boys' and Girls' School
Carmel, De Soto Parish
First teachers: Sisters Mary Magdalen, Elisa, Theresa, Johanna
Deiler, Churches

1890 St. John's German Evangelical-Lutheran School
Lake Charles, Calcasieu Parish; established by Zion Lutheran Church
of New Orleans
Pastor and first teacher: Pastor Hörnicke
Deiler, Churches; Hoffman

1892 St. Joseph House of Studies
Ponchatoula
First teacher: Rev. Jacob Ziegenfuss
Deiler, Churches

1895 Frenier German-English School
Tangipahoa Parish; one-room school, through eighth grade

First teacher: Mr. Hamel
Borel; Hoffman
1895 Keatchie German-English School
De Soto Parish
Hoffman
1901 Crowley German Language School
Acadia Parish
1914 Closed because of low attendance
Hoffman

CEMETERIES

New Orleans has always been noted for its cemeteries, the unique "cities of the dead" found throughout the densely populated older sections. They have been objects of fascination for visitors to the city as well as for each new generation of residents. In many ways the cemeteries reflect the city's history and culture. Because there was no separation of church and state in colonial Louisiana, cremation, banned by the Vatican, was not an option for the Catholic population of New Orleans. Consequently the only means of interment was in-ground burial. Because of the location of the city on a floodplain, these early burials were always problematical. The first settlers forced the wooden caskets of their dead into the natural levees formed by the banks of the Mississippi River. However, with seasonal floods, the buoyant caskets were pushed back up as the water table rose, exposing the saturated remains. To avoid the resulting weakening of the levee as well as the reappearance of coffins, the Catholic church established a cemetery (St. Louis No. 1) outside the limits of the settlement. There were many reasons for this plan. Human remains would wash away from the settled area during inundation, miasmas arising from burial sites would not foul the air, and contagion during epidemics would be less threatening. Locating graveyards away from the population center became the pattern of New Orleans as it grew. Old cemeteries were built over, relocated, or walled off from the residential areas, and new cemeteries were established beyond the city limits. The walled cemeteries, however, did not solve the problem of coffins and their remains floating to the surface when the water table rose.

The only solution was above-ground entombment. Early tombs were simple, simulating the appearance of small houses. Their construction made possible the unusual practice in New Orleans of burying succeeding generations of the same family in one burial site. As was the case with much of the layout of the city, the early cemeteries had no plan; new burial plots were simply added on to the existing ones. As in the population of the city itself, there was no separation by race, nationality, or religion until much later (the second half of the nineteenth century). As time went by the tombs of the deceased took on aspects of the homes of the living. Many of these above-ground burial structures became elaborate, reflecting the wealth of the deceased and the style of architecture in vogue at the time. With the turn of the twentieth century, land-draining water pumps were installed around the city, making below-ground burial possible for the first time. However, the residents of New Orleans preferred to continue their established tradition of burying the dead above ground in a variety of tombs.

The celebration of All Saints Day in New Orleans is unique among American cities. Municipal offices close on November 1 in the city as well as in other Louisiana Catholic strongholds. The celebration of this day traces back to the European Catholic festival of All Saints, observed since the dawn of Christianity. Like other Christian holidays (such as the city's Mardi Gras), it stemmed from pre-Christian pagan rites associated with the change of the seasons. The earliest celebrations were held by the Druids in honor of Samhain, Lord of the Dead, whose festival fell on November 1. Remnants of these rites were preserved in Christianized Europe and were brought by German immigrants to the New World. The fraternal order of Druids was organized as a benevolent society nationwide. The German Druid chapters in New Orleans took the name *Hain. Der Gross Hain* [Grand Grove] *von Louisiana,* which united the various state chapters under one umbrella, adopted the German motto, *Vereinigung, Friede, Eintracht* (Unity, Peace, Harmony) (see chapter 7, "Societies and Associations").

In ancient times All Saints Day marked the Celtic new year, the beginning of winter, and the end of the growth cycle in nature, with lengthening nights and colder days. The approaching somber weather engendered contemplation of deceased family members and remembrances of them. Throughout the ages religious rituals of honoring the dead and adornment of burial sites were practiced at this time of the year. In A.D. 609 Pope Boniface IV incorporated these pre-Christian ceremonies into the Catholic calendar, and by the end of the medieval period the celebration of All Saints Day was universal in Catholic Europe.

In New Orleans the custom had long been observed of bringing flowers and mementos (*immortelles*) to the family gravesite on November 1. It is still customary to clean, repair, replant, and whitewash the family tombs at the end of October in preparation for All Saints Day. On the day itself, crowds of cemetery visitors stroll among the gravesites, socializing with friends and relatives. The great number of tomb visitors requires mounted police at the entrances of the larger cemeteries. At one time, vendors of Creole specialties also hawked their wares at the cemetery entrances. Today a remnant of this custom can be found in the fruit and vegetable stand set up at the entrance to St. Louis No. 3 Cemetery by a fifth-generation German family.

The multitude of European Catholic immigrants who settled in New Orleans embraced the All Saints Day celebration of the city, none more enthusiastically than the Germans. The observances in New Orleans reflected the traditional German practice of making seasonal family visits to the graveyards to clean and replant the burial sites of deceased loved ones. The cemeteries were also used for Sunday outings. In good weather it was common for whole families to spend the day picnicking, strolling, and enjoying the parklike atmosphere of the *Friedhöfe* (graveyards). As the German sections of New Orleans became more and more densely populated, the cemeteries offered a familiar outdoors gathering place. There the children could play in safety while the adults walked among the monuments, enjoying the greenery and visiting with their neighbors.

Metairie Cemetery has been called the most elegant graveyard in the country. Many of its towering ornate monuments are visible from Metairie Road, originally a bayou, the banks of which provided high ground outside the city limits. The site was first developed in 1832 as a racetrack. In addition to racing it was occasionally used for municipal activities. The open spaces of the racetrack were ideal for the many activities of the German *Volksfest,* held there annually as a May Day celebration (see chapter 8). The Civil War and its aftermath, however, caused the closing of the racetrack. In 1872 the 150 acres of the racecourse were converted to a cemetery, which retained the oval shape of the track. The layout of Metairie Cemetery was patterned after the great suburban cemeteries of Mount Auburn in Boston and Greenwood in New York, with a spacious, parklike atmosphere as the background for elegant tombs and monuments. This was a departure from the other cemeteries of the city, which were small in size and surrounded by wall vaults.

Metairie Cemetery soon was patronized by most of the leading families of New Orleans. In this graveyard a number of prominent Germans and German-Americans of the later nineteenth and early twentieth centuries were buried. One example is the grave of the popular mayor of

New Orleans, Martin Behrman, a German-American of Jewish descent. Behrman dominated politics in New Orleans for a quarter-century and was mourned by 20,000 residents who crowded into the cemetery to attend his funeral. A unique aspect of the cemetery is the several hundred German-Jewish families buried there. These Jewish interments were among the few instances in the world where Jewish families did not choose to bury their dead in a cemetery consecrated by a synagogue. Even rabbis chose to be buried in Metairie Cemetery. The funeral of the first rabbi of Temple Sinai, James Koppel Gutheim, was said to have been the largest in New Orleans since the burial of Jefferson Davis. The inscription on the headstone of Simon Gumbel, a wealthy cotton broker and founder of the Sophie L. Gumbel Home, attests to the continuing German influence in the city: *Scheint die Sonne noch so schön, Einmal muss sie untergehen (Although the sun still shines so beautifully, one day it has to set)*. Michael Hahn, the German governor of Louisiana at the end of the Civil War, is also interred in Metairie Cemetery.

Another interesting note about this cemetery is that a number of its mausoleum and memorial designers and builders were German. So successful were they that, together, they made New Orleans the capital of this industry in the early twentieth century. For a number of decades they produced granite works for the entire nation, including the famous Confederate figures of Stone Mountain, Georgia, and the Philadelphia stone bridge. Perhaps the most noteworthy among these designers, builders, and sculptors was Albert Weiblen, who had emigrated from Germany in 1887. Although he came to the city without financial resources, he was able to build his firm into one of the largest in the South. In 1906 he moved his marble and

Weiblen Marble Company ad. *Courtesy of the Historic New Orleans Collection.*

stone works to City Park Avenue adjacent to Metairie Cemetery. He and his sons obtained most of the contracts for the monuments in this grave-yard and were largely responsible for the high quality in design and exe-cution of the memorials. In 1951 the Weiblen family was able to acquire a controlling interest in Metairie Cemetery, which they held until Albert's death. His widow continued the operation of the cemetery for almost two decades. Large oleander bushes that once graced Metairie Road were her contribution to the scenic view of the surrounding area.

Victor Huber and his three sons founded a successful business as producers of granite and marble headstones and decorative grave markers. Their importance in this business stemmed from their pur-chase of St. John Cemetery and their construction of Hope Mausoleum. St. John Cemetery was established in 1867 near the end of Canal Street by the St. John's First German Evangelical-Lutheran Congregation (see "Churches and Synagogues," above). When the city repaved Canal Street and billed the congregation for their share, they decided to sell the cemetery to Victor Huber, who was a member of the church and had supervised the cemetery's operations for some time.

Huber conceived the idea of building a community mausoleum on vacant ground in the rear of the cemetery, which, in time, was expand-ed to take up almost half of the area. His son Albert designed the struc-ture, which was named Hope Mausoleum and included Louisiana's first crematory within the building. The cemetery section of St. John's contains several interesting carved headstones from its pre-mausoleum days. Of note is the monument marking the grave of the well-known architect Richard Koch, who designed the entrance to Metairie Cemetery. He chose to have the German word *Wiedersehen* (until we meet again) engraved over clasped hands on his tombstone. In 1957 the remains from the Male and Female Lutheran Benevolent Society tomb in the Girod Street Cemetery were transferred to Hope Mausoleum. Christ Church Cathedral, the owner of this cemetery, had found that its maintenance had become too costly and had allowed it to fall into decay. When it was beyond salvaging, the church decided to demolish the cemetery, including the elegant and costly Lutheran tomb, which had contained seventy vaults. Christ Church arranged for all remains to be put into individual crypts in Hope Mausoleum, free of charge to the families of the deceased. The Hope Mausoleum section of the ceme-tery set an example of prudent land use in a city where space has always been at a premium. This concept has since been adopted in the newer cemeteries of the city.

There were several other smaller German stone and marble sculptors and designers in the monument business in New Orleans. Among them were Fredrick J. Birchmeier, Theodore Brune, Gottlieb Huber, Edwin Kursheedt, George Stroud, and Albert Rieker. Rieker was an exceptionally talented sculptor whose bronze children (cast in Geislingen-Am-Steig, Germany) adorn the Mathieu Vonderbank tomb in Metairie Cemetery. The bronze maiden adorning the tomb of the famous madam of Storyville, known as Josie Arlington, was cast in Düsseldorf, Germany. Josie was actually named Mamie Duebler, a German American born in Carrollton. The brothers Eugene and Daniel Warburg were also highly gifted marble cutters and sculptors. They were the sons of a German-Jewish immigrant and a Cuban-born Negress. Daniel's monuments in Metairie Cemetery and elsewhere were often graced by intricately entwined morning-glory vines, a motif for which he was well known.

In this section of New Orleans, bordering Metairie Road and City Park Avenue, a number of other graveyards were established. Originally this area, just beyond the city limits, offered the only accessible, undeveloped high land that could be used for burial purposes. Several of the older cemeteries in this area were also predominantly German. These were Cypress Grove, its extension, Greenwood Cemetery, and Odd Fellows Rest.

Cypress Grove was established in 1840 by the Firemen's Charitable and Benevolent Association of the city and was formerly named Firemen's Cemetery. Over half of the firemen of New Orleans were German immigrants. The year after its establishment, the remains of firemen who had been buried elsewhere were removed to this cemetery. More than a thousand fellow firemen, family, and friends attended the religious ceremonies and the procession down Canal Street to the reburial site. Later renamed Cypress Grove, it also became the burial place for many Protestant families from the Girod Street

Death notice of Emile Maier, July 30, 1883. *Courtesy of the Historic New Orleans Collection.*

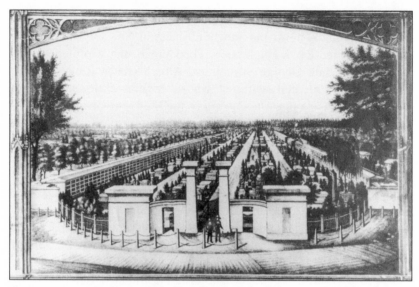

Cypress Grove. *Courtesy of Special Collections, Tulane University.*

Cemetery as it deteriorated through neglect. Several of the most ornate tombs in Cypress Grove were designed and constructed by Germans, the successful architect Theodore Brune, and the stone sculptor George Stroud. Stroud, who was a leading tomb builder in his day and erected many of the showiest tombs in Metairie Cemetery, was laid to rest in the main aisle of Cypress Grove.

Across the street is Greenwood Cemetery, also established by the Firemen's Charitable and Benevolent Association and an extension of Cypress Grove. It was the first above-ground cemetery not enclosed by walls. Acquired in 1852, its 150 acres made it comparable to Metairie Cemetery in size. The centerpiece of the cemetery is the Fireman's Monument, honoring twenty-three volunteer fire companies. Until 1891 when a professional fire department was organized in New Orleans, Fireman's Day, March 4, was a municipal holiday. It was customary on this day for the volunteer firemen of the city to parade down Canal Street. In 1853 the *Tägliche Deutsche Zeitung* (*Daily German Gazette*) reported a glittering all-German parade, a joint effort of the many German fire companies of the city. Outstanding in the cemetery is the magnificent cast-iron tomb of Isaac Newton Marks, enclosed by a Gothic-style iron fence.

Many of the early-nineteenth-century ironworkers of the city were of German origin, as the names Isenhart and Anheiser imply. By 1800 there were hundreds of foundries in the German states, accounting for the many highly skilled ironworkers who immigrated to the city. These replaced the traditional black artisans who had previously dominated the trade. A number of these Germans in time established ironworks in New Orleans (see chapter 5, "Trades, Businesses, and Professions"). The most well known was Hinderer's Ironworks, which continued in business until the mid-twentieth century. Frederick Hinderer had come to New Orleans before 1880 and began making iron furniture in partnership with another German, Frederick Daimler. Later he was associated with Wilhelm Spitz, who took over Hinderer's Ironworks after the founder's death.

Odd Fellows Rest is the other German-dominated cemetery at Canal Street and City Park Avenue. It was established in 1847 by the Grand Lodge of the Independent Order of Odd Fellows. The I.O.O.F. was an international benevolent society, which provided burial for its members and benefits for their families. Odd Fellows Rest was dedicated in 1849 with a grand procession led by two horse-drawn circus bandwagons and a funeral car bearing the remains of sixteen members gathered from other cemeteries. The elegant tomb of Teutonia Lodge No. 10, constructed about 1851, bears the German inscription *Freundschaft, Liebe und Wahrheit (Friendship, Love and Truth)*. Also of note in this cemetery is the Howard Association Memorial. During yellow-fever outbreaks, the New Orleans chapter of this association worked hand in hand with the *Deutsche Gesellschaft* (see chapter 2, "German Immigration to New Orleans") to assist indigent victims. Both organizations were particularly active during the great epidemic of 1853. After the battle against yellow fever ended in the early twentieth century the Howard Association disbanded.

Other predominantly German cemeteries are located in those sections of the city where German communities once flourished: the former cities of Lafayette and Carrollton, the Third District (now the Upper Ninth Ward), and Gretna on the West Bank. Some of these cemeteries were established by religious congregations, while others were municipally sponsored.

The City of Lafayette, which encompassed what is now known as the Upper Garden District/Irish Channel sections, has two municipal cemeteries, Lafayette No. 1 and 2. Lafayette Cemetery No. 1 resembles the older Creole cemeteries with its elegant tombs and wall vaults. The site was purchased from Cornelius Hurst in the 1830s and, like the Garden District itself, was divided into lots double the usual size.

Unlike the Creole cemeteries, however, it was built according to a plan, with two wide, intersecting walkways forming a cross. It stands in the middle of the fashionable Garden District, transformed by American enterprise into a thriving hub of commerce and palatial residences. A visitor to the suburb in the 1830s described the streets surrounding the cemetery as being dotted with stores marked with the skull and cross-bones, with elegant coffins and mortuary ornaments displayed in show windows. The yellow-fever epidemics of the city took a heavy toll on the immigrant population of the City of Lafayette as evidenced by the number of graves in this cemetery bearing German names and inscriptions. It is also the location of the tomb of the all-German Jefferson Fire Company No. 22, a many-vaulted structure erected in 1852 on one of the main aisles. The tomb is surrounded with an ornate cast-iron fence by Wood and Miltenberger and bears the emblem of the society at the top of its facade, a hand-pumper carved in marble. Also buried in this cemetery is Theodore von La Hache, the German-born founder of the New Orleans Philharmonic Society and compiler of the Catholic hymnal (see chapter 9). Lafayette Cemetery No. 2 is located farther along Washington Avenue, nearer the river. Here there is a preponderance of German gravesites, notable among which is the large monument of the *Deutsche Handwerker Verein* (German Craftsmen's Society), erected in 1868, three years after the cemetery was built.

Not far from these are two Catholic cemeteries, St. Joseph Cemetery No. 1 and No. 2, also located on Washington Avenue but on the lake side of St. Charles Avenue. St. Joseph Cemetery No. 1 was dedicated in 1854 by the St. Joseph German Orphan Asylum Association (see "German-Language Schools," above, and chapter 7, "Orphanages and Homes for the Aged"). The cemetery was established as a burial site for the German orphans, their families, and fellow immigrants of the City of Lafayette. Burial fees also provided support for the nuns of St. Mary's Assumption German Catholic Church and school. An annex was soon needed, so the block behind the cemetery was taken over in 1873 as St. Joseph Cemetery No. 2. When the city repaved the streets around these cemeteries and billed the Sisters of Notre Dame, they appealed to Archbishop Joseph Rummel for assistance. He relieved them of this liability by accepting the cemeteries for the diocese. The original wooden structure that preceded today's monumental St. Mary's Assumption Church was relocated to the Washington Avenue graveyard in 1863, just after the new church was finished. There it functioned as a mortuary chapel until 1997, when, amid much debate in the community, it was again moved to a site six blocks from its original location on Jackson Avenue. In St. Joseph No. 2 is the notable gravesite of Jacob Lechner with its lovely but rare cast-iron fence, designed in a rose-vine style. St. Joseph No. 2 also houses an interesting structure, a miniature Gothic chapel, the tomb of the German Redemptorist priests who served the three Catholic churches of this parish.

The four predominantly German cemeteries located in this area reflect the size of the City of Lafayette's German community. These cemeteries are testimonials to the high death toll among the immigrant population, which suffered from the many ills that afflict immigrants everywhere. In the German sections of New Orleans, the death rate was disproportionately high during the yellow-fever epidemics because of the lack of immunity that the native population had developed. Also located in the City of Lafayette was the Gates of Mercy (Shangarai Chassed) Cemetery, established in 1862 by the earliest German-Jewish congregation of New Orleans (see "Churches and Synagogues," above). Once located at Jackson Avenue and Saratoga Street, it held the remains of the early Jews of German background who came to New Orleans after the Louisiana Purchase. Prior to this, few Jews had settled in Louisiana because both they and all Protestants had specifically been banned by the *Code Noir,* put in force in the early colonial period by the French. The Gates of Mercy Cemetery was closed in 1957 and all remains reinterred in Hebrew Rest Cemetery on Elysian Fields. As in the case of Girod Street Cemetery, the growth of the city had raised the value of the land, resulting in the conversion of the graveyard to residential use.

In the former Third District neighborhood are the fascinating St. Roch Cemeteries No. 1 and No. 2. Many of the headstones in these cemeteries were engraved with verses in the German language. The votive chapel, the *Campo Sancto,* facing the entrance to St. Roch Cemetery No. 1, was modeled after the *Campo Sancto dei Tedeschi* (Sacred Chapel for the Germans) adjacent to St. Peter's Basilica in Rome. This chapel was built by Fr. Peter Leonhard Thevis, a German priest who arrived in New Orleans in 1867 during a raging yellow-fever epidemic. He remembered the devotions in his homeland made during plagues to St. Roch, a saint little known among Catholics in America. When his congregation was spared from the epidemic, he and his parishioners built a Gothic-style mortuary chapel to fulfill a promise to God that Thevis had made. The chapel contains a small room with realistic replicas of body parts and a collection of crutches and

Germans socializing in St. Roch Cemetery No. 1. *Courtesy of a private collection.*

braces. These ex-voto objects attest to the cures experienced by pilgrims praying for healing to St. Roch. The tomb of Father Thevis is located in front of the altar below the floor of the chapel. St. Roch Cemetery No. 1 is surrounded by wall vaults with fourteen niches, each displaying marble statues depicting the stations of the cross. On All Saints Day the cemetery is crowded with the faithful, who are led by a priest through the way of the cross. The participants make novenas at the stations and then participate in a Catholic mass held in the surrounding graveyard. St.

St. Roch Cemetery No. 1 mortuary chapel. *Courtesy of the Historic New Orleans Collection.*

Roch Cemetery No. 2, behind the original cemetery, was built in 1895 to provide more burial space. It also has a striking mortuary chapel dedicated to St. Michael, which functions as a vault-style tomb.

In this old section of town is another German-Jewish graveyard, Hebrew Rest Cemetery, established in 1872 by the Gates of Mercy congregation, which later formed Touro Synagogue. Orthodox Judaism requires in-ground burial, which the high water table in New Orleans prevents. The Reformed congregations establishing Hebrew Rest circumvented this by adopting coping-style gravesites. Copings are uncovered empty chambers framed by stone or brick, built up to three feet high off the ground. They allow multiple burials, each interment being covered with earth. Technically speaking, the coping burial is in the earth. There are also a number of lovely monuments, which Orthodox Jewry would forbid. A graceful angel strewing flowers adorns the Isaac Levy plot while a sorrowing young woman stands atop the gravestone of Moritz Keiffer. The inscriptions on both of these grave markers identify the occupants as having been born in Germany. Elaborate obelisks crafted from white bronze mark the graves of Harriette Levi and Simon Weil. They were cast by the local German-Jewish firm Coleman's White Bronze Works.

In Carrollton there are two German graveyards, St. Mary's Cemetery, formerly owned by the Catholic Church, and the municipal Carrollton Cemetery, also known as the Green Street Graveyard. The former was taken over by the city in 1921. The latter and far more significant cemetery was laid out in the rear of the town on high ground built up by the Macarty crevasse. Here is located the society tomb of *Der deutschen Freundschaftsbund* (The German Friendship League), dating to 1850. Other gravesites of note are those of Frederic Fischer, a German-born pioneer who came to Carrollton in 1839, and the twin tombs of the grocery magnates, the Lochte and Kirchoff families.

On the West Bank, the Gretna Hook and Ladder Cemetery bears mentioning. Gretna began as Mechanikham (Mechanics' Home), its German name derived from the origins and trades of the settlers. As time passed the Germans of the town formed volunteer fire companies, as did their fellow countrymen on the east bank of the river. A number of Germans are buried in this cemetery, which was established in 1859 by the Hook and Ladder Exempt Fire Company.

The following list of New Orleans area German cemeteries (i.e., cemeteries with a large German representation) is arranged according to dates of establishment. A listing of the more prominent German and German-American monuments in each cemetery is given, as are pertinent notes.

1830s Lafayette Cemetery No. 1

Washington Avenue between Coliseum and Prytania streets

Society tombs: *Jefferson Feuer Companie No. 22* (Jefferson Fire Company No. 22), erected 1852, shows hand-pumper fire engine and motto:

"Ready at the First Sound"; Order of Odd Fellows; Lafayette Hook and Ladder Company No. 1; monument of the *Deutsche Presbyterianische Gemeinde* (German Presbyterian Congregation)

Individual tombs: Frederick J. Birchmeier, stonemason and marble dealer; Theodore von La Hache, famous composer and organist

City purchased land for cemetery from Cornelius Hurst; Benjamin Buisson, city surveyor, laid out cemetery; many Germans and Irish buried there

1840 Cypress Grove (Firemen's Cemetery)

Canal Street at City Park Avenue

Society tombs: Baker's Benevolent Association (1863); Fire Company No. 10

Individual tombs: George Stroud; Stark and Letchford families (probably designed by Theodore Brune, erected by George Stroud)

Land for cemetery purchased by Firemen's Charitable and Benevolent Association

1844 St. Vincent de Paul Cemeteries I, II, III

1322 Louisa Street

Family tombs: Zaehringer, Nothacker, Frantz, Schoen

Jose Llula bought cemeteries in 1857; sold by his heirs to Albert Stewart in 1910

1847 Odd Fellows Rest

Canal Street and City Park Avenue

Society tombs: Tomb for I.O.O.F., Teutonia Lodge No. 10, name in pavement designates tomb of Southwestern Lodge No. 40

Cemetery bought by Odd Fellows, enlarged with donations from Firemen's Charitable and Benevolent Association, Henry Bier, and George Allan

1847 St. Mary Cemetery (Carrollton)

Adams Street between Spruce and Cohn, extending to Lowerline Street

German Catholic church, St. Mary's Nativity, established cemetery; city of New Orleans swapped land with church in 1921; now part of Carrollton Cemetery

1849 Carrollton Cemetery

Adams Street between Hickory and Birch, extending to Lowerline Street

Society tomb: *Die Deutsche Freundschaftsbund* (German Friendship League)

Individual tombs of German pioneers of Carrollton: Lochte, Kirchoff, Fischer, Thieler, Deibel

Originally owned by city of Carrollton; cemetery came under management of city of New Orleans when Carrollton annexed in 1874

1850 Lafayette Cemetery No. 2
Washington Avenue between Saratoga Street and Loyola Avenue
Society tomb: *Der Deutsche Handwerker Verein* (German Handworkers' Union)

1852 Greenwood Cemetery
120 City Park Avenue
Society tombs: 1874, Confederate Monument designed by architect Benjamin M. Harrod, erected by George Stroud; Swiss Society tomb; *Deutscher Louisiana Draymann Verein* tomb; tumular tomb of Benevolent and Protective Order of Elks erected by Albert Weiblen
Individual tomb: J. Hanno Deiler, historian, teacher, and musician, died July 20, 1909, buried in 1912 in wife's family tomb (Saganowsky) located at #48 Cypress
Land bought by Firemen's Charitable and Benevolent Association to extend Cypress Grove

1854 St. Joseph Cemetery No. 1
Washington Avenue between Saratoga and South Liberty streets
Society tombs: St. Georgius Society, Young Men's Benevolent Society
Individual tombs: Fabacher, Babst, Wegmann families
Established by St. Joseph German Orphan Asylum Association to provide burial for German immigrant families and revenue for School Sisters of Notre Dame, who administered orphanage

1859 Gretna Hook and Ladder Cemetery
Newton Street between Tenth and Eleventh streets, extending to Lafayette Avenue
Society tombs: Woodmen of the World, Orange Camp No. 8, Mulberry Camp No. 620
Individual tombs: Louis Oscar Fried, Gustave B. G. Kundert, George C. Kleinpeter
Gravesite of other Gretna pioneers: Strauss, Pflug, Strehle, Drinkhause, Weigel, Ehret, Steinbrunn, Loeschen, Stechelin, Zeyer, Gruner
Established by the Hook and Ladder Exempt Fire Company

1860 Hebrew Rest Cemetery
Elysian Fields Avenue between Pelopidas and Frenchmen streets
Heavy cast-iron gates; two squares of land

1862 Gates of Mercy Cemetery
Jackson Avenue at Saratoga Street
Established for pioneer Jews of German heritage; demolished in 1957; remains moved to Hebrew Rest Cemetery and marked by monument

1865 Masonic Cemetery

Bienville Street, between City Park Avenue and St. Anthony Street

Many Germans belonged to Masonic lodges

1867 St. John Cemetery/Hope Mausoleum

Canal Street between Bernadotte and North St. Anthony streets

St. John Evangelical Lutheran Congregation established cemetery as second Protestant cemetery in city; originally called First German Evangelical Lutheran St. John Cemetery; church operated until 1929; then purchased by Victor Huber and Sons, who developed Hope Mausoleum, 1931

1872 Metairie Cemetery

Pontchartrain Boulevard and Metairie Road

Among the many Germans buried here are (see chapter 9): Martin Behrman (section 48), memorial designed by Albert Weiblen; Gustave Adolphe Blaffer (section 04); Lucien Napoleon Brunswig (section 115); Charles F. Buck (section 89), memorial designed by Albert Weiblen; E. F. Del Bondio (section 105); Lawrence Fabacher (section 9); Rabbi Julian B. Feibelman (section 67); Louis Grunewald (section 04); Simon Gumbel (section 84); Rabbi James Koppel Gutheim (section 84); Michael Hahn (section 68), memorial designed by Albert Weiblen; Jacob Hassinger (section 04); Simon Hernsheim (section 123); Julius Koch (section 34); Julius Kruttschnitt (section 11); George Merz (section 108); Isidore Newman (section 84); Sigmund Odenheimer (section 37); Mel Ott (section 146); Joseph Reuther (section 73); William Schmidt (section 123); John G. Schwegmann (section 133); Edgar B. Stern, Edith Rosenwald Stern (section 123); Mathieu Vonderbank (section 05); Rev. Louis Voss (section 123); Albert Weiblen (section 55); Julius Weis (section 84); F. M. Ziegler (section 123); Hermann Zuberier (section 34)

Benjamin Morgan Harrod, architect; new entrance with fountain designed in 1961 by Richard Koch

1873 St. Joseph Cemetery No. 2

Sixth and South Liberty streets

Expansion of Cemetery No. 1; both cemeteries given to Archdiocese of New Orleans

1874 St. Roch No. 1 and No. 2

1725 St. Roch Avenue, between North Roman and North Derbigny streets

Individual tombs (in chapel): Fr. Peter Leonhard Thevis, Fr. Magnus Roth, John and Mary Neissing Lange (with memorial plaques), Lange children

Fr. Peter Leonhard Thevis established cemetery; modeled after *Campo Santo dei Tedeschi* adjacent to St. Peter's Basilica, Rome; mortuary chapel dedicated to St. Roch in 1876; contains ex-voto objects

Chapter Seven

Social Concerns

ORPHANAGES AND HOMES FOR THE AGED

Only after Bismarck unified the German states in 1871 was the concept introduced of government responsibility for the young and the old, the unemployed and the unemployable. It is interesting to note that the framework for the social net that exists in the United States (unemployment and disability insurance, Welfare, Social Security, Medicare, etc.) was patterned after the reforms introduced in Germany at the end of the nineteenth century.

The German communities of the New Orleans area were formed long before these concepts were put into practice in Germany. Assistance to the young and the old who had no family to provide care was seen as the responsibility of the community and its religious institutions. It was in this context that the Germans of New Orleans founded orphanages and homes for the aged and infirm.

Orphanages were needed as soon as the tide of immigration began. It brought to New Orleans a great number of children orphaned during the long passage across the Atlantic. The ships bringing German immigrants were usually overcrowded and under-provisioned, resulting in many deaths attributed to malnutrition, disease, and poor sanitation. The yellow-fever epidemics of New Orleans also took a disproportionately high toll on the immigrant population, which lacked the immunity developed by long-term residents. Another factor contributing to the need for orphanages was the inability of many immigrant parents to support their children, who were then placed in orphanages until their parents could provide for them.

Until the establishment of asylums specifically for German orphans, the *Deutsche Gesellschaft* attempted to fill this need. Records of the society show that almost a hundred orphans were placed with sympathetic private families or in the already overcrowded public asylums. As the situation became more critical, church and synagogue congregations stepped in and established German orphanages in New Orleans.

Cadets of St. Joseph's Orphan Asylum, from the Deutsches Haus Collection. *Courtesy of the Historic New Orleans Collection.*

The German Catholic St. Joseph's Orphan Asylum. In 1853, as German immigration was reaching its peak, the first of these institutions, St. Joseph's, was established. It was opened in the City of Lafayette by the St. Mary's Assumption Parish Association. First a temporary asylum was opened on First and Annunciation streets, then, the next year, a three-story brick building was erected at Josephine and Laurel streets, closer to the church. The association also purchased the adjoining block to be used as a burial ground for those who died inside the asylum. The complex was blessed in 1855 as St. Joseph's German Orphan Asylum Cemetery, with J. Hanno Deiler presiding at the groundbreaking ceremony and at subsequent fundraising events. By 1886 there were 200 children under care. Financial difficulties, which had developed as the number of orphans increased, forced the parish association to give up the orphanage as a charitable pursuit. The facility was then turned over to the School Sisters of Notre Dame.

The German Protestant Orphan Asylum. This was organized in 1866, chiefly through the efforts of the German Evangelical Church on Jackson Avenue. The block bounded by Webster, Camp, Chestnut, and State streets was purchased, and the frame house already on the property was used as a temporary asylum. In 1869 two three-story dormitories were built around a court with the former stable being converted to an administration building. Within twenty years the attendance at the asylum school reached almost ninety children. The education offered corresponded to that of the public schools, enabling the children from the asylum to transfer to the public school system. German was used until World War I.

The Bethlehem Orphan Asylum of the Evangelical-Lutheran Missouri Synod. This institution owed its founding chiefly to a society within St. Paul's Lutheran Church. The asylum was located at North Peters and Andry streets, where it opened its doors in 1883. That year a school was also established, attended by the eleven inmates of the asylum and eighteen children from the vicinity. The superintendents usually served as teachers in the school. In 1895, a larger building housing seventy-five orphans was erected as well as a larger schoolroom. After 1906 religious instruction, formerly given in both German and English, was taught in English only. But until World War I the German language was offered as a subject of study. The number of inmates between 1893 and 1903 ranged from twenty-three to seventy-two.

The Jewish Children's Home. In 1855, the Hebrew Benevolent Society established a combined orphans and widows home, located on Jackson Avenue and Chippewa Street. Later named the Jewish Widows and Orphans Home, it primarily accepted residents of German-Jewish stock. This establishment led to the founding of the Isidore Newman Manual Training School nearly fifty years later to teach a trade to the children of the asylum.

Germans who arrived with no language skills or trade were forced

Jewish Widows and Orphans Home, from *History of the Jews of Louisiana. Courtesy of Touro Infirmary Archives.*

to work as common laborers, paid barely enough to survive. Able-bodied new arrivals could only get work digging the canals of the city, laying railroad ties, or performing other unskilled tasks that paid little more than a dollar a day. Exhaustion, undernourishment, and disease combined to produce such a high fatality rate in the early 1850s that bodies were buried in mass, unmarked graves. Slaves, for whom the wealthy of New Orleans paid as much as $1,000 each, were far too valuable to be exposed to such rigorous working conditions.

Although the Germans were known for their industriousness, it was the exceptional immigrant who was able to climb out of poverty in his lifetime. Those who survived their working years were often unable to accumulate enough to support themselves in their old age. Once again the German communities looked to their religious institutions to care for the elderly and infirm. A number of facilities were established in the 1880s and 1890s to provide for this aging population. A Catholic home for the aged was the first such institution to be established. Under the auspices of the Little Sisters of the Poor it opened its doors to Protestants as well.

The German Protestant Home for the Aged and Infirm (*Das deutsche protestantische Heim für Alte und Gebrechliche*). The history of the German Protestant Home for the Aged dates back to 1885, when thirteen German Protestant churches joined together to establish a home for aged and destitute people of their own faith. The word *Altenheim* (home for the aged) was coined to describe it. A corner lot bordered by Magazine and Eleanor streets was purchased and a small house standing on the grounds was made ready. Within two years, applications for admittance exceeded the home's capacity, so a larger structure with room for thirty-six inmates was built. For five years the new building sufficed, but again so many applications were received that, in 1893, a wing was added. After another five years the space in the home proved inadequate, so a two-story building was added to the left wing. In 1951 a large, modern, one-story brick complex replaced these structures. This complex, today known as the Covenant Home, continues to house the elderly and infirm of the community. It accepts applicants of all faiths.

German Protestant Bethany Home (*Das deutsche protestantische Bethanienheim*). In 1889 the plan for a home for the aged Protestants of the Third District was conceived by a group of women from the Second German Presbyterian Church. Funds were raised to acquire property and to build a structure on the corner of North Claiborne and Allen Street. By 1895 the home established itself as independent of the Second German Presbyterian Church. Eight years later a two-story addition was built, which was replaced with a better-designed new addition in 1936. The main building was also renovated at this time. In 1965 the inmates were moved to a new site on Esplanade Avenue at Dorgenois Street, where a modern plant was built to meet the growing needs of the community. Ten years later the Bethany Society joined the Covenant Home, sharing a common board of directors and common problems, objectives, and goals.

Today the German orphan asylums have been disbanded since the state has taken over this role through foster homes and other social services. The exception is the Bethlehem Orphan Asylum, now known as the Bethlehem Children's Treatment Center in New Orleans East, run by the Lutheran Social Services of the South. However, two of the institutions originally set up by the German community for the aged and infirm have continued providing services, the Covenant Home on Magazine Street and the Bethany Home on Esplanade Avenue.

The New Orleans German orphanages and old-age homes are listed here by date of founding, date of closing when known, name, location, and notes.

Orphanages

1853- **German Catholic St. Joseph's Orphan Asylum** (for Boys
1939 and Girls)
2044 Laurel Street near Josephine
Demolished in 1939; St. Thomas Housing
Project then occupied site

1855- **Jewish Children's Home**
1966 Jackson Avenue and Chippewa Street
Superintendent: Michael Heyman (1890)
Established by Hebrew Benevolent Society

 1877 New structure designed by Thomas Sully erected on
St. Charles Avenue
Expanded to care for widows and children made destitute by Civil War and renamed the Jewish Widows and Orphans Home; occupied site of the Jewish Community Center; Isidore Newman Manual Training School established in 1903 to educate the home's residents

1866- **German Protestant Orphan Asylum**
1978 919 Webster Street

 1920 New building erected on State Street between Camp and Chestnut

 1979 Sold, demolished; only remaining building (stable) renovated as private home

1883-present	**Bethlehem Orphan Asylum**
	North Peters and Andry streets
	Institution now in operation as Bethlehem Children's Treatment Center, 4430 Bundy Road, New Orleans East, administered by Lutheran Social Services of the South
1890	**Fink Asylum for Protestant Widows and Orphans**
	3643 Camp Street between Antonine and Amelia
	Matron: Miss Z. Henderson
	Founded by Württemberg consul Johann David Fink; died 1856; willed his estate of $200,000 to establish asylum for widows and orphans; originally a raised Italianate house built in 1866 for Henry Rice

Old-Age Homes/Shelters

1860-67	**Asylum for Indigent Recuperating Germans** (*Asyl für mittellose deutsche Genesende*)
	Deutsche Gesellschaft established and oversaw shelter's operation
1885-present	**German Protestant Home for the Aged and Infirm** (*Deutsche protestantische Heim für Alte und Gebrechliche*)
	5919 Magazine Street
	Renamed Covenant Home
1889-present	**German Protestant Bethany Home** (*Deutsche protestantische Bethanienheim*)
	3535 Esplanade Avenue
	Now called Bethany Home
1899	**Julius Weis Home for Aged and Infirm Israelites**
	Near Touro Infirmary
	Established by Touro Infirmary and Hebrew Benevolent Society

SOCIETIES AND ASSOCIATIONS

The Germans of the towns and cities of Louisiana, as in other American states with a strong German presence, formed a number of societies. The most important of these was the *Deutsche Gesellschaft* (German Society), which assisted newcomers (see chapter 2, "German Immigration to New Orleans"). As early as 1843 the need for such an organization was recognized. Although it was founded in 1847, it was not officially chartered until 1851 as a chapter of the *Deutsche Gesellschaft* of New York. Within three years several local branches of the *Deutsche Gesellschaft* banded together to form a central committee of German societies. It provided salaried agents to meet every ship bringing German immigrants to the port to ensure

Deutsche Gesellschaft (German Society) publication celebrating eighty years of history. *Courtesy of the Historic New Orleans Collection.*

that they were safely escorted to riverboats for the next leg of their journey. German Society agents met these travelers in other destinations along the way as well. In New Orleans, assistance was provided in going through the customs procedure for those knowing no English or whose papers were not in order. When needed, food, clothing, and transportation costs were provided by the society, and relatives were contacted for additional help. A shelter was provided for the sick, the infirm, and orphaned children needing protection, all manned by volunteer members of the German community. Jobs were also found for the newcomers who remained in the city.

The German organizations of the state had varying purposes, but few were purely social. A number were dedicated to giving aid and support, not only to their fellow Germans, but also to the wider community. These benevolent societies supported the charitable works of the German churches while also adopting other worthy causes. In New Orleans the profits of the annual *Volksfest* (People's Festival) held to celebrate May Day were used to fund the Howard Association, a non-German relief organization. These funds were also offered to German societies whose charitable activities had caused them financial difficulties. In later years the *Turnverein* (Turners' Association) took over the sponsorship of the *Volksfest* and donated the profits to the German Protestant Orphan Asylum. The German orphan asylums and old-age homes, which were supported by the German churches and societies, were open to the entire community although applicants of German descent were given preference.

Fraternal organizations also served primarily as charitable agencies. The Germans of the New Orleans area were enthusiastic about the American penchant for such secret societies and lodges. The purpose of the lodges formed by the Germans was to assist their members in times of need.

Most of these organizations provided life insurance to the families of members, furnished burial plots, and paid funeral expenses. While these lodges promoted fraternity and good fellowship they also assisted the unemployed in finding jobs. By the turn of the century there were more than twenty-five such associations serving the German population.

Perhaps the most popular were the groves of the United Ancient Order of Druids. The *Magnolia Hain* (Magnolia Grove), chartered in 1836, was the first German Druid grove in the area. By 1853 the Germania Grove No. 29 had almost a hundred members. Five more groves were chartered in rapid succession and operated independently until their merger into the *Concordia Hain.* It, in turn, merged with the other Louisiana *Haine,* forming the *Gross Hain* of the state. This Grand Grove of the Druids, organized in 1857, kept all of its records in the German language for many years.

The Germans of the region also joined the Free Masons society. The first Masonic lodge was formed in 1853, followed by the Germania Lodge No. 46, whose hall still stands on Bienville Street. These merged into the Germania Free Masons Society, to which every German-speaking Free Mason could belong.

The Independent Order of Odd Fellows was another fraternal organization popular with the Germans of New Orleans. It was established as a secret society in eighteenth-century England to offer fellowship and mutual help for the common laboring man. Because the larger trades had their own benevolent organizations, the I.O.O.F. was meant for those working in various or "odd" trades. Two of the lodges, Teutonia No. 10 and Germania No. 29, built tombs for their members in Odd Fellows Rest.

As the name *Turnverein* implies (turners were gymnasts/tumblers), this important society was dedicated to the development of the mind as well as the body. The first New Orleans chapter of this nationwide organization was established in 1851. The forty charter members met for this purpose at Louis Stein's on Orleans Street in the First District. Dr. Benjamin Maas, elected president, proposed joining the national Turners' Association and adopting the statutes of the *Turnverein* of New York. Its membership immediately rose to 140 and met within two months in a converted house. The large number of members necessitated a second *Turngemeinde* (chapter), which was located at Union and

Turners' Hall, 938 Lafayette Street. *Photograph by Raymond Calvert.*

Young Turners. *Courtesy of a private collection.*

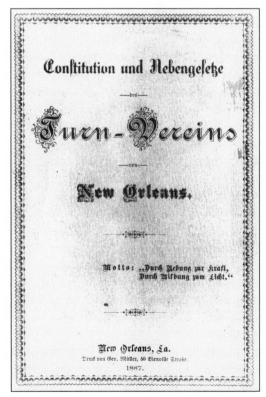

Constitution and Bylaws of the Turners' Association, 1887. *Courtesy of Special Collections, Tulane University.*

Admission ticket to performance of Turner Singers on January 22, 1905, at Turners' Hall. *Courtesy of a private collection.*

Carondelet streets in the Second District. In 1854 the *Turnverein* chapters were able to erect their own building on Lafayette Street, bordering the heavily German Fourth Municipality. The society sponsored a number of important activities. Its well-known *Turnschule* offered the children of members a full range of subjects, all taught in the German language. Excursions and hikes into the surrounding countryside were also organized by the Turners for their children's physical development. In addition to providing members and their families with exercise facilities and meeting rooms, Turners' Hall housed a library and an auditorium with a stage for the performance of German drama, dance, music, and song. This auditorium was the venue for regular Sunday evening cultural events. Balls, concerts, theater performances, and other forms of entertainment were offered to the members of the *Turnverein,* their families, and guests. The Turners had their own men's chorus but also lent their large auditorium to the many other German music and singing organizations of the city. The *Turnverein* also acted as a benevolent association and took over the administration of the German *Volksfest.* Late in 1917 the *Turnverein* was legally forced to use English in its correspondence, in direct contravention of its statutes requiring the use of German only.

The *Deutsche Companie* was founded by Solomon Marx in the early 1860s. Its purpose was to foster fellowship and promote the arts and sciences among the Jews of the city. The social affairs of the company ran the gamut from surprise parties to elaborate charity balls. To promote cultural pursuits the society maintained singing and dramatic groups and a circulating library. In 1872 the organization was renamed the *Harmonie Club.* Seven years later a sumptuous clubhouse was erected on Canal Street, now the location of the Boston Club. A similar organization was founded in 1891, the Young Men's Hebrew Association. This organization had the objective of establishing Jewish unity beyond congregation lines, within which intellectual, moral, and social improvement could be fostered. It leased quarters in Grunewald Hall, which unfortunately burned the next year. The decision was made to establish a permanent clubhouse, leading to the erection in 1896 of the ornate *Athenaeum* (Auditorium) at Clio Street and St. Charles Avenue. These two German-Jewish organizations had a Christian counterpart in the German organization *Schlaraffia,* founded in Prague in 1856. The New Orleans chapter was formed in 1930 to promote goodwill, art, and friendship, adopting the international motto *Kunst, Freundschaft und Humor* (Art, Friendship and Good Humor). Membership has always been limited to German speakers in all of the 300 chapters worldwide.

Athenaeum of the Young Men's Hebrew Association, St. Charles Avenue, from *History of the Jews of Louisiana. Courtesy of Touro Infirmary Archives.*

Trade and professional associations supported their members in their business pursuits and practices. Organizations for doctors, dentists, scientists, lawyers, teachers, etc., set standards for professional practice, shared knowledge, and made useful connections available. The draymen, dairymen, bakers, ironmongers, gardeners, mechanics, and other such tradesmen formed associations and unions to assure adequate pay and working conditions for their members. These organizations also had benevolent objectives. Quite a number, including one of the largest, the Louisiana German Draymen's Association, cared for the widows and orphaned children of its members. It also built a tomb in Greenwood Cemetery for the use of the membership. The *Allgemeiner Arbeiterbund* (General Workers Union), an organization for all workers, had branches in thirty cities. It assisted its members in cases of sickness, accident, and fire and provided them with old-age pensions and support for their widows and children.

The Germans of New Orleans organized societies to pursue almost every interest. The most numerous were church groups, but there were groups for political and literary discussion, for athletic activities, for pursuing both classical and popular music and song. The love of making music, combined with the German zest for parading, produced a number of marching bands. Jazz funeral processions and Mardi Gras marching bands are said to have been influenced by the German custom of brass-band parades. Even today many German villages in Bavaria proudly present their local brass bands, which parade in regional dress on holidays and for civic occasions.

The German's love of music and song was expressed in the formation of a number of singing societies in the city. New Orleans was the first city in the nation to organize a totally German singing club, the *Liederkranz,* founded in 1838. These societies met once or twice a week and gave frequent concerts and balls. Most singing societies were limited to male singers but a few formed mixed choruses. German festivals and celebrations of all kinds were almost always accompanied by performances of one or more *Gesängvereine* (singing associations). Some organizations even had their own singing groups within the membership, such as the *Turnverein,* the fraternal lodges, and the dramatic *Thalia Club.*

Volunteer military groups formed as early as the 1840s, not only to defend their adopted country when necessary, but also to accommodate the German love of drilling in uniform and discharging firearms. In 1845 the German newspaper the *Courier* reported that five German

German military organization preparing for parade, from the Deutsches Haus Collection. *Courtesy of a private collection.*

Joseph Sporrer's Military Band, 1893, from the Huber Collection. *Courtesy of the Historic New Orleans Collection.*

military companies regularly marched with knapsacks, freshly cleaned and oiled guns, blank cartridges, and firing sponges to Bayou St. John. There they met the German Louisiana Dragooners to exercise with arms and practice sharp-shooting. These volunteer militiamen received a subsidy from the state of Louisiana for maintaining their battle readiness. The German militias were able to furnish four companies for the Louisiana troops joining the Mexican War. During the Civil War two infantry regiments were primarily German, contributing two German generals to the Confederate forces. A favorite amusement of the militia was to form bands that gave outdoor concerts in the summer. At the turn of the century Joseph Sporrer's Military Band became well known for its Sunday concerts in City Park. The volunteer firemen also put on colorful exhibitions and parades, in addition to performing a real community service as firefighters.

The surprisingly large number of German societies that formed is partially explained by a need for local representation in the three widely separated German communities. During the 1850s, there was only one streetcar line linking Canal Street to Lafayette and Carrollton, which was quite expensive for the times (twenty-five cents). "Busses," which were drawn by mules, were cheaper but much slower. Since travel and communication between the separate German communities were limited, there was a need for local chapters in each area. In 1907, the *Deutsch-amerikanischer Staatsverband von Louisiana* (German-American State League of Louisiana) was organized. It was composed of about twenty German clubs and societies under the constitution of its parent organization, the National German-American Alliance, which had been formed seven years earlier in Philadelphia. The purpose of the alliance was to promote a sense of cohesiveness among German-Americans nationwide and to harness this power in a centralized organization. Beginning in 1910 the Louisiana League held annual events around October 6 called the *Deutsche Tage* (German Days) to commemorate the founding of Germantown in Pennsylvania in 1683. This effort was comprised of a number of speeches and events as symbols around which to rally the ethnic consciousness of the German-Americans of New Orleans. However, after the newness of the organization had worn off, inertia set in. The attendance at the monthly meetings dwindled, as did the support for the *Deutsche Tage,* which diminished every year. In 1914, on the eve of World War I, only twelve of the participating clubs sent delegates to the semiannual meeting. The end of the organization came in 1918 when the National Alliance was accused of high treason by the United States Senate and dissolved itself.

Almost 250 separate organizations are identified in the sections below. They are listed alphabetically according to type. Categories are: Benevolent, Cultural, Drama, Fraternal, German State/Regional, Heritage, Military, Music/Singing, Political, Religious, Rifle, Sports, Trade and Professional, and Volunteer Fire Companies. Founding dates, if known, are given, as are pertinent notes.

Benevolent Societies

1877 Allgemeine Wittwen und Waisen Kasse des vereinigten alten Ordens der Druiden von Louisiana (General Widows and Orphans Fund of the Ancient Order of the Druids of Louisiana)

1851 Baton Rouge Benevolent Society

1887 Claiborne deutscher Frauen Wohlthätigkeitsverein vom zweiten Distrikt (Claiborne German Women's Benevolent Association of the Second District)

1879 Clio Frauen Unterstützungsverein von New Orleans (Clio Ladies' Aid Society of New Orleans)

1847 Deutsche Gesellschaft von New Orleans (German Society of New Orleans), St. Peter Street at West de la Rue

1890 Deutscher Frauen Lafayette-Unterstützungsverein des dritten Distrikts (German Ladies' Aid Society of Lafayette of the Third District)

1884 Deutscher Louisiana Frauen Unterstützungsverein von New Orleans (German Ladies' Aid Society of Louisiana)

1883 Deutscher New Orleanser Frauen Unterstützungsverein (German Ladies' Aid Society of New Orleans)

? Deutscher Männer Unterstützungsverein (German Men's Assistance Association)

1882 Deutscher Unterstützungsverein des dritten Distrikts (German Assistance Association of the Third District)

1879 Deutscher Unterstützungsverein von Algiers, Louisiana (German Assistance Association of Algiers, Louisiana)

1886 Frauen Einigkeit Unterstützungsverein des zweiten Distrikts von New Orleans (United Ladies' Aid Society of the Second District of New Orleans)

1888 Frauen Unterstützungsverein Concordia (Concordia Ladies' Aid Society)

1885 Frauen Unterstützungsverein des dritten Distrikts in New Orleans, Louisiana (Ladies' Aid Society of the Third District in New Orleans)

1885 Frauen Wohlthätigkeitsverein vom Ersten Distrikt von New Orleans, Louisiana (German Ladies' Benevolent Association of the First District of New Orleans, Louisiana)

1889   German-American Benevolent Association of New Orleans
1921   German and Austrian Destitute Relief Commission of New Orleans, founded by the *Deutsche Gesellschaft* (German Society)
1885   Germania Frauen Einigkeit Unterstützungsverein von New Orleans (Germania United Ladies' Aid Society of New Orleans)
1880   Louisiana Frauen Unterstützungsverein (Louisiana Ladies' Aid Society)
?   Louisiana Wohltätigkeitsverein (Louisiana Benevolent Association)
?   Männer Unterstützungsverein des dritten Distrikts (Men's Assistance Association of the Third District)
?   Poydras deutsche Frauen Unterstützungsverein von New Orleans (Poydras German Ladies' Aid Society)
1870   Swiss Benevolent Association
?   United Brothers Benevolent Association
?   Washington Wohlthätigkeitsverein (Washington Benevolent Association)

Cultural Societies

1849   Deutsch-Amerikanischer Bildungsverein (German-American Culture Association)
1869   Deutscher Harmonie Club von New Orleans (Club for German Harmony, New Orleans); dedicated to promoting the arts among German Jews; membership about 500 men; successor organization of *Deutsche Companie*
1870   Germania Club; Custom House and Royal streets
1870   Nord-Deutscher Harmonie Club von Carrollton (North German Club for Harmony, Carrollton); for promoting the arts among German Jews
1849   Turngemeinde von New Orleans (Turners' Club of New Orleans, chapter of *Turnverein*)
1851   Turnverein von New Orleans (Turners' [Gymnasts'/Tumblers'] Association of New Orleans)
1891   Young Men's Hebrew Association; clubhouse (Athenaeum) at St. Charles Avenue and Clio Street

Drama Societies

1857   Deutsche philo-dramatische Gesellschaft (German Philo-Dramatic Society)
1837   Deutscher Nationalklub (German National Club); established German National Theater; director Oskar Guttmann
1853   Diletantenverein (Dilettantes' Association); director J. G. Meyer
1851   German Dramatic Club of New Orleans
1855   Liebhaber Theater Gesellschaft (Theater Lovers Society); director Johann Meinken, former member of Johann Rittig's troupe
1867   Orleans Dramatic Relief Association

1893   St. Boniface Dramatic Club of New Orleans, Louisiana
1854   Society of Adlersburg
1857   Thalia Club; dedicated to comedy and poetry
1875   Dramatische Gesellschaft (Drama Society); amateur local theater group

Fraternal Societies
Ancient Order of Good Fellows (Grand Lodge of Louisiana)
?   Arcanum Ark
?   Bismarck Grotto No. 1
?   Bismarck Hoch Erz [Highest Degree] Grotto No. 1
?   Oliver Grotto No. 2
?   Oliver Hoch Erz [Highest Degree] Grotto No. 2
?   Schiller Lodge No. 4; 82 Camp Street; meetings Monday evenings

Independent Order of Odd Fellows (1832)
?   Central Lager No. 11 (Central Camp No. 11)
?   Franklin Conclave No. 7
1859   Helvetia No. 44; Jefferson City
1853   Hermann Lodge No. 39; Marigny Building, Third District; meetings Wednesday evenings
1848   Independence Lodge No. 23
1849   I.O.O.F. Germania Lodge No. 29; Jefferson Hall, Fourth District; meetings Tuesday evenings; tomb in Odd Fellows Rest
1868   Oliver Conclave No. 16
1846   Teutonia Lodge No. 10; Room # 1, Odd Fellows Hall, Camp and Lafayette streets, meetings Tuesday nights; tomb in Greenwood Cemetery

Masonic Societies (F. & A.M.)
?   Alexander von Humbolt Lodge No. 22; 23 St. Charles Avenue; meetings Wednesday evenings
?   Disciples of Pythagoras No. 10; 23 St. Charles, meetings Friday evenings
?   Germania Assembly No. 15, Rainbow Order for Girls
1844   Germania Freimaurer Unterstützungsverein (Germania Free Masons Assistance Association)
?   Germania Lodge No. 46; St. Louis Street
?   Kosmos Lodge No. 171

Secret Societies
?   B.B.G.Y.M.
    Columbia Wigwam No. 2
    Louisiana Wigwam No. 1
?   O.D.H.S.

Louisiana Lodge No. 1
?   O.E.S.
Germania Chapter No. 190
?   S.W.M. (Heptasophs)
Guttenberg Conclave No. 5
Schiller Conclave No. 6
Washington Conclave No. 6

United Ancient Order of Druids (Grand Grove of Louisiana)

1856 Eichen Hain [Oak Grove] No. 2
1869 Germania Hain [Grove] No. 11
1857 Goethe Hain [Grove] No. 4; 32 Camp Street
1857 Gross Hain [Grand Grove] von Louisiana; motto: *Vereinigung, Friede, Eintracht* (Unity, Peace, Harmony)
1855 Magnolia Hain [Grove] No. 1; Claussen's Hall, corner Baronne and Perdido streets; 1861 moved to Toulouse near Marais Street
?   Magnolia Hoch Erz Kapitel No. 2 (Magnolia Highest Degree Chapter No. 2)
1857 Mispel Hain [Grove] No. 66; Tchoupitoulas Street
?   New Orleans Degree Grove No. 1; 82 Camp Street
?   New Orleanser Garden Hain [Grove] No. 1
?   Normal Supreme Arch Chapter No. 3
1857 Pioneer Hain [Grove] No. 3
?   Teutonia Hoch Erz Kapitel No. 1 (Teutonia Highest Degree Chapter No. 1)

Vereinigte (United) Order of Red Men

?   Lahaska Stamm [Tribe] No. 2
?   Osyka Stamm [Tribe] No. 1

Other

1884 Bärenklub (Bears' Club); carnival club fostering song and drama; met at Franz Willem's Bar on St. Charles Avenue across from St. Charles Hotel; secretary Georg Müller published humorous, satirical German newspaper *Narrhalle* as organ of Bear's Club
1862 Deutsche Companie (German Company); German-Jewish social club founded by Solomon Marx; forerunner of *Harmonie Club*
?   Deutscher Magnolia-Verein des vierten Distrikts (German Magnolia Association of the Fourth District)
1930 Schlaraffia; motto: *Kunst, Freundschaft und Humor* (Art, Friendship and Good Humor); men's German-speaking social club founded in Prague in 1856; over 300 chapters worldwide; membership by invitation only
1886 Teutonia Lodge No. 61, Ritter des Pythias Ordens (Order of the Knights of Pythias)

German State/Regional Associations

? Plattdeutscher Verein von New Orleans ([Speakers of] Low German [dialect] Association of New Orleans)

1888 Rhein-Pfälzer Unterstützungsverein von New Orleans (Rhineland-Palatinate Assistance Association of New Orleans)

1887 Schwaben Verein von New Orleans (Swabian Association of New Orleans)

? Schweitzer Gesellschaft von New Orleans ([Albert] Schweitzer Society of New Orleans)

1855 Schweizer Gesellschaft (Swiss Society)

? Schweizerbund, Sektion New Orleans (Swiss League, New Orleans Section)

Heritage Societies

1834 Deutsche Brüderschaft (German Brotherhood); Front, Levee, and Fourth streets; first social/heritage organization of Germans; originally founded to support the sick; chartered in 1838; rechartered in 1864

1835 Deutscher Freundschaftsbund von Carrollton (German Friendship League of Carrollton); established society tomb dated 1850 with twenty-four vaults in Carrollton Cemetery

1851 Deutscher Verein im dritten Distrikt (German Association in the Third District)

1853 Deutscher Verein im ersten [First] Distrikt

1853 Deutscher Verein im vierten [Fourth] Distrikt

1854-56 Deutscher Verein im zweiten [Second] Distrikt

1928 Deutsches Haus; founded by *Deutsche Gesellschaft, Turnverein,* and German singing societies; only continuously operating private ethnic clubhouse in New Orleans

Military Societies

1847 Battalion of Louisiana Volunteers; commanded by 1st Lt. Karl Fiesca, only German to reach such a high rank in Mexican War; batallion fought in Battle of Vera Cruz

1861 Deutsche Garde von New Orleans (German Guard of New Orleans)

1835 Deutsche Jäger Companie (German Hunters Company); commanded by *Kapitän* Heinrich Antz (developed out of the Steuben Guard, commanded by *Kapitän* Vincent Nolte, 1804); reactivated to fight in Mexican War; one of three companies to form all-German batallion

? Deutscher Militär-Verein von New Orleans (German Military Association of New Orleans)

1878 Deutsches (German) Regiment Company D

1856 Deutsches (German) Regiment von New Orleans

1848 German-American Battalion (German Guard) commanded by *Kapitän* Frederick Otto Eickholz

1879-   German Battalion; part of Louisiana state militia and guard
84

1861   German Home Guard No. 2, Fourth District

1861   German Independent Guard

1842   German Louisiana Fusiliers; commanded by *Kapitän* Carl Fieska

1842   German Orleans Fusiliers; commanded by *Kapitän* H. H. Wagner

1845   German Rifle Company H; commanded by *Kapitän* Theodore Grabau

1845   German Rifleman; commanded by *Kapitän* Heinrich Antz

?   German Veterans' Union

1851   Independent Winter Guard

1846   Jackson Guards; commanded by *Kapitän* Nikolaus Fidler; organized to fight in Mexican War

?   Lafayette Garde (guard)

1831   Louisiana Dragooner; commanded by *Kapitän* Maximilian F. Bonzano

1846   Louisiana Fuselier Companies No. 1 and No. 2; organized to fight in Mexican War; one of three companies to form all German batallion

1846   Montezuma Regiment; made up of four German companies organized to fight in Mexican War; officers of German companies: Maj. Karl Fiesca; Capt. George Dippacher (64 men); Capt. Karl Wirth (82 men); Capt. J. E. Bohler (62 men); Captain Romer (65 men)

1846   Regiment of Louisiana Volunteers; commanded of Colonel de Russy (fought in Mexican War); had two German companies commanded by Captains Christian Wirth and Frederich Otto Eichholz

1846   Schwarze Husaren (Black Hussars); commanded by *Kapitän* Theodore Bruning; German cavalry corps created by Capt. Charles Eckart of the German Louisiana Dragooners to fight in Mexican War

1884   Second Battalion Light Infantry, Louisiana Legion

1804   Steuben Guard; predecessor of the *Deutsche Jäger,* 1835; commanded by *Kapitän* Vincent Nolte

1851   Volunteer Companie A, Tenth Regiment

Music/Singing Societies

1856   Allgemeiner deutscher Musiker Verband von New Orleans (General German Music Alliance of New Orleans)

1857   Apollo Gesängverein (Apollo Singing Association)

1856   Beethoven Sängerbund (Beethoven Singers League)

1860   Carrollton Union

1838   Deutscher Liederkranz (German Singing Circle); believed to be first German singing society in U.S.; Dr. Authenrieth, first president; established fund for Hermann Monument in Detmold, Germany; in 1839 presented Haydn's *Creation* at St. Charles Hotel, in 1840 Romberg's *The Clock*

1889   Deutscher Liederkreis (German Song Circle) of the Fourth District;

members included leaders of German community Charles F. Buck, Joseph Voegtle, A. G. Ricks

1872 Deutscher Männer Gesängverein (German Men's Singing Association); Dr. Wilhoft, first president; Otto Weber, first music director; joined with Liederkranz to reorganize in 1878 as *Deutscher Liedertafel* (German Song Board); Ernst J. Wenck, first president; club at Canal Street and Exchange Alley; admitted non-Germans, women, and children; by 1881 had over 900 members

1873 Deutscher Männer Gesängverein vom sechsten Distrikt, New Orleans (German Men's Singing Association of the Sixth District)

1928 Deutsches Haus Sängerchor (Deutsches Haus Singers Chorus)

1885 Frohsinn (Glee Club); separated from Liedertafel; limited to Germans

1885 German Imperial Band; organized for Cotton Exposition

1866 Germania Men's Choir

1876 German Military Band

1874 Germania Quartet

1851 Gesängverein Sektion des Turnvereins von New Orleans (Singing Society Section of the Turners' Association of New Orleans)

1882 Harugari Männerchor von New Orleans (Harugari Men's Chorus); stated purpose was preservation of German song; frequently performed at *Volksfest* and other benefits

? Helvetia Sängerbund (Swiss Singers League)

? Mozart Verein (Mozart Association)

1882 New Orleans Quartette Klub; considered the most celebrated German singing society in the South; founder J. Hanno Deiler

1890s New Orleans (Tyrolean) Zither Club; organized by Victor Huber, Viennese composer and teacher

? Orpheus Quartet Club

1897 Schubert Verein ([Franz] Schubert Association)

1857 Unterstützungsverein der Musiker zu New Orleans (Assistance Association for Musicians in New Orleans)

1889 Vereinigte Sänger (United Singers); organized for laying-of-cornerstone ceremony for *Sängerhalle;* singers from Mobile also participated

Political Societies

1871 Bürger-Taxzahler-Arbeiter-Assembly von New Orleans (Citizens' Taxpaying Workers Assembly of New Orleans)

1854 Centralcomite der deutschen Vereine der ersten, zweiten, dritten und vierten Distrikts (Central Committee of the German Associations of the First, Second, Third and Fourth Districts)

1848 Centralverein zur Beförderung der Republik in Deutschland
(ca.) (Central Association for the Advancement of Germany as a Republic); dedicated to establishing German republic in the *Vaterland;* national

leaders: Karl Schurz and Gottfried Kinkel; Kinkel came to New Orleans to raise funds in 1848

1907 Deutsch-amerikanischer Staatsverband von Louisiana (German-American State League of Louisiana); formed by about twenty German organizations to promote German ethnicity

?   Freier Männerverein (Free Men's Association)

?   German Democratic Club of New Orleans

1867 German Republican Club

1909 Staatsverband für Louisiana von der deutsch-amerikanischen Nationalbund (Louisiana League of the National German-American Alliance); united the German-American societies of Louisiana under one central organization; continuation of *Centralcomite der deutschen Vereine* of 1854 (see above)

Religious Societies

Affiliated Religious Societies

1838 Association for the Relief of Jewish Widows and Orphans

1856 Deutscher christlicher Männerverein von New Orleans (German Christian Men's Association)

1866 Deutscher protestanten Waisenhaus Verein (German Protestant Orphan Asylum Association)

?   Deutscher römisch-katholischer Centralverein von Louisiana unter dem Schütze des heiligen Bonifazius, Apostels der Deutschen (German Roman Catholic Central Association of Louisiana under the Protection of St. Boniface, Apostle of the Germans)

1905 Frauen-Hilfsverein des deutschen protestantischen Heims für Alte und Gebrechliche (Ladies' Aid Society of the German Protestant Home for the Aged and Infirm)

1876 Frauen-Hilfsverein des deutschen protestantischen Waisenhauses (Ladies' Aid Society of the German Protestant Orphan Asylum)

1854- Hebrew Benevolent Society
1921

1847 Ladies' Hebrew Benevolent Society of New Orleans

1900 Provident Aid Association; Jewish charitable association founded
(ca.) by Simon Gumbel

1867 Young Men's Hebrew Benevolent Society

Church-Related Organizations

1915 Altar Society of the Clio Street Evangelical Church

1925 Altar Society of the First Evangelical Church

1915 Christlicher Männer-Unterstützungsverein der Clio Strasse evangelischen Kirche (Christian Men's Assistance Association of the Clio Street Evangelical Church)

?   Christlicher Männer-Unterstützungsverein der ersten deutschen protestantischen Gemeinde von New Orleans (Christian Men's Assistance Association of the First German Protestant Congregation)

? Deutscher Chor der Clio Strasse evangelischen Kirche (German Choir of the Clio Street Evangelical Church)

1931 Deutscher christlicher Männerverein der zweiten deutschen presbyterischen Kirche (German Christian Men's Association of the Second German Presbyterian Church)

1879 Deutscher christlicher Unterstützungsverein der zweiten deutschen presbyterischen Kirche (German Christian Assistance Association of the Second German Presbyterian Church)

1854 Deutscher St. Joseph Waisenverein (German St. Joseph's Orphan Association)

? Erste deutsche evangelische Gemeinde im sechsten Distrikt (First German Evangelical Congregation in the Sixth District)

1925 Evangelical Brotherhood of the First Evangelical Church

? Frauen Altarverein der St. Heinrich Kirche im sechsten Distrikt (Ladies' Altar Society of St. Henry's Church in the Sixth District)

1880 Frauen Unterstützungsverein der Craps Strasse methodisten Kirche (Ladies' Aid Society of the Craps Street Methodist Church)

1853 Frauenverein, Zion Lutheran Church (Ladies' Society)

1915 Frauen-Wohlthätigkeitsverein der Clio Strasse evangelischen Kirche (Ladies' Benevolent Society of the Clio Street Evangelical Church)

1886 Frauen-Wohlthätigkeitsverein, erste deutsche protestantische Gemeinde von New Orleans, Louisiana (Ladies' Benevolent Society, First German Protestant Congregation of New Orleans, Louisiana)

1925 Frauen-Wohlthätigkeitsverein (Ladies' Benevolent Society) of the First Evangelical Church

1915 Gleaners Society of the Clio Street Evangelical Church

1925 Gleaners Society of the First Evangelical Church

1915 Heidenkind-Waisenverein der Clio Strasse evangelischen Kirche (Unbaptized Orphans' Association of the Clio Street Evangelical Church)

1925 Helping Hands Society of the First Evangelical Church

1915 Krankencomite der Clio Strasse evangelischen Kirche (Clio Street Evangelical Church Committee for the Sick)

1855 Missionsverein der Clio Strasse evangelischen Kirche (Missions Association of the Clio Street Evangelical Church)

1915 Nähschule der Clio Strasse evangelischen Kirche (Sewing School of the Clio Street Evangelical Church)

1867 St. Anna Benevolent Society (Holy Trinity Church)

1880 St. Bonifazius Wohlthätigkeitsverein der deutschen katholischen St. Bonifazius-Kirche (St. Boniface Benevolent Association of the German Catholic Church of St. Boniface)

1874 St. Heinrich Altarverein zur Unterstützung der kranken Mitglieder (St. Henry's Altar Society for the Support of Ailing Members)

1890 St. Heinrich deutscher katholischer Wohlthätigkeitsverein (St. Henry's German Catholic Benevolent Association)

1880s St. Helena Frauenverein der St. Bonifazius Kirche zu New Orleans, Louisiana (St. Helena Ladies' Society of the St. Boniface Church in New Orleans, Louisiana)

1867 St. Joseph School, Church and Benevolent Society (Holy Trinity Church)

1856 St. Maria Himmelfahrt gemeinshaftliche katholische Wohlthätigkeits-Gesellschaft (St. Mary's Assumption Catholic Congregation Benevolent Society)

?   St. Marien Altarverein (St. Mary's Altar Society)

1915 Tabetha Verein der Clio Strasse evangelischen Kirche (Tabetha Society of the Clio Street Evangelical Church)

1925 Usher's Club of the First Evangelical Church

1925 Young Men's Fellowship Club of the First Evangelical Church

Rifle Clubs

1851 Deutsche Schützengesellschaft (German Shooting Society)

1888 Deutscher Schützenverein von New Orleans (German Shooting Association of New Orleans)

1860 Gulf Coast Scharfschützen (Gulf Coast Sharpshooters)
(ca.)

?   Scharfschützen Companie (Sharpshooters' Company)

?   Swiss Rifle Club

1870 Turner Schützen (Turner [*Turnverein*] Shooters)

Sports Clubs

1849 German Pedestrian Society of Carrollton

1900 Pyramid (Turner gymnasts/tumblers)

1912 Vierzehntes Turnbezirk von New Orleans (Turners of New Orleans, Fourteenth Chapter)

Schützenhalle (shooting gallery) proposed for the Third American *Bundes-Schiessen* (Rifle Association) competition, Louisiana Cotton Centennial Exhibition, 1884. *Courtesy of the Historic New Orleans Collection.*

Trade and Professional Associations

1850   Allgemeiner Arbeiterverein (General Workers Union); founded by carpenters, tailors, shoemakers, draymen, and metalworkers

1854   Association of Cigar Makers and Factory Workers

1853   Association of Coffee House Owners

1850   Bakers Benevolent Society; 120 members; meetings held at Dauphine and Elysian Fields

1853   Bund der Barbiere (Barbers' Union)

1854   Deutscher Handwerker Verein des vierten Distrikts in New Orleans (German Handworkers' Association of the Fourth District)

?   Deutsche Lehrerverein (German Teachers' Association)

1854   Deutscher Louisiana Draymannsverein von New Orleans (German-Louisiana Draymen's Association of New Orleans); meetings held at Engine House #7; tomb for members in Greenwood Cemetery

1889   Gambrinus Unterstützungsverein deutscher Bräuerei-Arbeiter von New Orleans (Gambrinus Assistance Society for German Brewery Workers of New Orleans)

1878   Gärtner gegenseitige Unterstützungs-Gesellschaft von New Orleans (Gardener's Mutual Assistance Society of New Orleans)

1854   German Mechanics' Society, Fourth District

1854   German Screwmen's Association

?   Louisiana Draymen's Association

1854   Louisiana Gewerbe Verein (Louisiana Business Association)

1878   New Orleans Bäcker Gesellen Verein (German Bakers' Apprentices Association)

?   New Orleans Bräumeister Verein (New Orleans Brewmasters Association)

1874   New Orleans deutscher Cottonpress Arbeiter Unterstützungsverein (German Cotton Press Workers' Assistance Association of New Orleans)

1853   Schreiner Arbeiter (Cabinetmakers)

?   Schuh- und Stiefelmacher Bund (Shoe and Bootmakers' League)

1854   Tischler Unterstützungsverein (Joiners Assistance Association)

1852   Verein deutscher Ärtze (Association of German Physicians)

1881   Vereinigte Schneider Unterstützungs-Gesellschaft von New Orleans (United Tailors' Assistance Society of New Orleans)

1854   Vereinigter Schuhmacher Bund (United Shoemakers' League)

Volunteer Fire Companies

?   David Crockett Ladies' Auxiliary

1841   David Crockett Steam Fire Company No. 1; first called Gretna Fire Company No. 1; oldest continuously active volunteer fire company in the United States

1885   Gretna Haken und Leiter Exempt Wohlthätigkeitsverein (Gretna Hook and Ladder Benevolent Society)

1885   Gretna Hook and Ladder Company No. 1
(ca.)

1836   Home Hook and Ladder Company No. 1, Faubourg Bouligny, Jefferson City; Marengo and Live Oak streets

1845   Jefferson Feuer Companie No. 22 (Jefferson Fire Company No. 22), Tchoupitoulas between Philip and Soraparu streets, Fourth District; motto: "Ready at the First Sound"; tomb located in Lafayette Cemetery No. 1, shows 1852 hand-pumper fire engine

1843   Louisiana Spritzen Companie No. 10 (Louisiana Dousing [Fire] Company), Dumaine Street; engine house also used for German church services

1900   Mechanics' Fire Company No. 1; Gretna

1861   Mechanics' Fire Company No. 6; Commerce Street

1846   Pioneer Fire Engine Company No. 1, Faubourg East Bouligny, Jefferson City; Magazine between General Pershing and Milan streets

1854   Vigilant Feuer Companie No. 3 (Vigilant Fire Company No. 3)

1834   Volunteer Fire Department #10, St. Claude Avenue and Rampart Street

1884   William Tell Hook and Ladder Company; Newton and Third streets, Gretna

CHAPTER EIGHT

Entertainment

To a great extent, life in the German communities of the New Orleans area reflected the way of life left behind in the *Vaterland* (fatherland, i.e., German states). Socializing in these communities centered around the family and its celebrations of birthdays, anniversaries, and holidays, around festivals and activities of the German community, around the church and its support groups, and around the innumerable other organizations and societies to which the Germans belonged.

The home was the center for observing family occasions with friends. Birthdays, engagements, anniversaries, and such were celebrated with drinking, dining, and dancing to the music of small ensembles. Elaborate buffets were prepared by the housewife, who took the opportunity to show off her culinary talents. Christmas Eve, like Easter, centered on the family's children, but Christmas and the day after were given over to socializing among the adults. Sumptuous Christmas parties were put on at home, while many of the German associations rented public or private facilities. *Sylvesterabend* (New Year's Eve) was likewise an occasion for adult entertainment in the German clubs, halls, and hotels of New Orleans.

Despite the strong Mediterranean/Catholic influences in the city, which had turned the population away from the puritanical Sunday practices of most American cities, the "excessive German carousing" on this holy day was sharply criticized by many factions in the city. The German Sunday was not just a day for going to church and remaining quietly at home but rather a day for visiting friends, playing cards, and attending Sunday-night dances. The many beer gardens and dancehalls offered large, pleasant surroundings for these weekend activities. They also served as venues for the meetings and social events of the many German organizations of the city.

On Sundays the men of the German community liked to participate in the shooting contests sponsored by the German military organizations. Afterward the organizations often paraded to City Park to give band concerts, a practice begun in 1889 by Joseph Sporrer's military band. German families would often spend the whole afternoon and evening in the park, staying until after dark to watch the free moving pictures, which were projected on a screen at the bandstand.

After church in the summer months, families also liked to take picnic baskets on the train to the amusement parks of Milneberg, West End, and Spanish Fort, or to the north shore of Lake Pontchartrain. Spanish Fort was also frequently the site for presentations by the *Liedertafel* singing society, another favorite weekend entertainment of the German community. In the mild New Orleans winters the whole family visited the beer gardens and halls, most of which provided *Familienbälle* (family dancing) on weekend evenings (see chapter 5, "Breweries and Beer Gardens").

The native German love of civic celebrations was well received in New Orleans, which was already noted for its public carnival and many parades. One illustration was the event put on by the German community for the inauguration of Michael Hahn as governor of Louisiana. Hahn, who was a native German and preferred his own language to English, was unloved in the general community. He was widely considered a traitor to the Confederacy because of his close ties to the Union while the city was occupied during the Civil War. His election in 1864 was possible only because of stringent voting qualifications imposed by the Union. Nevertheless his inauguration as governor was a great occasion for the whole city because it marked the return of civil government after military occupation. Since there was no structure large enough for the ceremonies, Lafayette Square, across from the city hall, was designated as the site. The tree trunks in this urban park were whitewashed, their branches were hung with decorative vines, the walks were spread with fresh shells, and an amphitheater surrounding a raised speakers' platform was built. The square was also decorated with an array of flags and Chinese lanterns. At sunrise a 100-gun salute was fired to announce the occasion to the populace, which soon packed the surrounding streets. A 300-piece band played, choruses of children sang, and church bells rang to open the ceremonies and introduce the speeches. That evening, parades wound through the streets, and a brilliant ball was held at the French Opera House.

German theater was an integral part of life in the German community of the New Orleans area. This tradition, which was brought from the *Vaterland,* encountered a corresponding love of the performing arts in the natives of New Orleans. German theater did not refer to buildings but rather to productions in the German language, which were put

German community gathering on Lafayette Square for inauguration of Gov. Michael Hahn, 1864. *Courtesy of the Historic New Orleans Collection.*

on in theaters all over the city. The American, Pelican, St. Charles, Creole Ballroom, and Gaiety theaters were particularly popular venues. Of great importance to the German community was the well-appointed auditorium of the *Turnverein* (Turners' Association), which was regularly used for both amateur and professional performances. There were also several structures built specifically to house German-language productions, beginning in 1839 with the first German theater at Magazine Street and Delord (now Howard Avenue). A performance in German on December 22 had the distinction of being the first to take place on any stage in America, predating New York's German theater by two weeks. Under the management of Adolph Icks, this theater ran a series of German productions that, according to the *Daily Picayune,* played to full houses. Ferdinand's *Yd'sche Truppe* (Yiddish Troupe) was so successful despite the language barrier that hundreds had to be turned away. Several years later Rudolph Riese, formerly of the German Theater of Philadelphia, undertook a new venture in a theater on the corner of Nayades (St. Charles) and Polymnia streets. He and Louisa Thielemann also staged performances on Old Levee Street (Decatur). These efforts to establish professional German theater in New Orleans remained spotty in the 1830s and 1840s. Nevertheless 1845 marked the first German-language performance in America of

Goethe's *Faust,* twenty years earlier than the date commonly accepted. But it was not until the next decade that the German-language theater became well established.

Most notable among the buildings erected in New Orleans for the performing arts was the National Theater, an elegant Greek Revival structure originally built in 1856 as Werlein Concert Hall to house musical events. It was located at Baronne and Perdido streets (later the De Soto Hotel site, now Le Pavillon Hotel). Shortly thereafter it was leased by Wilhelm Boettner, who redecorated the entire building, enlarged the stage, and added a bar, restaurant, and flower stand. For the 1859-60 season Boettner opened the building as a German theater. It was widely recognized as one of the finest of its kind in America.

Up to this point a great number of productions had been staged by various thespian societies in New Orleans, which delayed the development of professional German theater until the 1850s. Foremost of these local drama groups was the German *Diletantenverein* (Dilettantes' Association) of New Orleans, an organization of accomplished young Germans directed by J. G. Meyer. In the 1850s outstanding theater companies, such as those of Christian and Louisa Thielemann and W. C. Adlersberg, began to include New Orleans on their circuits, bringing internationally renowned performers to the city. After a short run a decade earlier, the Thielemanns, directors of the German theater in St. Louis and Chicago, put on thirty-one performances in New Orleans in the first six months of 1851. With the return of W. C. Adlersberg from Cincinnati in 1854, German theater in New Orleans reached its zenith.

Johann Rittig and his wife left Adlersberg to form their own troupe and drafted their talent from the *Diletantenverein.* The national theater troupes had inspired a higher level of professionalism in the local companies, which now could give accomplished performances. The Rittigs adopted the *Turnverein* theater for their regular Sunday-night productions. Their performances were so popular that they expanded to three productions a week and moved to the larger American Theater. Guest artists were brought in from other cities as German theater became continuous, supported by these visiting performers and local dramatic clubs.

Fewer German theater pieces were produced during the Civil War. In 1862, a German theater site was established by Friedrich Brooks for his German City Theater group in Armory Hall, at Camp and Poydras streets. Competing with this drama group was the Lafayette Volkstheater established at the same time in Eagle Hall at Prytania and Felicity streets. Another troupe opened up in Lusitanos Hall in 1863, offering one- and two-act farces, which were popular at the time. In 1865 it moved to the St. Charles Opera House, where it took on more serious works, including Schiller's *Wilhelm Tell.* Later that year, however, Gustav Ostermann rented the French Opera House twice a week, including its scenic facilities. He not only gave performances of Schiller's works, including *Wilhelm Tell,* but also presented Goethe's *Faust.* With the superior facilities of the French Opera House at his disposal, Ostermann was soon successful in driving out the other theater troupes trying to operate under wartime conditions.

As soon as the war ended German theater blossomed. In 1865 41 different German plays were performed, topped by 69 in 1870 and reaching an all-time high of 128 productions the next year. This year, 1871, marked the unification of the German states by Bismarck, resulting in the founding of the German Empire. This momentous event in Europe had a unifying effect on the German community of New Orleans, giving it a feeling of prestige and sense of pride in its unique culture. A renaissance of German theater resulted, bringing famous actors from Germany such as Fanny Janauschek and Elizabeth von Stamwitz. Audiences swelled, assisted by the highest rate of immigration to the city since the Civil War had begun.

The popularity of German theater in its day was also due to the *Gemütlichkeit* (warm, pleasant, informal atmosphere) afforded by a dramatic evening. The programs were similar to those of other theaters of this period, having one long comedy or tragedy followed by a farce in conclusion. In the German theater, however, food and drink were served during the performance, followed by a ball in the theater itself or in a nearby hall. Because of the popularity of German drama, most of the theaters in the city staged plays in that language. At least two thousand performances by over two hundred playwrights were recorded between 1839 and 1890.

In the 1880s interest in German theater gradually declined as the German community became more assimilated. In the next decade only irregular performances by local amateur groups were given. By the turn of the century, when second- and third-generation Germans had lost interest in the language and culture of the fatherland, German theater disappeared from New Orleans.

One of the most important cultural pursuits fostered by the Germans of the region, however, was music. Their love of music was manifested not only in attendance at symphony and opera performances but also in the musical activities in which the Germans themselves took part. A number of German singing societies developed, the first in 1838, named the *Deutscher Liederkranz* (German Singing Circle). Not only did these singing societies practice old favorites but they also wrote their own music. J. C. Viereck's arrangement of the well-known Confederate marching song "Dixie" was first published in New Orleans by Werlein's Music Company. In addition to the more formal singing societies, small neighborhood instrumental groups were organized, which met

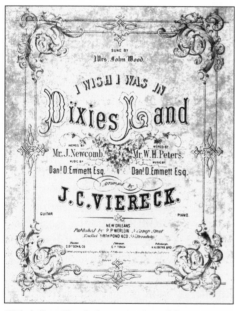

"Dixie" Confederate marching song arranged by Joseph Viereck, first published by Werlein's Music Company. *Courtesy of the Historic New Orleans Collection.*

Philip Werlein's Music Store, Canal Street. *Courtesy of the Louisiana Collection, Earl K. Long Library, University of New Orleans.*

weekly in members' homes. These groups relished the sheer joy of playing the familiar German compositions as well as the socializing that a *Musikabend* (evening of music) afforded.

The culmination of this love of song was the selection of New Orleans as the site for the 1890 annual convention of the North American *Sängerbund* (Singers' Society). A hall was built at Lee Circle for the occasion. In October of 1889 festivities were organized to celebrate the laying of the cornerstone of this *Sängerhalle*. A parade formed on Canal Street led by Mayor Shakespeare and the president of the *Sängerhalle* Committee, Jacob Hassinger. These dignitaries were followed by the consul generals of the city and state and municipal officials, all on horseback or in carriages. Twelve bands, the various singing societies and other German associations, military companies, turners, etc., followed on foot.

The *Sängerhalle* was built on the granite-block foundations of the Masonic Temple, which had been laid facing Lee Circle fifteen years earlier. Because construction had not continued, the Grand Lodge of the State of Louisiana placed this substructure at the disposal of the *Sängerfest* Committee. The growing *Halle* was decorated with flags and streamers for the cornerstone event, as were many houses on the parade route. The crowd filled all the available space around Lee Circle, while the parade participants filed onto the grandstand erected for the event. An orchestra opened the ceremonies, followed by a round of choruses from the *Vereinigte Sänger* (United Singers), many speeches, and the laying of the cornerstone by President Hassinger. At the close of the ceremonies the local singing clubs and bands led the guests to Coliseum Hall for a banquet and more songs and speeches. Special recognition was given to the local singers as well as to the Mobile singing society, which had traveled to New Orleans for the occasion.

The *Sängerhalle* for the twenty-sixth North American Singers' Association festival was a huge, ornate structure built to house 1,700 singers from sixty-four different German singing societies, a 100-piece orchestra, and 6,400 spectators. This songfest was a three-day affair, which took place in February of 1890. Each of the six performances was a sellout, with people standing in the streets just to hear the singing. Until that time, no presentation in the city had attracted such large audiences.

The songfest, given by these men's choruses from all over the country, was a great cultural and financial success. It helped to continue the interest in German music and song in the community long past the turn of the century. In 1953, more than sixty years later, the North American

Cover of program for *Sängerfest* held February 1890. *Courtesy of a private collection.*

Sängerbund chose New Orleans for a second time as the site for its annual convention. Although German culture had been suppressed as a result of the world wars, the *Sängerbund* enjoyed a successful series of performances.

A number of other culturally oriented events was sponsored by the German community in the tradition of the *Vaterland.* An interesting example was the three-day commemoration of the 100th birthday of the most popular of all the German dramatists and poets, Friedrich Schiller. The entire city took part in this festival, with numerous houses and ships in the port displaying German and American flags. A performance of one of Schiller's most beloved plays, *Die Räuber* (*The Robbers*), served as a prefestival event. The main celebration began the next day, on November 10, 1859, with a parade in which the mayor, other city dignitaries, and the German organizations of the city took part. Beginning with three marching bands the parade wound through the French Quarter and the American sector to the St. Charles Theater on Poydras Street. The central point of interest was the Schiller float, created in the form of a temple of the Muses, decorated with sixteen shield-shaped portraits of the most celebrated writers of all time. Behind, on a high pedestal, was the bust of the poet, garlanded with laurel leaves and a gilded necklace. This bust of Schiller was later presented to the city and installed in the Fisk Public Library. The opening ceremonies at the St. Charles Theater were conducted by the first president of the *Deutsche Gesellschaft* (see chapter 2, "German Immigration to New Orleans"), after which various musical groups and choruses performed compositions honoring Schiller. That evening in Odd Fellows Hall, elaborately decorated for the occasion, a drama with orchestration was held. On the third night, the Schiller festival closed with an elegant ball also held in Odd Fellows Hall (see *Deutsche Zeitung,* Nov. 6, 1898). The festival of

1869 for the natural scientist and geographer Alexander von Humboldt and the Franz Schubert festival of 1897, honoring the 100th birthday of this famous composer, were other notable celebrations.

In the German tradition of spring wine festivals, an annual *Maifest* (May Day celebration) was held, also known as the *Deutsches Volks- und Schützenfest* (German Folk and Shooting Festival). This affair,

Volksfest or German May Day festival held annually in New Orleans at the Union Race Course, from *Frank Leslie's Illustrated Newspaper*, May 28, 1859. *Courtesy of a private collection.*

inaugurated in 1854, soon became the amusement highlight of the German community's year. The *Volksfest* lasted all day, with most of the German organizations taking some part in the program. It began early with a parade of military and fire companies bearing the American, German, and Swiss flags. Brass bands, decorated floats, and horse-drawn wagons followed, tracing a route along Canal Street to Union Race Course. There, booths with food and drink, platforms for dancing, gambling, racing, shooting contests, competitive games, and other entertainments were provided for the enjoyment of the German community. The profits were given to organizations such as the *Deutsche Gesellschaft* and the Howard Association, which benefited the German as well as the wider community.

The *Harmonie Club,* a Jewish men's organization for promoting the arts, put on an annual parade, with brass bands led by a grand marshal. After parading downtown, the members took the streetcar to Carrollton, where they were greeted by the club's president in his carriage, drawn by three horses draped in the colors of the German flag. The Carrollton club members then joined in, and all proceeded amid a cannon salvo to the Carrollton Garten, a German restaurant, where the revelry continued far into the night (see *Tägliche Deutsche Zeitung,* Apr. 20, 1880). On October 6, 1883, a bicentennial jubilee was held at Spanish Fort to

Harmonie Club, from *History of the Jews of Louisiana.* *Courtesy of Touro Infirmary Archives.*

commemorate the arrival of the first German colonists in America. For a period, October 6 was celebrated as German Day, with a parade and presentations honoring the contributions of the Germans and German-Americans to the city, region, and nation. German Day was later revived by the Louisiana League of the National German-American Alliance, an organization uniting the separate societies of the state under one central umbrella (see chapter 7, "Societies and Associations").

The typical German male participated in one of the many volunteer military or fire companies, which frequently paraded in showy uniforms on weekends and civic occasions. The native love for dressing up, parading, and dancing endeared the Mardi Gras activities of the city to the Germans. During the Carnival season the various German societies gave a number of street parades and festive balls, all well attended by their members, families, and friends. Of note was the annual *Liedertafel* (Song-Board) ball held by this singing society at Grunewald Hall, always festooned with flowers both inside and out for these occasions (see *Daily Picayune,* Feb. 4, 1883).

In 1893, a year after the hall burned, Louis Grunewald built a six-story hotel with 200 rooms on the site at the corner of Canal and Baronne streets. In 1908 he enlarged the hotel with an elaborate fourteen-story structure containing 400 rooms, with the main entrance on Baronne. Its curious basement nightclub, the Cave, said to be the first nightclub in America, attracted considerable patronage and comment. To disguise the many pipes, conduits, and beams, 700,000 pounds of concrete and stucco had been fashioned into stalagmites and stalactites, with figures of naked ladies interspersed among the cocktail tables. Although this curiosity disappeared long ago, the hotel, renamed the Roosevelt, then the Fairmont, still holds its premier position among the hotels of the city.

Whenever German naval ships arrived at the port, the community proudly paraded to the docks. Amid great ceremony in honor of the officers, the ships were officially inspected by designated dignitaries. Afterward, spectacular banquets were held in a hotel or hall in the community, with German song, dancing, and many speeches. One notable occasion involved the presentation of a flag by the German citizens of the City of Lafayette, which was to be transported to the senate of the city-state of Bremen. The custom of ship inspections is still practiced by the German community when military ships arrive in the port.

Other pastimes involved calisthenics and gymnastics rather than tennis, golf, or team sports. The *Turnverein* owned a large building

Grunewald Hall, Canal and University Place. *Courtesy of Special Collections, Tulane University.*

Liedertafel program, April 11, 1882, for performance at Grunewald Hall. *Courtesy of Special Collections, Tulane University.*

housing a gymnasium, theater, library, and hall for meetings, banquets, and balls. Men well into middle age performed regular workouts, as physical culture was considered essential for achieving a "refined humanity." German children were expected to build healthy, sturdy bodies through gymnastics and long hikes. Instead of American sports, they practiced folk dancing, weightlifting, and pyramid building.

Gardening was another pastime the Germans cultivated. Just as in the *Vaterland,* the German housewife in America planted flowers wherever space permitted. Lush yard and patio plantings were sources of pride for every German household. German immigrants were drawn to the nursery and florist business and were said to have introduced the concept of colorful flower gardens to New Orleans. These furnished a German alternative to the all-white Creole garden, which was traditionally based on smell. John Fredrick Nau, in his *German People of New Orleans, 1850-1900,* maintained that the wealthier Germans, who moved from the Irish Channel into the adjacent area, were responsible for this section being named the Garden District.

Many of the forms of entertainment enjoyed by the Germans centered on the home or the outdoors. Those New Orleans area establishments where they came together to eat, drink, dance, and socialize are listed alphabetically in this section. The dates they were established (*date*) and/or referenced (*cited*) in an article, advertisement, etc., are noted. Additionally, the establishment locations and owners are given, when known (see also chapter 5, "Trades, Businesses, and Professions").

Bars/Saloons/Taverns

date   cited

1910 **(ca.)**	**Brewer's Bar** Piety and Burgundy streets *Schwegmann*
1864	**Erster Felsenkeller** Georg Merz *Deiler*
1870s	**Hambacher's Schloss** Exchange Alley *Deiler; Nau*
1870s	**Hatry's** St. Louis Street *Deiler; Nau*
1870s	**Hosch's** Coliseum Street *Deiler; Nau*
1910 **(ca.)**	**Hurstel's Bar** St. Claude Avenue between Independence and Pauline streets *Schwegmann*
1870s	**Kölner Dom** South Rampart Street "Küster" Mäusebach *Deiler; Nau*
1856	**Kroft's**

Conti Street
1863   Common Street
Deiler

1850   **Krost Beer Parlor/Saloon**
(ca.)   Orleans Street
Christian Krost
1870s   15-17 St. Charles Street
Val Merz
Sängerfest; Nau

1910   **Nunnemacher's Bar**
(ca.)   Upper Ninth Ward
Schwegmann

1860   **Orleans Public House**
131-33 Chartres Street
Mrs. C. Lachenmeyer
Gardner 1860

1920s   **Passauer's**
Magazine Street, Irish Channel
Called Parasol's by locals
Soards 1920

1860   **Hugo Redwitz**
(ca.)   49 Customhouse Street
1890   632 Common Street
Albert Heim
Nau; Deiler

1870s   **Seeliger's**
St. Mary's Market
Charles Seeliger
Deiler; Nau

1913   **Geo. W. Springer's New Royal Café & Billiard Hall**
130 Royal Street
Motto: "Live and let live"
Sängerfest

1870s   **Stegle's**
Two bars in vicinity of Orleans Street
Deiler

1860   **Joseph Voegtle's Saloon**
(ca.)   Corner Poydras Street and St. Charles Avenue
Sängerfest; Nau

1913   **Wagner House**
622 Iberville Street
Emile S. Schwertz
Sängerfest

1940   **Frederick Wisser's Café & Grocery**

Fourth and Huey P. Long Avenue, Gretna
Capt. Rick Wisser
Jeff. Parish Review, 1940

Restaurants/Coffeehouses

Coffeehouses also sold beer, wine, and spirits and rented rooms

1856		**Begué's Restaurant**
		823 Decatur Street
		Hypolite Begué
		Building dates to 1830
	1929	Tujague's Restaurant took over
		NOPL
1897		**Brunies (Big Corner) Restaurant**
		400 Second Street, Gretna
		Gretna Diamond Jubilee Coll.
1859		**Bruning's Restaurant**
		East and West End, Lake Pontchartrain
	1937	"Captain" John, Teddy Bruning
		Thoede
1870s		**Canterbury House**
		Chartres Street
		Deiler; Nau
1860s		**Cosmopolitan Restaurant**
		124 Bourbon Street
		Joseph Voegtle
		Nau
1860s		**Fabacher's Coffee, Beer & Boarding House**
		Gravier Street near Magnolia
		Joseph Fabacher
		Nau
1880		**Fabacher's Restaurant and Oyster House**
		137 Royal Street
	1887	Purchased by Lawrence Fabacher from father, Joseph; Lawrence then sold restaurant to brothers Anthony, Joseph, and Peter to go into brewing business
	1916	Fabacher Bros. Ladies & Gentlemen's Restaurant
		410-15 St. Charles Avenue
		Nau; City of N.O.; Gardner 1916
	1903	**Gluck's Restaurant**
		124 Royal Street
		Henry Gluck
		Zacherie
	1903	**Goebel's**

106 Royal Street
Zacherie

1904   Julius Groetsch's Restaurant & Wine Vaults
Magazine Street and Jackson Avenue
City of N.O.

1860   Mrs. J. Heinen's Boarding House
Chartres and St. Louis streets
Gardner 1860

1860   Frank Huber's
10 Royal Street
Gardner 1860

1891   Kolb's German Tavern
125 St. Charles Avenue
Konrad Kolb
Formerly Merz's Café

1990   Closed
Nau

1870s   Kossuth House
Royal Street
Charles Seeliger
Deiler; Nau

1913   Lehmann's Café & Men's Rooming House
Baronne Street
H. O. Lehmann
Sängerfest

1890   Meyer's House & Restaurant
100 St. Charles Street
Bernhard Meyer
Sängerfest

1860   Mueller's
(ca.)   117 Royal Street
Johann Mueller

1850   Phoenix Coffee House & Saloon
(ca.)   Carrollton Avenue and Hampson Street, Carrollton
Mahe

1860   Schmitt's Restaurant & Saloon
(ca.)   143 Gravier Street, near St. Charles Avenue
John Schmitt
Nau

1860   Stevedore's Exchange & Coffee House
(ca.)   Rudolph von Weinmann
Nau

1913   Vonderbank's Restaurant
126-30 Common Street

Mathieu Vonderbank
Sängerfest

1913   **White Hall Coffee House**
St. Louis Street
Anderson White
For bachelors only, with bowling
Sängerfest

1860   **Wolfskul's**
(ca.)   Third and Water streets
Heinrich Wolfskul
Nau

1860   **Zum Schwan**
(ca.)   Joseph Lochert
Nau

1860   **Zur Fliege**
(ca.)   243 Bienville
Famous for Bratwurst and Braunschweiger sausage
Nau

Hotels

1860   **Cosmopolitan Hotel**
(ca.)   128 Bourbon Street; facade also on Royal Street
Joseph Voegtle
Nau

1880   **Fabacher's Hotel**
708-16 Iberville, later Customhouse Street
Lawrence Fabacher and brothers: Joseph, Peter, and Anthony
Nau; City of N.O.

1893   **Hotel Grunewald**
Canal and Baronne streets on site of Grunewald Hall (burned 1892)
Louis Grunewald
    1908   14-story structure built on Baronne Street; later renamed the Roosevelt, "The Largest and Finest Hotel in the South"; currently the Fairmont Hotel

1890   **Hotel Herwig**
(ca.)   Grand Isle
Plantation-style hotel, destroyed by 1893 hurricane
Jeff. Parish Review, 1937

1890   **Hotel Krantz**
(ca.)   Grand Isle
25 refurbished slave cabins, dining room/dancehall
Swanson

1916   **Ocean Beach Hotel**

Menu from Fabacher's Restaurant and Hotel, established 1880. *Courtesy of the Historic New Orleans Collection.*

First Grunewald Hotel, 1893, Canal and Baronne streets, from Engelhardt, *City of New Orleans. Courtesy of the Louisiana Collection, Earl K. Long Library, University of New Orleans.*

Hotel Vonderbank, Magazine Street near Gravier, from Engelhardt, *City of New Orleans. Courtesy of the Louisiana Collection, Earl K. Long Library, University of New Orleans.*

Grand Isle
August Muller
Swanson

1890   **Hotel Oleander**
(ca.)   Grand Isle
John Ludwig
Jeff. Parish Review, 1937

1860   **Hotel Schmitt** (formerly St. James Hotel)
(ca.)   38-42 Magazine Street
John Schmitt
Nau

1860   **Hotel Vonderbank**
(ca.)   36-44 Magazine Street
Charles Dormitzer
Sängerfest; Nau

THEATER

German Theater Buildings

1866 **German National Theater**
(also known as) **Werlein Hall**
Baronne and Perdido streets
Architect: William Thiel; builders: Schneider & Zuberier
Seating for 1,300 people; cost $160,000
Tägliche Deutsche Zeitung, Oct. 14, 1866, p. 8, c. 1

1839   **(First) German Theater**
Magazine Street and Delord (now Howard Avenue)
    1850   Fire destroyed theater and 40 other buildings in City of Lafayette
Nau; Deiler

1840   **(Second) German Theater**
Polymnia and Nayades streets (now St. Charles Avenue)
Directors: Rudolph Riese and Louisa Thielemann
Moehlenbrock

1845   **German Theater**
Old Levee (now Decatur) between Barracks and Hospital streets
Directors: Rudolph Riese and Louisa Thielemann
Deiler

1849   **(New) German Theater**
Camp and Poydras streets
Established by F. Brooks
Director: Philip Horowitz
Balls held after every performance

1850   Destroyed by fire one year after opening; reopened shortly
after fire
*Deutsche Zeitung, Nov. 18, 1849, p. 2; Deutsche Zeitung, May
30, 1850, p. 3; Deiler; Moehlenbrock*

?   **German Theater**
St. Peter and St. Claude streets
Cruse

1853   **Turnverein Auditorium/Theater**
Turners' [Gymnasts'] Hall
Lafayette Street
Soards 1867

German drama was also performed at the Saint Charles Opera Hall, the
Athenaeum, the Academy of Music, the French Opera House, the Grand
Opera House, and the American and Werlein halls as well as those noted in the
text.

Movie/Variety Theaters

1910   **Fichtenberg's Penny Wonderland**
(ca.)   711 Canal Street; first movie house in New Orleans
Henry Fichtenberg, also owned movie theaters: Alamo,
1027 Canal Street; Dream World, 635 Canal Street
Schwegmann

1889   **Iron Theater**
Orleans Street
Frederick William Stempel, known as Senior Faranta, the India
Rubber Man

1900   Elysian Fields and Burgundy streets
Cruse

CHAPTER NINE

Prominent Germans and German-Americans

This section begins with the biographies of three men, without whom the story of the Louisiana Germans could not be told. Their scholarly work laid the foundation for subsequent research into the field of the German heritage of Louisiana. Much of the material used by them to trace the history and influence of the Germans of this state has been lost or is no longer accessible. Thanks to their efforts, this vital information has been preserved and forms a broad base of knowledge upon which subsequent research can build.

J. HANNO DEILER

John Hanno Deiler was born at Altötting, Upper Bavaria, on August 8, 1849, as the second son of Konrad and Magdalena Deiler. His father was a Bavarian royal-court musician and a descendent of an old Nüremberg family. Deiler attended the public schools in his hometown and received training in music from his father as well as from a Bavarian court composer. In 1866 he won a scholarship to the Royal Normal College of Munich and graduated from that institution with honors in 1868. He then held government appointments as a teacher in several schools. While teaching in Munich, he furthered his own education at the Royal Polytechnic Institute and at the University of Munich.

In 1871 Deiler accepted a position in New Orleans as principal of St. Boniface German Catholic School. He arrived early in 1872 to begin this work and also served as organist for

J. Hanno Deiler. *Courtesy of the Historic New Orleans Collection.*

St. Boniface Church. Later that year he married Wilhelmina Saganowski, daughter of a Hungarian engineer. His brother Aloys Deiler, who immigrated with him, also served as an organist and music teacher in New Orleans.

In 1879 John Hanno became professor of German at the University of Louisiana (now Tulane) in conjunction with the chairmanship of German at Newcomb College, the women's division. It was Deiler's ambition to elevate the cultural milieu for Germans nationwide and cultivate a taste for German literature, culture, and music in New Orleans. Toward these ends he served for many years as president of the *Deutsche Gesellschaft* (German Society), the most important German organization of the city. He also served as president of the New Orleans German Gazette [*Deutsche Zeitung*] Publishing Company, which put out the most important and longest-running German-language newspaper of the city. Deiler helped establish a number of German cultural organizations. In 1882 he founded and served as president of the New Orleans Quartet Club, which was dedicated to the preservation of German culture and song. He was also active in attracting German immigrants to Louisiana, making an extended trip to Germany with the state commissioner of immigration. To this end he also wrote a pamphlet, "Louisiana, a Home for German Immigrants," thousands of copies of which were circulated. Deiler collected much of the material known as the German Archives for the History of the Germans in the South, in the possession of the *Deutsches Haus* in New Orleans. (This archive is now on extended loan to the Historic New Orleans Collection.)

Through Deiler's efforts, the twenty-sixth annual singing festival (*Sängerfest*) of the North American Singers' Association (*der Nordamerikanischen Sängerbund*) was held in 1890 in New Orleans. For this event Deiler served as director-general and leader of the mass choruses (see chapter 8). He went on to represent the New Orleans association the next year at the *Sängerfest* in Vienna and attended the German *Sängerfest* of 1896 in Stuttgart. While there he was unanimously elected president of the national *Sängerbund* by the convention, its highest honor. He was elected president again in 1903.

Deiler contributed to numerous German and American periodicals and also wrote extensively about the Germans who had immigrated to America. His research focused on the history of Germans in the United States, especially in Louisiana. His publications on this topic included many articles and the book *Settlement of the German Coast of*

Louisiana and the Creoles of German Descent. He also published a number of long pamphlets, including "Germany's Contribution to the Present Population of New Orleans," "The Redemption System in the State of Louisiana," "History of European Immigration to the United States from 1820 to 1896," "History of the German Society of New Orleans," "History of the New Orleans German Press," "History of the German Churches in Louisiana," and "A Forgotten German Colony" (see bibliography). In addition to these works Professor Deiler wrote a number of papers and addresses on various subjects. In 1898 the German Kaiser, Wilhelm I, recognized his achievements and services to the German people in the United States by inducting him into the Order of the Crown, an honor that bestowed knighthood upon him.

After twenty-eight years as professor of the German language and literature at Tulane, Professor Deiler resigned in 1907. Heart trouble forced him to move to the quieter atmosphere of Covington, Louisiana. He died at his summer home on July 21, 1909, and he was buried in the Saganowski tomb of his wife's family in Greenwood Cemetery, New Orleans.

LOUIS VOSS

Louis Voss was born in 1856 in the German state of Schleswig-Holstein. He immigrated to Chicago in 1872 and then entered the German Theological Seminary of Newark, New Jersey. Upon graduation in 1879 he went back to Germany to take a postgraduate course in Leipzig. When he returned to America in 1880 he accepted a call as pastor of the first German Presbyterian church in New Orleans, the First Street Presbyterian Church. He and Irene Gaschen, whom he later married, conducted the church school in both German and English until 1883. Voss also served as instructor in Greek and German at Tulane University beginning in 1892, later replacing J. Hanno Deiler. The

Louis Voss, from *History of the German Society of New Orleans,* 1927. *Coutesy of a private collection.*

restoration of the teaching of German in the public schools in 1931 was made possible partly through his efforts. His essay entitled "Why German Should Be Studied" stressed the importance of the German language from a practical, scientific, and literary point of view.

Pastor Voss was a charter member of the board of directors of the German Protestant Home for the Aged and Infirm. In the course of his service to the residents of this home, he edited the *Altenheimbote* for thirty-six years. This was a monthly newsletter, which contained articles on current events in Germany, events of importance in New Orleans, and spiritual messages for the residents. Voss also served as clerk of the Presbytery of New Orleans beginning in 1892 and as director of the Presbyterian Synod of Louisiana in 1901. Additionally he was associate editor of the *Southwestern Presbyterian* for many years. Voss was also an active member of the German community, serving as celebratory speaker on many occasions as well as holding important positions in the *Deutsche Gesellschaft* and the *Deutsches Haus.*

As an author he wrote two prize essays entitled "Eldership" and "Confirmation." He also wrote two books, *The Beginnings of Presbyterianism in the Southwest* and *History of the German Society,* the latter important to the documentation of German history in New Orleans. It was republished with an informative introduction by Don Heinrich Tolzmann as *Louisiana's German Heritage: Louis Voss' Introductory History.* Voss also was the author of a number of pamphlets and articles.

In recognition of his scholarship on German Presbyterianism and the Louisiana Germans and German heritage, Tulane University conferred upon him the degree of Doctor of Divinity in 1913. Voss died in New Orleans on February 6, 1936.

JOHN FREDRICK NAU

John Fredrick Nau was born on October 8, 1910, in Nagercoil, British India, the son of a Lutheran missionary. When he was four his parents took him to Germany, where he lived through World War I until 1921. His formal schooling began there. In 1921 he came to the United

John Fredrick Nau. *Photograph by Raymond Calvert.*

States in the company of his parents, three brothers, and three sisters. After a brief stay in Ohio his family moved to New Orleans later that year. There he attended St. John Lutheran Parochial School, from which he graduated in 1925. That same summer he moved with his parents to Greensboro, North Carolina, where he attended Greensboro High School for one year. He then entered Concordia College in Conover, North Carolina, to prepare for ministry in the Lutheran church. Upon finishing his undergraduate work at Concordia in the spring of 1930, he entered Concordia Seminary in St. Louis. From 1932 to 1934 he served as assistant pastor at Salem Evangelical Lutheran Church of Buffalo, New York, and the next year taught at Emmanuel Lutheran College of Greensboro, North Carolina. He completed his studies at Concordia Seminary in the spring of 1936.

After returning to Emmanuel Lutheran College for another year, he accepted a call to Christ Evangelical Lutheran Church in Pascagoula, Mississippi. After serving this congregation for three and a half years, in 1939 he married Johanna Leonora Hasenkampf of New Orleans. The couple had three children, John Jr., Henry, and Carolyn.

Redeemer Evangelical Lutheran Church of New Orleans extended a call to Nau in 1940, which he readily accepted. While serving this congregation he studied at Tulane University, receiving the degree of master of arts in history in 1948.

Later that year he accepted the pastorate of the Messiah and Holy Trinity Evangelical Lutheran congregations of Columbia, South Carolina, where he also enrolled in graduate school. At the University of South Carolina he continued his studies leading toward a doctoral degree, which he received in 1954. He then accepted a teaching position with Mississippi Southern College in Hattiesburg, where he served as professor of history and chairman of the Department of Religion and Philosophy for a number of years. Upon his retirement he and his wife settled in Hattiesburg, where he died in 2001.

In addition to these three giants in the field of Louisiana's German heritage, seven others were named by Nau in his history of the Germans of New Orleans: Jacob Hassinger, founder of the *Deutsche Zeitung,* the most important and longest-published German newspaper in New Orleans; Frederick Loeber, house surgeon of Touro Infirmary and recipient, along with Deiler, of the German Order of the Crown; Loeber's associate at Touro, William Kohlmann; Fritz Jahncke, who paved the streets of New Orleans at a time when less than 20 of the 500 miles of street were passable during the rainy season; Gustav Seegers, who developed a monopoly on sewing machines at the turn of the twentieth century; A. G. Ricks, the largest manufacturer of boots, shoes, and gaiters in the country; and Henry L. Frantz, who donated his fortune from manufacturing coffins and providing mortuary services to establish the Lutheran Bethlehem Orphan Asylum.

It is impossible to include in this listing all of the prominent Germans of the state of Louisiana. Because of the subjectivity of judging who should be included, published sources recognizing prominent Germans and German-Americans have been relied upon to compile this listing. It has been limited to immigrants who came to Louisiana from the German-speaking states of Europe and their children. In the case of a few outstanding German-Americans of the third generation, exceptions were made, which are denoted in the listing with asterisks. This section does not include all prominent Germans and German-Americans named in other chapters. For each listing the following information, if known, is given: name, profession, birth date, immediate family members, date of coming to Louisiana, contributions to the community, personal information, and death date. General notes and the source(s) of information follow.

PROMINENT GERMANS AND GERMAN-AMERICANS

Karl J. R. Arndt
Academic historian; native of Germany; served as professor of German at Louisiana State University for twelve years, then Clark University, Worcester, Massachusetts; assembled material on Germantown, Louisiana; published extensively on German religious colonies in U.S.; died in 1995.
Society for German American Studies (SGAS)

Ferdinand Beer
Founder of export firm Central American Trading Co.; born in Germany, 1845; began dry goods, cotton business in New Orleans; married Emma Friedlander, five children; then established trading company and commission business headquartered both in New Orleans and Nicaragua; member of Temple Sinai, Free Masons, B'Nai Brith; died in 1909.
Fortier

Elizabeth Kettenring Begué
Restaurateur, culinary artist; born in Bavaria, 1831; came to New Orleans in 1853; husbands Louis Dutrey, then Hypolite Bégué; in 1853

opened Dutrey's Place in the French Market, later renamed Begué's Exchange; "Sundays at Bégue's" became fashionable because of her "French Market Breakfast," popularized by Cotton Centennial of 1886; died in 1906.

La. Biog.

Martin Behrman

Mayor of New Orleans, elected five times: 1904-20, 1925-26; son of German-Jewish cigar maker who died early; converted to Catholicism; attended German-American School, where instructed by J. Hanno Deiler; leader of Democratic machine; known for anti-integration, white supremacist policies; model of assimilated German; belonged to no German organizations.

Berchtold

Michael Biegel

Politician, cofounder of Ponchatoula; born in Bavaria, 1824; married Catherine Hoffman, five children; appointed by Governor Warmoth to develop Ponchatoula; elected alderman, postmaster; died in 1876.

La. Biog.

Gustave Adolph Blaffer

Banker, founder of Germania Savings Bank; born in New Orleans, 1849, of German parents, John Auguste Blaffer and Anna Ostermann; father built mansion at 1328 Felicity Street in 1869 designed by Charles Lewis Hillger; died in 1924.

Voss; Irwin

Peter Blaise

Brewer; born Freymig, Alsace-Lorraine, 1838; married Josephine Hauck of New Orleans; introduced lager beer at Southern Brewery, founded New Hope Brewery, early steam brewery in New Orleans; president of Standard Brewing Company; organized New Orleans Brewing Association; died in 1910.

Voss

James Hubert Blenk

Catholic clergyman, seventh archbishop of New Orleans, 1906-17; born in Neustadt, Bavaria, 1856, of James Marcus Blenk and Catherine Witteman; became Catholic at twelve, educated by Redemptorists, Marists, ordained 1885; came to New Orleans 1906; president of Jefferson College; pastor of Holy Name of Mary Catholic Church, Algiers; helped found Notre Dame Seminary, Loyola University, Xavier University, Daughters of Katherine Drexel; established first Catholic school board, became superintendent, founded Federation of

Catholic Societies, Holy Name societies, supported Knights of Columbus; died in 1917.

La. Biog.; Biog. & Hist. Memoirs

Ewald Hermann Boelitz

Founded *Louisiana Staatszeitung* (Louisiana State Newspaper) in 1850; born in Frankfurt-am-Oder, Brandenburg, 1819; divorced wife in New Orleans, gave her control of *Louisiana Staatszeitung,* which she sold to employees, 1865; main rival to Joseph Cohn and *Deutsche Zeitung;* returned to Brandenburg to claim inheritance; died in Osterode, Harz Mountains, in 1866 at age forty-seven (see chapter 5, "The German-Language Press").

Deiler, Presse

John Baptiste Bogaerts

Clergyman, Catholic priest; born in Olmen, Belgium, 1840; of Belgium/German descent; came to New Orleans in 1863 with large group of clergy recruited by Archbishop Odin; ordained as deacon, then priest in New Orleans; organized parish in Gretna, became pastor of St. Joseph's Catholic Church; transferred to New Orleans to St. Henry's in 1871 while also acting as vicar-general of archdiocese; became chancellor of archdiocese and pastor of St. Mary's Assumption in 1891, St. Anna's 1901; instrumental in moving St. Joseph Abbey (Benedictine monastery) from Gessen (Tangipahoa Parish) to St. Tammany; died in 1935.

Calvert

Maximilian Ferdinand Bonzano

Physician, politician; born in Ehringen, Württemberg, 1821; came to New Orleans in 1835; began as typesetter, then apothecary's apprentice with Curlius Riddels, brother of German teacher; studied medicine, became assistant physician at Charity Hospital; appointed director of the U.S. Mint by President Polk; became inspector and engineer of lighthouse, president of first organized union in New Orleans, drafter of emancipation ordinance for Louisiana; elected to Congress in 1864, named tax collector for Louisiana by Lincoln, then representative of Republican Electoral College; named surveyor general by Grant in 1874, dismissed from this post by Gov. Michael Hahn, but remained in different positions at Mint until 1884; then retired to Hermitage Plantation in St. Bernard Parish on land formerly chief quarters for General Jackson in Battle of New Orleans; set up laboratory and pursued scientific studies until death in 1894; gave valuable collection to Howard-Tilton Library (Tulane) in New Orleans.

Deiler, Presse

Joseph Augustus Briedenborn

First Coca-Cola bottler; born in Vicksburg, Mississippi, 1866, as one of eight children, father Henry immigrated from Hamburg at age seventeen; Joseph worked in father's confectionery store serving new fountain drink from Atlanta, recognized potential, imported and bottled drink in 1894; married Ann Schlottman in 1889, three children; moved to Louisiana, established first Coca Cola bottling plant in Monroe in 1913; died in 1952 at age eighty-six.
Puneky

Theodore Brune

Architect, mausoleum designer/builder; born in Hanover, Germany; helped make New Orleans center of memorial monument business for many years; designed and built most of elaborate mausoleums on "Millionaire's Row" in Metairie Cemetery; designed Mater Dolorosa Church, St. Joseph Abbey Church; died in 1932; buried in abbey cemetery (see chapter 4, "Public and Commercial Buildings").
Irvin; Gandolfo

Lucien Napoleon Brunswig*

Wholesale pharmaceutical manufacturer; born 1854 of German background; built mansion on Prytania Street; married Annie Mercer, son and two daughters; died in 1943; buried in Metairie Cemetery; large pyramid tomb inspired by German design.
City of New Orleans; Guide; Architecture III

Charles F. Buck

Legislator; Louisiana state senator from Second District, spokesman for German community; born in Durrheim, Baden, 1841; came to New Orleans in 1852; parents died in yellow-fever epidemic of 1853; married Mary Weidner, five children; attended Louisiana State Seminary, Alexandria; began law practice 1867, became city attorney; school board member, math and Latin professor, spoke French and German, Shakespeare scholar; member of dramatic clubs, *Deutsche Gesellschaft* (thirty-three years), *Frohsinn;* Germania Lodge, Louisiana grand master, thirty-third-degree Mason, first president of German-American State Alliance (1910) and vice-president 1916-17, delegate to National German-American Alliance, president of German Protestant Orphan Asylum (thirty-eight years); died in 1918.
Voss; Nau; Berchtold

John Christian Buehler

Planter; Buehler's Plains, south of Baton Rouge, named for him; German native; married fellow German Christiana Seither, seven children;

owned land in Baton Rouge, which sold to city for municipal burial ground (Magnolia Cemetery); owned Winters Plantation; came to New Orleans in 1840, established bakery business; died in 1866. Son Eugene born in New Orleans, 1860; established Buehler Building Supply; president of Teutonia Bank.

LLVMC; Nau

Anthony Frederick Bultmann

Businessman, undertaker; born in New Orleans, 1853 of German parents, Anthony Bultmann (baker) and Magdalena Koehler; one of four children; married Ida Maurer, five children; purchased William Feltman's undertaking business, founded Bultmann Mortuary Service, 1883; also established livery business; director of Orleans Manufacturing Company (see chapter 5, "Trades, Businesses, and Professions").

Voss; Deiler, Ansiedler; Biog. & Hist. Memoirs

Michael Cambre (Kammer)

Pioneer farmer, social and business leader on German Coast; born in Breisgau, Bodensee, 1723; married Catherine Jacob, three sons, progenitor of large family; members took part in Galvez expedition, War of 1812, Civil War; his plantation (at Reserve) became part of St. John the Baptist Parish; died in 1810.

La. Biog.

Elizabeth Magnius Cohen

First female practicing physician in Louisiana; born in New York, 1820, of German parents; came to New Orleans to treat yellow fever; died in 1921.

La. Biog.

Heinrich Theodore Romanoff Cohen

Newspaperman, appointed coeditor, business manager of *Louisiana Staatszeitung* in 1853; Polish Jew converted in Berlin to Christianity to marry woman he had seduced; claimed given name Romanoff at christening by godfather, king of Russia; came in conflict with one of editors of *Deutsche Zeitung,* pistol duel took place, Cohen shot in the abdomen, but recovered; died of yellow fever in 1853.

Deiler, Presse

Joseph Cohn

Newspaperman, bookstore owner, notary; born in Hamburg, 1817; came to New Orleans in 1841; three children; began as typesetter; 1848 bought *Deutsche Courier,* sold after five years, founded *Deutsche Zeitung;* one of most important owners/editors of German newspapers

in New Orleans; credited with founding of *Deutsche Gesellschaft* in 1843, which became viable in 1847; died in 1882 (see chapter 5, "The German-Language Press").
Clark, Liberals; Deiler, Presse; Nau
Solomon Cohn
Developer; German native; moved to Carrollton in 1836, established Carrollton's first industry, ropewalk between Levee and Second streets; elected to first city council of Carrollton in 1845; developer of New Orleans and Carrollton railroad and village of Carrollton along with Karl Zimpel and others.
Chase; Gill
Peter Czackert
Catholic Clergyman; Redemptorist priest; born in Bohemia, 1820, of German heritage; came to New Orleans in 1842; built German Catholic congregation in Fourth District; founded St. Mary's Assumption Church; returned to city in 1847 from call to Pittsburgh to establish Redemptorists with Brother Louis Kenning; died of typhus in 1848; buried in front of altar of original St. Mary's Assumption Church (see chapter 6, "Churches and Synagogues").
Nau; Calvert
Alfred David Danziger*
Lawyer, businessman; born in New Orleans, 1884, grandfather Theodore Danziger, German native and pioneer merchant of New Orleans; Alfred specialized in successions and real estate, owned half-interest in LaSalle and Jung hotels; active in anti-Klan work; secretary of Isidore Newman Manual Training School, director of Milne Home for Boys, Jewish Children's Home; member Masons, Elks, B'nai B'rith, Young Men's Hebrew Association, Temple Sinai.
Chambers
Emile Ferdinand del Bondio
Commission house owner, wholesale grocer; born in Mainz, 1842; came to New Orleans in 1860; married Clara A. Hassinger; established commission house on Poydras and South Peters after Civil War; built mansion on Camp Street; director of *Times-Democrat* newspaper, board of German Protestant Orphan Asylum, German Society; died in 1904.
Voss; Soards 1867
Hermann Bacher Deutsch
Journalist, author; born in Breux, Austria, 1889; never married; writer for *Times-Picayune,* former *States Item,* where became chief editorial

writer, daily columnist; known as "Bunny" Deutsch; wrote nonfiction and novels; died in 1970.

La. Biog.; LLMVC

Albert Diettel

Architect; born in Dresden, Germany, where worked as mason and railroad engineer; came to New Orleans in 1849; designed Third Presbyterian Church (Holy Redeemer Catholic Church), St. Mary's Assumption Church, Southern Brewing Company, St. Elizabeth's Children's Home, Grunewald Hall, Gates of Mercy (Congregation Shangari Chassed), St. John the Baptist Church, St. Peter and Paul Church, Hebrew Rest Cemetery; died in 1896 (see chapter 4, "Public and Commercial Buildings").

Lane; Irvin

William Drews

Architect, builder; born in German-speaking Pomerania, 1825; set up carpentry shop in City of Lafayette with Charles Hillger; married Prussian Emilie Manski (died at thirty-three), two children, also raised two orphaned nephews; with Hillger designed and built over fifteen residences and stores, St. Joseph Orphan Asylum, First Street Presbyterian Church, First German Lutheran Church; fell into debt at end of Civil War, left New Orleans; death date unknown (see chapter 4, "Public and Commercial Buildings").

Irvin

Frederick Adam Earhart

Pharmacist, politician; city council member 1920-49; Louisiana senator 1912-20; born in New Orleans, 1875, of German parents, Valentine Adam Earhart and Christine Adele Breitling; graduated from Loyola University, where taught pharmacy, established successful chain of pharmacies in city; married Ida May Hailes, seven children; member of Constitutional Convention of 1921, Commissioner of Public Utilities; consolidated city's five railroad stations into Union Passenger Terminal; appointed chairman of Civil Service Commission by Mayor Martin Behrman; secretary of State Board of Pharmacy; served in Spanish-American War, World War I; Earhart Boulevard named for him; member of F.&A.M., Druids, Masons: W.O.W. and Ben Hur orders; died at seventy-seven in New Orleans in 1952.

Brown; Times-Picayune, June 16, 1996, D-8

John Ehret*

Politician for thirty-four years; descendent of Gretna German pioneering families; appointed first mayor of Gretna by Louisiana governor,

1913-17; cofounded Good Government League with next mayor, Charles F. Gelbke, to reform Jefferson Parish politics and incorporate Gretna to achieve self-government; served as police juryman for Third Ward; Jefferson Parish assessor for more than decade; vice-president of Gretna Exchange and Savings Bank, later reorganized as First National Bank of Jefferson; had West Bank beer distributorship for New Orleans Brewing Company for thirty years; owned Jefferson Ice Company; died in 1930.

Zwelling; Thoede, Jeff. Parish; Chambers

Dietrich Einsiedel

Architect, contractor; born in Saxony, 1852; came to New Orleans in 1881; designed and built Crescent Brewing Company, Appelbie Brewing Company, Jackson Brewery, Algiers Brewing Company, Swartz Brewing, New Orleans Rice Milling Company, Young Men's Canal Street Club, Adeline Center; member of *Turnverein,* Democratic Party.

Biog. & Hist. Memoirs

August Erath

Businessman, politician; born in German-speaking Switzerland, 1843; came to New Orleans in 1860, moved to New Iberia in 1876; established brewery, soda and seltzer water factory, ice factory; large hardware business; built opera house and Masonic Hall for city; elected mayor; town of Erath in Vermilion Parish named after him.

Perrin; Leeper

Joseph Henry Fabacher

Farmer, businessman; born in New Orleans, 1858, of native German Franz Joseph Fabacher of Büsenberg and Magdelena Frey of Rosenweiler, Alsace; married Dora Ginkel, ten children; settled town of Fabacher with other German nationals, introduced rice culture in Acadia Parish; postmaster in Frey, Louisiana; died in 1910.

Lawrence Fabacher

Restaurateur, founder of Jax Brewery; brother of Joseph, born in Crowley, 1863, on parents' rice plantation; came to New Orleans in 1880; established Fabacher's Restaurant on Royal Street; married German-American Antoinette Wagner, seven children; sold restaurant to brother Peter; founded Jax Brewery in 1895, largest brewery in South; built castle-like mansion at 5707 St. Charles Avenue; died in 1923 (see chapter 5, "Breweries").

La. Biog.; Nau; Deiler, Ansiedler; D'Antoni, N.O. Magazine

Johann David Fink

German consul from Württemberg; willed $200,000 for founding of

Fink Asylum for Protestant Widows and Orphans, at Camp and Orleans; left fortune to stepbrother's abandoned wife and twelve children; died in New Orleans in 1857; originally buried in Girod Street Cemetery; remains moved to Valence Street Cemetery when Girod cemetery demolished.

Deiler, Presse; Voss; Architecture III

William Fitzner

Architect; born in Leipzig, 1845; came to New Orleans at age fourteen to join sister Emelie, wife of architect Charles Hillger; settled in City of Lafayette, opened carpentry shop with brother Gustave and Hillger (partnership with Hillger ended 1860); successively married three Germans from City of Lafayette, Salomea Schutterle, Caroline Hoppemeyer, and Anna Blattner; designed St. Mary's Dominican Academy, Louisiana Brewing Company, Louisiana Avenue Methodist Church, Crescent Jute Manufacturing Company, Lane Cotton Mills (four-story brick addition), Weckerling Brewing Company, Lafayette Brewing Company, Standard Brewing Company; noted for preference for Italianate style; active member of Masonic Union Lodge No. 12; went bankrupt, left New Orleans in 1865; died in 1914 (see chapter 4, "Public and Commercial Buildings").

Irvin; Nau

Henry L. Frantz

Mortician, funeral director, owner and operator of Frantz & Schoen Funeral Directors and Embalmers, had carriage and livery business; born in Saar Union, Alsace-Lorraine, September 8, 1846; came to New Orleans in 1857; married Johanna Waldo of Third District; reared six orphaned children of relatives; in partnership with Jacob Schoen since 1874; councilman; director and vice-president of Southern Brewing Company; director of City Park Improvement Association; vice-president of Orleans Manufacturing Company; director and vice-president of Bethlehem Orphan's Asylum; president of Louisiana Fire Company No. 10, treasurer of Young Men's Benevolent Association, vice-president of Funeral Directors Association of Louisiana, president of New Orleans Funeral Director Association, member St. Paul's Evangelical Lutheran Church (see chapter 5, "Trades, Businesses, and Professions").

Voss; Biog. & Hist. Memoirs

William Franz

Mechanic, businessman; born in Wiebersviller, Alsace-Lorraine, 1845, one of eight children; father Swabian; family of wall builders, clockmakers, and blacksmiths; parents came to New Orleans in 1857; married

Wilhelmina Koepf; established Franz and Company, mechanics; founder of Third District Homestead, member for twenty years of Orleans Parish School Board; officer, president (1911-15) of German Society; director, president of German Protestant Home for the Aged and Infirm.
Voss

Herman Frasch

Inventor, developer, philanthropist; born in Oberrot near Gaildorf, Bavaria, 1851; married Romalda Berkin, Elizabeth Blee, three children; developed Frasch process for producing sulfur; established Union Sulfur Company making U.S. world leader in sulfur production; also developed processes for mining salt, caustic soda, waxed paper, white lead, linseed oil; received Perkins Medal in 1912; developed Herman Frasch Park as gift to city of Sulfur, Louisiana; died in 1914; buried in Gaildorf, Germany.
La. Biog.

Julius Freihan

Cotton factor, businessman, philanthropist; born in Breslau, 1834; came to New Orleans in 1888; owner of mercantile conglomerate on Bayou Sara, St. Francisville; member of Cotton Exchange; president of Lane Cotton Mills; supported West Feliciana Parish public schools, Hebrew Rest Cemetery in St. Francisville, Audubon Park in New Orleans; Royal Arch Mason, Temple Sinai; died in 1904.
La. Biog.

Anton Joseph Frey

Businessman, founder of L. A. Frey and Sons, Inc., Third District; born in Öttweiler, Alsace, 1848; came to New Orleans in 1864; married Apollonia Morrell, seven children; Frey and Sons became national meat processing and packing business, famous for German sausage; five of six sons joined business; died in 1892.
Deiler, Ansiedler

Joseph Fromherz

Architect, engineer, builder, contractor; born in New Orleans; father Joseph, native German, mother Barbara Zimmer from Alsace; entered contracting business of father-in-law Ferdinand Reutsch, also native German; Joseph began as professor of mathematics in St. Landry Parish; in 1880 established partnership with J. A. Muir until Muir's death in 1911, then with Albert Drennen; formed new company with two sons in 1918; contractor for innumerable public buildings including Abram's Building, Jewish Orphans Home, Grunewald Hall, New Orleans National Bank, American Sugar Refinery (first building in

New Orleans to use pilings), House of Good Shepherd, Little Sisters of the Poor, St. Francis of Assisi Church, Notre Dame Seminary; restored Our Lady of Guadeloupe; responsible for parts of U.S. Naval Station, D. H. Holmes, Liberty Theater, Lafayette Hotel, Tulane-Newcomb Building, Loyola Stadium, Union Brewery, Standard Brewery, Spanish Fort; saved St. Louis Cathedral from demolition by strengthening foundation; also built many private buildings/residences in New Orleans area; died in New Orleans in 1925.
Chambers

Francis Leon Gassler
Catholic clergyman, missionary in Louisiana; born in German-speaking Switzerland, 1864; ordained 1893; served in Iota, Louisiana, in New Orleans at Annunciation Church, became Catholic vicar-general, dean in Baton Rouge, served at St. Joseph's, where enlarged church, and at Our Lady of the Lake Hospital, staffed Catholic High School, broadcast Sunday liturgies; wrote history of St. Joseph's Church; died in 1944 in Baton Rouge.
La. Biog.; Baudier

Charles F. Gelbke*
Mayor of Gretna for twenty-two years (second, fourth, and sixth mayor, 1917-49), physician, surgeon for Texas Southern Pacific Railroad; born in Tangipahoa Parish, of German stock; put self through college and medical school (Tulane); as physician concerned with public health, implemented citywide water infiltration system; coroner of Jefferson Parish; cofounder of Good Government League with previous mayor, John Ehret, to reform Jefferson Parish politics; instrumental in incorporation of first, second, and third wards of Jefferson Parish as Gretna in 1913; ran on Gelbke-Schaffler "German" ticket with Bender, Gessler, Gegenheimer, Gehring, Schurb, Huber; died in 1951.
Zwelling; Thoede, City Hall; Chambers

Hermann B. Gessner
Physician; born in New Orleans, 1872, of George Gessner of Sondershofen, Bavaria (father prominent in Revolution of 1848, served in Civil War in Washington Artillery) and Josephine Nicks of Bremen; parents came to New Orleans in late 1840s; Hermann got medical degree at Tulane, where later served as professor of surgery; married Jessie Hayes, four children; played major role in eradicating yellow fever in New Orleans area after outbreak of 1905; served as surgeon in Spanish-American War; visiting surgeon at Charity Hospital, Touro Infirmary.
Fortier; La. Portraits

Johann Georg Goentgen
Cofounder of Germantown, Louisiana, teacher, librarian, advisor and secretary to Count de Leon von Proli (spiritual leader of colony that became Germantown, first called Dutchtown, 1835); born a German native in Bornheim, 1791; came to Louisiana in 1833; assumed "fatherhood" of three children of Count de Leon and common-law wife Magdelena Heuser; died in 1858 in Germantown.
La. Biog.; Deiler, Colonie

Sidonius Goette, Jr.
Politician; born in Donaldsonville, 1859; one of six children; father, from German state of Baden, brought family to New Orleans in 1842; Jr. developed father's shoe business in Donaldsonville to largest in Louisiana; elected alderman in 1885, then mayor (donated salary back to city); built waterworks, municipal wharf, president of Phoenix Steam Fire Company #11 and of Donaldsonville Ice Co., director of city bank; managed Phoenix Opera.
Biog. & Hist. Memoirs; Perrin

Daniel Johannes Goos
Businessman in Lake Charles, civic leader; born in Föur, Schleswig-Holstein, 1815; married Katherine Moeling, fifteen children; developed sawmills, lumber mills; lumber schooners ran blockade during Civil War, supplied lumber for Kiel Canal, Germany; brought Germans to Lake Charles after Civil War to work in lumber mills; Lutheran church member; died in 1898.
La. Biog.

Louis Grunewald
Businessman; born in Bavaria, 1827, as one of five children, mother immigrated as widow to New Orleans in 1841 but died of yellow fever shortly after arrival; wife Marie Louise Schlinder; founder of Grunewald Music Store, built Grunewald Hall, Canal Street, then Grunewald Hotel (later Roosevelt, Fairmont); treasurer twenty-sixth *Sängerfest* in New Orleans; died in 1915.
Nau

Luke Gruwe
Catholic clergyman, monk, priest; born in Liesborn, Westphalia, 1849; trained as draftsman; entered monastery at St. Meinrad, Indiana, ordained in 1882; founding prior of St. Joseph Priory at Gessen, Louisiana; rector of the seminary and college; recalled to St. Meinrad in 1902, where served as prior for many years.
Deiler, Churches; Defrange

Simon Gumbel

Founder of Gumbel and Company, cotton brokerage; born in Bavaria, 1832; came to New Orleans in 1846; married Sophie Lengsfield; began as peddler; became wholesaler of notions; built first cottonseed mill, then rice mills, owned extensive rice lands; built mansion at Prytania, Philip, and First streets designed by William Fitzner; treasurer of Relief of Jewish Widows and Orphans Association, managed Jewish Orphans Home; founder of Sophie L. Gumbel Home; B'nai B'rith, *Harmonie Club;* treasurer Provident Aid Society; died in 1909. Son Henry Elias became businessman in New Orleans; in 1869 took over father's business, also president of Lafayette Sugar Refining Co., Eagle Bag Co. in New Orleans, Pelican and Amelia cotton presses, vice-president of U.S. Irrigation and Rice Milling Co.
LLMVC; Jews of La.; Irwin; Fortier

Charles Christian Gutekunst

Engineer of Atchafalaya Basin, businessman, politician; born in Hork as native German, 1848; came to New Orleans in 1870; married Elouise Mendoza, eight children; settled in St. Martinville; served as justice of peace and on police jury, Louisiana Democratic Convention delegate twice; died in 1923.
La. Biog.

James Koppel Gutheim

Rabbi; born in Warburg, Westphalia, 1817; came to New Orleans in 1850; married Emilie Jones; served at Shangari Chassed (dedicated 1851), Dispersed of Judah (dedicated 1857), first rabbi of Temple Sinai (1870); officer of Relief of Jewish Widows and Orphans Association; president of Hebrew Benevolent Association, vice-president of Touro Infirmary; member Orleans Parish School Board, Conference of Charities, New Orleans Auxiliary Sanitary Association, Louisiana Educational Society, Louisiana Historical Society, Red Cross, Society of Civics; avid defender of Confederacy; died in 1886, buried in Metairie Cemetery (see chapter 6, "Cemeteries").
Jews of La.

Georg Michael Hahn

Legislator, governor of Louisiana, newspaperman; born in Klingenmünster, Palatinate, 1830; brought to New Orleans in 1835 by mother, widow with five children, who died in 1841 of yellow fever leaving all children to well-meaning people; Michael talented, allowed to go to high school since crippled (had to use crutches whole life), unsuited to physical work, graduated with distinction, studied law under Roselius, in 1852 passed bar at age twenty-two; became member

of New Orleans School Board, later president; in politics was known to Stephen Douglas, gave decisive speech May 8, 1860, in Lafayette Square in favor of Union; successfully opposed Louisiana constitutional amendment to prevent naturalized citizens from voting, holding office; after fall of New Orleans in Civil War joined Union administration, excellent speaker, trusted by General Butler, brought to President Lincoln's attention, who sought his advice in matters relating to South; elected twice to U.S. House of Representatives (1862-63, 1885-86); elected governor of Louisiana 1864; U.S. senator in 1865; in Washington declared self for general suffrage of Negroes, arousing bad feelings among Louisiana party members, later resulting in Mechanics' Institute riot, July 31, 1866, in which Hahn badly wounded by gunshot; in 1867 began publishing *New Orleans Republican;* later served as administrator of Charity Hospital; director of U.S. Mint (1869); founded association to create Union Party in Louisiana; later founded, edited *True Delta,* only English newspaper in Louisiana representing Republicans; retired 1871 to St. Charles Parish, where laid out Hahnville on own sugar plantation; published *St. Charles Herald* newspaper; served as school director in St. Charles Parish; always popular in own district: 1872 elected to state legislature; 1879-89 district judge; 1884 elected to U.S. House of Representatives, where served twice as speaker; died alone in Washington hotel room in 1886 (see chapter 2, "German Immigration to New Orleans").
La. Biog.; Deiler, Presse; Voss; Körner

Henry Hardtner

"Father of Forestry" in Louisiana; born in Pineville, 1870, of E. J. Hardtner, German immigrant; married Juliet Doerr, three children; formed sawmill partnership with father and others; became chairman of Louisiana Commission on National Resources; brought U.S. Forestry Service to Louisiana; elected to Louisiana legislature, 1910; in 1913 established first reforestation effort in Louisiana, which became first Louisiana fish and game preserve; died in 1935.
Puneky

Jacob Hassinger

Newspaperman, businessman; born in Rehborn, Bavaria, 1828; came to U.S. in 1841; married German Catherine Schuber, born Artzheim; owner of Joseph Cohn's *German Gazette,* editor of *Deutsche Zeitung;* founder of Germania Savings Bank; president of *Sängerfest* of 1890; greatly esteemed in German community; died in 1903 (see chapter 5, "The German-Language Press").
Voss; Nau

Rudolf S. Hecht
Banker, businessman, civic leader; born in Ansbach, Germany, June 3, 1885; came to New Orleans in 1906; married Lynne Watkins (daughter of Supreme Court justice), three daughters; founder, president of Hecht and Company, investment bankers; president Hibernia Bank; board member Mississippi Delta Shipping Line, American Institute of Banking, Port Commissioners, American Bankers Association; member Pickwick Club, Metairie Country Club; died in 1956.
Voss; La. Biog.

Lewis Heerman
Surgeon; native of Germany; distinguished himself in naval medical history; burned the *Philadelphia* in harbor of Tripoli in 1892; commended by Congress; sent to New Orleans as naval hospital surgeon; married Eliza Potts, five sons; purchased buildings on Esplanade to establish naval hospital with own funds; died in residence on Camp and Julia in 1933.
Architecture IV

Alexander Julius Heinemann*
Developer of Pelican Stadium and baseball franchise; born 1876 of German stock; began as soft-drink vendor in stands, became general manager of team, established Pelican Stadium on Tulane and Carrollton, called Heinemann Park until 1938; ruined by 1929 financial crash, committed suicide in 1930.
Huber, Pictorial History

Maximillian Heller
Rabbi, scholar, writer, religious leader; born in Prague, Bohemia, 1860, of German/Czech parents, Seligman Heller and Mathilde Kassowitz; married Ida Ammie Marks; graduated from Hebrew Union College, Cincinnati; professor of Hebrew language and literature (Tulane); in 1886 became rabbi of Temple Sinai (for forty years), circuit rider; president of Conference of American Rabbis; member American Jewish Historical Society, American Oriental Society, Round Table, Jewish Widows and Orphans Home; died in 1929.
La. Biog.; Korn; Fortier

Samuel Hermann
Financier, merchant banker; dealt in loans, mortgages, bank stocks, and real estate in America, Europe, and West Indies; born in Frankfurt-am-Main, 1807; married Marie E. Becnel, widow of Pierre Brou of German Coast; owned two merchant vessels for import-export business; built Hermann-Grima House in 1831 at 820 St. Louis Street, now

historic house museum; board of City Bank, director of New Orleans Gas, Light and Banking; co-financed German plays at American Theater and balls following performances.

La. Portraits

Simon Hernsheim

Manufacturer, owner of La Belle Creole Tobacco Factory with brothers; born in New Orleans, 1839, of German parents; married Ida Roehl, born in Elberfeld, Germany; produced perique cigarettes with tobacco grown only in St. James Parish; owned mansion at Seventh and St. Charles Avenue, now Columns Hotel; patron of public libraries; died in 1898.

Biog. & Hist. Memoirs

Matthew Herzog

Planter; born on Magnolia Plantation, Natchitoches Parish, 1857; father German national, acquired Magnolia Plantation through marriage, prosperous planter and slave owner. Son Ambrose became lawyer, businessman; rebuilt plantation house destroyed by Union soldiers; acquired Little Rivers Plantation; died in New Orleans in 1921.

Chambers

Charles Lewis Hillger

Architect; born in Germany, 1830; immigrated to New Orleans, designed German Protestant Orphan Asylum, Temple Sinai, Zion Lutheran Church, Jackson Avenue Evangelical Church, new facade for Trinity Episcopal Church, Rayne Memorial Methodist Church; died in 1879 (see chapter 4, "Public and Commercial Buildings").

Irwin

Victor Huber

Cemetery owner, memorial craftsman, musician; born in Vienna, 1875, came to New Orleans in 1891; married Eleonora Reisig, three sons; founded Victor Huber & Sons, producers of granite and marble cemetery headstones and decorative grave markers, built tombs in Metairie and other cemeteries, purchased St. John Cemetery, constructed Hope Mausoleum; talented musician, composer, and music teacher, expert on Tyrolean zither, in 1890s organized the New Orleans Zither Club, developed Victor Huber Zither Method published in 1899 by Louis Grunewald's music company; directed New Orleans Quartet Club, choir of St. John Lutheran Church; founding member, president of *Deutsches Haus* 1934-36; died in 1942.

Leonard Victor Huber (son)

Businessman, historian, civic leader; born 1903; married Audrey

Wells, two sons; built Louisiana's first crematorium in Hope Mausoleum; president of Louisiana Landmarks, board of Vieux Carré Survey, Friends of Cabildo, Keys Foundation, Beauregard House, Louisiana Historical Association, Louisiana State Museum, Philharmonic Symphony; received Harnett Kane Award; died in 1984 (see chapter 6, "Cemeteries").
La. Biog.

Marks Isaacs
Merchant, philanthropist; born in Edenkoben, Palatinate, 1851; married Lilly Oppenheim, two sons; founded dry goods store on Canal Street (became Maison Blanche); also established Marks Isaacs on Canal Street; built mansion on St. Charles Avenue; member *Harmonie Club,* Young Men's Hebrew Association, Touro Infirmary, Jewish Widows and Orphans Home, Touro Synagogue; died in 1910.
Fortier; La. Portraits

Edward Jacobs
Planter, banker; born in Pomerania, Prussia, 1822; came to Shreveport in 1884; married Palestine Cole, twelve children; established National Bank of Shreveport; owned cotton plantation; died in 1896.
La. Biog.

Fritz Jahncke
Entrepreneur, founder of Jahncke Services; born in Hamburg, 1848; married Margaret Lee, three sons all in business; brought Schillinger cement patent from New York firm to New Orleans, established Jahncke Services; paved streets previously only banquettes or mud, also imported German flagstones for paving, supplied building materials and cement for many public buildings of city; owned fleet of barges and tugboats; introduced hydraulic dredge to city; helped develop port of New Orleans and New Basin Canal; established Jahncke Shipbuilding Company with shipyard in Madisonville, built ships for World War I effort; dredged Bogue Lusa Creek (for construction of world's largest lumber mill) creating city of Bogalusa; died in 1911; three sons continued Jahncke Services after father's death: Paul acted as vice-president of Jahncke Services; Ernest served as engineer (see below); Walter served as secretary-treasurer, also vice-president of Allied Building Council, president of Contractors and Dealers Exchange of New Orleans; sons dedicated fountain in front of New Orleans Museum of Art in father's memory.

Ernest Lee Jahncke (son)
Engineer for Jahncke Services; built seawall from West End to Spanish

Fort; president of Commerce Association of New Orleans, member Louisiana General Assembly, American Society of Civil Engineers; noted for ouster from International Olympic Committee for stand against American participation in 1936 Olympics held in Hitler's Berlin (see chapter 5, "Trades, Businesses, and Professions").
Nau; Jahncke

Emile Johns
Music teacher, book and music store owner; German native; established Emile Johns & C. P. Manouvrier Company with fellow German, who served as American consul in Panama; store at 113 Chartres Street, outlet for Playel pianos; opened second store on St. Charles, expanded into printing and bookbinding; captain of German Louisiana Dragoners, cofounder with Manouvrier of first German singing society (*Liederkranz*); died in Paris in 1860 as result of operation.
Deiler, Presse

Andreas Jung (Juan)
Colonial civil officer (commandant) appointed by governor ca. 1770; German national; ship chandler and builder in New Orleans, landowner on Bayou St. John and North Shore.

Peter Jung*
Furniture, hotel business; descendent of Andreas Jung; born in New Orleans, 1858; founder and president of Crescent (iron) Bed Company ca. 1900; proprietor of Jung Hotel; owned portion of Christmas Plantation sold by son to National Park Service for development of Jean Lafitte National Park and Preserve.
Voss; Swanson, Barataria

Leopold Kaplan
Pioneer of Louisiana rice industry, real-estate developer; born in Most, Poland, 1872, of German parents; came to Acadia Parish in 1888; started as peddler; married twice, one son; reclaimed land, developed rice mills in Crowley area; established churches, Kaplan Memorial Hospital; founded Kaplan (Vermilion Parish); died in Crowley in 1944.
La. Biog.; Story of La.; Perrin

Leopold Kaufman
Merchant banker, civic leader; born in Gundershofen, Alsace, 1851; came to Lake Charles in 1879; married Pauline Raas, two children; founded First National Bank of Lake Charles, Temple Sinai; owned largest mercantile business in Southwest Louisiana; donated Kaufman Hall, funded McNeese State University; died in Lake Charles in 1937.
La. Biog.; Perrin

J. H. Keller
Manufacturer, philanthropist; born in Zurich, Switzerland, 1830; came to New Orleans in 1848 at age eighteen; began as locksmith, finisher, and employee in soap factory; in 1849 founded J. H. Keller Soap Works located in City of Lafayette, largest soap manufacturer in South, with over twenty soap products; built home on adjoining plot; also built Keller Market at Magnolia and Felicity, with shade trees, running water, and lights; established Keller School at Jackson and Freret in 1873 (now McDonough 38); supported orphan asylums, YMCA.
City of New Orleans

Louis Kenning
Cofounder of Redemptorist Order in New Orleans; kept journal in German of events at Redemptorist Convent; teacher in first school in St. Mary's Assumption Parish; survived yellow-fever epidemics while ministering to stricken during twenty-seven-year tenure at St. Mary's; died in 1875; buried in St. Mary's Assumption Church.
Calvert

Georg Kleinpeter
Dairy farmer, German pioneer in agriculture; claimed Dutch (*Deutsch*) Highlands; first to grow sugarcane successfully on high ground; built first cotton gin, 1790. Son Jean Baptiste continued sugarcane enterprise, was first to erect steam sugar mill, 1832; house restored, relocated to Louisiana State University's Rural Life Museum.
Deiler, Ansiedler, Presse

John Klorer
City engineer of New Orleans; born in New Orleans, 1874; father German immigrant who established confectionery business; state Board of Engineers, president of Louisiana Engineering Society; ran unsuccessfully for mayor of New Orleans on "German" ticket with George Froeling, John Vetter, Alfred Danziger; member of Elks, Catholic societies.
Kendall

Abraham Klotz
Merchant, sugar planter; born in Uhrweiler, Alsace, 1836; brought by father Solomon Klotz to Louisiana in 1855; began as peddler, clerk in father's store, then established own store; married Julia Abraham, two children, then raised sister Pauline's five children; fought in Civil War; became sugar manufacturer in Donaldsonville, Assumption Parish; owner of Star and Klotzville plantations; member Touro Infirmary, Bikur Cholim (Donaldsonville), Masons, Army of Northern Virginia,

supporter of Jewish Widows and Orphans Home in New Orleans.
Jews of La.; Biog. & Hist. Memoirs

Hermann Klumpp

German consul of New Orleans; born in Germany; president of
German Society 1890-91, member thirty years, officer twenty years;
died in 1894; eulogy delivered by J. Hanno Deiler.
Deutsches Haus Coll., HNOC; Voss

Julius Koch

Architect; born in Stuttgart, 1857, came to New Orleans in 1885; married Anna Frotscher; thirty-second-degree Mason, Shriner; died in
1918. Son Richard was born in New Orleans, 1899; continued architectural firm with Samuel Wilson (Koch & Wilson), leading firm for
historic restoration in Louisiana; died in 1971.
Voss

Joseph Koegerl

Catholic priest; born in Bavaria, 1844; came to New Orleans in 1868;
assistant pastor under Father Thevis at Holy Trinity Church, pastor of
St. Boniface's Church 1870-90; brought J. Hanno Deiler as organist
and teacher at school, pastor of St. Peter's Church in Covington 1890-
1916; lifelong benefactor and friend of Benedictines; died in 1926.
Calvert

Ferdinand Otto Koelle

Protestant clergyman; born in Elberfeld, German-speaking
Switzerland, 1839; educated for ministry; came to New Orleans in
1868 as pastor of Second German Presbyterian Church (now Claiborne
Avenue Presbyterian Church); organizer and first president of
Protestant Home for Aged, founded German Protestant Bethany Home;
died in 1904.
Voss; Nau

William Kohlmann

Physician; born in Rheinpfalz, 1863; trained at Heidelberg and
Würzburg universities in Germany; came to New Orleans in 1891; out-
standing surgeon, widely published in Europe; worked with Frederick
Loeber at Touro Infirmary, helped establish hospital as one of best in
South; Orleans Parish Medical Association, La. State Medical
Association, American Medical Association; member of *Harmonie
Club,* Touro Synagogue.
Nau; La. Portraits

Samuel Kohn

Real-estate developer; born in German-speaking Bohemia; emigrated from Hamburg in 1805; bought half-interest in tavern on Bayou St. John, became partner in Chartres Street gambling enterprise; made fortune in banking and land speculation; developed New Orleans and Carrollton Railway, land in Carrollton; owned most of the city center of Jefferson; died in 1853, leaving business interests to brother Joachim, two nephews, Carl and Edward.

Architecture VII

Konrad Kolb

Restaurateur, retail and wholesale grocery and delicatessen business; born in Bavaria, 1874; came to New Orleans in 1891; bought Kolb's German Tavern (Merz's Café); also operated farm on Gentilly Road; member of Louisiana German-American *Staatsverband, Turnverein, Harugari Männerchor.*

Voss

Hiram Kostmeyer

Physician, surgeon, medical educator (Tulane); born in New Orleans, 1883; mother Catherine Eichborn, German national; political activist in White League, fought "Carpetbagger" regime; became instructor in gynecology at Tulane, surgeon at Charity Hospital and for Illinois Central Railroad; member of Orleans Parish Medical Association, Louisiana State Medical Association, American Medical Association; Worshipful Master, Blue Lodge of Masonic Order.

Fortier; La. Portraits

John Krantz

Businessman; born in Thedinghausen as German native circa 1850; came to America at age eighteen; made fortune in New Orleans ice business; bought about twenty-five slave cabins and created hotel, Krantz Place, on Grand Isle in 1876; partner in development of New Orleans-Fort Jackson-Grand Isle Railroad; owned two steamers for transportation between New Orleans and Grand Isle; developed gambling on steamers and hotel; Protestant, built interdenominational chapel on hotel grounds; property and boats destroyed by 1893 hurricane.

Reeves, Grand Isle

Rudolph Krause

Businessman; born in Schlawe, Prussia, 1863; came to Louisiana in 1890; began as bookkeeper and treasurer of lumber company in Westlake, Louisiana; established Krause & Managan Lumber Company in Lake Charles; vice-president of Murray-Brooks Hardware Co., First National Bank, president of Lake Charles Trust & Savings Bank.

La. Biog.

Ernest Kruttschnitt
Attorney with Roselius; born in New Orleans, 1852, of John
Kruttschnitt, German consul general, and Penina Benjamin; Democrat,
anti-lottery; member Orleans Public School Board, Pickwick Club.
Biog. & Hist. Memoirs
Joseph Kundek (Kundig or Kundeck)
Catholic clergyman, missionary priest; born in Croatia, 1810, of German
parents; ordained August 18, 1833; went from Archdiocese of Agram,
Croatia, to Leopoldine Foundation in Vienna to volunteer for missions in
America; installed as rector of mission at Jasper, Indiana in 1838; came
to New Orleans in 1843; worked in diocese, built first German Catholic
church in New Orleans, called Church of Our Lady of the Assumption
(site of later St. Mary's Assumption Church); persuaded Benedictine
monastery in Einsiedeln, German-speaking Switzerland, to establish St.
Meinrad Abbey in Indiana; sent as priest to German Catholic colony in
Roberts Cove; established St. Joseph Abbey; died in Jasper, 1857.
Kleber
Paul H. Kurzweg
Businessman; born in Plaquemine, Iberville Parish, 1882, of Julius
Kurzweg, cooper, born in Neustettin, Pomerania, 1838, immigrated to
South Louisiana; Paul joined Iberville Wholesale Grocery Company;
then organized St. Mary Groceries, merged with Consolidated
Wholesale Grocery Company in 1921, became vice-president; then
moved to Morgan City, became director of Morgan City Bank and
Trust Company; acquired sugarcane plantation east of Morgan City.
Chambers
Theodore von La Hache (Hacke)
Musician, composer, music publisher; born in Dresden, Saxony, 1823;
studied with Karl Gottlieb Reissiger; organist for St. Theresa's Church,
choirmaster at St. Patrick's; married Emilia Johnston, eight children;
member Harmonic Association, Odd Fellows; died in 1869; collection
of music at La Hache Music Library, New Orleans Public Library.
La. Coll., NOPL; Fields
John Lange
Pioneer of Third District, entrepreneur, philanthropist; born a German
native, 1820; came to New Orleans in 1838; married Mary Anna
Neissing, six children; developed large salvage business, popularized
concept of recycling; donated land, gave financial support to Father
Thevis for *Campo Sancto* (St. Roch's Cemetery); died in 1900.
N.O. Archdiocesan Cemeteries

Conrad Leithman
"Father of baseball" in South; born in Bavaria, 1839; managed Robert E. Lee baseball team for twenty years (1860s-1870s); built Sportsman Park on New Basin Canal, city's first baseball park; died in 1911.
Daily States Item, June 22, 1911

Count de Leon/Count Leon von Proli
Religious mystic, utopian, founder of religious sect that settled Germantown in 1835; born Maximilian Bernhard Müller in Kostheim, near Mainz, Germany, 1788, of uneducated parents; led sect to George Rapp's Harmony Society in Economy, Pennsylvania, in 1831; established own religious commune in Philipsburg, Pennsylvania; then came to Grand Ecore in 1833; died in Natchitoches in yellow-fever epidemic of 1834.

Countess de Leon (Elisa Heuser)
Cofounder of Germantown; common-law wife of Proli, Count de Leon; born in Frankfurt, Germany, 1798; parents Johann and Anna Maria Heuser prevented marriage to Proli; came to Louisiana with Proli's followers in 1834; after Proli's death moved colony away from Red River to Germantown, Webster Parish; took over leadership with Dr. Goentgen; three illegitimate children (raised by Goentgens); colony flourished until after Civil War, abandoned 1871; died in Hot Springs, Arkansas, date unknown.
La. Biog.; Krouse

Louis Leonhard
Businessman, philanthropist, legislator; born in Kaiserslautern, Rheinpfalz, 1840; came to New Orleans in 1853; married Josephine Schueler; owner of Leonard & Sons Department Store, Louisa and Dauphine streets; elected to Louisiana state legislature; officer of Metropolitan Bank; president Third District Building Association, State Homestead League; director, German Protestant Home for the Aged and Infirm; finance secretary for *Sängerfest* of 1890; died in 1900.
Altenheimbote

Otto Lerch
Physician, medical writer, watercolorist, pianist; born in Prenzlau, 1855; came to Louisiana in 1890; married Elizabeth Tory, Katherine Wren; first to practice internal medicine as specialty; introduced Wasserman test for syphilis to New Orleans; chair of Clinical Medicine at New Orleans Polyclinic, School of Medicine, Tulane University; died in 1948.
La. Biog.

J. L. Leucht

Rabbi; established Touro Synagogue; born in Hesse-Darmstadt, 1844; came to New Orleans in 1868; married Mathilde Kahn, 1869, three children; became assistant to Rabbi Gutheim, then rabbi of Touro Synagogue on Carondelet Street; responsible for new synagogue on St. Charles; member of Louisiana State School Board, president of Louisiana State Prisons and Asylums Commission, vice-president of Touro Infirmary; supporter of Jewish Widows and Orphans Home; president of Red Cross, Kingsley House.

Nau; La. Portraits; Fortier; Myers

Frederick Loeber

Physician; house surgeon of Touro Infirmary 1869-1901; trained in France, Germany, America; received Order of the Crown from German Kaiser in 1899; awarded Times-Picayune Loving Cup; built mansion on Coliseum Street; died in 1901. Three daughters: Maud and Edith (Ballard) became physicians; Florence first woman admitted to law school in Louisiana, president of Louisiana Woman's Suffrage Association.

Nau

John Ludwig* (King John)

Merchant; German-American born and raised on Grand Isle; operated grocery and general store begun by father ca. 1880; led way for agricultural reconstruction of Grand Isle after 1893 hurricane; developed large terrapin farm ca. 1900, supplying restaurants in South and on East Coast with turtle meat (produced 35,000-50,000 lb. annually); developed new agricultural methods on island resulting in greatly improved productivity.

S. Reeves, Grand Isle; Jeff. Parish Review

Karl Aloys Luzenberg

Physician; born in Verona, Italy, 1805, of German parents, father Joseph Godfrey Luzenberg of old noble Austrian family; Karl immigrated to America with family in 1819, studied medicine in Philadelphia, came to New Orleans in 1828 as assistant at Charity Hospital; married Mary Clement, daughter of New York banker/merchant, three children; in 1829 became house surgeon, chief administrator of Charity Hospital; left New Orleans to study further in Europe (1832-34); returned to New Orleans and founded private Franklin/Luzenberg Hospital on Elysian Fields, Medical College of Louisiana (forerunner of Tulane Medical School) where served as professor of surgery, and Medical Surgical Society of Louisiana; introduced

surgical amphitheater, developed cataract surgery; director of Marine Hospital but lost appointment as Henry Clay supporter (opposed Polk); director of New Orleans Drainage Company; cofounder in 1839 of Natural History Society of Louisiana, president in 1843; president Philharmonic Symphony; alderman, First District; died in 1848 of heart attack at age forty-three.
Deiler, Presse; La. Biog.; Körner; Voss; Fortier

Francis Joseph (Maurice) Masquelet
Catholic clergyman, parish priest; born in Gabville, near Strasbourg, Alsace, 1795; ordained in native country; came to U.S. in 1830s; assisted priest in Pittsburgh in 1833, then Fr. P. Czackert at St. Marie (Picquet's settlement), Illinois; brought parents and rest of family from Alsace to Teutopolis; came to New Orleans in 1842; worked among Germans at St. Mary's Assumption and Holy Trinity churches (1844-49); built first Holy Trinity church in *Faubourg des Allemands* (Third District); returned to North and later to Alsace, where died in 1873.
Calvert

Anton Menge
Inventor; native of Westphalia, Prussia; came to New Orleans in late 1820s; began as coppersmith, moved to Plaquemines Parish; married Catherine Conrad, originally of Saxony, in 1844; established copper and brass foundry; invented Menge Elevator Dredge in 1859, revolutionized canal dredging; designed fire engine after Civil War, became active fireman; member Plaquemines Parish Police Jury; died in 1866. Son Joseph became civil engineer; born in New Orleans, 1846; improved father's dredge, in 1878 acquired nine patents, established Menge Patent Pumps on Tchoupitoulas Street, in 1882 developed draining and irrigating pumps used nationwide; also invented machine separating chaff from rice.
Menge

Valentine Merz
Restaurateur, philanthropist; born in Indiana, 1855, of German parents; came to New Orleans in 1868; worked for uncle George Merz, owner of Old Canal City Beer Brewery; then took over agencies for Blatz Brewing and Anheuser-Busch; bought Jules Kruse Saloon; acquired co-ownership of Merz Saloon & Restaurant, Orleans Street, moved location to Common Street, sold business to Konrad Kolb; Kolb's became longest-surviving German restaurant in city, closed 1990; president of New Orleans Brewing Co., built Dixie Brewing Co.; board of Interstate Bank; donated funding for zoo in Audubon Park, formerly called Merz Memorial Zoo.
Voss; Deiler, Presse

Sally Miller/Salome Müller
Redemptioner; born in Langensoultzbach, Württemberg, in 1814; came to New Orleans in 1818 with parents Daniel (cobbler) and Dorothea Müller, sister and infant brother, all died of yellow fever except Sally and sister (ages four and six); Sally became indentured servant under redemption system; sold into slavery by John Fritz Miller (as Negress named Mary) to Louis Belmonti; bore one son by fellow (Negro) slave in 1828; German community successfully sued for her freedom in 1844 (lawsuit went to Supreme Court); Sally was set free but counter-sued by John F. Miller for fraud to save own reputation.
La. Biog.; Deiler, Redemptionsystem; Wilson, La. Hist.

Georg Müller (alias Georg Gumbel)
Publisher; born in Dienheim near Oppenheim, 1839; educated in French, English, learned book publishing business; drafted into papal Swiss regiment in Italy as youth; came to New Orleans in 1866; founded German military battalion (was captain); amassed fortune as publisher for thirty years; board of German Protestant Orphans Asylum, secretary to *Frohsinn, Liedertafel, Gesangfest* of 1881; *Schweizergesellschaft* (Swiss Society); married unsuccessfully late in life; moved to San Diego; died in 1898 at age fifty-nine.
Nau; Deiler, Presse

Herman L. Neugass*
Athlete, sprinter in 100- and 220-yard dash; New Orleans resident of German-Jewish parentage; known as "Human Bullet" and "Green Wave" as college student at Tulane University; refused to participate in 1936 Olympics in Hitler's Berlin; died in Washington, 1991.
Times-Picayune, June 11, 1935; Zwelling

Isidore Newman, Sr.
Banker, philanthropist; born in Kaiserslautern, 1838; came to New Orleans in 1853; married Rebecca Kieffer in 1868, seven children; began as bookkeeper for Henry Stern; founded Isidore Newman & Son, investment bankers; built mansion at 3804 St. Charles Avenue; organizer, president of New Orleans Stock Exchange; helped state and city government fund debt; electrified Carrollton railroad; developed Touro Infirmary; founded Isidore Newman Manual Training School; endowed Home for Jewish Widows and Orphans, Audubon Park expansion; built Home for Incurables, awarded Times-Picayune Loving Cup in 1903; president, *Harmonie Club,* member Hebrew Benevolent Association; died in 1909.
Jews of La.; La. Biog.; City of New Orleans

Vincent Nolte
Cotton speculator; born in Livorno, Italy, 1779, of German parents; grew up in Hamburg; apprenticed at fifteen at father's German import-export firm in Livorno; came to New Orleans in 1806, stayed twenty years; served as captain in the German Steuben Guards, founded own business in 1812 as agent for Barings (London), Hope House (Amsterdam), associated with Rothschilds; then became independent cotton trader, invested in cotton presses, wharves, ships; fought in Battle of New Orleans as grenadier; friend of French patriot Lafayette; returned to Hamburg, established own import house; lost fortune through fraud; jailed in England for breach of contract; later took service job to survive; at seventy-four wrote two-volume work *Fünfzig Jahre in beiden Hemisphären* (*Fifty Years in Both Hemispheres*), appearing in Hamburg in 1853; attracted attention in New Orleans through criticisms of important figures in city, descriptions of bad conditions in Battle of New Orleans; related wanderings throughout world, model for *Anthony Adverse;* died in Hamburg in 1854.
Deiler, Presse; La. Biog.; Körner; Biog & Hist. Memoirs

Edward William Alton Ochsner*
Surgeon, academician; first to discover smoking as cause of lung cancer and heart disease; born in Kimball, North Dakota, 1896, as third-generation German-American; parents Edward Philip Ochsner and Clara Leda Schontz; family coat-of-arms registered in courthouse in Zurich in 1605; did surgical residency at universities of Zurich and Frankfurt; came to New Orleans in 1927; married Isabel Lockwood (four children), Jane Kellog Sturdy; appointed professor of surgery at Tulane; taught Michael DeBakey; wrote six complete books, twenty-four chapters in other books, 500 articles, performed 20,000 operations; member of American Cancer Society, American College of Surgeons, American Medical Association, International Cardiovascular Society, Pan American Medical Association, cofounder of Ochsner Clinic and Hospital, president of Ochsner Foundation; awarded Times-Picayune Loving Cup in 1930; also chosen as Rex, king of Carnival; died in 1981.
Deutsches Haus Coll., HNOC; La. Biog.; Southerner

Sigmund Odenheimer
Businessman, president of Lane Cotton Mills; born in Odenheim, Baden, 1860; studied engineering in Karlsruhe; married Pauline Freyhan, three children; owned mansion at 5225 St. Charles Avenue; associate of Lehman, Stern & Company, Maginnis Mills; noted for

inventing cotton bagging for cotton bales, to replace jute bagging; member of state Board of Health; president of New Orleans International Trade Exhibition; president of Louisiana German-American *Staatsverband,* member of *Turnverein, Deutsche Gesellschaft, Harugari, Männerchor, Harmonie Club,* Young Men's Hebrew Association, Temple Sinai; died in 1945.
Voss; Southerner; Jews of La.; La. Portraits; Fortier

Melvin ("Mel") Thomas Ott*
Major league baseball player (New York Giants); born in Gretna, 1909, of German stock; joined Giants at age sixteen, right fielder, power hitter despite small stature, led National League in homeruns six times, set record for 511 homeruns; managed Giants for seven years; elected to Hall of Fame, 1951; died in car accident in New Orleans in 1958; Mel Ott Sports Park in Gretna dedicated in his memory; called Pride of Gretna.
Zwelling; Gretna Diamond Jubilee Coll.; Thoede, City Hall; Huber, Pictorial History

Stanley Ott*
Catholic clergyman, third bishop of Baton Rouge; born in Gretna, 1927, of German stock; educated at St. Joseph, Notre Dame seminaries, North American College, Rome; ordained in Rome, 1951; received Ph.D. in theology from Gregorian University, Rome; served as chaplain at Catholic Center, Louisiana State University, rector of St. Joseph Cathedral and other posts in Baton Rouge; appointed auxiliary bishop of New Orleans, 1976, bishop of Baton Rouge, 1983; died of cancer in 1992.
Calvert

Karl Postl (alias Charles Sealsfield)
Journalist, novelist; born in Poppitz, Moravia, 1793, of German parentage; came to U.S. in 1823; acquired Louisiana plantation; described Louisiana in *Life in the New World;* ranked in German states as author above Irving and Cooper; died in Solothurn, Switzerland, in 1864.
La. Biog.

Ludwig von Reizenstein
Draftsman/artist, civil engineer, literary satirist, ornithologist/zoologist; born in Streitberg near Forschheim, Franken, 1829, father Baron Alexander von Reizenstein was lord chamberlain, royal advisor to Ludwig I, king of Bavaria; studied in Freising and at University of Munich, where became member of bodyguards for Lola Montez, mistress to Ludwig I; royal scandal forced him to emigrate in 1848, came to New Orleans in 1849; published weekly newspaper *Der Alligator* and serialized his *Geheimnisse* [*Secrets*] *von New Orleans* in *Louisiana*

Staatszeitung; fought in Civil War; tried through mathematical calculations to beat Louisiana and Havana lotteries, lost everything; supported self through literary writings, author of many articles in *Scribner's* and *Century Magazine;* expert on birds and insects, flora and fauna of Louisiana, in 1875 discovered new species of butterfly at Spanish Fort, confirmed by Smithsonian Institution; many architectural renderings by him in New Orleans Notarial Archives; died in 1888 at age fifty-nine (see chapter 5, "The German-Language Press").
Nau; Clark, Liberals; La. Biog.; Deiler, Presse

Johann Reuss

Sugar planter, real-estate developer; native of Hesse-Darmstadt, came to Louisiana ca. 1850; married Helena Lotz; owner of Allemania, Germania, Ashland, Elsie, Cuba, and Chatham plantations; founded Hohen Solms (named for German principality Hollenzollern) south of Baton Rouge; owned large land holdings in Ascension Parish and on west bank of Mississippi; died in 1898. Son George became commission merchant; born in New Orleans, 1858; married Bertha Spor, first-generation German-American, four children; inherited Ashland Plantation, renamed it Belle Helene after mother; drained thousands of acres in vicinity; member of school board, built public high school in Donaldsonville as memorial to daughter; member of B.P.O.E., Lodge No. 1153, German Lutheran Church.
Biog. & Hist. Memoirs; River Road; La. Portraits; Fortier

Joseph Reuther

Businessman, educator; born in Deidesheim, Rheinpfalz, 1848; immigrated with parents, Henry Jacob Reuther (baker) and Marie Leidenheimer, to New Orleans in 1866; established Reuther's Bakery, most up-to-date plant in city; later sons merged it with Sunshine Bakery; elected to school board in 1908; prominent in introducing German into public high schools; board of Metropolitan Bank, president of Orleans Homestead Association, president of German Society; died in 1934 (see chapter 6, "German-Language Schools").
Voss; Architecture V

Adolph Gustave Ricks

Leather merchant; born in Hamburg, 1842; came first to Texas, then Baton Rouge, later to New Orleans; served in Confederate army; was largest manufacturer of boots, shoes, and gaiters in country; president of Metropolitan Bank, manager of New Orleans Brewing Co.; member of city council, New Orleans commissioner of public finance; commissioner of Milne Asylum; thirty-second-degree Mason, president of

Odd Fellows, member of German Society, *Frohsinn,* First German Evangelical Church; died in 1925.
Voss; Nau; City of New Orleans; Fortier

Christian Roselius

Attorney general of Louisiana; born in Thedinghausen near Bremen, 1803; came to New Orleans in 1820 at sixteen as redemptioner; served for two and one-half years at *Louisiana Advertiser* to repay cost of voyage; worked at *Louisiana Courier;* in 1827 published *Halcyon* (literary weekly); linguistically talented, mastered French, German, English; passed bar 1828, became civil and criminal lawyer at Davezac law office; wife head of girl's school, three children; became attorney general of Louisiana 1841-43; professor of civil law at Tulane University, 1850-73; dean of law school; elected to Louisiana constitutional conventions of 1845 and 1852; nominated to state supreme court on Whig ticket in 1853 but defeated; talented politician, speaker for Whig party, but opposed by *Staatszeitung* and Louisiana natives as foreigner; in 1861 nominated to secession convention but refused to sign the secession ordinance; offered partnership with Daniel Webster but declined; during Civil War served Confederacy in Jefferson Parish Mounted Guard; appointed chief justice of New Orleans during Reconstruction (refused); was theater enthusiast; had large library in mansion at 515 Broadway, New Orleans, once whole square; did not take part in German life of city although noted for philanthropy, lived entirely for studies, family; died in 1873.
Nau; Clark, Civil War; Deiler, Presse; Körner; Laguaite; La. Biog.; Rightor

Charles Rossner

Dentist, oral surgeon; born in Gretna, 1906; father *Burgermeister* (mayor) of Herzogweiler, Germany; married Helen Louise Gates, five children; served as colonel in World War II; first to use acupuncture in oral surgery; staff member of Eye, Ear, Nose and Throat Clinic at Touro for fifty years; chief of staff of Louisiana State University Dental Clinic; also staff member of Ochsner Medical Foundation Hospital, Tulane Medical School; died in 1983; Rossner memorial lecture given annually by Touro and Louisiana State University School of Dentistry.
La. Biog.

Joseph Francis Rummel

Catholic clergyman, prelate, ninth archbishop of Archdiocese of New Orleans, 1935-64; born in Steinmauern, Baden, 1876; came to New Orleans in 1935, established schools, organizations, institutional

desegregation; supporter of rights of labor; established forty-eight new parishes, seventy school buildings, active in Refugees, U.S.O. charitable program; established Confraternity for Christian Doctrine, Council of Catholic Women, Catholic Youth Organization, Catholic Physicians' Guild, Council of Catholic Men, Christian Family Council; died in 1964.
Calvert

Frederick W. Salmen
Businessman; native of German-speaking Switzerland; immigrated at age twelve; founded Salmen Brick & Lumber Co. in Slidell, largest building-materials business in Louisiana; made Slidell model industrial town.
Chambers

Louis J. Salomon*
First Mardi Gras Rex, king of Carnival, 1872; born 1839 of German-Jewish heritage, converted to Catholicism in 1862; son of Ezekiel Salomon, owner of Levi & Salomon cotton factorage; great-grandson of Prussian immigrant Hyam Salomon; enlisted in Confederate army, then joined father's private bank; named Rex as one of organizers and highest fundraiser ($5,000) for parade in honor of visiting Russian prince Alexis; original parade a mile long, led by king on horseback in borrowed costume, preceded by decorated white bull (*Boeuf Gras*), 60,000 viewers; moved to New York, where became member of New York Stock Exchange; died in 1941; buried in New York.
Korn; Schwegmann; Laborde, N. O. Magazine

Christian Sans
Protestant clergyman; born in Westphalia, Prussia, 1813; came to New Orleans in 1840; organized first German Lutheran congregation, located in Phoenix Fire Station in Third District; also a sister congregation in Lafayette as well as mission in Freetown; first to start German-language school using Pestalozzian and Prussian educational methods, employed Ueber brothers as teachers; founded Second Protestant Church and school on corner of Craps and Port; left city in 1843 for New York, where married Ann Mary Ueber, sister of John and Jacob Ueber; continued to build German congregations and churches in New York, Wisconsin, and Illinois; died in 1891.
Zwelling; Deiler, Churches

Paul Schaeuble
Clergyman, Catholic priest, Benedictine monk, first abbot of St. Joseph Abbey, 1903-31; born in Segeten, Baden, 1863; ordained 1889; came to New Orleans in 1890, joined St. Meinrad Abbey; became pastor of St. Boniface Parish, prior of St. Joseph Abbey in 1902, abbot in

1903; moved abbey to St. Benedict, reconstructed abbey after fire of 1907; named chaplain at Carville in 1932, then St. Gertrude Convent at Ramsey; died in 1955.
Calvert

Adam Schlösser
Planter; born in Rheinland, 1824; came to New Orleans in 1848 with wife Martha Stengel, had fourteen children; acquired 700 acres on western shore of Lake Pontchartrain; in 1849 joined brother Martin, stave maker from Rheinland, first settler (1836) in this cypress swamp; together they developed stave and cordwood business, exporting products to German states; then began vegetable farming, became one of largest cabbage growers in South supplying Chicago via Illinois Central Railroad, beating Midwestern farmers to market; with other German farmers developed 4,000 acres for vegetable farming between Frenier (Schlosser) and Ruddock, one of most lucrative farms in country; died in 1906 (see chapter 3, "German Settlements and Place Names").
Biog. & Hist. Memoirs; Borel

Jacob Schoen
Mortician, partner of Henry L. Frantz; born in Eiglach near Worstadt, Hesse-Darmstadt, 1841; came to New Orleans in 1859; worked as longshoreman, then became undertaker; formed partnership with Frantz 1874-79, then with oldest son, Philip; three sons continued the successful and long-standing mortuary business (see chapter 5, "Trades, Businesses, and Professions").
Voss

Bernard Schott
Meatpacker; German immigrant, began as butcher in stall #15 of Poydras Market, then opened small shop in Upper Ninth Ward as pork butcher shortly after marriage in 1877; five of sons joined business, developed into large meatpacking house; he died in 1909; grandsons continued business, sold in 1985.
Zwelling; Architecture V

Charles Schueler
Commissioner of Agriculture and Immigration of Louisiana; born in Mähringen, Württemberg; settled in Baton Rouge; in 1907 traveled back to Germany with J. Hanno Deiler to recruit German farmers for Louisiana; placed advertisements in *Das Echo* and other newspapers in Berlin area, produced few results.
Voss

Julius Schwabacher

Produce and commission-house broker; born in Württemberg, 1850s; came to Louisiana in 1870 with brothers Max and Morris; founded J. & M. Schwabacher with offices in Chicago, Kansas City, St. Louis; member of Chicago Board of Trade, New Orleans Board of Trade; director of Germania National Bank, Chalmette Homestead.

Jews of La.

Henry Schwartz

Decorator, merchant, real-estate developer; cofounder of Heath, Schwartz & Co.; decorated French Opera House, Vonderbank Hotel, St. Charles Hotel, Planter's Club (Thibodaux), Ocean Club Hotel (Grand Isle); manager of coal interests in Pennsylvania, land in Mississippi and Louisiana; member New Orleans Board of Trade, president of Wall Paper Decorative Association, St. John Rowing Club.

Biog. & Hist. Memoirs

Louis Schwarz

Book dealer, insurance company owner; born in Brakwede near Bielefeld in Westphalia, 1819; came to New Orleans in 1846; worked at bookstore of Heimish and Co., purchased business, moved it to Chartres Street near Canal, where very successful for years; cofounder of Teutonia Insurance Company; founder, board member of *New Orleans Journal,* newspaper rivaling *Deutsche Zeitung;* secretary of *Deutsche Gesellschaft,* member German Theater Company, German Protestant Orphan Asylum; in 1890 retired to extensive property on Tchoupitoulas Street; died in 1893.

Deiler, Presse

Garrett Schwegmann, Sr.

Founded first Schwegmann grocery store; born in Osnabruck-Hanover, 1839; immigrated to New Orleans, began cleaning privies; joined Union Army Company D of Second Regiment, Louisiana Infantry, wounded; then worked as butter clerk at Henke's Grocery; married Henke's daughter Mary at Holy Trinity Church, ceremony performed by Father Thevis; five children; original store established in 1869 on Piety Street, died in 1930; buried in St. Roch Cemetery. Brother John W. developed supermarket concept for grocery store(s); married Mary Frey, daughter of Anton Joseph Frey; rented brother's store on Piety Street in 1939, converted it to self-service, reduced prices 10 percent; developed first Schwegmann Giant Supermarket with sons John Jr., Anthony, and Paul, at St. Claude and Elysian Fields in 1946. Son John Jr. developed business into extensive grocery chain with wholesale transport division; established ten Schwegmann Giant Supermarkets; entered politics, elected Public Service Commissioner in New Orleans, three times to state legislature; supermarkets subsequently failed and were sold.

Francis-Xavier Seelos

Catholic clergyman, Redemptorist priest, missionary, born in Füssen, Bavaria, 1819; came to New Orleans in 1866; pastor of St. Mary's Assumption Church (which houses Seelos Museum); died of yellow fever in 1868; beatified by Pope John Paul II at St. Peter's Basilica in Rome in 2000.

La. Biog.

Louise von Seybold

Native of Munich, Bavaria; married Antoine Valsin Marmillion, builder of plantation house on San Francisco Plantation, owned by his father, Edward Marmillion; three daughters; as mistress of San Francisco decorated home; sold plantation in 1879 after husband died; returned to Munich with children; died in 1904.

San Francisco Plantation (SFP) Archives

Albert Stein

Engineer, designer of New Orleans waterworks; born in Düsseldorf, 1792; built Miami bridge near Hamilton, Ohio in 1817; in 1822 built first waterworks run by steam pumps in Cincinnati; went to Philadelphia as artist for Milson's Ornithologue; then went to New Orleans, where built city's first waterworks, began operation in 1849, twenty-eight streets from levee to the rear section of the city fed through central pipeline; later built waterworks in Richmond, Lynchburg, Nashville, Mobile; also Appomatox Canal at Petersburg, Alabama; died in 1876 at the age of eighty-four in Mobile, where family owned waterworks.

Deiler, Presse

Maurice Stern

Financier, philanthropist; born in Emershausen, Bavaria, 1855; came to New Orleans in 1871; married Hanna Bloom in 1883, three children; joined Lehman, Abraham & Company as partner, then as president, renamed it Lehman-Stern; vice-president of Lane Cotton Mills, director of Whitney Bank, Morgan State Bank, International Land Improvement Company, New Orleans Cotton Exchange, Board of Trade, treasurer of Southern States Land & Timber Co., officer of Sugar Exchange, member of state Board of Education, Progressive Union, Eye, Ear, Nose & Throat Hospital, president of Temple Sinai, trustee of Touro Infirmary, board member of Jewish Widows and Orphans Home, executive committee of Hebrew Union College, Cincinnati, member of B'nai B'rith, *Harmonie Club;* died in 1919.

Edgar Bloom Stern (son)

Financier, cotton broker, philanthropist; born in New Orleans, 1886; graduated from Harvard; married Edith Rosenwald Sulzberger, daughter of Sears & Roebuck magnate, Julius Rosenwald (Edith attended school in Germany); served in World War I; developed Lincoln Beach; funded Country Day School, Newcomb Nursery School, served on Orleans Parish School Board; trustee of Tuskegee Institute, board of United Negro College Fund; president of board of Dillard University, Flint-Goodrich Hospital; president of New Orleans Cotton Exchange, Community Chest; trustee of Howard-Tilton Library, Rosenwald Fund, International House, Trade Mart, WDSU-TV, Tulane University, Ford Foundation; Council on Foreign Relations; Federal Reserve Bank of Atlanta; received presidential appointment to Committee on Education Beyond High School; died in Utah in 1959; widow donated mansion with extensive gardens to city, now publicly owned as Longue Vue House and Gardens.

La. Biog.; Jews of La.; La. Portraits; Fortier; Myers

Sol Stern

Businessman: exporter, manufacturer, inventor; one of first in South to begin manufacture of fertilizer, established business in 1869, accepted consignments from farmers of produce, poultry in exchange for fertilizer, which shipped all over world; also established large-scale moss business, 1882; invented hitching fastener for floats, wagons; member of Chamber of Commerce.

City of New Orleans

Erich Sternberg

Mayor of Baton Rouge, merchant, real-estate developer; born in Aurich, Bavaria, 1907; came to Louisiana in 1936; married Lea Knurr, three children; founded Goudchaux Department Store, Sternberg Realty, Fifteen-Fifty Realty; director of City of Hope Hospital, board of B'nai Israel Temple; Mason; died in Baton Rouge in 1965.

La. Biog.

John F. Stumpf

Physician, pharmacist; born in Louisiana of German parents; married Louise Ruch, sons Archibald, Louis, Alvin; Stumpf established drugstore in New Orleans in 1876, then moved to Gretna in 1887; opened Stumpf's Drug Store on First Street; active in Good Government League, led to incorporation of Gretna; after John's death in 1911 son Archibald took over business; Archibald had three sons: A. Louis,

Norman P., John Frederick; Louis operated second Stumpf's Drug Store at Huey P. Long and Third Street; Norman ("Pat") became pharmacist and managed third Stumpf's Drug Store in west bank shopping center; John F. became dentist, retired in 1954 to develop Stumpf's Westside Shopping Center as founder and co-owner, died in 1957.

Alvin Stumpf* (son)

Pharmacist, businessman, legislator; developed John Stumpf's Son(s) with brothers and father, who founded business; manufactured Stumpf's Magic Hoodoo, arsenic-based insecticide patented by father; Alvin later became sole owner, invented Rust-Away, developed over forty related products, exported all over Caribbean; credited with helping to eliminate yellow fever in Panama during digging of canal; carried on Stumpf family interests with brother Archibald in Westside Shopping Center after death of Archibald's son John F. Stumpf; Alvin also involved in development of Veterans Highway, second Greater New Orleans Mississippi River Bridge; director of First National Bank of Jefferson Parish, member of Mississippi River Bridge Authority, chairman of Jefferson Parish Red Cross, sponsor of parish athletic teams for youth, many other civic organizations; elected to state legislature in 1930, served a number of terms as Louisiana state senator from Tenth District; Stumpf Boulevard and Stumpf's Westside Shopping Center named for family.

Story of La.; La. Bus. & Prof. Directory

Peter Leonhard Thevis

Clergyman, Catholic priest; born in Cologne; came to New Orleans in 1867; pastor of Holy Trinity Church, 1870-93; instrumental in establishing German colony in Roberts Cove in 1881; to fulfill promise to saint for saving congregation of Holy Trinity during yellow-fever epidemic of 1867, built St. Roch *Campo Sancto* mortuary chapel with own hands; had traveled to Bavaria and Hungary to visit other mortuary chapels; structure considered excellent example of Gothic architecture; Good Friday procession to stations of cross in cemetery still annual rite in New Orleans; died in 1893; memorial to Father Thevis in chapel (see chapter 6, "Churches and Synagogues").

Nau; Times-Picayune, Dixie Roto, Oct. 26, 1969

William Thiel

Architect; born in Fischhausen, East Prussia, 1812; trained as cabinetmaker; came to New Orleans in 1851; naturalized 1855; in 1860 formed partnership with Albert Diettel; designed Gates of Mercy, Gates of Prayer (Shangarai Tefiloh), Temme Derech synagogue (Polish-Jewish Congregation), Odd Fellows Hall, *Turnverein,* German National Theater; vice-president of German Society, Quitmann Lodge

(Master in Masons), Odd Fellows Delta Lodge No. 15; died in 1870 (see chapter 4, "Public and Commercial Buildings").
Deutsches Haus Coll., HNOC; Irvin

Louisa Thielemann
Actress and theater director; German national; with Rudolph Riese directed first German theater in New Orleans on Old Levee Road between Barracks and Hospital streets; director of German National Theater in New Orleans; funded traveling German theater troupe; she and husband credited with establishing professional German theater in city (see chapter 8).
Deiler, Presse; Nau

Joseph Voegtle
Legislator, hotel owner; born in Freiburg, Baden, 1853; came to New Orleans in 1870; Louisiana state senator from Third District for fourteen years; member of Sewerage and Water Board, postmaster of New Orleans, 1914; proprietor of Voegtle's Saloon and Cosmopolitan Hotel; director of Canal Bank; first president of German-American State League of Louisiana; officer, financial secretary, director of *Deutsche Gesellschaft;* founding member, president of *Frohsinn;* director of German Protestant Orphan Asylum; died in 1916.
Voss; Berchtold; Nau

Leon Toll Von Zinken
Distinguished military officer in Prussian army; immigrated to New Orleans; during Civil War served as colonel in Twentieth Louisiana Regiment under Brig. Gen. August Reichard, also Prussian; very successful in training recruits, wounded several times; involved in politics after war, celebrated in circles sympathetic to Confederacy; figurehead publisher of *New Orleans Journal;* newspaper failed (see chapter 5, "The German-Language Press").
Nau; Deiler, Presse

Edward Henry Walsdorf
Pharmacist; born in New Orleans, 1872, to German parents, August Walsdorf and Josephine Schaller; married Delia Stewart, three children; established chain of drugstores, taught pharmacology at Tulane University; president of Louisiana State Board of Pharmacy and Pharmaceutical Association, represented five states to National Association of Boards of Pharmacy, member of Grand Consistory, thirty-second-degree Scottish Rite Mason, member of Jerusalem Temple, Order of Eastern Star, Knights of Pythias, Odd Fellows, Ancient Order of Druids, Royal Order of Moose.
Voss

John F. Wegmann

Businessman; born in New Orleans, 1878, as second of eleven children; father native of Bavaria, mother from Alsace; educated at St. Mary's Assumption *Deutsche Schule;* president of Lafayette Fire Insurance Co., vice-president of New Orleans School Board; medical writer, worked for reform in medical and university education, established sanitary code for Louisiana State Board of Health.
Fortier

Albert Weiblen

Stone and marble mason; born in Metzingen, Württemberg, 1857; came to U.S. in 1883 to study banking; came to New Orleans in 1906; established Weiblen Marble and Granite and Weiblen Stone Mountain Granite corporations; two sons, both in business; built many local monuments, mausoleums, fountains, altars; numerous contracts outside of New Orleans; died in 1957 at 100 years of age. Son George completed job of carving of Stone Mountain Confederate figures; owned Metairie Cemetery 1951-69; widow continued operating cemetery for two decades until sold (see chapter 6, "Cemeteries").
Voss; Architecture III; Gandolfo; Gill

Bertrand Weil

Businessman, legislator; born in Alexandria, 1859, of John Weil of Bavaria; father came to New Orleans in early 1840s, began as peddler, opened store in Alexandria, had ten children; son Bertrand began as clerk in father's store, formed partnership with brother and brother-in-law, Weil Bros. & Bauer; became largest holder of real estate in Alexandria, one of largest Louisiana plantation owners; donated clinic/hospital for poor to city; president of Rapides Parish Police Jury, state senator (1910-24), vice-president of Rapides Bank and Trust, member of Masons, Shriners, Elks.
Chambers

Julius Weis

Philanthropist, cotton factor, banking and insurance executive; born in Klingen, 1826; came to New Orleans in 1845; married Caroline Mayer from Natchez, seven children; began as peddler, then merchant (partner to Leon Godchaux), slave owner before Civil War; founded J. Weis & Son, international banking institution; built mansion at Jackson Avenue and Chestnut (designed by Charles Hillger); founded Julius Weis Home for Aged and Infirm Israelites, Jewish Widows and Orphans Asylum; supported Hebrew Educational Society; president, director of Touro Infirmary, Hebrew Benevolent Association; member of Young Men's Hebrew Association; died in 1909.
Jews of La.; Irvin; Nau; Myers

Philip Peter Werlein
Music store proprietor; born in Rheinkreis, Bavaria, 1812; immigrated
to Louisiana; married Margaret Halsey, four children; established girl's
school in Clinton; relocated to New Orleans in 1853, formed partnership with William Mayor; published "Dixie," marching song of
Confederacy; served Confederacy in Civil War in New Orleans Home
Guard; forced to leave city during Union occupation (business confiscated by Federal troops, stock sold at auction, but rebuilt after war);
proprietor of well-known store on Canal Street; member Odd Fellows;
died in 1885; original Werlein's on Canal Street later moved to smaller store on Decatur with branches in two suburbs (see chapter 8).
La. Biog.; Nau; La. Portraits
William Dietrich White (anglicized from Witte)
German pioneer from Baden; came to Gretna in 1840s; had seven children, among them Lilly White Ruppel, August (Gustavus) White,
William J. White; served as fireman, became president of David
Crockett Fire Company; William D. White Masonic lodge in Gretna
named for him. Son William J. worked as smith for U.S. Mint in New
Orleans, tax collector for Gretna, died in 1916. Grandson William
("Bill") John White elected mayor of Gretna (1950-85), attorney; born
in Gretna, 1910; married Wilhelmina Kraus; World War II veteran; as
mayor supported construction of Mississippi River Bridge (built in
1958), extended paving and lighting of Gretna streets; home construction; responsible for new Jefferson Parish courthouse, modernization
of Gretna sewage system, new city incinerator, waterworks; active in
local, state, and national bar associations, Veterans of Foreign Wars,
Chamber of Commerce, American Legion, Lions, Rotary clubs,
Masonic lodge. William Richard ("Dick") White born in Gretna, 1901,
brother of mayor; married Helen Hock; became career banker; president
of Gretna Exchange and Savings Bank reorganized as First National
Bank of Jefferson; supported parish oil industry, Jefferson Parish Police
Jury, parish school board and highway commission, Mississippi River
Bridge Authority; active in Gretna Rotary Club, Lions Club, West Bank
Boy Scouts, Red Cross, Community Chest, David Crockett Fire
Company No. 1, other civic associations; Shriner, Mason.
La. Bus. & Prof. Directory; Story of La.; Gretna Diamond Jubilee Coll.
Charles F. W. Wieck
Merchant, real-estate developer; born a German native, where trained
as carpenter and builder, came to U.S. in 1858, moved to Baton Rouge
in 1860; wife Catherine Wagenblast also born in German state, five

children; entered general merchandising business, acquired real estate and large plantation in Baton Rouge area; member of city council, Masons in Baton Rouge, Knights Templar in New Orleans; died in 1889. Son Charles entered father's business; developed Sumter House, luxury hotel in Baton Rouge; president of Wieck Realty Company, owner of Wieck Building; active in Democratic party, Baton Rouge Chamber of Commerce, member of Masonic orders in Baton Rouge, Jerusalem Temple, Knights of Pythias.
Chambers

Louis Alfred Wiltz*
Mayor of New Orleans, legislator, speaker of Louisiana House of Representatives, governor of Louisiana; born in New Orleans, 1843; descendent of Joseph Wiltz, German Coast pioneer from Thruingia; grandson of Laurent Wiltz, landowner in Marigny in 1780s and in Faubourg Plaisance (later Jefferson City), divided for development in 1807 into forty-two lots with central thoroughfare Grand Course Wiltz, now Louisiana Avenue; Louis Alfred attended Ueber (German-language) School; began political career as clerk of Second District Court; enlisted in Confederate army at age eighteen, served in Civil War in New Orleans Artillery, captain of Chalmette regiment; after war married Marie Bienvenu, seven children; developed mercantile business, elected state legislator in 1868, then alderman, then in 1872 mayor of New Orleans at age twenty-nine; elected to state house of representatives, then governor of Louisiana in 1879; established Bureau of Agriculture and Immigration, built railroads, improved public health; member of Fusion party (combination of Democrats and Liberals), rival of Republican Michael Hahn; died of tuberculosis in 1881 while in office.
La. Biog.; Nau; Voss

Charles Wirth
Merchant, real-estate developer; born in Freudenstadt, Württemberg, 1851; came to New Orleans in 1864; married Josephine Hauck, two sons; founded Wirth's Grocery Store on Magazine Street in 1872; developed Wirth Place (between Freret and Magnolia) and surrounding area; elected to city council; president and largest stockholder of Standard Brewing Company, producer of *Wirthbräu* (Wirth Brew); charter member of Old Firemen's Homestead; president of Imperial Realty and Charles Wirth Realty companies; president of German Protestant Orphan Asylum; member of Jackson Avenue Evangelical Church, Odd Fellows, Ancient Order of Druids; died in 1936.
Voss; Nau

Edward Wisner
Real-estate developer, philanthropist; born in 1860 of German and Dutch parentage; came to Louisiana in 1888; reclaimed millions of acres of "meadow" land in area surrounding Lockport; settled in New Orleans in 1900, developed land; Wisner Boulevard and Wisner Education Wing of New Orleans Museum of Art named after family.
Fortier

William George Zetzmann*
Businessman, civic leader, established Zetz Seven-Up Bottling Company (plants in New Orleans, Baton Rouge); born in New Orleans, 1894, of German-American parentage; sold father's ice-manufacturing business in 1917 to develop bottling business; chairman of board of Louisiana State Public Works under four governors, founding member and president of International House and International Trade Mart, officer of Mississippi Valley Association, New Orleans Railroad Terminal, Audubon Park Commission; received Times-Picayune Loving Cup Award in 1942.
La. Directory

Francis Michael Ziegler
Merchant; born in Oberndorf-am-Neckar, Württemberg, 1811; co-owner of large wholesale grocery business (Schmidt & Ziegler) founded in New Orleans in 1845, partnership with William Schmidt lasted fifty years; Schmidt noted for his mansion in Garden District; Ziegler helped erect Lee Circle Monument; he and Schmidt buried side by side in twin Gothic tombs in Metairie Cemetery; both died in 1901 (see chapter 5, "Trades, Businesses, and Professions").
Voss; City of New Orleans; Architecture III

Karl Frederick Zimpel
Surveyor, architect, engineer, mapmaker, contractor; born in Prussia, 1801; served under Kaiser Friedrich Wilhelm I; came to New Orleans in 1830 as engineer for New Orleans and Carrollton railroad; became city surveyor and engineer, laid out and developed Carrollton in 1833 on site of Macarty Plantation, once uppermost part of Governor Bienville's 1719 land grant; drew New Orleans Topographical Map (first map of Carrollton, 1834); designed and built Bank of New Orleans, Banks Arcade, Bishop's City Hotel, Orleans Cotton Press (largest in city); remodeled Charity Hospital; Zimple Street (Carrollton) named after him; returned to Prussia in 1837, where died (see chapter 4, "Public and Commercial Buildings").
Deiler, Presse; Chase; Irvin

Bibliography

PRIMARY SOURCES

Archives and Manuscripts Division and Louisiana/Special Collections. Earl K. Long Library, University of New Orleans (cited as *Special Colls., U.N.O. Library*).

Archives Nationales, Paris, *Archives des Ministère des Colonies, Series C 13 A; G 1; C 13 C*, vol. 464 (see chapter 1).

Archivo General de Indias, Seville, *Seccion 11 A. Papeles de Cuba*, legato 216 B (see chapter 1).

Deutsches Haus Collection. Microfilm of records available at the Deutsches Haus, 200 South Galvez Street, New Orleans.

Diamond Jubilee Festival: Holy Trinity Church and Free Parochial School (1853-1928). New Orleans: Archives of the Archdiocese of New Orleans, 1928 (cited as *Diamond*).

Echo of the Clio Street Evangelical Church. Deutsches Haus Collection, Historic New Orleans Collection. Williams Research Center, New Orleans (cited as *Deutsches Haus Coll., HNOC*).

Festschrift des deutsch-amerikanischen Nationalbundes, Staatsverband für Louisiana, October 5, 1913 [*Program for the Fourth Annual Celebration of German Day by the German-American National Association; Louisiana Chapter*] (n.p., 1913). Special Collections. Tulane University Library, New Orleans (cited as *Festschrift*).

Fink Asylum (Delachaise House) Records, 1874-1924; John D. Find's Will, 1860; *Haber Papers*. Vertical files, Louisiana and Lower Mississippi Valley Collection. Hill Memorial Library, Louisiana State University (cited as *LLMVC*).

German Consular Records, 1837-72: Bavaria 1858-72; Duchy of Nassau 1851-62; Prussia 1837-72.

German, Germans, Deutsche categories, German Newspapers; Works Progress Administration Newspaper File. Special Collections. New Orleans Public Library (cited as *NOPL*).

Gretna; A Self Portrait in Retrospect. A Photographic Exhibit

Commemorating Gretna's Diamond Jubilee. Louisiana/Special Collections. Earl K. Long Library, University of New Orleans (cited as *Gretna Diamond Jubilee Coll.*).

Inventory of the Church and Synagogue Archives of Louisiana: Jewish Congregations and Organizations. Louisiana Historical Records Survey, Department of Archives. Hill Memorial Library, Louisiana State University (see chapter 7).

San Francisco Plantation Archives. River Road, Louisiana (cited as *SFP Archives*).

Souvenir of the Diamond Jubilee of the St. John's Evangelical Lutheran Congregation of New Orleans, Louisiana, May 5-8, 1927 (see chapter 6).

Special Collections. Tulane University Library, New Orleans (cited as *Special Colls., Tulane Library*).

Zwelling, Shomer, interpretive planner; Jeff Kennedy Associates, Inc., designers; Jennifer Blazes, National Park Service, producer. German-American Cultural Center Exhibit Plan Notebook, 1997 (cited as *Zwelling*).

SECONDARY SOURCES

American Institute of Architects, New Orleans Chapter. *A Guide to New Orleans Architecture.* New Orleans: American Institute of Architects, 1974 (cited as *Guide*).

Arndt, Karl J. R., and May E. Olson. *Deutsch-amerikanische Zeitungen und Zeitschriften, 1732-1955 [German-American Newspapers and Magazines].* Heidelberg: Quelle & Meyer Verlag, 1961 (cited as *Arndt, Zeitungen*).

————. *Die deutschsprachige Presse der Amerikas 1732-1968: Geschichte und Bibliographie [The German-Language Press of America, 1732-1968: History and Bibliography].* Pullach/Munich: Verlag Dokumention, 1973 (cited as *Arndt, Presse*).

Baudier, Roger. *The Catholic Church in Louisiana.* New Orleans: A. W. Hyatt, 1939 (cited as *Baudier*).

The Behrman Administration of the Municipality of New Orleans, Hon. Martin Behrman, Mayor, 1904-1908-1912. New Orleans: American Printing, 1912 (cited as *Behrman*).

Berchtold, Raimond. "The Decline of German Ethnicity in New Orleans, 1880-1930." M.A. thesis, University of New Orleans, 1984 (cited as *Berchtold*).

Biographical and Historical Memoirs of Louisiana, Chicago: Goodspeed, 1892 (cited as *Biog. & Hist. Memoirs*).

Blake, Siva M. "The Company of the Indies and John Law's Germans 1717-1731." M.A. thesis, Middle Tennessee State University, 2001 (see chapter 1).

Blume, Helmut. *The German Coast during the Colonial Era, 1722-1803: The Evolution of a Distinct Cultural Landscape in the Lower Mississippi Delta during the Colonial Era: with Special Reference to the Development of Louisiana's German Coast.* Trans., ed., annot. Ellen C. Merrill. Destrehan, La.: German-Acadian Coast Historical and Genealogical Society, 1990 (see chapter 1).

Boling, Yvette G., and M. T. Duffard, comp. *Federal Census, 1850. Jefferson Parish, Louisiana.* Reprint, Jefferson, La.: n.p., 1986 (cited as *1850 Census*).

Borel, J. B. "The German Lost Coast." *Gretna Chronicles, Newsletter of the Gretna Historical Society* (May 1998) (cited as *Borel*).

Brasseaux, Carl A. "The Long Road to Louisiana: Acadian Exiles in the Britain Incident." *Gulf Coast Historical Review* 1, no. 1 (1985): 24-38 (see chapter 1).

Briede, Kathryn Claire. "A History of the City of Lafayette." M.A. thesis, Tulane University, 1937 (cited as *Briede*).

Brown, David, comp. *A History of Who's Who in Louisiana Politics.* New Orleans: n.p., 1916 (cited as *Brown*).

Bruns, Mrs. Thomas. *Louisiana Portraits: Colonial Dames of Louisiana.* N.p., n.d. (cited as La. Portraits).

Cable, Mary. *Lost New Orleans.* Boston: Houghton Mifflin, 1980 (cited as *Cable*).

Calvert, Raymond Neil. "The German Catholic Churches of New Orleans, 1836-1898." M.A. thesis, Notre Dame Seminary, 1986 (cited as *Calvert*).

Chambers, Henry Edward. *A History of Louisiana, Wilderness-Colony-Province-Territory-State-People.* 3 vols. Chicago: The American Historical Society, 1925 (cited as *Chambers*).

Champigny, Chevalier de. *Etat présent de la Louisiane avec toutes les Particularités de cette Province d'Amèrique.* The Hague: n.p., 1776 (see chapter 1).

Chase, John. *Frenchmen, Desire, Good Children and Other Streets of New Orleans.* 1960. Reprint, Gretna, La.: Pelican, 2004 (see chapter 3).

Christovich, Mary Louise, Roulhac Toledano, Betsy Swanson, and Pat

Holden. *New Orleans Architecture.* Vol. 2, *The American Sector.* Gretna, La.: Pelican, 1972 (cited as *Architecture II*).

Christovich, Mary Louise, Sally Kittredge Evans, and Roulhac Toledano. *New Orleans Architecture.* Vol. 5, *The Esplanade Ridge.* Gretna, La.: Pelican, 1977 (cited as *Architecture V*).

The City of New Orleans, The Book of the Chamber of Commerce and Industry of Louisiana and other Public Bodies of the Crescent City. New Orleans: Geo. W. Engelhardt, 1894 (cited as *City of New Orleans*).

Clark, Robert. "German Liberals in New Orleans, 1840-60." *Louisiana Historical Quarterly* (1937): 137-51 (cited as *Clark, Liberals*).

Clark, Robert T. "The New Orleans German Colony in the Civil War." *Louisiana Historical Quarterly* 20: 991-1015 (cited as *Clark, Civil War*).

Cohen, H. and F., ed., comp. *Cohen's New Orleans and Southern Directory. Jefferson City, Gretna, Algiers, and McDonogh; Lafayette, Baton Rouge.* New Orleans: Daily Delta Printers, 1849-56 (cited as *Cohen*).

Conrad, Glenn R. "Alsatian Immigration, 1753-1759." *New Orleans Genesis* 14 (1975): 221-26 (see chapter 1).

———. "Emigration Forcée: A French Attempt to Populate Louisiana, 1716-1720." *Proceedings of the Fourth Meeting of the French Colonial Historical Society* (1979) (see chapter 1).

———, ed., comp. *A Dictionary of Louisiana Biography.* 2 vols. Lafayette: Louisiana Historical Association and Center for Louisiana Studies, University of Louisiana at Lafayette, 1988 (cited as *Conrad, La. Biog.*).

Cruse, Boyd, and Merle Horton. *Signor Feranta's Iron Theater.* New Orleans: Historic New Orleans Collection, 1982 (cited as *Cruse*).

Cuming, F. *Sketches of a Tour to the Western Country through the States of Ohio and Kentucky; a Voyage down the Ohio and Mississippi Territory and Part of West Florida, 1807-1809.* Pittsburgh: n.p., 1810 (see chapter 1).

Curry, Mary Grace. *Gretna: A Sesquicentennial Salute.* Metairie, La.: Jefferson Parish Historical Commission, 1986 (cited as *Curry*).

Dabney, Thomas Ewing. *One Hundred Great Years.* Baton Rouge: Louisiana State University Press, 1944 (cited as *Dabney*).

D'Antoni, Edward J. "An Almost Mythical World." *New Orleans Magazine* (December 2002): 47-51 (cited as *D'Antoni, N.O. Magazine*).

Davis, Edwin Adams. *The Story of Louisiana.* 3 vols. New Orleans: J. F. Hyer, 1960 (cited as *Story of La.*).

Defrange, Jonathan, O.S.B. *Centuries of Grace, a Pictorial History of St. Joseph Abbey and Seminary.* St. Benedict, La.: St. Joseph Abbey, n.d. (cited as *Defrange*).

Deiler, J. Hanno. *Die ersten Deutschen am unteren Mississippi und die Creolen deutscher Abstammung* [*The First Germans on the Lower Mississippi and the Creoles of German Descent*]. New Orleans: Selbstverlag, 1904 (see chapter 1).

————. *Eine vergessene deutsche Colonie. Eine Stimme zur Vertheidigung des Grafen de Leon, alias Proli, alias Bernhard Müller* [*A Forgotten German Colony. A Voice in Defense of Prince Leon, alias Proli, alias Bernhard Müller*]. New Orleans: Selbstverlag, 1900 (cited as *Deiler, Colonie*).

————. "Germany's Contribution to the Present Population of New Orleans with a Census of the German Schools." Paper presented to the New Orleans Academy of Science, April 27, 1886; printed in *The Louisiana Journal of Education* (May 1886) (cited as *Deiler, Schools*).

————. *Geschichte der deutschen Gesellschaft von New Orleans, mit einer Einleitung: die europäische Einwanderung nach den Vereinigten Staaten von 1820 bis 1896. Festschrift zum goldenen Jubiläum der deutschen Gesellschaft* [*History of the German Society of New Orleans with an Introduction: the European Immigration to the United States from 1820 to 1896. A Publication in Honor of the Golden Jubilee of the German Society*]. New Orleans: Selbstverlag, 1897 (see chapter 2).

————. *Geschichte der New Orleanser deutschen Presse. Nebst andern Denkwürdigkeiten der New Orleanser Deutschen* [*History of the New Orleans German Press. Along with Other Memorable Events Concerning the New Orleans Germans*]. New Orleans: Selbstverlag, 1901 (cited as *Deiler, Presse*).

————. *A History of the German Churches in Louisiana (1823-1893).* Trans. Marie Stella Condon. Lafayette: University of Louisiana at Lafayette, 1983; German title: *Geschichte der deutschen Kirchengemeinden im Staate Louisiana* (cited as *Deiler, Churches*).

————. *Louisiana. Ein Heim für deutsche Ansiedler* [*Louisiana. A Home for German Settlers*]. New Orleans: Deutsche Gesellschaft von New Orleans, Druck der New Orleans deutschen Zeitung, 1895 (cited as *Deiler, Ansiedler*).

————. *Settlement of the German Coast of Louisiana and the Creoles of German Descent.* Philadelphia: American Germanica Press, 1909. Reprint, with a preface, chronology, and index by Jack Belsom, Baltimore: Genealogical, 1969 (see chapter 1).

————. *Zur Geschichte der Deutschen am unteren Mississippi. Das Redemptionsystem im Staat Louisiana* [*A History of the Germans on the Lower Mississippi. The Redemption System in the State of Louisiana*]. New Orleans: Selbstverlag, 1889 (see chapter 2).

————. *Zur Geschichte der Deutschen am unteren Mississippi und die deutsche Einwanderung über New Orleans* [*A History of the Germans on the Lower Mississippi and the German Immigration via New Orleans*]. New Orleans: Selbstverlag, 1889 (see chapter 2).

Des Loziers, Baudry. *Voyage à la Louisiane et sûr le Continent de l'Amèrique Septentrionale, fait dans les Années 1794 à 1798.* Paris: Imprimeur-Librarie, Palais du Tribunat, 1802 (see chapter 1).

"Dispatches of the Spanish Governors of Louisiana, 1763-1789." In *Survey of Federal Archives in Louisiana.* New Orleans: n.p., 1937-38 (see chapter 1).

Ditchy, Jay K. "Early Census Tables of Louisiana." *Louisiana Historical Quarterly* 13 (1930): 205-29 (see chapter 1).

Dixon, Richard Remy. *Algiers, My Home Town.* Gretna: Rau's Ex-Cel Printing, 1990 (cited as *Dixon*).

Dufour, Charles L. *Ten Flags in the Wind: The Story of Louisiana.* New York: Harper & Row, 1967 (see chapters 1, 2).

Duvallon, B. *Vue de la Colonie espagnole du Mississippi ou des Provinces de la Louisiane et Floride occidentale, en l'Année 1802.* Paris: n.p., 1803 (see chapter 1).

Edwards, Richard. *Edwards' Annual Directory of the City to the Inhabitants, Institutions, Incorporated Companies, Manufacturing Establishments, Business Firms, etc., of New Orleans and its Suburbs.* New Orleans: Southern, 1869, 1870, 1872, 1873 (cited as *Edwards* with year).

Engelhardt, George W. *New Orleans, Louisiana, The Crescent City: the Book of the Picayune also of the Public Bodies and Business Interests of the Place, prepared for the New Orleans Picayune.* New Orleans: Engelhardt, 1904 (cited as *Engelhardt*).

Faye, Stanley. "The Arkansas Post of Louisiana: French Domination." *Louisiana Historical Quarterly* 26 (1943): 661-70 (see chapter 1).

Ficklin, John R. *History of Reconstruction in Louisiana.* Baltimore: n.p., 1910 (see chapter 2).

Fields, Warren C. "The Life and Works of Theodore von LaHache." Vol. 1, "LaHache's Life from His Birth in Dresden to His Death in New Orleans." Vol. 2, "A Reproduction of Selected Works by LaHache." Ph.D. dissertation, University of Iowa, 1973 (see chapter 9).

Florence, Robert. *New Orleans Cemeteries.* New Orleans: Batture Press, 1997 (see chapter 6).

Forsyth, Alice D., and Earlene Zeringue. The German Pest Ships, 1720-21. New Orleans: Genealogic Research Society of New Orleans, 1969 (see chapter 1).

Fortier, Alcée. *Louisiana, with a Supplementary Biography.* 2 vols. Madison: n.p., 1914 (see chapter 7).

―――, ed. *Louisiana: Comprising Sketches of Parishes, Towns, Events, Institutions, and Persons, Arranged in Encyclopedic Form, 1856-1914.*, 3 vols. 1909. Reprint, New Orleans: Century Press, 1914 (cited as *Fortier*).

Franz, Alexander. *Die erste Auswanderung in das Mississippithal. Eine kritische Würdigung* [*The First Wave of Immigration into the Mississippi Valley. A Critical Evaluation*]. Frankfurt: n.p., 1912 (see chapter 1).

―――. *Die Kolonisation des Mississippitales bis zum Ausgange der französischen Herrschaft. Eine kolonial-historische Studie* [*The Colonization of the Mississippi Valley during the French Dominion. A Colonial Historical Study*]. New York: G. Wigand, 1906 (see chapter 1).

Friends of the Cabildo. *New Orleans Architecture.* Vol. 7, *Jefferson City.* Gretna, La.: Pelican, 1989 (cited as *Architecture VII*). Vol. 8, *The University Section.* Gretna, La.: Pelican, 1997 (cited as *Architecture VIII*).

Gandolfo, Henri A. *Metairie Cemetery, an Historical Memoir: Tales of Its Statesmen, Soldiers and Great Families.* New Orleans: Stewart Enterprises, 1984 (cited as *Metairie Cemetery;* see chapter 6).

Gardner, Charles. *Gardner's New Orleans Directory including Jefferson City, Gretna, Carrollton, Algiers and McDonoghville.* New Orleans: Bulletin Book & Job Printing Establishment, 1860, 1861, 1869, 1916 (cited as *Gardner* with year).

Gibson, John. *Gibson's Guide and Directory of the State of Louisiana and the Cities of New Orleans and Lafayette, Embracing an Historical Notice of the State, its Boundaries, Products, and Government, and an Historical Notice of the City of New Orleans from its Foundation.* New Orleans: J. Gibson, 1838 (cited as *Gibson, Guide*).

―――. *Historical Epitome of the State of Louisiana with an Historical Notice of the City of New Orleans, Views and Descriptions of its Public Buildings.* New Orleans: J. Gibson, 1840 (cited as *Gibson, La.*).

Gill, Donald A. *Stories behind New Orleans Street Names.* Chicago: Bonus Books, 1992 (see chapter 3).

Giraud, Marcel. *Histoire de la Louisiane française.* Vol. 3, *L'Epoque de John Law (1717-1720).* Paris: Presses Universitaires de France, 1966. Vol. 4, *La Louisiane après le Système de Law (1721-1723).* Paris: Presses Universitaires de France, 1974. Vol. 5, *La Compagnie des Indes (1723-1731).* Paris: Presses Universitaires de France, 1987 (see chapter 1).

Graham, L., ed., comp. *Graham's Crescent City Directory: Embracing also a Separate Record of Jefferson City, Carrollton, Algiers, Gretna and Milneburg.* New Orleans: Graham Publications, 1867, 1868 (cited as *Graham* with year).

Gurtner, George. *Historic Churches of Old New Orleans.* New Orleans: Friends of St. Alphonsus, 1996 (cited as *Gurtner*).

Heinz, Jakob. *"Kurpfälzer Blut in Louisiana"* ["Palatinate Blood in Louisiana"]. *Pfälzische Heimatkunde* 22 (1926): 12-17 (see chapter 1).

Hennepin, Louis. *Beschreibung der Landschafft Louisiana welche, auf Befehl des Königs in Frankreich, neulich gegen Südwesten Neu-Frankreichs in America entdecket worden. Nebenst einer Landcart und Bericht von den Sitten und Lebens-Art der Wilden in selbiger Landschafft. In frantzösischer Sprache heraus gegeben durch P. Ludwig Hennepin, nun aber ins Teutsche übersetzt* [Description of the Country of Louisiana in Southwest New France in America, which Has Been Discovered and Claimed upon the Order of the King of France. Also a Map and Report about the Customs and Way of Life of the Indians in the Country. Published in French by Hennepin, translated into German]. Nürnberg: Otto Press, 1689 (see chapter 1).

Hill, R. R. *Descriptive Catalogue of the Documents relating to the History of the United States in the Papeles Procedentes de Cuba, Archivo General des Indias.* Washington, D.C.: n.p., 1916 (see chapter 1).

History of the Jews of Louisiana, their Religious, Charitable and Political Life. New Orleans: New Orleans Jewish Historical, ca. 1905 (cited as *Jews of La.*).

Hoffman, Beryl May. "German Education in New Orleans." M.A. thesis, Tulane University, 1939 (cited as *Hoffman*).

Huber, Leonard V. *New Orleans: A Pictorial History.* 1971. Reprint, Gretna, La.: Pelican, 1991 (cited as *Huber, Pictorial Hist.*).

Huber, Leonard V., Peggy McDowell, and Mary Louise Christovich. *New Orleans Architecture.* Vol. 3, *The Cemeteries.* Gretna, La.: Pelican, 1974 (cited as *Architecture III*).

Irvin, Hilary. "The Impact of German Immigration on New Orleans Architecture." *Louisiana History* 27, no. 4 (fall 1986): 375-406 (cited as *Irvin*).

"J. Hanno Deiler, eine Würdigung" ["A Salute to J. Hanno Deiler"]. *German American Annals* 7 (September-October 1909): 277-79 (see chapter 9).

Jackson, Wesley. "German Baptists of Mowata Form Unique Congregation." *New Orleans Times-Picayune* (January 27, 1974), sec. 2, p. 6 (cited as *Jackson*).

Jefferson Parish Annual Review. Jefferson, La.: Official Publication of the Police Jury, 1937-38, 1947, 1954 (cited as *Jeff. Parish Review* with year).

Jewell, Edwin L., ed., comp. *Crescent City Illustrated. The Commercial, Social, Political and General History of New Orleans.* New Orleans: n.p., 1873 (cited as *Jewell*).

Kearns, Melinda K. "St. Roch Will Never Die: A Folklore Study of a New Orleans Cemetery." M.A. thesis, Northwestern State University of Louisiana at Natcitoches, 1997 (cited as *Kearns*).

Kendall, John Smith. *History of New Orleans.* Vol. 3. Chicago: Lewis, 1922 (cited as *Kendall*).

Kleber, Albert, O.S.B. *History of St. Meinrad Archabbey, 1854-1954.* St. Meinrad, Ind.: Grail Publications, 1954 (cited as *Kleber*).

Koerner, Gustav. *Das deutsche Element in den Vereinigten Staaten von Nordamerika, 1818-1848* [*The German Element in the United States of North America, 1818-1848*]. Cincinnati: A. G. Wilde, 1880 (see chapter 2).

Kolp, John L. "Suburbanization in Uptown New Orleans: Lafayette City, 1833-52." M.A. thesis, University of New Orleans, 1973 (cited as *Kolp*).

Kondert, Reinhart. "Charles Frederick D'Arensbourg, 1693-1777." *New Orleans Genesis* 20 (1981): 395-401 (see chapter 1).

————. "German Immigration to French Colonial Louisiana: A Reevaluation." *Proceedings of the French Colonial Historical Society* 4 (April 6-8, 1978): 70-81 (see chapter 1).

————. "The Germans of Acadia Parish." *Louisiana Review* (summer 1977, April 1978): 19-37 (cited as *Kondert, Acadia Parish*).

————. *The Germans of Colonial Louisiana, 1720-1803,*

American-German Studies. Vol. 5. Stuttgart: Verlag Hans-Dieter Heinz, Academic Publishing House, 1990 (see chapter 1).

———. The New Orleans German Society. Paper presented at Deutsches Haus, n.d., New Orleans (see chapter 2).

Konrad, William Robinson. "The Diminishing Influence of German Culture in New Orleans since 1865." M.A. thesis, Tulane University, 1940; *Louisiana Historical Quarterly* 24 (1941): 127-67 (cited as *Konrad*).

Korn, Bertram Wallace. *Early Jews of New Orleans.* Waltham, Mass.: American Jewish Historical Society, 1969 (cited as *Korn*).

Krouse, Rita Moore. *Fragments of a Dream. The Story of Germantown.* Ruston: n.p., 1962 (cited as *Krouse*).

La Harpe, Bernard de, Jean Baptiste. *Journal historique de l'Etablissement des Français à la Louisiane.* Trans. Joan Cain and Virginia Koenig; ed., annot. Glenn R. Conrad. Lafayette: Center for Louisiana Studies, University of Louisiana at Lafayette, 1971 (see chapter 1).

Laborde, Errol. "A King and a Prayer." *New Orleans Magazine* (February 2004): 44-46 (cited as *Laborde, N.O. Magazine*).

Laguaite, Jeannette Kay. "The German Element in New Orleans, 1820-1860." M.A. thesis, Tulane University, 1940 (cited as *Laguaite*).

Lane, Mills. *Architecture of the Old South: Louisiana.* New York: Abbeville Press, 1990 (cited as *Lane*).

Le Conte, René. *Les Allemands à la Louisiane au XVIII siècle.* N.p., n.d. (see chapter 1).

Le Gac, Charles. *Memoir of Charles Le Gac, Director of the Company of the Indies in Louisiana, 1718-1721.* Trans. Olivia Blanchard. New Orleans: Survey of Federal Archives in Louisiana, 1938 (see chapter 1).

Le Page du Pratz. *Histoire de la Louisiane. The History of Louisiana.* Trans., ed. Joseph G. Tregle, Jr. Baton Rouge: Louisiana American Revolution Bicentennial Commission, Louisiana State University Press, 1975 (see chapter 1).

Ledet, Wilton Paul. "The History of the City of Carrollton." M.A. thesis, Tulane University, 1937 (see chapter 6).

Leeper, Clare D'Artois. *Louisiana Places* and *1976, 1977 Supplements.* Baton Rouge: Legacy, 1976 (cited as *Leeper* and *Leeper Supplement* with year).

Leslie, Frank. *Frank Leslie's Illustrated Newspaper.* New York: n.p., 1859 (cited as *Leslie*).

Louisiana, A Guide to the State Works Projects Administration, State of Louisiana. New York: Hastings House, 1941 (cited as *La. Guide*).

The Louisiana Newspaper Project Printout, April 1990. Baton Rouge: Louisiana Newspaper Project, Louisiana State University Libraries, 1990 (cited as *Louisiana Newspapers, 1990*).

Louisiana Newspapers 1794-1941: A Union List of Louisiana Newspaper Files Available in Offices of Publishers, Libraries and Private Collections in Louisiana. Louisiana Historical Records Survey, Division of Community Service Programs, Work Projects Administration. Baton Rouge: Hill Memorial Library, Louisiana State University, October 1941 (cited as *Louisiana Newspapers, 1941*).

McCord, Stanley Joe. "A Historical and Linguistic Study of the German Settlement at Roberts Cove, Louisiana." Ph.D. dissertation, Louisiana State University, 1969 (cited as *McCord*).

McMullan, T. N., ed., and Louisiana Library Association. *Louisiana Newspapers 1794-1961; A Union List of Louisiana Newspaper Files Available in Public, College and University Libraries in Louisiana*. Baton Rouge: Louisiana State University Libraries, 1965 (cited as *Louisiana Newspapers, 1965*).

Mahe, John Albert. "The Development of a Town at Carrollton." M.A. thesis, Tulane University, 1976 (cited as *Mahe*).

Menge Patent Pumps. Estate Joseph Menge Patentees, J. Westerfield, manager. New Orleans: n.p., n.d. Special Collections. Tulane University Library, New Orleans (cited as *Menge*).

Moehlenbrock, Arthur H. "The German Drama on the New Orleans Stage." *Louisiana Historical Quarterly* 26 (1943): 360-627 (cited as *Moehlenbrock*).

Morrison, Betty L. *A Guide to the Highway Historical Markers in Louisiana*. Gretna, La.: Her Printers, 1977 (see chapter 3).

Myers, W. E. *Israelites of Louisiana, Their Religious, Civic, Charitable and Patriotic Life*. New Orleans: Myers, 1901 (cited as *Myers*).

Mygott & Company's Directory. Comp. W. H. Raney. New Orleans: L. Pesson & B. Simm, 1857 (cited as *Mygott*).

National Encyclopedia of American Biography. Vol. 9. New York: White, 1907 (see chapter 9).

Nau, John Fredrick. *The German People of New Orleans, 1850-1900*. Leiden: E. Brill, 1958 (cited as *Nau*).

New Orleans Archdiocesan Cemeteries. New Orleans: n.p., n.d. (see chapter 6).

Official Text-Book and Programmes of the Twenty-Sixth Sängerfest of the

North-American Sängerbund Held at New Orleans, La., February 12-15, 1890. New Orleans: Crescent, 1890 (cited as *Sängerfest*).

O'Neill, Charles E., ed. *Charlevoix's Louisiana: Selections from the History and the Journal of Pierre F. X. de Charlevoix.* Baton Rouge: Louisiana American Revolution Bicentennial Commission, n.d. (see chapter 1).

Perrin, William Henry, ed. *Southwest Louisiana Biographical and Historical Survey.* N.p.: Gulf, 1891 (see chapter 9).

Pitts & Clarke (*sic*), ed., comp. *New Orleans Directory for 1842, Comprising the Names, Residences and Occupations of the merchants . . . and Citizens of New Orleans, Lafayette, Algiers and Gretna. Together with Historical Notices of the State of Louisiana, the City of New Orleans; a Record of the Victims of the Epidemic of 1841, and the Details of the General Business of the City of New Orleans.* New Orleans: Pitts & Clarke, 1842 (cited as *Pitts & Clarke*).

Polk, R. L., ed., comp. *Polk's New Orleans City Directory.* New Orleans: R. L. Polk, 1938, 1947, 1962 (cited as *Polk* with year).

Prim, Rev. J. B. *The Church of the Holy Trinity.* New Orleans: n.p., 1908 (cited as *Prim*).

Puneky, Claire, ed. *Louisiana Leaders by Louisiana Pen Women.* Baton Rouge: Claitor's, 1970 (cited as *Puneky*).

Rattermann, H. K. *"Die Mississippi Seifenblase: ein Blatt aus der Geschichte der Besiedlung des Mississippi Thales"* ["The Mississippi (Soap) Bubble: A Page from the History of the Settlement of the Mississippi Valley"]. *Der Deutsche Pionier* (September 1875): 147-53 (see chapter 1).

Reeves, Sally Kittredge Evans, Frederick Stielow, and Betsy Swanson. *Grand Isle on the Gulf: An Early History.* Metairie, La.: Jefferson Parish Historical Commission, 1979 (cited as *Reeves, Grand Isle*).

Reeves, William D. *Westwego, from Cheniere to Canal.* Comp. Daniel Alario, Sr., and Pat Legendre. *Jefferson Parish Historical Series, Monograph no. 19. Westwego, La.: Jefferson Parish Historical Society, 1996* (cited as *Reeves, W.*).

Reinders, Robert C. *End of an Era: New Orleans, 1850-1860.* 1964. Reprint, Gretna, La.: Pelican, 1989 (cited as *Reinders*).

Rightor, Henry, ed. *Standard History of New Orleans, Louisiana, Giving a Description of the Natural Advantages, Natural History, Settlement, Indians, Creoles, Municipal and Military History, Mercantile and Commercial Interests, Banking, Transportation,*

Struggles against High Water, the Press, Educational etc. Chicago: Lewis, 1900 (cited as *Rightor*).

Robichaux, Albert J. *German Coast Families: European Origins and Settlement in Colonial Louisiana.* Rayne, La.: Hebert, 1997 (see chapter 1).

————. "History of Kraemer, Louisiana." *New Orleans Genesis* (1983): 394-402 (cited as *Robichaux*).

Robin, C. C. *Voyage to Louisiana, 1803-1805.* Trans. Stuart Landry. New Orleans: Pelican, 1966 (see chapter 1).

Rowland, Dunbar, and Albert G. Sanders, ed. *Mississippi Provincial Archives, 1704-1742; French Dominion.* 3 vols. Jackson: Mississippi Department of Archives, 1927-32 (see chapter 1).

Samuel, Martha Ann Brett, and Ray Samuel. *The Great Days of the Garden District and the Old City of Lafayette.* 1961. Reprint, New Orleans: Parents' League, Louise S. McGehee School, 1974 (cited as *Samuel*).

Schwarz, Jonathan L. "German Communities and Their Impact on South Louisiana." M.A. thesis, University of Louisiana at Hammond, 1989 (cited as *Schwarz*).

Schwegmann, John, Jr., and Mary E. White. Articles in *Times Picayune-States Item* appearing on July 28, August 1, August 4, 1969. Reprinted and expanded in "Just Like Meeting an Old Friend." *Times-Picayune-States Item* (weekly series on Wednesdays, June 1 through September 30, 1978) (cited as *Schwegmann*).

Scott, Liz. "When Werlein's Brought Music to Canal." *New Orleans Magazine* (April 1998): 20-22 (cited as *Scott*).

Seventy-Fifth Anniversary, Jahncke Services Inc. New Orleans: Searcy & Pfaff, 1950 (cited as *Jahncke*).

Skaggs, William E., and J. B. Lux, ed. *Louisiana Business and Professional Directory.* Baton Rouge: Louisiana State Publications, n.d. (cited as *La. Directory*).

Smith, Helen. "Fine Homes Now Stand on Site of Orphanage." *New Orleans Times-Picayune* (December 27, 1986), Real Estate sec., pp. 12-13 (cited as *Smith*).

Soards, L., ed., comp. *Soards New Orleans City Directory.* New Orleans: Soards, 1867, 1870, 1874, 1880, 1884, 1888, 1890, 1891, 1898, 1902, 1909, 1916 (cited as *Soards* with year).

The Southerner, Addenda. New Orleans: Southern Editors' Association, 1944 (cited as *Southerner*).

Springer, Annemarie. *Nineteenth Century German-American Church Artists.* Bloomington: Indiana University Press, 2001 (cited as *Springer*).

Stall, Gaspar J. *Buddy Stall's Crescent City.* New Orleans: n.p., 1995 (cited as *Stall*).

Sternberg, Mary Ann. *Along the River Road.* Baton Rouge: Louisiana State University Press, 1996 (cited as *River Road*).

Surrey, N. M. Miller. *Calendar of Manuscripts in Paris Archives and Libraries Relating to the Mississippi Valley to 1803.* Washington, D.C.: Carnegie Institution, Department of Historical Research, 1926 (see chapter 1).

Swanson, Betsy. *Historic Jefferson Parish, from Shore to Shore.* 1975. Reprint, Gretna, La.: Pelican, 2003 (cited as *Swanson*).

————, ed. *Terre Haute de Barataria: An Historic Upland on an Old River Distributary Overtaken by Forest in the Barataria Unit of the Jean Lafitte National Historical Park and Preserve.* Harahan, La.: Jefferson Parish Historical Commission, 1991 (cited as *Swanson, Barataria*).

Thoede, Henry. *A History of Jefferson Parish and Its People.* Gretna, La.: Distinctive Printing, 1976 (cited as *Thoede, Jeff. Parish*).

Thoede, Henry J. *City Hall, Gretna, Louisiana.* Gretna, La.: C & C Printing, 1964 (cited as *Thoede, City Hall*).

Toledano, Roulhac, Sally Evans, and Mary Louise Christovich. *New Orleans Architecture.* Vol. 4, *The Creole Faubourgs.* Gretna, La.: Pelican, 1974 (cited as *Architecture IV*).

Toledano, Roulhac B., and Mary Louise Christovich. *New Orleans Architecture.* Vol. 6, *Faubourg Tremé and the Bayou Road.* Gretna, La.: Pelican, 1980 (cited as *Architecture VI*).

Villiers du Terrage, Marc de. *Les dernières Années de la Louisiane française.* Paris: n.p., 1903 (see chapter 1).

Voss, Louis. *German Coast of Louisiana.* Hoboken, N.J.: Triangle Press, 1928 (see chapter 1).

————. *History of the German Society of New Orleans with an Introduction giving a Synopsis of the History of the Germans in the United States with Specific Reference to Those in Louisiana, Written at the Request of the German Society and Published on the Occasion of its Eightieth Anniversary, Celebrated on December 6, 1927.* New Orleans: Sendker Printing, 1927. Republished as *Louisiana's German Heritage, Louis Voss' Introductory History.* Ed. Don Heinrich Tolzmann. Bowie, Md.: Heritage Books, 1994 (cited as *Voss*).

————, ed. *Altenheimbote* (monthly newsletter of German Protestant Home for the Aged). Deutsches Haus Collection, Historic New Orleans Collection. Williams Research Center (cited as *Altenheimbote*).

Waldo, J. Curtis. *Waldo's New Orleans Illustrated Visitor's Guide*. New Orleans: J. C. Waldo, 1880 (cited as *Waldo*).

Wallace, J. *The History of Illinois and Louisiana under French Rule*. Cincinnati: n.p., 1893 (see chapter 1).

Wharton, G. M. *The New Orleans Sketch Book by "Stahl," author of "The Port Folio of a Southern Medical Student."* Philadelphia: A. Hart, 1853 (see chapter 5).

Whitaker, A. P. "The Commerce of Louisiana and the Floridas at the End of the Eighteenth Century." *Hispanic American Historical Review* 8 (1928): 190-203 (see chapter 1).

Whitbread, Leslie. *Place Names of Jefferson Parish*. Metairie, La.: Jefferson Parish Historical Commission, 1977 (cited as *Whitbread*).

Wilson, Carol. "Sally Müller, the White Slave." *Louisiana History* 40, no. 2 (1999): 133-53 (see chapter 9).

Wilson, Samuel, Jr. *A Guide to the Architecture of New Orleans, 1699-1959*. New York: Reinhold, 1959 (cited as *Wilson*).

Wilson, Samuel, Jr., and Bernard Lemann. *New Orleans Architecture*. Vol. 1, *The Lower Garden District*. Gretna, La.: Pelican, 1998 (cited as *Architecture I*).

Young, Bright. "Statement of Sugar and Rice Crops Made in Louisiana, 1885-86." *La Bouchereau*. Special Collections. Tulane University Library, New Orleans (cited as *Young*).

Zacharie, James S. *New Orleans Guide: with Descriptions of the Roots to New Orleans, Sites of the City Arranged Alphabetically, also, Outlines of the History of Louisiana*. New Orleans: F. F. Hansell, 1903 (cited as *Zacharie*).

Index